A MANUAL OF
ANGLO-CATHOLIC DEVOTION

ANDREW BURNHAM is Bishop of Ebbsfleet, a Provincial Episcopal Visitor in the Province of Canterbury. After an earlier career as a musician and teacher, he served as a priest in parishes in Nottinghham until, in January 1995, he became Vice-Principal of St Stephen's House, Oxford. He was also appointed to the Church of England Liturgical Commission in 1995 and played a part, both in the Commission and in General Synod, in forming the liturgies of *Common Worship*. Married with two chidlren, he lives in Oxford.

A Manual of Anglo-Catholic Devotion

Compiled by Andrew Burnham

CANTERBURY
PRESS
Norwich

© in this compilation Andrew Burnham 2001

First published in 2001 by The Canterbury Press Norwich
(a publishing imprint of Hymns Ancient & Modern Limited
a registered charity)
St Mary's Works, St Mary's Plain
Norwich, Norfolk, NR3 3BH

All rights reserved. No part of this publication which is
copyright may be reproduced, stored in a retrieval
system, or transmitted, in any form or by any means,
electronic, mechanical, photocopying, recording or
otherwise, without the prior permission of the publisher.

A catalogue record of this book is available
from the British Library

ISBN 1–85311–354–9

Typeset by Regent Typesetting, London
and printed in Great Britain by
Biddles Ltd, Guildford and King's Lynn

For Hannah and Dominic

Contents

Introduction	xiii
Sources and Acknowledgements	xix
The Illustrative Work of Martin Travers	xxi
Angelus Domini **and** *Regina Caeli*	1
Before Praying	3
I PRAYER IN THE MORNING	5
Morning Prayers	7
Morning Prayer	19
The Office of Lauds *on Sundays and Feast Days*	19
The Office of Lauds *on Weekdays*	33
Morning Prayer in Traditional Language	49
II PRAYER DURING THE DAY	59
Prayer During the Day	61
Midday Prayer	71
III INITIATION AND HEALING	81
Baptism and Confirmation	83
Decision and Profession of Faith at Baptism	83
Commission at Confirmation	85
Emergency Baptism	86

Reconciliation: Sacrament of Penance	87
Preparation	87
Confession	91
Thanksgiving	93
Prayers for the Sick	95
Prayer for the Sick	95
Prayer for the Dying	99

IV THE EUCHARIST   103

Preparation for Mass	105
The Mass	109
A Form of Preparation	109
Order One	114
Eucharistic Prayers for Order One	134
Order One in Traditional Language	153
Thanksgiving after Mass	173

V THE CHURCH'S YEAR   177

Calendar	179
Table of Moveable Feasts	200
Advent	203
Propers and Readings	203
Other Prayers	208
Antiphons	210
Christmas and the Annunciation of the Lord	213
Propers and Readings	213
Other Prayers	219

Epiphany and Feasts of the Lord — 221
- Propers and Readings — 221
- Other Prayers — 228

Ordinary Time before Lent — 229
- Propers and Reading — 229
- Other Prayers — 238

Lent — 239
- Propers and Readings — 239
- Other Prayers — 245
- Seven Penitential Psalms — 246

Passiontide — 253
- Propers and Readings — 253
- Other Prayers — 261
- Stations of the Cross — 263

Easter — 285
- Propers and Readings — 285
- Other Prayers — 292

Ascension and the Seventh Sunday of Easter — 293
- Propers and Readings — 293
- Other Prayers — 297

Pentecost — 299
- Propers and Readings — 299
- Other Prayers — 303

Trinity Sunday — 305
- Propers and Readings — 305
- Other Prayers — 309

Corpus Christi — 311
- Propers and Readings — 311
- Other Prayers — 315
- Visit to the Blessed Sacrament — 316
- Benediction — 320

Sacred Heart — 323
- Propers and Readings — 323
- Other Prayers — 327
- Act of Consecration to the Sacred Heart of Jesus — 328
- Litany of the Sacred Heart — 329

Ordinary Time: Monday after Pentecost until the end of October — 331
- Propers and Readings — 331
- Other Prayers — 352
- Pilgrimage — 353

Our Lady — 363
- Propers and Readings — 363
- Other Prayers — 368
- Prayers to Our Lady — 371
- The Shrine of Our Lady of Walsingham — 375
- The Rosary — 380
- Litany of Loreto — 394

The Saints — 397
- Propers and Readings — 397
- Other Prayers — 409
- Prayers of Holy Men and Women — 411
- Litany of the Saints — 416

The Faithful Departed — 419
- Propers and Readings — 419
- Other Prayers — 423

The King and the Kingdom: Ordinary Time in November and Christ the King	425
Propers and Readings	425
Other Prayers	434
Act of Dedication to Christ the King	435

VI PSALMS AND CANTICLES 435

Psalms	437
Canticles	557

VII PRAYER IN THE EVENING 591

Evening Prayers	593
Intercessions	603
Evening Prayer	625
The Office of Vespers *on Saturdays and on the Eve of Solemnities*	625
The Office of Vespers *on Sundays and Solemnities* *and daily as required*	634
Evening Prayer in Traditional Language	649
Night Prayer	
The Office of Compline *on Saturdays and on the Eve of Solemnities* *and daily as required*	655
The Office of Vespers *on Sundays and Solemnities* *and daily as required*	662
Final Anthems to the Blessed Virgin Mary	668

Introduction

A Manual...

A MANUAL is, by definition, a handbook. With the information technology revolution, a manual has come to mean for some an essential tool for accessing what is otherwise inaccessible and for others a book which itself is maddeningly inaccessible. The best manuals enable the user to escape from them. They remain available and easy to consult. The worst gather dust or are pulped. Prayer manuals and primers have abounded, particularly since the end of the fifteenth century. The 'prymer' of the English late mediaeval period would contain typically the 'Little Office of the Blessed Virgin Mary', the Seven Penitential Psalms, the 'Songs of Ascents' (Psalms 120–134), the litany, and offices for the dead. Much would be in English at a time when Latin was the language of the liturgy.

A Manual of Anglo-Catholic Devotion began as an attempt to mark one of the great milestones of the Christian pilgrimage, the great Jubilee Year 2000, and the dawning of the third millennium. At first it was intended that the manual might reflect the new and more settled stage of liturgical development marked by the Church of England's *Common Worship*. As the project developed, it became clear that too much remains uncertain. To give an example, it would be a bold person who would guess what wording of the Lord's Prayer will be dominant in England in thirty years' time.

Since so much remains uncertain about how liturgies will develop, *A Manual of Anglo-Catholic Devotion* is content to be true to itself and does not pretend to mark any definitive stage in the history of liturgy. It sees wisdom in the language policy of the Church of England back in the 1990s, which allowed historical texts in 'exclusive' language to remain intact but required new texts to be in 'inclusive' language with regard to human beings. Accordingly, some prayers in this manual, though by no means all, are in the traditional English in which they were written. But there is no attempt to rework language about God. Whilst it is right to explore a range of biblical metaphors and similes in our attempts to pray, we are surely lost if we move away from the God who, through his only-begotten Son, has revealed himself as our Father.

One of the emphases of the blossoming of the liturgical movement in the twentieth century was that the prayer of the people of God is corporate. People are not spectators at the liturgy but participants, and the tradition of leaving the priest to offer the Mass whilst the faithful click their rosaries or buy and sell in the church porch is now long past. The Mass is not a theatrical production for spectators but a drama workshop in which all present have a part to play. Yet the fresh discovery of the corporate worship of the people of God – in itself welcome – seems to have been accompanied by a decline in personal prayer and devotion that was not entirely foreseen. One senses an increasing unease, for instance, about the sacrament of reconciliation – how well used is it? – and about holy communion – what preparation is made for this awesome sacrament? Is there any link between devotional decline and the increased emphasis on the corporate? It is a question to be thoroughly investigated, though there is almost certainly no simple answer.

... of Anglo-Catholic ...

In the nineteenth century, 'Anglo-Catholic' asserted the historic claims of the Church of England – the Church of Augustine and Anselm, as well as the Church of Cranmer and Laud – to be the Catholic Church in England. The distinctive claims of Roman Catholicism, especially as regards England, were thought to be erroneous. As Article XXXVII of the Thirty-Nine Articles said, 'The Bishop of Rome hath no jurisdiction in this Realm of England.' At the same time, there was a fascination with the culture and fashions of contemporary Roman Catholicism, especially the continental variety. The Ritualists, in particular, were concerned to recover for the Church of England all the privileges of Catholicism: the Mass at the centre of the Christian life, the Reserved Sacrament as a sign of God's promise to tabernacle among his people, the place of Our Lady, the celebration of seven sacraments (and in particular Penance and Extreme Unction), and the joy and wonder of Catholic worship, with its appeal to all five senses.

Made defiant by the verdict of Pope Leo XIII in 1896 that the Anglican Church lacked Catholic orders, Anglo-Catholicism continued to grow in the first half of the twentieth century. In the last thirty or forty years of the twentieth century, thoughtful Anglo-Catholics wondered whether they had 'lost the battle but won the war': Anglo-Catholicism was in steep decline:

Introduction

meanwhile Anglicanism, world-wide, had accepted so much of what Anglo-Catholics had campaigned for. Perhaps Anglo-Catholicism was 'a grain of wheat' which 'if it dies . . . bears much fruit' (John 12:24), a not inappropriate image for a movement whose energy and focus is the Mass.

At the same time, ecumenical understanding was growing, especially since the Second Vatican Council, and Anglo-Catholics – and indeed Anglicans as a whole – became much less certain that the distinctive claims of Rome must be rejected. Some Anglo-Catholics began to style themselves 'Anglican Catholics' (or even 'Catholic Anglicans'). The Anglican-Roman Catholic International Commission explored, amongst other things, Roman ideas of primacy and the role of the successor of Peter. Anglicans became more relaxed about the role of the Roman Catholic Church in the British Isles and were as likely, it seems, to refer to 'Catholics' when they meant 'Roman Catholics' as Anglicans of an earlier generation were to refer rather rudely to 'Romans'. Since one of the conceits of Anglo-Catholicism has been to use the word 'Catholic' as a synonym for 'Anglo-Catholic', there has been increasing ambiguity – not among the general public, for people know full well that a 'Catholic' is a 'Roman Catholic' – but within Church circles. It is for that reason that – unlike *A Manual of Catholic Devotion* (Church Literature Association, 1950), subtitled 'for Members of the Church of England' – this book is called more straightforwardly *A Manual of Anglo-Catholic Devotion.*

Some Anglo-Catholics in the 1990s were less convinced that they had lost a battle and won a war. Perhaps instead they had 'won the battle and lost the war'. A painful division between those who whole-heartedly welcomed the priesting of women and those who believed that the priesting of women was either impossible or ecumenically inexpedient was one indication of a war lost. Another indication was that 'Catholic', for Anglicans, was becoming an aesthetic and even sensual thing, devoid of doctrinal and theological rigour. The battle for lovely things like votive candles in cathedrals and holy week liturgies in parish churches was won, but the war – and the 'vision glorious' of the Tractarian pioneers of the Anglo-Catholic revival – was all but lost. Some Anglo-Catholics sought refuge in Roman Catholicism and Orthodoxy. Others bided their time, praying for, and working for, 'a Catholic moment' when there would be a substantial realignment of Catholics in England, and perhaps further afield, a moment not of individual submission but of ecclesial reconciliation. Others still, it has to be said, continued to believe in the vocation of Anglicanism as a whole to be a bridge between Protestant and Catholic Christianity in the search of all the churches to respond faithfully to the prayer of Jesus 'that they may all be one' (John 17:21).

This thumbnail sketch of Anglo-Catholicism is intended simply to explain some of the editorial decisions in the book. *A Manual of Anglo-Catholic Devotion* is not a political book but a prayer book. It is for those who would like to use it, however they define themselves, and whether or not they are Anglicans. Amongst readers there will be those who have been nourished by the language of the Book of Common Prayer who nonetheless find prayers in modern English helpful. There will be those who have little or no experience of praying in an older register of language and are impatient that only a few of the older prayers in this collection are modernised. There will be those for whom some aspects of Catholic sacramental piety have not been part of their living out of the Christian life so far. Similarly there are prayers from sources which some might regard as partisan. It is hoped that those who would define the word 'Catholic' more narrowly will none the less welcome this book as an assistance to others in what has been called 'the Catholic project'.

. . . Devotion

A Manual of Anglo-Catholic Devotion includes much that is helpful for corporate prayer and, as is usual nowadays, bases some material for daily personal praying on the public prayer of the office. Recognizing, however, that without personal devotion the liturgy of the Church becomes dry, formal and remote – or cloying and trivial – the manual is unashamedly a resource for personal praying. Personal praying (there is no such thing as 'private prayer') requires that what is called an 'office' be recognizably that of the Church (and the use of versicles and responses and the first person plural is a reminder of that) but a manual can do no more than provide digests and examples of what is available in office books and resources for authorised public services. At the time of writing the Church of England's *Common Worship* Office Book is yet to be completed and the difficult decision has been taken that the offices in this manual, therefore, though indebted to the popular Daily Office of the Society of Saint Francis (*Celebrating Common Prayer*) – itself both a very accessible resource in its own right and a pilot project for the new Church of England Office – should have much in common too with parts of the Roman Catholic *Divine Office*, which is still the nearest thing in a divided world to a universal paean of praise. Those who wish to explore the Office further will move on in due course, whether to the full provision of *Common Worship* or to the *Divine Office*.

Christians, when praying, should have the Scriptures open before them. The person who attends midweek mass, regularly or occasionally, will be following, for the most part, the daily cycle of readings given in *A Manual of Anglo-Catholic Devotion*, the Eucharistic Lectionary as used by both Anglicans and

Introduction

Roman Catholics. The Sunday and Holy Day cycle here is mostly that of the *Common Worship* Principal Lectionary (CWPL). The readings may be followed in the usual missals but it would be easier and more fruitful to use the Bible, especially if it has the Apocrypha included.

There are many individual biblical verses and short readings in the manual. They have been chosen not least because of their quality as starting points for meditation and wordless prayer. Most Scripture here is from the New Revised Standard Version (NRSV), which is the version used except when otherwise indicated. Quite often the Revised Standard Version (RSV) has been preferred and this is noted after the biblical reference.

The difficult decision has been taken to exclude poetry and devotional readings – other than scriptural ones – from the manual. Mediaeval carol texts and the poetry of amongst others, Donne, Herbert and Hopkins, might well have been included but have been left out. For those who seek it, none of this material is hard to find. Robert Atwell's anthologies (*Celebrating the Saints,* Canterbury Press, 1998; *Celebrating the Seasons,* Canterbury Press, 1999) provide a good daily diet (and a handsome substitute for the long-awaited optional Lectionary promised in paragraph 161 of the *General Instruction on the Liturgy of the Hours*).

There are about thirty hymns included in the manual. Two or three are well-known classics of Catholic devotion that could not have been omitted. Others are recent translations of ancient hymns. A good hymn will stand the test of being used, even without music, for personal praying of the office. And, as Augustine reminds us, singing is a way of praying twice over. Many of the hymns will be all the more valuable for not being the ones that are encountered over and over again in church on Sundays. The convention that office hymns are set to long metre tunes *(LM)* has not been observed in every case and there is usually therefore a reference to a number in *Hymns for Prayer and Praise* (Canterbury Press, 1996) so that those who want to sing may find appropriate music.

A Manual of Anglo-Catholic Devotion has a simple shape. Material for use in the morning and during the day (both informal resources and offices) is at the front of the book. Material for use in the evening and at night (both informal resources and offices) is at the back of the book. Sections on 'Initiation and Healing' and the Mass are in the middle of the book, followed by a selection of material for the Church's Year. This section is both a resource for enriching daily prayer – with hymns, collects, readings and canticles – and the location for devotions which emerge from the mystery that a feast or season celebrates. Thus Advent Antiphons, Penitential Psalms, Stations of the Cross, Benediction, the Rosary, the Litany of the Saints and

Vespers for the Dead are to be found with the season with which they are most obviously associated.

A generation ago many Anglo-Catholics were formed in the faith by *A Manual of Catholic Devotion*. *A Manual of Anglo-Catholic Devotion* is a very different book, attempting however to do something very similar over half a century later. I take the opportunity to thank Christine Smith of Canterbury Press, for encouragement, help and extraordinary patience and Julian Litten for suggesting the use of Martin Travers' illustrations. The largest debt is to my wife, Cathy, and children, Hannah and Dominic, not least for enduring neglect as – after dinner, at weekends, and at holiday time – I have so often disappeared upstairs to the little study in the attic to work on the manual.

Prayer eventually becomes an ascent towards wordless contemplation, as the saints teach us, but, for words to become fewer and fewer, there have to be some words to begin with. Not only that but, as in other things, it is often those who themselves are not very advanced who are best able to help others. If this is so, then I am indeed well-qualified to provide by way of *A Manual of Anglo-Catholic Devotion* what a good manual should provide, some assistance in accessing what is otherwise inaccessible.

Andrew Burnham
Oxford
St Teresa Benedicta of the Cross 2000

Sources and Acknowledgements

Every effort has been made to trace copyright ownership of items included in this volume. The publisher would be grateful to be informed of any omissions.

(1) Extracts from *Common Worship: Services and Prayers for the Church of England*, Church House Publishing, 2000, are © The Archbishops' Council 2000 and are reprinted by permission
(2) *The Book of Common Prayer*
(3) *A Daily Office SSF*, by permission of the Society of St Francis
(4) © Stanbrook Abbey, Callow End, Worcester WR2 4TD
(5) Excerpts from the English translation of *The Roman Missal* © 1973, International Committee on English in the Litergy, Inc. (ICEL); excerpts from the English translation of *Rite of Penance* © 1974, ICEL; excerpts from the English translation of *A Book of Prayers* © 1982, ICEL. All rights reserved.
(6) © Martin, Israel, *The Pain that Heals,* Hodder and Stoughton, 1981, permission sought.
(7) © Ampleforth Abbey Trust
(8) Andrew Burnham
(9) Woodgate, M. V., *Father Congreve of Cowley,* SPCK, 1956
(10) Ed. Lemopoulos, Georges, *Let us pray to the Lord*, World Council of Churches, 1996
(11) Dix, Dom Gregory, *The Shape of the Liturgy*, Dacre Press, 1945, permission sought.
(12) © Spink, Kathryn, *In the Silence of the Heart*, SPCK, 1983, by permission of the publisher
(13) *Forward in Faith Prayer Book*
(14) *The Divine Office,* © William Collins Sons & Co. Ltd
(15) © ELLC
(16) *After the Third Collect*, Mowbray, 1952
(17) Milner-White, Eric, *A Procession of Passion Prayers*, SPCK, 1966, by kind permission of the Friends of York Minster
(18) Milner-White, Eric and Briggs, G. W. *Daily Prayer*, © Oxford University Press, 1941
(19) *The Sunday Missal*, © 1984, William Collins Sons & Co. Ltd

Sources

(20) Counsell, Michael ed., *2000 Years of Prayer*, Canterbury Press Norwich, 1999
(21) Silk, David, *Prayers for use at the Alternative Services*, © Mowbray, Cassell, 1980
(22) Pope John XXIII, *Journal of a Soul*, tr. White, Dorothy, © Geoffrey Chapman (a division of Cassell Ltd), 1980
(23) *Order of Christian Funerals*
(24) Buckley, Michael, *The Catholic Prayer Book*, published and copyright 1999 by Darton, Longman & Todd Ltd, and used by the permission of the publishers
(25) Pope John Paul II, *Prayers and Devotions*, The K. S. Giniger Company, 1984, permission sought
(26) Oliver, Stephen, ed., *Pastoral Prayers*, SPCK, 1995
(27) Anselm, tr. and © Ward, Benedicta, SLG, *Prayers and Meditations of Saint Anselm*, Penguin Classics, 1973
(28) *The Book of Common Prayer*, © Church Pension Fund, used by permission, 1979, ECUSA
(29) © Markby, Peter, Church Pastoral Aid Society
(30) © Linzey, Andrew, *Animal Rites: Liturgies of Animal Care*, SCM Press, 1999
(31) Pascal, Blaise, tr. Van de Weyer, Robert, *Selected Writings from Blaise Pascal*, Hunt & Thorpe, 1991
(32) *Book of Common Order of the Church of Scotland*, Saint Andrew Press, Edinburgh, 1994
(33) © Christian Aid
(34) tr. Bridges, Robert Ambrose? (1844–1930), from *the Yattendon Hymnal*, by permission of Oxford University Press
(35) *Hymns for Prayer and Praise*, Canterbury Press Norwich, © 1995, Panel of Monastic Musicians, Mount Saint Bernard Abbey, Coalville, Leicester LE67 5UL
(36) From *Hymns for Prayer and Praise* ibid. © 1995 Saint Mary's Abbey, West Malling, Kent NE19 6JX
(37) From *The Book of Common Prayer 1979*, ibid., tr. Bland Tucker, F., (1895–1984) © Church Pension Fund, used by permission
(38) ©1969 Quinn, James, SJ and Chapman, Geoffrey, a Cassell imprint, Wellington House, Strand, London WC2R 0BB
(39) Cousins, Ewart, ed., *The Tree of Life*, SPCK, 1978, © Paulist Press
(40) Obbard, Elizabeth Ruth, *A Walsingham Prayer Book*, Canterbury Press Norwich, 1997
(41) Finnegan, Seán ed., *A Book of Hours*, Canterbury Press Norwich, 1997
(42) © 1989 Wright, Ralph, OSB, GIA Publications Inc., 7404 South Mason Avenue, Chicago, Illinois 60638. All rights reserved.
(43) *Pilgrim's Manual*, © Walsingham College Trust Association Ltd
(44) John of the Cross, tr. Allison Peers, Edgar *The Complete Works of Saint John of the Cross*, Burns & Oates, 1934, revised 1953
(52) A.B.

The Illustrative Work of Martin Travers, ARCA FBS MGP

The illustrations between pages 382 and 392 are drawn from *The People's Rosary Book*, a publication issued by the Society of St Peter and St Paul in 1924, and are the work of artist/designer Martin Travers (b. 1886; d.1948).

Baptised Howard Martin Otto, Travers was brought up at Goodmanchester, Huntingdon, and educated at Tonbridge School, Kent, in the surrounding countryside of which he gained an appreciation of old buildings, especially churches. Outwardly a shy and reserved man, he began his career as the pupil of the architect Sir John Ninian Comper, and ended it as a competent book illustrator, prolific designer of ecclesiastical fixtures and fittings, and Tutor in Stained Glass at the Royal College of Art.

By his mid-twenties Travers was manifesting a distaste towards the Rev'd Percy Dearmer's promotion of an invented ceremonial tied down to the second year of the reign of Edward VI. Writing in 1916 he said, 'The history of the attempted revival of the "English Use" is the story of a lost opportunity. If only the eminent liturgical authorities, and the gifted authors who sought to popularise their discoveries, had set themselves to reform ritual and ceremonial on the lines upon which these things had taken root in our Churches, the ritual divergences and the ceremonial chaos – now ten times more confounded than ten years ago – would long ere this have been banished and put to flight . . . A very corrupt following of the Western usage has become popular or at least common in our Churches, so that simple and dignified ceremonies are made fussy, elaborate, and absurd. Hosts of red-robed acolytes stand about aimlessly in sanctuaries, wearing white gloves and strange caps, meaningless processions are performed on every double feast carrying nothing but banners and candles and going nowhere in particular.'[1]

The establishment of the Society of SS Peter and Paul in 1911 as a reaction by some extreme catholics in the Church of England to Percy Dearmer's *The Parson's Handbook* (1910), promoted the Continental Baroque, on the understanding that England would have followed continental ritual and ceremonial had not the Refomation 'interfered', thus the Continental Baroque was seen as the 'resumption of an arrested development.'[2] The Society of SS Peter and Paul thought that a catholic revival could best achieved through the publication of missals, office books and popular Mass books, and who better to illustrate them than Martin Travers, the reactionary *enfant-terrible* of the 'British Museum Rite'.

To some extent, Travers' illustrations failed to get his message of 1916 across, for nothing could be more English than his rendition of the continental baroque; indeed, the same can be said of his contemporaries, Alec Hunter, W Lawson and T. Noyes Lewis. Nevertheless, they have a delicacy of line and execution which, in recalling the strength of the catholic movement during the teens and twenties of the last century, also display a timeless sentimentality and a deep love towards Our Lady. He is buried in Goodmanchester churchyard.

Julian W. S. Litten

1. M Travers, *Pictures of the English Liturgy*, vol. 2, London, Society of SS Peter and Paul, 1916, 3–4
2. Mgr Ronald Knox in P. Anson, *Fashions in Church Furnishing*, London, Faith Press, 1960, 316

Angelus Domini and *Regina Caeli*

Angelus Domini

The angel of the Lord declared unto Mary,
and she conceived by the Holy Spirit.

Hail Mary, full of grace,
the Lord is with thee.
Blessed art thou among women
and blessed is the fruit of thy womb, Jesus.
Holy Mary, Mother of God,
pray for us sinners, now, and at the hour of our death.

Behold the handmaid of the Lord:
be it unto me according to thy word.

Hail Mary . . .

The Word was made flesh,
and dwelt among us.

Hail Mary . . .

V/ Pray for us, O holy Mother of God,
R/ that we may be made worthy of the promises of Christ.

Let us pray.

Pour forth, we beseech you, O Lord, your grace into our hearts, that we to whom the incarnation of Christ, your Son, was made known by the message of an angel, may by his passion and cross be brought to the glory of his resurrection, through Christ our Lord.

Regina Caeli

Instead of the Angelus *in Eastertide*

Joy to thee, O Queen of heaven, alleluia.
He whom thou wast meet to bear, alleluia.
As he promised hath arisen, alleluia.
Pour for us to him thy prayer, alleluia.

V/ Rejoice and be glad, O Virgin Mary, alleluia,
R/ for the Lord has risen indeed, alleluia.

O God, by the resurrection of your Son, our Lord Jesus Christ, you have brought joy to the whole world: grant that, by the help of his mother the Virgin Mary, we may obtain the joys of everlasting life; through Christ our Lord.

Before Praying

The Spirit helps us in our weakness; for we do not know how to pray as we ought, but that very Spirit intercedes with sighs too deep for words. And God, who searches the heart, knows what is the mind of the Spirit, because the Spirit intercedes for the saints according to the will of God. We know that all things work together for good for those who love God, who are called according to his purpose.

Romans 8:26–28

It is Christ who prays in every soul in whom he dwells.

R. H. Benson

Aperi Domine

Open my mouth, O Lord, to bless your holy name;
cleanse my heart from all evil, vain, and wandering thoughts;
enlighten my understanding and enkindle my feelings.
So may I pray attentively, devoutly and worthily
and be fit to be heard in the presence of your divine majesty.
Through Christ our Lord.

Liturgia Horarum (tr. AB) (8)

I PRAYER IN THE MORNING

Morning Prayers

Morning Prayers may begin with the Angelus *or* Regina Caeli *(see page 1).*

1 Adoration

Make the sign of the cross and say:

In the name of the Father, and of the Son, and of the Holy Spirit.

O Christ, our Morning Star, Splendour of Light Eternal, shining with the glory of the rainbow, come and waken us from the greyness of our apathy and renew in us your gift of hope.

The Venerable Bede (20)

or

I laid me down and slept, and rose up again,
for thou Lord sustained me:
all love, all glory, be to thee.

Thomas Ken, Directions for Prayers

or

As I rejoice in the gift of this new day,
so may the light of your presence, O God,
set my heart on fire with love for you;
now and for ever.

A Daily Office SSF* (3)

Gloria Patri

Glory be to the Father, and to the Son, and to the Holy Spirit:
as it was in the beginning, is now and ever shall be,
world without end.

or

Glory to the Father, and to the Son, and to the Holy Spirit:
as it was in the beginning, is now, and shall be for ever.

In Praise of Creation

Verses from Psalm 104 may be used:

1 O Lord, how manifold are your works! *
   In wisdom you have made them all;
   the earth is full of your creatures.
2 All of these look to you *
   to give them their food in due season.
3 When you give it them, they gather it; *
   you open your hand and they are filled with good.
4 When you hide your face they are troubled; *
   when you take away their breath,
     they die and return again to the dust.
5 When you send forth your spirit, they are created, *
   and you renew the face of the earth.
6 May the glory of the Lord endure for ever; *
   may the Lord rejoice in his works;
7 I will sing to the Lord as long as I live; *
   I will make music to my God while I have my being.

   Glory . . .

Psalm 104:26, 29–33, 35

For the whole of Psalm 104, see page 509.

Instead of Psalm 104, any psalm or canticle, particularly one of the following, may be used:

A Song of Creation (*Benedicite omnia opera*)	page 24 or 53
Psalm 8	page 440
Psalm 19 (part one)	page 445
Psalm 65	page 481
Psalm 67	page 482
Psalm 145	page 551

2 Bible Reading

Daily Bible Reading may be part of Prayer During the Day, see page 61.
For the reading scheme, see THE CHURCH'S YEAR, pages 177–433.

Advent	page 203
Christmas *and the Annunciation of the Lord*	page 213
Epiphany *(until Candlemas) and Feasts of the Lord*	page 221
Ordinary Time *(3 February until Shrove Tuesday)*	page 229
Lent	page 239
Passiontide	page 253
Eastertide	page 285
Ascension Day	page 293
Pentecost *(Friday after Ascension until Pentecost)*	page 299
Trinity	page 305
Corpus Christi	page 311
Sacred Heart	page 323
Ordinary Time *(Monday after Pentecost until the end of October)*	page 331

Our Lady	page 363
Saints	page 392
Faithful Departed	page 419
The King and the Kingdom *(Christ the King and Ordinary Time in November)*	page 425

3 Spiritual Reading

Use either a daily anthology or continue reading a suitable book.

4 Reflection

Reflect quietly on the reading.

One or more of the following prayers may help:

Veni, Sancte Spiritus

Come, Holy Spirit, fill the hearts of your faithful
and kindle in them the fire of your love.
Send forth your Spirit and they shall be made
and you will renew the face of the earth.

Act of Faith

My God, I believe in you and all that your Church teaches, because you have said it, and your word is true.

Act of Hope

My God, I hope in you, for grace and for glory, because of your promises, your mercy and your power.

Act of Love

My God, I love you with all my heart and above all things, and for your sake I love my neighbour as myself.

Act of Contrition

My God, I am very sorry for all the sins by which I have offended you, and I resolve by the help of your grace not to sin again.

Act of Consecration

My God, I give myself to you, in union with the offering of Jesus Christ on the cross and in the holy sacrifice of the Mass.

5 Offering of the Day

Think now about the day ahead: its joys and difficulties, its opportunities for loving God and your neighbour. Remember those you will meet, those whom you may help or harm. If you will be alone, remember those who are near and dear and those whom you can support in prayer.

Prayer to the Guardian Angel

O angel of God,
appointed by divine mercy to be my guardian,
enlighten and protect,
direct and govern me
this day.

Any one of the following may be used or they may be used for the different days of the week: (i) on Sunday, (ii) on Monday etc.

Morning Offering (i)

Lord Jesus Christ,
take all my freedom,
my memory, my understanding, and my will.
All that I have and cherish
you have given me.
I surrender it all to be guided by your will.
Your grace and your love are wealth enough for me.
Give me these, Lord Jesus,
and I ask for nothing more.

Prayer of Self-Dedication to Jesus Christ (5)

Morning Offering (ii)

Father,
you have brought us
to the beginning of a new day.
Your hand is upon us to care for and protect us.
We offer you our lives and hearts.
May we always do your will
and love our neighbour as ourselves.

Ampleforth (7)

Morning Offering (iii)

Father, we offer to you this day
all our thoughts, words and actions,
all our sufferings and disappointments,
and all our joys.
And we unite our lives
with that of your beloved Son, Jesus Christ.

Ampleforth (7)

Morning Offering (iv)

O my God, I believe in thee,
do thou strengthen my faith.
All my hopes are in thee,
do thou secure them.
I love thee with my whole heart,
teach me to love thee daily more and more.
I am sorry that I have offended thee,
do thou increase my sorrow.
I adore thee as my first beginning.
I aspire after thee as my last end.
I give thee thanks as my constant benefactor.
I call upon thee as my sovereign protector.
Vouchsafe, O my God,
    to conduct me by thy wisdom,
    to restrain me by thy justice,

    to comfort me by thy mercy,
    to defend me by thy power.
To thee I desire to consecrate all my thoughts,
    words, actions and sufferings;
that henceforward I may think of thee, speak of thee,
and willingly refer all my actions to thy greater glory,
and suffer willingly whatever thou shalt appoint.
Lord, I desire that in all things thy will may be done,
because it is thy will,
and in the manner that thou willest.
I beg of thee
    to enlighten my understanding,
    to inflame my will,
    to purify my body,
    and to sanctify my soul.

Richard Challoner
The Garden of the Soul

Morning Offering (v)

O Lord, grant me to greet the coming day in peace.
Help me in all things to rely upon your holy will.
In every hour of the day reveal your will to me.
Bless my dealings with all who surround me.
Teach me to treat all that comes to me throughout the day
    with peace of soul,
    and with firm conviction that your will governs all.
In all my deeds and words guide my thoughts and feelings.
In unforeseen events let me not forget that all are sent by you.
Teach me to act firmly and wisely,
    without embittering and embarrassing others.
Give me the strength to bear the fatigue of the coming day
    with all that it shall bring.
Direct my will, teach me to pray,
    pray you yourself in me.

Prayer at the beginning of the day,
Metropolitan Philaret of Moscow (19th cent.) (10)

Morning Offering (vi)

Let the healing grace of your love, O Lord, so transform me that I may play my part in the transfiguration of the world from a place of suffering, death and corruption to a realm of infinite light, joy and love. Make me so obedient to your Spirit that my life may become a living prayer, and a witness to your unfailing presence.

Martin Israel (6)

Morning Offering (vii)

O Jesus, through the most pure heart of Mary,
I offer you all the prayers, works,
sufferings and joys of this day,
for the intentions of your Divine Heart.

Ampleforth (7)

Other suitable prayers

O my God,
whatever is nearer to me than thou,
things of this earth and things more naturally pleasing to me
will be sure to interrupt the sight of thee,
unless thy grace interfere.
Keep thou my eyes, my heart,
from any such miserable tyranny.
Break my bonds, raise my heart.
Keep my whole being fixed on thee.
Let me never lose sight of thee,
and while I gaze on thee,
let my love of thee grow more and more every day.

John Henry Newman

We, your servants, offer you, O God, prayers and intercessions
on behalf of the peace of the churches
and the tranquillity of the monasteries;
keep your ministers in righteousness,
forgive sinners who turn to you,
make the rich generous in almsgiving,
provide for the poor,
support the widows,
educate the orphans,

Morning Prayers

sustain the aged,
guard the youth by your cross,
gather the dispersed,
convert those in error;
and let our prayers and intercessions prevail with you,
and we will offer praise and honour
to you high Trinity, now and always and for ever.

Morning Prayer,
Syrian Liturgy (10)

God grant me the serenity
to accept the things I cannot change,
courage to change the things I can,
and wisdom to know the difference.

Reinhold Niebuhr

Make me worthy, Lord, to serve those throughout the world who live and die in poverty and hunger. Through my hands give them this day their daily bread, and by my understanding love, give peace and joy.

Mother Teresa of Calcutta*

Christ be with me, Christ within me,
Christ behind me, Christ before me,
Christ beside me, Christ to win me,
Christ to comfort and restore me.

Christ beneath me, Christ above me,
Christ in quiet, Christ in danger,
Christ in hearts of all that love me,
Christ in mouth of friends and stranger.

Saint Patrick's Breastplate

6 Collect and Lord's Prayer

Either the Collect for the Day or one of these prayers may be said:

Prayer on a Sunday

O God, who makest us glad with the weekly remembrance of the glorious resurrection of thy Son our Lord: vouchsafe us this day such a blessing

through thy worship, that the days which follow it may be spent in thy favour,
through the same Jesus Christ our Lord.

William Bright

Prayer on a Weekday

Almighty and everlasting God,
we thank you that you have brought us safely
to the beginning of this day.
Keep us from falling into sin
or running into danger,
order us in all our doings
and guide us to do always
what is righteous in your sight;
through Jesus Christ our Lord.

*Book of Common Prayer * (2)*

For those who love you, Lord,
you have prepared blessings which no eye has seen;
fill our hearts with longing for you,
that, loving you in all things and above all things,
we may obtain your promises,
which exceed every heart's desire.

ICEL (5)

The morning's praying is summed up in the prayer which Jesus himself taught:

Pater Noster

Our Father, who art in heaven,
hallowed be thy name;
Thy kingdom come,
Thy will be done, on earth as it is in heaven.
Give us this day our daily bread,
and forgive us our trespasses,
as we forgive those who trespass against us;
and lead us not into temptation,
but deliver us from evil.
For thine is the kingdom, the power and the glory,
for ever and ever.

7 Conclusion

One of the following endings is used:

God be in my head, and in my understanding.
God be in mine eyes, and in my looking.
God be in my mouth, and in my speaking.
God be in my heart, and in my thinking.
God be at my end, and at my departing.

Sarum Primer 1514

or

Blessing and honour, thanksgiving and praise,
more than we can utter, more than we conceive
be unto thee,
O most adorable Trinity, Father, Son and Holy Ghost,
by all angels, all men, all creatures,
for ever and ever.

or

To God the Father, who first loved us,
and made us accepted in the Beloved:
To God the Son, who loved us,
and washed us from our sins in his own blood:
To God the Holy Ghost,
who sheds the love of God abroad in our hearts
be all love and all glory for time and eternity.

Thomas Ken

Let us bless the Lord.
Thanks be to God.

May the Lord bless us, and keep us from all evil,
and bring us to everlasting life.

or

Let us bless the Lord.
Thanks be to God.

May the divine assistance remain with us always.

If the Angelus *was not used earlier, there may follow:*

Ave Maria

Hail Mary, full of grace,
the Lord is with thee.
Blessed art thou among women
and blessed is the fruit of thy womb, Jesus.
Holy Mary, Mother of God,
pray for us sinners, now, and at the hour of our death.

Morning Prayer

The Office of Lauds on Sundays and Feast Days

Items marked (+) are also available in traditional language, see Morning Prayer in Traditional Language, pages 49–58.

In The Propers *(see pages 203–431) festal and seasonal alternatives are available for items marked (*).*

Advent *page 203*

Christmas *page 213*
and the Annunciation of the Lord

Epiphany *(until Candlemas)* *page 221*
and Feasts of the Lord

Ordinary Time
(3 February until Shrove Tuesday) *page 229*

Lent *page 239*

Passiontide *page 253*

Eastertide *page 285*

Ascension Day *page 293*

Pentecost
(Friday after Ascension until Pentecost) *page 299*

Trinity *page 305*

Corpus Christi *page 311*

Sacred Heart *page 323*

Ordinary Time
(Monday after Pentecost until the end of October) *page 331*

Our Lady *page 363*

Saints *page 397*

Faithful Departed *page 419*

The King and the Kingdom
(Christ the King and Ordinary Time in November) *page 425*

V/ O Lord, open our lips.   *or*   V/ Lord, open our lips.
R/ And our mouth shall   R/ And we shall praise
proclaim your praise.   your name.

Invitatory

Jubilate Deo (+)

1 O be joyful in the Lord, all the earth; *
   serve the Lord with gladness
     and come before his presence with a song.
2 Know that the Lord is God; *
   it is he that has made us and we are his;
     we are his people and the sheep of his pasture.
3 Enter his gates with thanksgiving;
   and his courts with praise; *
     give thanks to him and bless his holy name.
4 or the Lord is gracious; his love is everlasting, *
   and his faithfulness endures from generation to generation.

   Glory . . .

Psalm 100

At Easter, the Easter Anthems may be used (see pages 583–590).

Office Hymn (*)

Splendor Paternae Gloriae

O splendour of God's glory bright,
True light begotten of his light,
Full light of light, light's living spring,
O day, our days illumining.

Come, righteous sun of heavenly love,
Pour down your radiance from above;
And shed the Holy Spirit's ray
On every thought and sense today.

With prayer the Father we implore,
The Father glorious evermore:
Almighty, source of grace and power,
Be with us in temptation's hour,

To guide whatever we may do,
With love all envy to subdue,
To give us grace to bear all wrong,
Transforming sorrow into song.

All laud to you, O Father be,
To you, O Son, eternally;
To you, the Spirit, equal praise
From joyful hearts we ever raise.

LM
Ambrose? (34)
tr. Robert Bridges*
Hymns for Prayer and Praise 221

Psalmody (on Sunday, Solemnities and Feasts)

Psalm (on Sunday, Solemnities and Feasts)

Either *(Sunday, Week 1)*

Psalm 63:1–9

1 O God, you are my God; eagerly I seek you; *
   my soul is athirst for you.
2 My flesh also faints for you, *
   as in a dry and thirsty land where there is no water.
3 So would I gaze upon you in your holy place, *
   that I might behold your power and your glory.
4 Your loving-kindness is better than life itself *
   and so my lips shall praise you
5 I will bless you as long as I live *
   and lift up my hands in your name.

6 My soul shall be satisfied, as with marrow and fatness, *
     and my mouth shall praise you with joyful lips,
7 When I remember you upon my bed *
     and meditate on you in the watches of the night.
8 For you have been my helper *
     and under the shadow of your wings will I rejoice.
9 My soul clings to you; *
     your right hand shall hold me fast.

   Glory . . .

***or** (Sunday, Week 3)*

Psalm 93

1 The Lord is king and has put on glorious apparel; *
     the Lord has put on his glory
     and girded himself with strength.
2 He has made the whole world so sure *
     that it cannot be moved.
3 Your throne has been established from of old; *
     you are from everlasting.
4 The floods have lifted up, O Lord,
     the floods have lifted up their voice *
     the floods lift up their pounding waves.
5 Mightier than the thunder of many waters,
     mightier than the breakers of the sea, *
     the Lord on high is mightier.
6 Your testimonies are very sure; *
     holiness adorns your house, O Lord, for ever.

   Glory . . .

***or** (Sunday, Weeks 2 and 4)*

Psalm 118

1 O give thanks to the Lord, for he is good; *
     his mercy endures forever.
2 Let Israel now proclaim, *
     'His mercy endures for ever.'

3 Let the house of Aaron now proclaim, *
    'His mercy endures for ever.'
 4 Let those who fear the Lord proclaim *
    'His mercy endures for ever.'
 5 In my constraint, I called to the Lord; *
    the Lord answered and set me free.
 6 The Lord is at my side; I will not fear; *
    what can flesh do to me?
 7 With the Lord at my side as my saviour, *
    I shall see the downfall of my enemies.
 8 It is better to take refuge in the Lord *
    than to put any confidence in flesh.
 9 It is better to take refuge in the Lord *
    than to put any confidence in princes.
10 All the nations encompassed me, *
    but by the name of the Lord I drove them back.
11 They hemmed me in, they hemmed me in on every side, *
    but by the name of the Lord I drove them back.
12 They swarmed about me like bees;
    they blazed like fire among thorns, *
    but by the name of the Lord I drove them back.
13 Surely, I was thrust to the brink, *
    but the Lord came to my help.
14 The Lord is my strength and my song, *
    and he has become my salvation.
15 Joyful shouts of salvation *
    sound from the tents of the righteous.
16 'The right hand of the Lord does mighty deeds;
    the right hand of the Lord raises up; *
    the right hand of the Lord does mighty deeds.'
17 I shall not die, but live *
    and declare the works of the Lord.
18 The Lord has punished me sorely, *
    but he has not given me over to death.
19 Open to me the gates of righteousness, *
    that I may enter and give thanks to the Lord.
20 This is the gate of the Lord; *
    the righteous shall enter through it.
21 I will give thanks to you, for you have answered me *
    and have become my salvation.

22 The stone which the builders rejected *
   has become the chief cornerstone.
23 This is the Lord's doing, *
   and it is marvellous in our eyes.
24 This is the day that the Lord has made; *
   we will rejoice and be glad in it.
25 Come, O Lord, and save us we pray. *
   Come, Lord, send us now prosperity.
26 Blessed is he who comes in the name of the Lord; *
   we bless you from the house of the Lord.
27 The Lord is God; he has given us light; *
   link the pilgrims with cords
   right to the horns of the altar.
28 You are my God and I will thank you; *
   you are my God and I will exalt you.
29 O give thanks to the Lord, for he is good; *
   his mercy endures for ever.

   Glory . . .

Canticle (on Sunday, Solemnities and Feasts)(*)

Either *(Sunday, Weeks 1 and 3)*

A Song of Creation (+)
Benedicite omnia opera

1 Bless the Lord all you works of the Lord: *
   sing his praise and exalt him for ever.
2 Bless the Lord you heavens: *
   sing his praise and exalt him for ever.
3 Bless the Lord you angels of the Lord: *
   bless the Lord all you his hosts;
   bless the Lord you waters above the heavens: *
   sing his praise and exalt him for ever.
4 Bless the Lord sun and moon: *
   bless the Lord you stars of heaven;
   bless the Lord all rain and dew: *
   sing his praise and exalt him for ever.
5 Bless the Lord all winds that blow: *

    bless the Lord you fire and heat;
    bless the Lord scorching wind and bitter cold: *
    sing his praise and exalt him for ever.
6 Bless the Lord dews and falling snows: *
    bless the Lord you nights and days;
    bless the Lord light and darkness: *
    sing his praise and exalt him for ever.
7 Bless the Lord frost and cold: *
    bless the Lord you ice and snow;
    bless the Lord lightnings and clouds: *
    sing his praise and exalt him for ever.
8 O let the earth bless the Lord: *
    bless the Lord you mountains and hills;
    bless the Lord all that grows in the ground: *
    sing his praise and exalt him for ever.
9 Bless the Lord you springs: *
    bless the Lord you seas and rivers;
    bless the Lord you whales and all that swim in the waters: *
    sing his praise and exalt him for ever.
10 Bless the Lord all birds of the air: *
    bless the Lord you beasts and cattle;
    bless the Lord all people on earth: *
    sing his praise and exalt him for ever.
11 O people of God bless the Lord: *
    bless the Lord you priests of the Lord;
    bless the Lord you servants of the Lord: *
    sing his praise and exalt him for ever.
12 Bless the Lord all you of upright spirit: *
    bless the Lord you that are holy and humble in heart;

    Bless the Father, the Son and the Holy Spirit: *
    sing his praise and exalt him for ever.

The Song of the Three 35–65
ELLC (15)

or *(Sunday, Weeks 2 and 4)*

A Song of the Three (+)
Benedictus es

1 Blessed are you, the God of our ancestors, *
   worthy to be praised and exalted for ever.
2 Blessed is your holy and glorious name, *
   worthy to be praised and exalted for ever.
3 Blessed are you, in your holy and glorious temple, *
   worthy to be praised and exalted for ever.
4 Blessed are you who look into the depths, *
   worthy to be praised and exalted for ever.
5 Blessed are you, enthroned on the cherubim, *
   worthy to be praised and exalted for ever.
6 Blessed are you on the throne of your kingdom, *
   worthy to be praised and exalted for ever.
7 Blessed are you in the heights of heaven, *
   worthy to be praised and exalted for ever.

Bless the Father, the Son and the Holy Spirit: *
worthy to be praised and exalted for ever.

The Song of the Three 29–34
ELLC (15)

Lauds Psalm (on Sunday, Solemnities and Feasts)

Either *(Sunday, Week 1)*

Psalm 149

1 Alleluia.
   O sing to the Lord a new song; *
   sing his praise in the congregation of the faithful.
2 Let Israel rejoice in their maker; *
   let the children of Zion be joyful in their king.
3 Let them praise his name in the dance; *
   let them sing praise to him with timbrel and lyre
4 For the Lord has pleasure in his people *
   and adorns the poor with salvation.
5 Let the faithful be joyful in glory; *

Morning Prayer

    let them rejoice in their ranks;
6 With the praises of God in their mouths *
    and a two-edged sword in their hand;
7 To execute vengeance on the nations *
    and punishment on the peoples;
8 To bind their kings in chains *
    and their nobles with fetters of iron;
9 To execute on them the judgement decreed: *
    such honour have all his faithful servants.
    Alleluia.

Glory . . .

or *(Sunday, Weeks 2 and 4)*

Psalm 150

1 Alleluia.
    O praise God in his holiness; *
        praise him in the firmament of his power.
2 Praise him for his mighty acts; *
    praise him according to his excellent greatness.
3 Praise him with the blast of the trumpet; *
    praise him upon the harp and lyre.
4 Praise him with timbrel and dances; *
    praise him upon the strings and pipe.
5 Praise him with ringing cymbals; *
    praise him upon the clashing cymbals.
6 Let everything that has breath *
    praise the Lord.
    Alleluia.

Glory . . .

or *(Sunday, Week 3)*

Psalm 148

1 Alleluia.
    Praise the Lord from the heavens; *
    praise him in the heights.

2 Praise him, all you angels of his; *
    praise him, all his host.
3 Praise him, sun and moon; *
    praise him, all you stars of light.
4 Praise him, heaven of heavens, *
    and you waters above the heavens.
5 Let them praise the name of the Lord, *
    for he commanded and they were created.
6 He made them fast for ever and ever; *
    he gave them a law which shall not pass away.
7 Praise the Lord from the earth, *
    you sea monsters and all deeps;
8 Fire and hail, snow and mist, *
    tempestuous wind, fulfilling his word;
9 Mountains and all hills, *
    fruit trees and all cedars;
10 Wild beasts and all cattle, *
    creeping things and birds on the wing;
11 Kings of the earth and all peoples, *
    princes and all rulers of the world;
12 Young men and women,
    old and young together; *
    let them praise the name of the Lord.
13 For his name only is exalted, *
    his splendour above earth and heaven.
14 He has raised up the horn of his people
    and praise for all his faithful servants, *
    the children of Israel, a people who are near him.
    Alleluia.

Glory . . .

Scripture Reading

The first reading appointed for the day (see the Propers, pages 203–431).

or

Short Reading (*)

This is the covenant that I will make with the house of Israel after those days, says the Lord: I will put my law within them, and I will write it on their hearts; and I will be their God, and they shall be my people. No longer shall they teach one another, or say to each other, 'Know the Lord,' for they shall all know me, from the least of them to the greatest, says the Lord; for I will forgive their iniquity, and remember their sin no more.

Jeremiah 31:33–34

Short Responsory

R/ You are the Christ, the Son of the living God. Have mercy on us.
R/ You are the Christ, the Son of the living God. Have mercy on us.
V/ You are seated at the right hand of the Father.
R/ You are the Christ, the Son of the living God. Have mercy on us.
V/ Glory . . . Holy Spirit.
R/ You are the Christ, the Son of the living God. Have mercy on us.

Divine Office (14)

Refrains (*)

Seek the Lord while he may be found, call upon him while he is near.

Isaiah 55:6 (RSV)

God is spirit, and those who worship him must worship in spirit and in truth.

John 4:24 (RSV)

Gospel Canticle: Benedictus

The Song of Zechariah (+)

Refrain (*as above or as in the Propers*)

1. Blessed be the Lord the God of Israel, *
   who has come to his people and set them free.
2. He has raised up for us a mighty Saviour, *
   born of the house of his servant David.

3 Through his holy prophets God promised of old *
    to save us from our enemies,
    from the hands of all that hate us,
4 to show mercy to our ancestors, *
    and to remember his holy covenant.
5 This was the oath God swore to our father Abraham: *
    to set us free from the hands of our enemies,
6 free to worship him without fear, *
    holy and righteous in his sight
    all the days of our life.
7 And you, child, shall be called the prophet of the Most High, *
    for you will go before the Lord to prepare his way,
8 to give his people knowledge of salvation *
    by the forgiveness of all their sins.
9 In the tender compassion of our God *
    the dawn from on high shall break upon us,
10 to shine on those who dwell in darkness and the shadow of death, *
    and to guide our feet into the way of peace.

   Glory . . .

Luke 1:68–79
ELLC*(15)

Refrain *(repeated)*

Prayers

The day is offered to God.

If set prayers are desired, some or all of the following petitions may be adapted and used (and see pages 14–15):

Govern and direct your holy Church;
fill it with love and truth;
and grant it that unity which is your will . . .

Give us boldness to preach the gospel in all the world,
and make disciples of all the nations . . .

Enlighten *N* our bishop, and all who minister, with knowledge and
    understanding,
that by their teaching and their lives they may proclaim your word . . .

Give your people grace to hear and receive your word,
and to bring forth the fruit of the Spirit . . .

Bring into the way of truth all who have erred and are deceived.

Strengthen those who stand;
comfort and help the faint-hearted;
raise up the fallen;
and finally beat down Satan under our feet . . .

from the Litany (1)

Our Father

The Lord's Prayer is said here or after the Collect.

Collect (*)

The collect of the day (or season) is said

or

Eternal God and Father,
you create us by your power
and redeem us by your love:
guide and strengthen us by your Spirit,
that we may give ourselves in love and service
to one another and to you;
through Jesus Christ our Lord.

Common Worship (1)

Te Deum (Sunday, Solemnities and Feasts only)(+)

We praise you, O God,
we acclaim you as the Lord;
all creation worships you,
the Father everlasting.
To you all angels, all the powers of heaven,
the cherubim and seraphim, sing in endless praise:
Holy holy holy Lord, God of power and might:

heaven and earth are full of your glory.
The glorious company of apostles praise you.
The noble fellowship of prophets praise you.
The white-robed army of martyrs praise you.
Throughout the world the holy Church acclaims you;
Father of majesty unbounded;
your true and only Son, worthy of all praise,
the Holy Spirit, advocate and guide.

You, Christ, are the King of glory,
the eternal Son of the Father.
When you took our flesh to set us free:
you humbly chose the Virgin's womb.
You overcame the sting of death:
and opened the kingdom of heaven to all believers.
You are seated at God's right hand in glory:
we believe that you will come and be our judge.
Come then Lord and help your people:
bought with the price of your own blood;
and bring us with your saints:
to glory everlasting.

The Te Deum *may end here.*

Save your people Lord and bless your inheritance.
Govern and uphold them now and always.

Day by day we bless you.
We praise your name for ever.

Keep us today, Lord, from all sin:
have mercy on us, Lord, have mercy.

Lord show us your love and mercy:
for we have put our trust in you.

In you, Lord, is our hope:
let us never be put to shame.

ELLC* (15)

Ending

The Lord bless us, and keep us from all evil, and bring us to everlasting life.
Amen.

Morning Prayer

The Office of Lauds on Weekdays

Items marked (+) *are also available in traditional language, see Morning Prayer in Traditional Language, pages 49–58.*

In The Propers *(see pages 203–431) festal and seasonal alternatives are available for items marked (*).*

Advent	*page 203*
Christmas *and the Annunciation of the Lord*	*page 213*
Epiphany *(until Candlemas) and Feasts of the Lord*	*page 221*
Ordinary Time *(3 February until Shrove Tuesday)*	*page 229*
Lent	*page 239*
Passiontide	*page 253*
Eastertide	*page 285*
Ascension Day	*page 293*
Pentecost *(Friday after Ascension until Pentecost)*	*page 299*
Trinity	*page 305*
Corpus Christi	*page 311*
Sacred Heart	*page 323*
Ordinary Time *(Monday after Pentecost until the end of October)*	*page 331*

Our Lady *page 363*

Saints *page 397*

Faithful Departed *page 419*

The King and the Kingdom
(Christ the King and Ordinary Time in November) *page 425*

V/ O Lord, open our lips.   *or*   V/ Lord, open our lips.
R/ And our mouth shall proclaim your praise.   R/ And we shall praise your name.

Invitatory (+)

Venite, exultemus Domino

1 O come, let us sing to the Lord; *
    let us heartily rejoice in the rock of our salvation.
2 Let us come into his presence with thanksgiving; *
    and be glad in him with psalms.
3 For the Lord is a great God; *
    and a great king above all gods.
4 In his hand are the depths of the earth; *
    and the heights of the mountains are his also.
5 The sea is his, for he made it, *
    and his hands have moulded the dry land.
6 Come, let us worship and bow down *
    and kneel before the Lord our Maker.
7 For he is our God; *
    we are the people of his pasture and the sheep of his hand.

8 O that today you would listen to his voice! *
    'Harden not your hearts as at Meribah,
    on that day at Massah in the wilderness,
9 'When your forebears tested me, and put me to the proof, *
    though they had seen my works.
10 'Forty years long I detested that generation and said, *
    "This people are wayward in their hearts;
    they do not know my ways."
11   'So I swore in my wrath, *
      "They shall not enter into my rest."'

    Glory . . .   *Psalm 95*

Office Hymn (*)

Ecce iam noctis tenuatur umbra

See, now the shadows of the night are fading,
Sunlight arising, dawn of day in splendour;
Spirit enlightened, to the mighty Father
Pray we devoutly,

That in his mercy he may always keep us,
Eager and ready for his holy service;
Then may he give us, of a father's goodness,
Joy in his kingdom.

This may he grant us, God for ever blessed,
Father eternal, Son and Holy Spirit:
His is the glory filling all creation,
Ever resounding.

Alcuin? (35)
Hymns for Prayer and Praise 223

Psalms (see pages 437–558)

Either the psalms for the day:

	Week 1	Week 2	Week 3	Week 4
Monday	5	42	84	90
Tuesday	24 *(see below)*	43	85	101
Wednesday	36	77	86	108
Thursday	57	80	87	143
Friday	51 *(see below)*	51	51	51
Saturday	119:145–152 *(19)*	92	119:145–152 *(19)*	92

or Psalms 24 or 51

Psalm 24 *(any weekday)*

1 The earth is the Lord's and all that fills it, *
   the compass of the world and all who dwell therein.
2 For he has founded it upon the seas *

     and set it firm upon the rivers of the deep.
3 'Who shall ascend the hill of the Lord, *
     or who can rise up in his holy place?'
4 'Those who have clean hands and a pure heart, *
     who have not lifted up their soul to an idol,
     nor sworn an oath to a lie;
5 'They shall receive a blessing from the Lord, *
     a just reward from the God of their salvation.'
6 Such is the company of those who seek him, *
     who seek your face, O God of Jacob.

7 Lift up your heads, O gates;
     and be lifted up, you everlasting doors; *
     and the King of glory shall come in.
8 'Who is the King of glory?' *
     'The Lord, strong and mighty,
     the Lord who is mighty in battle.'
9 Lift up your heads, O gates;
     be lifted up, you everlasting doors; *
     and the King of glory shall come in.
10 'Who is this King of glory?' *
     'The Lord of hosts,
     he is the King of glory.'

    Glory . . .

or

Psalm 51 *(on Friday)*

1 Have mercy on me, O God, in your great goodness; *
     according to the abundance of your compassion
     blot out my offences.
2 Wash me thoroughly from my wickedness *
     and cleanse me from my sin.
3 For I acknowledge my faults *
     and my sin is ever before me.
4 Against you only have I sinned *
     and done what is evil in your sight,

5 So that you are justified in your sentence *
 and righteous in your judgement.
6 I have been wicked even from my birth, *
 a sinner when my mother conceived me.
7 Behold, you desire truth deep within me *
 and shall make me understand wisdom
 in the depths of my heart.
8 Purge me with hyssop and I shall be clean; *
 wash me and I shall be whiter than snow.
9 Make me hear of joy and gladness, *
 that the bones you have broken may rejoice.
10 Turn your face from my sins *
 and blot out all my misdeeds.
11 Make me a clean heart, O God, *
 and renew a right spirit within me.
12 Cast me not away from your presence *
 and take not your holy spirit from me.
13 Give me again the joy of your salvation *
 and sustain me with your gracious spirit;
14 Then shall I teach your ways to the wicked *
 and sinners shall return to you.
15 Deliver me from my guilt, O God,
 the God of my salvation, *
 and my tongue shall sing of your righteousness.
16 O Lord, open my lips *
 and my mouth shall proclaim your praise.
17 For you desire no sacrifice, else I would give it; *
 you take no delight in burnt offerings.
18 The sacrifice of God is a broken spirit; *
 a broken and contrite heart, O God, you will not despise.
19 O be favourable and gracious to Zion; *
 build up the walls of Jerusalem.
20 Then you will accept sacrifices offered in righteousness,
 the burnt offerings and oblations; *
 then shall they offer up bulls on your altar.

 Glory . . .

Canticle (*)

Monday (*)

A Song of David

Refrain: Splendour and majesty are yours, O God; *
 you are exalted as head over all.

1 Blessed are you, God of Israel, for ever and ever; *
 for yours is the greatness, the power,
 the glory, the splendour and the majesty.
2 Everything in heaven and on earth is yours; *
 yours is the kingdom, O Lord,
 and you are exalted as head over all.
3 Riches and honour come from you *
 and you rule over all.
4 In your hand are power and might; *
 yours it is to give power and strength to all.
5 And now we give you thanks, our God, *
 and praise your glorious name.
6 For all things come from you, *
 and of your own have we given you.

 Glory . . .

Refrain: Splendour and majesty are yours, O God; *
 you are exalted as head over all.

1 Chronicles 29:10b-13,14b
Common Worship (1)

or

Week 1, A Song of David, *Canticle 4, as above.*

Week 2, A Song of God's Servants, *Canticle 30, page 580.*

Week 3, A Song of Peace, *Canticle 6, page 561.*

Week 4, A Song of the Lord's Salvation, *Canticle 14, page 567.*

Tuesday (*)

A Song of God's Reign

Refrain: See what the Lord our God has done *
 and exalt him in the sight of the living.

1 Blessed be God, who lives for ever, *
 whose reign endures throughout all ages.
2 Declare God's praise before the nations, *
 you who are the children of Israel.
3 For if our God has scattered you among them, *
 there too has he shown you his greatness.
4 Exalt him in the sight of the living, *
 because he is our God and our Father for ever.
5 Though God punishes you for your wickedness, *
 mercy will be shown to you all.
6 God will gather you from every nation, *
 from wherever you have been scattered.
7 When you turn to the Lord
 with all your heart and soul, *
 God will hide his face from you no more.
8 See what the Lord has done for you *
 and give thanks with a loud voice.
9 Praise the Lord of righteousness *
 and exalt the King of the ages.

Glory . . .

Refrain: See what the Lord our God has done *
 and exalt him in the sight of the living.

Tobit 13:1–6
A Daily Office SSF (3)

or

Week 1, A Song of God's Reign, *Canticle 25, as above.*

Week 2, A Song of the Living, *Canticle 11, page 564.*

Week 3, A Song of Trust in the Lord, *Canticle 9, page 563.*

Week 4, The Prayer of Azariah in the Furnace, *Canticle 32, page 581.*

Wednesday (*)

The Song of Hannah

Refrain: Blessed are those who believe, *
for what God has promised will be fulfilled.

1 My heart exults in the Lord; *
   my strength is exalted in my God.
2 My mouth derides my enemies, *
   because I rejoice in your salvation.
3 There is no Holy One like you, O Lord, *
   nor any Rock like you, our God.
4 For you are a God of knowledge *
   and by you our actions are weighed.
5 The bows of the mighty are broken, *
   but the feeble gird on strength.
6 Those who were full now search for bread,*
   but those who were hungry are well fed.
7 The barren woman has borne sevenfold, *
   but she who has many children is forlorn.
8 Both the poor and the rich are of your making; *
   you bring low and you also exalt.
9 You raise up the poor from the dust, *
   and lift the needy from the ash heap.
10 You make them sit with the rulers *
   and inherit a place of honour.
11 For the pillars of the earth are yours *
   and on them you have set the world.

   Glory . . .

Refrain: Blessed are those who believe, *
for what God has promised will be fulfilled.

1 Samuel 2:1–8
A Daily Office SSF (3)

or

Week 1, A Song of God's Mercy, *Canticle 27, page 578.*

Week 2, The Song of Hannah, *Canticle 3, as above.*

Morning Prayer

Week 3, A Song of the Might of the Lord, Canticle 10, page 564.

Week 4, A Song of the Bride, Canticle 18, page 570.

Thursday (*)

A Song of Deliverance

Refrain: All the earth, shout and sing for joy, *
     for great in your midst is the Holy One.

1 'Behold, God is my salvation; *
   I will trust and will not be afraid;
2 'For the Lord God is my strength and my song, *
   and has become my salvation.'
3 With joy you will draw water *
   from the wells of salvation.
4 On that day you will say, *
   'Give thanks to the Lord, call upon his name;
5 'Make known his deeds among the nations, *
   proclaim that his name is exalted.
6 'Sing God's praises, who has triumphed gloriously; *
   let this be known in all the world.
7 'Shout and sing for joy, you that dwell in Zion, *
   for great in your midst is the Holy One of Israel.'

   Glory . . .

Refrain: All the earth, shout and sing for joy, *
     for great in your midst is the Holy One.

Isaiah 12:2–6
A Daily Office SSF (3)

or

Week 1, A Song of the Shepherd, Canticle 21, page 573.

Week 2, A Song of Deliverance, Canticle 8, as above.

Week 3, A Song of God's Herald, Canticle 12, page 565.

Week 4, A Song of Jerusalem our Mother, Canticle 19, page 571.

Friday (*)

A Song of Solomon

Refrain: Many waters cannot quench love; *
 neither can the floods drown it.

1 Set me as a seal upon your heart, *
 as a seal upon your arm;
2 For love is strong as death
 passion fierce as the grave; *
 its flashes are flashes of fire,
 a raging flame.
3 Many waters cannot quench love, *
 neither can the floods drown it.
4 If all the wealth of our house
 were offered for love, *
 it would be utterly scorned.

 Glory . . .

Refrain: Many waters cannot quench love; *
 neither can the floods drown it.

Song of Solomon 8:7–8
A Daily Office SSF (3)

or

Week 1, A Song of God the Saviour, *Canticle 15, page 568.*

Week 2, A Prayer of Habakkuk, *Canticle 24, page 575.*

Week 3, A Song of Entreaty, *Canticle 20, page 572.*

Week 4, A Song of Thanksgiving from a Liberated People, *Canticle 26, page 577.*

Saturday (*)

The Song of Moses and Miriam

Refrain: In your unfailing love, O Lord, *
    you lead the people whom you have redeemed.

1 I will sing to the Lord, who has triumph triumphed gloriously, *
    the horse and his rider have been thrown into the sea.
2 The Lord is my strength and my song *
    and has become my salvation.
3 This is my God whom I will praise *
    the God of my forebears whom I will exalt.
4 The Lord is a warrior, *
    the Lord is his name.
5 Your right hand, O Lord, is glorious in power: *
    your right hand, O Lord, shatters the enemy.
6 At the blast of your nostrils, the sea covered them; *
    they sank as lead in the mighty waters.
7 In your unfailing love, O Lord, *
    you lead the people whom you have redeemed.
8 And by your invincible strength *
    you will guide them to your holy dwelling.
9 You will bring them in and plant them, O Lord, *
    in the sanctuary which your hands have established.

   Glory . . .

Refrain: In your unfailing love, O Lord, *
    you lead the people whom you have redeemed.

Exodus 15:1b-3,6,10,13,17
Common Worship (1)

or

Week 1, The Song of Moses and Miriam, *Canticle 1, as above*

Week 2, A Song of the Rock, *Canticle 2, page 558*

Week 3, A Song of the Knowledge of Wisdom, *Canticle 29, page 579*

Week 4, A Song of Ezekiel, *Canticle 23, page 574*

Lauds Psalm (see pages 21–28)

Either the psalms for the day:

	Week 1	Week 2	Week 3	Week 4
Monday	29	19:1–6	96	135
Tuesday	33	65	67	144:1–10
Wednesday	47	97	98	146
Thursday	48	81	99	147:1–12
Friday	100	147:13–21 (see below)	100	147:13–21 (see below)
Saturday	117	8	117	8

or

Psalm 147 (part two)

13 Sing praise to the Lord, O Jerusalem; *
    praise your God, O Zion;
14 For he has strengthened the bars of your gates *
    and has blest your children within you.
15 He has established peace in your borders *
    and satisfies you with the finest wheat.
16 He sends forth his command to the earth *
    and his word runs very swiftly.
17 He gives snow like wool *
    and scatters the hoarfrost like ashes.
18 He casts down his hailstones like morsels of bread; *
    who can endure his frost?
19 He sends forth his word and melts them; *
    he blows with his wind and the waters flow.
20 He declares his word to Jacob, *
    his statutes and judgements to Israel.
21 He has not dealt so with any other nation; *
    they do not know his laws.
    Alleluia.

  Glory . . .

Scripture Reading

The first reading appointed for the day (see the Propers, pages 203–431)

or

Short Reading (*)

Let no evil talk come out of your mouths, but only what is useful for building up, as there is need, so that your words may give grace to those who hear. And do not grieve the Holy Spirit of God, with which you were marked with a seal for the day of redemption. Put away from you all bitterness and wrath and anger and wrangling and slander, together with all malice, and be kind to one another, tender-hearted, forgiving one another, as God in Christ has forgiven you.

Ephesians 4:29–32

Short Responsory

R/ I call with my whole heart; answer me, O Lord.
R/ I call with my whole heart; answer me, O Lord.
V/ I will keep your commandments.
R/ I call with my whole heart; answer me, O Lord.
V/ Glory . . . Holy Spirit.
R/ I call with my whole heart; answer me, O Lord.

Psalm 119:145

Refrains (*)

Welcome with meekness the implanted word that has the power to save your souls.

James 1:21

You will do well to be attentive to this as to a lamp shining in a dark place, until the day dawns and the morning star rises in your hearts.

2 Peter 1:19–20

Man shall not live by bread alone, but by every word that proceeds from the mouth of God.

Matthew 4:4 (RSV)

My sheep hear my voice. I know them, and they follow me.

John 10:27

Gospel Canticle: Benedictus

(The Song of Zechariah) (+)

Refrain *(as above or as in the Propers)*

1 Blessed be the Lord the God of Israel, *
   who has come to his people and set them free.
2 He has raised up for us a mighty Saviour; *
   born of the house of his servant David.
3 Through his holy prophets God promised of old *
   to save us from our enemies,
   from the hands of all that hate us,
4 to show mercy to our ancestors *
   and to remember his holy covenant.
5 This was the oath God swore to our father Abraham: *
   to set us free from the hands of our enemies,
6 free to worship him without fear, *
   holy and righteous in his sight
   all the days of our life.
7 And you, child, shall be called the prophet of the Most High, *
   for you will go before the Lord to prepare his way,
8 to give his people knowledge of salvation *
   by the forgiveness of all their sins.
9 In the tender compassion of our God *
   the dawn from on high shall break upon us,
10 to shine on those who dwell in darkness and the shadow of death, *
   and to guide our feet into the way of peace.

   Glory . . .

Luke 1:68–79
ELLC* (15)

Refrain (*repeated*)

Prayers

The day is offered to God.

If set prayers are desired, some or all of the following petitions may be adapted and used (and see pages 14–15):

In the work of redemption, God has shown us the dignity of human work.
O Lord, bless us in our work.

We bless you, O Lord, for bringing us to this day:
we thank you for protecting us and for giving us all we need . . .

Assist us, Lord, in our daily tasks:
help us to serve you responsibly in the world,
and work always for the coming of your kingdom . . .

Make holy all those who labour – workers and craftsmen,
  and those in business and commerce:
sustain all whose calling is to care for others . . .

Give hope and purpose to those who have no work,
the unemployed and those whose working lives have ended . . .

Help the sick and comfort the afflicted:
be with us and with all whom we meet today . . .

AB (8)

Our Father

The Lord's Prayer is said here or after the Collect.

Collect (*)

The collect of the day (or season) is said:

or (+)

Almighty and everlasting God,
we thank you that you have brought us safely
to the beginning of this day.

Keep us from falling into sin
or running into danger,
order us in all our doings
and guide us to do always
what is righteous in your sight;
through Jesus Christ our Lord.

Book of Common Prayer* (2)

Ending

The Lord bless us, and keep us from all evil, and bring us to everlasting life. Amen.

Morning Prayer

Morning Prayer in Traditional Language

O Lord, open thou our lips.
And our mouth shall shew forth thy praise.

O God, make speed to save us.
O Lord, make haste to help us.

Glory be to the Father, and to the Son:
and to the Holy Ghost;
**As it was in the beginning, is now, and ever shall be:
world without end. Amen.**

Praise ye the Lord.
The Lord's Name be praised.

Invitatory

Venite, exultemus Domino

1 O come, let us sing unto the Lord: *
　　let us heartily rejoice in the strength of our salvation.
2 Let us come before his presence with thanksgiving: *
　　and show ourselves glad in him with psalms.
3 For the Lord is a great God: *
　　and a great King above all gods.
4 In his hand are all the corners of the earth: *
　　and the strength of the hills is his also.
5 The sea is his and he made it: *
　　and his hands prepared the dry land.
6 O come, let us worship and fall down: *
　　and kneel before the Lord our Maker.

7 For he is the Lord our God: *
    and we are the people of his pasture, and the sheep of his hand.
8 Today if ye will hear his voice, harden not your hearts: *
    as in the provocation,
    and as the day of temptation in the wilderness.
9 When your fathers tempted me: *
    proved me, and saw my works.
10 Forty years long was I grieved with this generation, and said: *
    It is a people that do err in their hearts,
    for they have not known my ways.
11 Unto whom I sware in my wrath: *
    that they should not enter into my rest.

Glory be to the Father, and to the Son: *
and to the Holy Ghost;
As it was in the beginning, is now, and ever shall be: *
world without end. Amen.

Psalm 95
Book of Common Prayer (2)

or

Jubilate Deo

1 O be joyful in the Lord, all ye lands: *
    serve the Lord with gladness,
    and come before his presence with a song.
2 Be ye sure that the Lord he is God: *
    it is he that hath made us and we are his;
    we are his people and the sheep of his pasture.
3 O go your ways into his gates with thanksgiving,
    and into his courts with praise: *
    be thankful unto him, speak good of his Name.
4 For the Lord is gracious, his mercy is everlasting: *
    and his truth endureth from generation to generation.

Glory be to the Father, and to the Son: *
and to the Holy Ghost;
As it was in the beginning, is now, and ever shall be: *
world without end. Amen.

Psalm 100
Book of Common Prayer (2)

Psalms

Day of the Month	Psalm
Day 1	4–5
Day 2	11
Day 3	15–16
Day 4	19–21
Day 5	24–26
Day 6	30–31
Day 7	35
Day 8	38, 40
Day 9	45–47
Day 10	51
Day 11	56–57
Day 12	62–64
Day 13	67
Day 14	71–72
Day 15	75–76
Day 16	79–81
Day 17	86–87
Day 18	90–92
Day 19	95–97
Day 20	100–102
Day 21	105:1–22
Day 22	108
Day 23	112–113
Day 24	116–118
Day 25	119:33–72 *(5–9)*

Day 26	119:105–144 *(14–18)*
Day 27	120–125
Day 28	132–135
Day 29	139–140
Day 30	144–146

First Lesson

The first reading appointed for the day (see the Propers, pages 203–431).

or

Short Reading

Watch yourself, my son, in everything you do, and discipline yourself in all your conduct. And what you hate, do not do to anyone. Do not drink wine to excess or let drunkenness go with you on your way. Give some of your food to the hungry, and some of your clothing to the naked. Give all your surplus as alms, and do not let your eye begrudge your giving of alms. Seek advice from every wise person and do not despise any useful counsel. At all times bless the Lord God and ask him that your ways may be made straight and that all your paths and plans may prosper.

Tobit 4:14b-16, 18–19a

Te Deum

We praise thee, O God; we acknowledge thee to be the Lord.
All the earth doth worship thee, the Father everlasting.
To thee all angels cry aloud, the heavens, and all the powers therein.
To thee cherubim and seraphim continually do cry.
Holy, holy, holy, Lord God of Sabaoth;
Heaven and earth are full of the majesty of thy glory.
The glorious company of the apostles praise thee.
The goodly fellowship of the prophets praise thee.
The noble army of martyrs praise thee.
The holy Church throughout all the world doth acknowledge thee:
the Father of an infinite majesty;

thine honourable, true and only Son;
also the Holy Ghost the Comforter.

Thou art the King of Glory O Christ.
Thou art the everlasting Son of the Father.
When thou tookest upon thee to deliver man,
 thou didst not abhor the Virgin's womb.
When thou hadst overcome the sharpness of death,
 thou didst open the kingdom of heaven to all believers.
Thou sittest at the right hand of God, in the glory of the Father.
We believe that thou shalt come to be our Judge.
We therefore pray thee, help thy servants,
 whom thou hast redeemed with thy precious blood.
Make them to be numbered with thy saints in glory everlasting.

The Te Deum *may end here.*

O Lord, save thy people and bless thine heritage.
Govern them and lift them up for ever.

Day by day we magnify thee;
and we worship thy name ever world without end.

Vouchsafe, O Lord, to keep us this day without sin.
O Lord, have mercy upon us, have mercy upon us.

O Lord, let thy mercy lighten upon us, as our trust is in thee.
O Lord, in thee have I trusted; let me never be confounded.

Book of Common Prayer* (2)

or

Canticle

A Song of Creation
Benedicite omnia opera

  1 O all ye Works of the Lord, bless ye the Lord: *
     praise him, and magnify him for ever.
  2 O ye Angels of the Lord, bless ye the Lord: *
     praise him, and magnify him for ever.
  3 O ye Heavens, bless ye the Lord: *
     praise him, and magnify him for ever.

4 O ye Waters that be above the Firmament, bless ye the Lord: *
    praise him, and magnify him for ever.
5 O all ye Powers of the Lord, bless ye the Lord: *
    praise him, and magnify him for ever.
6 O ye Sun and Moon, bless ye the Lord: *
    praise him, and magnify him for ever.
7 O ye Stars of Heaven, bless ye the Lord: *
    praise him, and magnify him for ever.
8 O ye Showers and Dew, bless ye the Lord: *
    praise him, and magnify him for ever.
9 O ye Winds of God, bless ye the Lord: *
    praise him and magnify him for ever.
10 O ye Fire and Heat, bless ye the Lord: *
    praise him, and magnify him for ever.
11 O ye Winter and Summer, bless ye the Lord: *
    praise him, and magnify him for ever.
12 O ye Dews and Frosts, bless ye the Lord: *
    praise him, and magnify him for ever.
13 O ye Frost and Cold, bless ye the Lord: *
    praise him, and magnify him for ever.
14 O ye Ice and Snow, bless ye the Lord: *
     praise him, and magnify him forever.
15 O ye Nights and Days, bless ye the Lord: *
    praise him, and magnify him for ever.
16 O ye Light and Darkness, bless ye the Lord: *
    praise him, and magnify him for ever.
17 O ye Lightnings and Clouds, bless ye the Lord: *
    praise him, and magnify him for ever.
18 O let the Earth bless the Lord: *
    yea, let it praise him, and magnify him for ever.
19 O ye Mountains and Hills, bless ye the Lord: *
    praise him, and magnify him for ever.
20 O all ye Green Things upon the earth, bless ye the Lord: *
    praise him, and magnify him for ever.
21 O ye Wells, bless ye the Lord: *
    praise him, and magnify him for ever.
22 O ye Seas and Floods, bless ye the Lord: *
    praise him, and magnify him for ever.
23 O ye Whales, and all that move in the Waters, bless ye the Lord: *
    praise him, and magnify him for ever.

Morning Prayer

24 O ye Fowls of the Air, bless ye the Lord: *
   praise him, and magnify him for ever.
25 O all ye Beasts and Cattle, bless ye the Lord: *
   praise him, and magnify him for ever.
26 O ye Children of Men, bless ye the Lord: *
   praise him, and magnify him for ever.
27 O let Israel bless the Lord: *
   praise him, and magnify him for ever.
28 O ye Priests of the Lord, bless ye the Lord: *
   praise him, and magnify him for ever.
29 O ye Servants of the Lord, bless ye the Lord: *
   praise him, and magnify him for ever.
30 O ye Spirits and Souls of the Righteous, bless ye the Lord: *
   praise him, and magnify him for ever.
31 O ye holy and humble Men of Heart, bless ye the Lord: *
   praise him, and magnify him for ever.
32 O Ananias, Azarias and Misael, bless ye the Lord: *
   praise him, and magnify him for ever.

Glory be to the Father, and to the Son: *
and to the Holy Ghost;
As it was in the beginning, is now, and ever shall be: *
world without end. Amen.

from The Song of the Three Holy Children 35–66
Book of Common Prayer* (2)

Second Lesson

The second reading appointed for the day (see the Propers, pages 203–431).

or

Short Reading

In our prayers for you we always thank God, the Father of our Lord Jesus Christ, for we have heard of your faith in Christ Jesus and of the love that you have for all the saints, because of the hope laid up for you in heaven. You have heard of this hope before in the word of the truth, the gospel that has come to you. Just as it is bearing fruit and growing in the whole world, so it has been bearing fruit among yourselves from the day you heard it and truly comprehended the grace of God.

Colossians 1:3–6

Gospel Canticle: Benedictus

The Song of Zechariah

1 Blessed be the Lord God of Israel: *
    for he hath visited and redeemed his people;
2 And hath raised up a mighty salvation for us: *
    in the house of his servant David;
3 As he spake by the mouth of his holy prophets: *
    which have been since the world began;
4 That we should be saved from our enemies: *
    and from the hands of all that hate us;
5 To perform the mercy promised to our forefathers: *
    and to remember his holy covenant;
6 To perform the oath: *
    which he sware to our forefather Abraham;
7 That we being delivered out of the hands of our enemies: *
    might serve him without fear;
8 In holiness and righteousness before him: *
    all the days of our life.
9 And thou child shalt be called the Prophet of the Highest: *
    for thou shalt go before the face of the Lord to prepare his ways;
10 To give knowledge of salvation unto his people: *
    for the remission of their sins,
11 Through the tender mercy of our God: *
    whereby the day-spring from on high hath visited us;
12 To give light to them that sit in darkness,
    and in the shadow of death *
    and to guide our feet into the way of peace.

Glory be to the Father, and to the Son: *
and to the Holy Ghost;
As it was in the beginning, is now, and ever shall be: *
world without end. Amen.

Luke 1:68–79
Book of Common Prayer (2)

Creed

I believe in God,
the Father almighty,
maker of heaven and earth.
And in Jesus Christ, his only Son, our Lord,
who was conceived by the Holy Ghost,
born of the Virgin Mary,
suffered under Pontius Pilate,
was crucified, dead and buried.
He descended into hell.
The third day he rose again from the dead;
he ascended into heaven
and sitteth on the right hand of God the Father almighty.
From thence he shall come to judge the quick and the dead.
I believe in the Holy Ghost;
the holy catholic church,
the communion of saints,
the forgiveness of sins,
the resurrection of the body;
and the life everlasting.

Book of Common Prayer (2)

Lord, have mercy upon us.
Christ, have mercy upon us.
Lord, have mercy upon us.

Our Father

Our Father, which art in heaven,
hallowed be thy name;
Thy kingdom come,
Thy will be done, in earth as it is in heaven.
Give us this day our daily bread,
and forgive us our trespasses,
as we forgive them that trespass against us;
and lead us not into temptation,
but deliver us from evil.

O Lord, shew thy mercy upon us.
And grant us thy salvation.

O Lord, save the Queen.
And mercifully hear us when we call upon thee.

Endue thy ministers with righteousness.
And make thy chosen people joyful.

O Lord, save thy people.
And bless thine inheritance.

Give peace in our time, O Lord.
Because there is none other that fighteth for us, but only thou, O God.

O God, make clean our hearts within us.
And take not thy Holy Spirit from us.

Collect of the Day

Collect for Peace

O God, who art the author of peace and lover of concord, in knowledge of whom standeth our eternal life, whose service is perfect freedom: Defend us thy humble servants in all assaults of our enemies; that we, surely trusting in thy defence, may not fear the power of any adversaries; through the might of Jesus Christ our Lord.

Book of Common Prayer (2)

Collect for Grace

O Lord our heavenly Father, almighty and everlasting God, who hast safely brought us to the beginning of this day: Defend us in the same with thy mighty power; and grant that this day we fall into no sin, neither run into any kind of danger; but that all our doings may be ordered by thy governance, to do always that is righteous in thy sight; through Jesus Christ our Lord.

Book of Common Prayer (2)

The grace of our Lord Jesus Christ,
and the love of God,
and the fellowship of the Holy Ghost,
be with us all evermore.

2 Corinthians 13
Book of Common Prayer (2)

II PRAYER DURING THE DAY

Prayer During the Day

Prayer During the Day may begin with the midday Angelus *or* Regina Caeli *(see page 1).*

1 Bible Reading

Daily Bible Reading may be part of Prayer During the Day.
For the reading scheme, see THE CHURCH'S YEAR, pages 203–431.

Advent	*page 203*
Christmas *and the Annunciation of the Lord*	*page 213*
Epiphany *(until Candlemas)* *and Feasts of the Lord*	*page 221*
Ordinary Time *(3 February until Shrove Tuesday)*	*page 229*
Lent	*page 239*
Passiontide	*page 253*
Eastertide	*page 285*
Ascension Day	*page 293*
Pentecost *(Friday after Ascension until Pentecost)*	*page 299*
Trinity	*page 305*
Corpus Christi	*page 311*
Sacred Heart	*page 323*

Ordinary Time	*page 323*
(Monday after Pentecost until the end of October)	*page 331*
Our Lady	*page 363*
Saints	*page 397*
Faithful Departed	*page 419*
The King and the Kingdom	
(Christ the King and Ordinary Time in November)	*page 425*

2 Spiritual Reading

Use either a daily anthology or continue reading a suitable book.

3 Meditation

Our Creation

Preparation

Place yourself in the presence of God and ask him to inspire you.

Considerations

1 Consider that a few years ago you were not in the world at all, that you were nothing. Where was your soul then? The world had already lasted so long and you were not known.
2 God has raised you from this nothingness and made you what you are, purely out of his goodness. He had no need of you.
3 Consider what nature God has given you; the highest in the visible world, capable of eternal life and perfect union with him.

Spiritual Acts and Resolutions

1 *Humble yourself*

Humble yourself before God, saying in your heart with the psalmist:

My lifetime is as nothing in your sight. What is man, that you should be mindful of him? *(Psalm 39:5; 8:4)*

My soul, I was in the depths of nothingness and would still be there had not God drawn me out. If I were still there, what could I have done?

2 *Give thanks to God*

My good and great Creator, how much I owe you! In your mercy you decided to raise me from my nothingness to make me what I am. What can I possibly do to give you worthy praise or thank you enough for your immeasurable goodness?

3 *Acknowledge your sinfulness*

My Creator, instead of uniting myself to you in loving service, my disordered desires have made me a rebel and I have cut myself off from you. I have preferred sin and dishonoured you, forgetting that you are my Creator.

4 *Kneel down in worship*

Know, my soul, that the Lord is God: it is he that has made us and we are his. *(Psalm 100:2)*

5 *Resolve anew*

From now on I will no longer put myself first: by myself I am nothing. What have I to glory in? I am dust and ashes, and even less than that! What have I to be proud of? In order to humble myself I will take the necessary steps, bear with humiliation, and change my life. I shall follow my Saviour, honour the nature he has given me, align myself with his will, and, in obedience, accept the guidance of my spiritual director.

Conclusion

1 *Thanksgiving*

Bless the Lord, O my soul, and all that is within me bless his holy name. *(Psalm 103:1)*

In his goodness he has lifted me from nothingness and in his mercy created me.

2 *Offering*

My God, with all my heart I offer you the life you have given me; I dedicate it and consecrate it to you.

3 *Petition*

Strengthen me, O God, in these desires and resolutions. Holy Mary, commend them to your Son's mercy.

Our Father

Hail Mary

Your prayer complete, wander back in spirit among your thoughts and gather a bouquet of spiritual flowers to perfume your whole day.

adapted A.B., from Saint Francis de Sales
From Introduction to the Devout Life

4 *The Jesus Prayer*

This prayer should be recited slowly and many times over. It may be synchronized with breathing. Breathe in during the first half (addressing God) and breathe out during the second (acknowledging sins).

Lord Jesus, Son of the living God:
be merciful to me, a sinner.

or

Lord Jesus, Son of God:
have mercy on me a sinner.

5 *Practising the Presence of God*

Prayer of Charles de Foucauld

My Father, I abandon myself to you. Do with me as you will. Whatever you may do with me I thank you. I am prepared for anything. I accept anything, provided your will is fulfilled in me and in all creatures. I ask for nothing more, my God. I place my soul in your hands. I give it to you, my God, with all the love of my heart, because I love you. And for me it is a necessity of love, this gift of myself, this placing of myself in your hands without reserve in boundless confidence, because you are my Father.

(20)

For everything there is a season, and a time for every matter under heaven:
a time to be born, and a time to die;
a time to plant, and a time to pluck up what is planted;

a time to kill, and a time to heal;
a time to break down, and a time to build up;
a time to weep, and a time to laugh;
a time to mourn, and a time to dance;
a time to throw away stones, and a time to gather stones together;
a time to embrace, and a time to refrain from embracing;
a time to seek, and a time to lose;
a time to keep, and a time to throw away;
a time to tear, and a time to sew;
a time to keep silence, and a time to speak;
a time to love, and a time to hate;
a time for war, and a time for peace.

Ecclesiastes 3:1–8

Friday Afternoon: Prayer to Christ Crucified

O kind and loving Jesus,
I kneel here before you,
asking you most fervently
to put into my heart
the virtues of faith, hope and charity,
with true contrition for my sins
and a firm purpose of amendment.
Help me to contemplate with sorrow
your five precious wounds,
while I remember David's prophecy:
They have pierced my hands and my feet;
they have counted all my bones.

Stanbrook Abbey (4)

Christ has no body now on earth but yours,
no hands but yours, no feet but yours;
yours are the eyes through which is to look out
Christ's compassion to the world,
yours are the feet with which he is to go about doing good,
and yours are the hands with which he is to bless us now.

Saint Teresa of Avila

Lord, bless my going out and coming in,
from this time forth, for evermore.

Thomas Ken,
Directions for Prayers

Auguries of Innocence

To see the world in a grain of sand,
And a heaven in a wild flower;
Hold infinity in the palm of your hand,
And eternity in an hour.

William Blake

To the Christian

I give you the end of a golden string:
Only wind it into a ball –
It will lead you in at Heaven's gate,
Built in Jerusalem's wall.

William Blake

If I cannot work or rise from my chair or my bed,
love remains to me;
I can pray.

George Congreve SSJE (9)

Teach us to pray often, that we may pray oftener.

Jeremy Taylor

Set a watch, O Lord, upon our tongue:
that we may never speak the cruel word which is untrue;
or, being true, is not the whole truth;
or being wholly true, is merciless;
for the love of Jesus Christ our Lord.

G. W. Briggs* (18)

Grace

Bless us, O Lord, and these gifts
which we receive from your bounty.

Bless, O Lord, this food to our use and ourselves to your service.
Through Christ our Lord.

Prayer during the Day

Lord, grant that whether I eat or drink, or whatever I do,
I may do all to thy glory.

Thomas Ken
Directions for Prayers

Praise God from whom all blessings flow.
Praise him all creatures here below.
Praise him above angelic host.
Praise Father, Son and Holy Ghost.

Thomas Ken

We give you thanks
for all your gifts,
almighty God,
living and reigning
now and for ever.

ICEL (5)

Work

Prosper thou the works of my hands, O Lord;
O, prosper thou my handiwork.

Thomas Ken
Directions for Prayers

Behold, O Lord God, our strivings after a truer and more abiding order. Give us visions that bring back a lost glory to the earth, and dreams that foreshadow the better order which you have prepared for us. Scatter every excuse of frailty and unworthiness: consecrate us all with a heavenly mission: open to us a clearer prospect of our work. Give us strength according to our day gladly to welcome and gratefully to fulfil it; through Jesus Christ our Lord.

B. F. Westcott

Most loving Lord, give me a childlike love of thee, which may cast out all fear.

Edward Bouverie Pusey

O merciful Lord Jesus, forget not me, as I have forgotten thee.
Christina Rossetti

Lord, make me a saint according to your own heart, meek and humble.
Mother Teresa of Calcutta (12)

Act of spiritual communion

I believe in you, Lord Jesus,
present in the most holy sacrament of the altar.
I love you above all things, and I long to receive you into my soul.
Though I cannot now receive you in the sacrament,
I pray you to come none the less spiritually into my heart.
I embrace you and I unite myself to you,
for you are already within me, as I am in you.
Let me never be separated from you.
traditional, adapted AB. (8)

Prayer before a meeting

Come, Holy Spirit, fill the hearts of your faithful
and kindle in them the fire of your love.
Send forth your Spirit and they shall be made
and you will renew the face of the earth.

Let us pray.

Lord, unite us to yourself in the bond of love
and keep us faithful to all that is true.

As we gather in your name,
may we temper justice with love,
so that all our decisions may be pleasing to you,
and earn the reward promised to good and faithful servants.
You live and reign with the Father, and the Son,

(13)

At the end of a meeting

The grace of our Lord Jesus Christ,
the love of God
and the fellowship of the Holy Spirit
be with us all evermore.

2 Corinthians 13:14

6 Thanksgiving

Almighty God, Father of all mercies, we thine unworthy servants do give thee most humble and hearty thanks for all thy goodness and loving-kindness to us and to all men; [particularly to those who desire now to offer up their praises and thanksgivings for the late mercies vouchsafed unto them]. We bless thee for our creation, preservation, and all the blessings of this life; but above all for thine inestimable love in the redemption of the world by our Lord Jesus Christ, for the means of grace, and for the hope of glory. And we beseech thee, give us that due sense of all thy mercies, that our hearts may be unfeignedly thankful, and that we shew forth thy praise, not only with our lips, but in our lives; by giving up ourselves to thy service, and by walking before thee in holiness and righteousness all our days; through Jesus Christ our Lord, to whom with thee and the Holy Ghost be all honour and glory, world without end.

Edward Reynolds

or

Almighty God, Father of all mercies,
we your unworthy servants
give you most humble and hearty thanks
for all your goodness and loving-kindness.
We bless you for our creation, preservation,
    and all the blessings of this life;
but above all for your immeasurable love
in the redemption of the world
by our Lord Jesus Christ,
for the means of grace, and for the hope of glory.
And give us, we pray,
such a sense of all your mercies
that our hearts may be unfeignedly thankful,

and that we show forth your praise,
not only with our lips but in our lives,
by giving up ourselves to your service,
and by walking before you,
in holiness and righteousness, all our days;
through Jesus Christ our Lord,
to whom with you and the Holy Spirit,
   be honour and glory,
for ever and ever.

Edward Reynolds* (3)

I thank thee, O God; for the pleasures thou hast given me through my senses: for the glory of the thunder, for the mystery of music, the singing of birds and the laughter of children. I thank thee for the delights of colour, the awe of the sunset, the wild roses in the hedgerows, the smile of friendship. I thank thee for the sweetness of flowers and the scent of hay. Truly, O Lord, the earth is full of thy riches.

Edward King* (20)

7 Conclusion

Let us bless the Lord.
Thanks be to God.

May the Lord bless us, and keep us from all evil,
and bring us to everlasting life.

or

Let us bless the Lord.
Thanks be to God.

May the divine assistance remain with us always.

Midday Prayer

Midday Prayer begins with the Angelus *or* Regina Caeli *(see page 1).*

V/ O God, make speed to save us.   *or*   *V/* O God, come to our aid.
R/ O Lord, make haste to help us.   *R/* O Lord, make haste to help us.

Glory . . . Amen.

(Except in Lent) Alleluia.

Office Hymn

Rector potens, verax Deus

O God of truth and Lord of power,
With order ruling time and change,
Whose splendour shines in morning light,
Whose glory burns in midday fire:

Extinguish every flame of strife
And banish every wrong desire;
Grant health of body and of mind,
Create in us true peace of heart.

To God the Father glory be,
All glory to his only Son
And to the Spirit, Paraclete,
In time and in eternity.

LM
Ambrose? (36)
Hymns for Prayer and Praise 239

Prayer during the Day

Psalmody

Either Psalms 126 and 127 (see pages 536–537) or Psalms 128 and 129 (see pages 537–538) may be used in place of the psalms below.

Psalms *(see pages 435–556)*

Either *the psalms for the day and week:*

	Week 1	Week 2	Week 3	Week 4
Sunday	118	23 *(see below)* 76	118	23 *(see below)* 76
Monday	19:7–14 7	119:41–48 *(6)* 40	119:89–96*(12)* *(see below)* 71	119:129–136 *(17)* 82 120
Tuesday	119:1–8 *(1)* *(see below)* 13 14	119:49–56 *(7)* 53 54	119:97–104 *(13)* 74	119:137–144 *(18)* 88
Wednesday	119:9–16 *(2)* *(see below)* 17	119:57–64 *(8)* 55	119:105–112 *(14)* 70 75	119:145–152 *(19)* 94
Thursday	119:17–24 *(3)* *(see below)* 25	119:65–72 *(9)* 56 57	119:113–120 *(15)* 79 80	119:153–160 *(20)* 128 129
Friday	119:25–32 *(4)* 26 28	119:73–80 *(10)* *(see below)* 59 60	22	119:161–168 *(21)* *(see below)* 133 140
Saturday	119:33–40 *(5)* *(see below)* 34	119:81–88 *(11)* 61 64	119:121–128 *(16)* 34	119:169–176 *(22)* 45

or *using the following one-week cycle:*

Sunday

Psalm 23

1 The Lord is my shepherd; *
    therefore can I lack nothing.
2 He makes me lie down in green pastures *
    and leads me beside still waters.
3 He shall refresh my soul *
    and guide me in the paths of righteousness for his name's sake.
4 Even though I walk through the valley of the shadow of death,
        I will fear no evil; *
    for you are with me;
    your rod and your staff, they comfort me.
5 You have spread a table before me
        in the presence of those who trouble me; *
    you have anointed my head with oil
    and my cup shall be full.
6 Surely, goodness and loving mercy shall follow me
        all the days of my life, *
    and I will dwell in the house of the Lord for ever.

Glory . . .

Monday

Psalm 19 (part two)

7 The law of the Lord is perfect, reviving the soul; *
    the testimony of the Lord is sure
    and gives wisdom to the simple.
8 The statutes of the Lord are right and rejoice the heart; *
    the commandment of the Lord is pure
    and gives light to the eyes.
9 The fear of the Lord is clean and endures for ever; *
    the judgements of the Lord are true
    and righteous altogether.
10 More to be desired are they than gold,
        more than much fine gold, *
    sweeter also than honey,
    dripping from the honey-comb.

11 By them also is your servant taught *
    and in keeping them there is great reward.
12 Who can tell how often they offend? *
    O cleanse me from my secret faults!
13 Keep your servant also from presumptuous sins
    lest they get dominion over me; *
    so shall I be undefiled,
    and innocent of great offence.
14 Let the words of my mouth and the meditation of my heart
    be acceptable in your sight, *
    O Lord, my strength and my redeemer.

    Glory . . .

Tuesday

Psalm 119

1 Aleph

1 Blessed are those whose way is pure, *
    who walk in the law of the Lord.
2 Blessed are those who keep his testimonies *
    and seek him with all their whole heart,
3 Those who do no wickedness, *
    but walk in his ways.
4 You, O Lord, have charged *
    that we should diligently keep your commandments.
5 O that my ways were made so direct *
    that I might keep your statutes.
6 Then I should not be put to shame, *
    because I have regard for all your commandments.
7 I will thank you with an unfeigned heart, *
    when I have learned your righteous judgements.
8 I will keep your statutes; *
    O forsake me not utterly.

    Glory . . .

Wednesday

Psalm 119

2 Beth

9 How shall young people cleanse their way *
   to keep themselves according to your word?
10 With my whole heart have I sought you; *
   O let me not go astray from your commandments.
11 Your words have I hidden within my heart, *
   that I should not sin against you.
12 Blessed are you, O Lord; *
   O teach me your statutes.
13 With my lips have I been telling *
   of all the judgements of your mouth.
14 I have taken greater delight in the way of your testimonies *
   than in all manner of riches.
15 I will meditate on your commandments *
   and contemplate your ways.
16 My delight shall be in your statutes *
   and I will not forget your word.

   Glory . . .

Thursday

Psalm 119

3 Gimel

17 O do good to your servant that I may live, *
   and so shall I keep your word.
18 Open my eyes, that I may see *
   the wonders of your law.
19 I am a stranger upon earth; *
   hide not your commandments from me.
20 My soul is consumed at all times *
   with fervent longing for your judgements.
21 You have rebuked the arrogant; *
   cursed are those who stray from your commandments.

22 Turn from me shame and rebuke, *
   for I have kept your testimonies.
23 Rulers also sit and speak against me, *
   but your servant meditates on your statutes.
24 For your testimonies are my delight; *
   they are my faithful counsellors.

   Glory . . .

Friday

Psalm 119

4 Daleth

25 My soul cleaves to the dust; *
   O give me life according to your word.
26 I have acknowledged my ways and you have answered me; *
   O teach me your statutes.
27 Make me understand the way of your commandments, *
   and so shall I meditate on your wondrous works.
28 My soul melts away in tears of sorrow; *
   raise me up according to your word.
29 Take from me the way of falsehood; *
   be gracious to me through your law.
30 I have chosen the way of truth *
   and your judgements have I laid before me.
31 I hold fast to your testimonies; *
   O Lord, let me not be put to shame.
32 I will run the way of your commandments, *
   when you have set my heart at liberty.

   Glory . . .

or

Psalm 22

1 My God, my God, why have you forsaken me, *
   and are so far from my salvation,
   from the words of my distress?
2 O my God, I cry in the daytime,

     but you do not answer; *
     and by night also, but I find no rest.
3 Yet you are the Holy One, *
     enthroned upon the praises of Israel.
4 Our forebears trusted in you; *
     they trusted, and you delivered them.
5 They cried out to you and were delivered; *
     they put their trust in you and were not confounded.
6 But as for me, I am a worm and no man, *
     scorned by all and despised by the people.
7 All who see me laugh me to scorn; *
     they curl their lips and wag their heads, saying,
8 'He trusted in the Lord; let him deliver him; *
     let him deliver him, if he delights in him.'
9 But it is you that took me out of the womb *
     and laid me safe upon my mother's breast.
10 On you was I cast ever since I was born; *
     you are my God even from my mother's womb.
11 Be not far from me, for trouble is near at hand *
     and there is none to help.
12 Mighty oxen come around me; *
     fat bulls of Bashan close me in on every side.
13 They gape upon me with their mouths, *
     as it were a ramping and a roaring lion.
14 I am poured out like water;
     all my bones are out of joint; *
     my heart has become like wax
     melting in the depths of my body.
15 My mouth is dried up like a potsherd;
     my tongue cleaves to my gums; *
     you have laid me in the dust of death.
16 For the hounds are all about me,
     the pack of evildoers close in on me; *
     they pierce my hands and my feet.
17 I can count all my bones; *
     they stand staring and looking upon me.
18 They divide my garments among them; *
     they cast lots for my clothing.
19 Be not far from me, O Lord; *
     you are my strength; hasten to help me.

20 Deliver my soul from the sword, *
    my poor life from the power of the dog.
21 Save me from the lion's mouth,
    from the horns of wild oxen. *
    You have answered me!
22 I will tell of your name to my people; *
    in the midst of the congregation will I praise you.
23 Praise the Lord, you that fear him; *
    O seed of Jacob, glorify him;
    stand in awe of him, O seed of Israel.
24 For he has not despised nor abhorred the suffering of the poor;
    neither has he hidden his face from them; *
    but when they cried to him he heard them.
25 From you comes my praise in the great congregation; *
    I will perform my vows
    in the presence of those that fear you.
26 The poor shall eat and be satisfied; *
    those who seek the Lord shall praise him;
    their hearts shall live for ever.
27 All the ends of the earth
    shall remember and turn to the Lord, *
    and all the families of the nations shall bow before him.
28 For the kingdom is the Lord's *
    and he rules over the nations.
29 How can those who sleep in the earth
    bow down in worship, *
    or those who go down to the dust kneel before him?
30 He has saved my life for himself;
    my descendants shall serve him; *
    this shall be told of the Lord for generations to come.
31 They shall come and make known his salvation,
    to a people yet unborn, *
    declaring that he, the Lord, has done it.

Glory . . .

Saturday

Psalm 119

5 He

33 Teach me, O Lord, the way of your statutes *
 and I shall keep it to the end.
34 Give me understanding and I shall keep your law; *
 I shall keep it with my whole heart.
35 Lead me in the path of your commandments, *
 for therein is my delight.
36 Incline my heart to your testimonies *
 and not to unjust gain.
37 Turn away my eyes lest they gaze on vanities; *
 O give me life in your way.
38 Confirm to your servant your promise, *
 which stands for all who fear you.
39 Turn away the reproach which I dread, *
 because your judgements are good.
40 Behold, I long for your commandments; *
 in your righteousness give me life.

Glory . . .

Short Readings

Owe to no one anything, except to love one another; for the one who loves another has fulfilled the law. The commandments, 'You shall not commit adultery; You shall not murder; You shall not steal; You shall not covet;' and any other commandment, are summed up in this word, 'Love your neighbour as yourself.' Love does no wrong to a neighbour; therefore love is the fulfilling of the law.

Romans 13:8–10

or

Let everyone be quick to listen, slow to speak, slow to anger; for your anger does not produce God's righteousness. Therefore rid yourselves of all sordidness and rank growth of wickedness, and welcome with meekness the implanted word that has the power to save your souls. But be doers of the word, and not merely hearers who deceive themselves.

James 1:19b-22

Collect (*)

The collect of the day (or season) is said.

or

Almighty God,
we thank you for the gift of your holy word.
May it be a lantern to our feet,
a light to our paths,
and a strength to our lives.
Take us and use us
to love and serve
in the power of the Holy Spirit
and in the name of your Son,
Jesus Christ our Lord.

Common Worship (1)

Ending

V/ Let us bless the Lord.   *or*   **V/** Let us praise the Lord.
R/ Thanks be to God.   **R/** Thanks be to God.

III INITIATION AND HEALING

Baptism and Confirmation

Decision and Profession of Faith at Baptism

The Decision and Profession of Faith may be used for the examination of conscience, at night, or in preparation for the Sacrament of Reconciliation, or in preparation for the Renewal of Baptismal Promises at Easter.

Decision

Do you reject the devil and all rebellion against God?
I reject them.
Do you renounce the deceit and corruption of evil?
I renounce them.
Do you repent of the sins that separate us from God and neighbour?
I repent of them.

Do you turn to Christ as Saviour?
I turn to Christ.
Do you submit to Christ as Lord?
I submit to Christ.
Do you come to Christ, the way, the truth and the life?
I come to Christ.

Common Worship (1)

Profession of Faith

Do you believe and trust in God the Father?
I believe in God, the Father almighty,
creator of heaven and earth.

Do you believe and trust in his Son Jesus Christ?
I believe in Jesus Christ, his only Son, our Lord,

who was conceived by the power of the Holy Spirit,
born of the Virgin Mary,
suffered under Pontius Pilate,
was crucified, died and was buried;
he descended to the dead.
On the third day he rose again;
he ascended into heaven,
he is seated at the right hand of the Father,
and will come again to judge the living and the dead.

Do you believe and trust in the Holy Spirit?
**I believe in the Holy Spirit,
the holy catholic church,
the communion of saints,
the forgiveness of sins,
the resurrection of the body;
and the life everlasting.**

Common Worship (1)

Commission at Confirmation

The Commission at Confirmation may be used for the examination of conscience, at night, or in preparation for the Sacrament of Reconciliation, or in preparation for the Renewal of Baptismal Promises at Easter.

Will you continue in the apostles' teaching and fellowship,
in the breaking of bread, and in the prayers?
With the help of God, I will.

Will you persevere in resisting evil,
and, whenever you fall into sin, repent and return to the Lord?
With the help of God, I will.

Will you proclaim by word and example
the good news of God in Christ?
With the help of God, I will.

Will you seek and serve Christ in all people,
loving your neighbour as yourself?
With the help of God, I will.

Will you acknowledge Christ's authority over human society,
by prayer for the world and its leaders,
by defending the weak, and by seeking peace and justice?
With the help of God, I will.

May Christ dwell in your hearts through faith,
that you may be rooted and grounded in love
and bring forth the fruit of the Spirit.

Common Worship (1)

Emergency Baptism

In an emergency, a lay person may be the minister of baptism, and should subsequently inform those who have the pastoral responsibility for the person so baptized. For other notes and texts, see Common Worship.

The following form is sufficient:

The minister pours water on the person to be baptized, saying:
I baptize you in the name of the Father, and of the Son, and of the Holy Spirit.
Amen.

The minister may then say the Lord's Prayer and the Grace or a blessing.

Common Worship (1)

Reconciliation: Sacrament of Penance

1 Preparation

Careful preparation is necessary for the Sacrament of Penance. The following stages are suggested.

Reading

The Ten Commandments

I am the Lord your God.
You shall have no other gods before me.
You shall not make for yourself a graven image.
You shall not take the name of the Lord your God in vain.
Remember the Sabbath day to keep it holy.
Honour your father and your mother.
You shall not kill.
You shall not commit adultery.
You shall not steal.
You shall not bear false witness against your neighbour.
You shall not covet.

from Exodus 20:2–17

The Beatitudes

Blessed are the poor in spirit,
   for theirs is the kingdom of heaven.
Blessed are those who mourn,
   for they will be comforted.
Blessed are the meek,

for they will inherit the earth.
Blessed are those who hunger and thirst for righteousness,
    for they will be filled.
Blessed are the merciful,
    for they will receive mercy.
Blessed are the pure in heart,
    for they will see God.
Blessed are the peacemakers,
    for they will be called children of God.
Blessed are those who are persecuted for righteousness' sake,
    for theirs is the kingdom of God.

Matthew 5:3–10

The Lord's Summary of the Law

Our Lord Jesus Christ said,
The first commandment is this:
'Hear, O Israel, the Lord our God is the only Lord.
You shall love the Lord your God with all your heart,
with all your soul, and with all your mind,
and with all your strength.'

The second is this:
'Love your neighbour as yourself.'
There is no other commandment greater than these.

Mark 12:29–31

The Call to Perfection

Be perfect as your heavenly Father is perfect.

Matthew 5:48

The Golden Rule

In everything do to others as you would have them do to you.

Matthew 7:12

Reconciliation

God's Forgiveness

If we say that we have no sin, we deceive ourselves, and the truth is not in us. If we confess our sins, he who is faithful and just will forgive us our sins and cleanse us from all unrighteousness.

1 John 1:8–9

If anyone does sin, we have an advocate with the Father, Jesus Christ the righteous; and he is the atoning sacrifice for our sins, and not for ours only but also for the sins of the whole world.

1 John 2:1b-2

Examination of Conscience

This may include the making of a list, later to be destroyed, and the answering of such questions as these:

The Story so far

Father I have sinned against heaven and before you; I am no more worthy to be called your son.

Luke 15:21

How long is it since my last confession?
Do I sincerely want a new start?
Did I forget to mention or deliberately omit anything serious last time?
Did I complete the penance I was given?
Did I make restoration for any injury to others?

Love of God

You shall love the Lord your God with all your heart, with all your soul, and with all your mind, and with all your strength.

Mark 12:30

Do I love God?
Do I make an idol of money, possessions or sex?
Do I blaspheme by taking the name the name of the Lord in vain?
Do I study and listen to the Word of God and try to obey God's
    commandments?
Do I go to Mass regularly on Sundays and holy days?
Do I keep Sunday as a holy day?
Do I say my prayers regularly?

Love of Neighbour

Love your neighbour as yourself.

Mark 12:31

Have I hated others?
Do I love my family and friends?
Have I been faithful to my spouse?
Have I been kind and helpful to my children?
Have I honoured my mother and my father?
Do I contribute my share to the Church?
Do I contribute generously to good causes?

Have I lived up to the commission I received at confirmation?
Am I a peacemaker and an example to others of Christian living?
Do I keep my conscience in good repair?
Do I hunger and thirst for righteousness and speak up for my beliefs and principles?
Have I respected the integrity of creation – animals and natural resources?
Do I encourage my family and children to live a Christian life?
Do I visit the bereaved and the lonely, the sick and the imprisoned?

Have I stolen from others?
Have I cheated my spouse, my employer, my employee or others?
Have I made restitution of what I have stolen?
Have I damaged others' good name?
Have I been quarrelsome?
Have I thought ill of others and used others for my own ends?
Have I exploited others sexually?

The Way of Perfection

Be perfect as your heavenly Father is perfect.

Matthew 5:48

Do I fast and practise self-control?
Have I followed what my conscience tells me?
Have I tried to acquire habits of wisdom and understanding?
Have I wallowed in self-pity?
Have I allowed myself to be consumed by ambition, bitterness or disappointment?

Have I wasted money?
Have I kept my word?

Have I been proud?
Have I coveted other people's possessions or spouse?
Have I indulged impurity?
Have I been envious of others?
Have I been greedy?
Have I been angry?
Have I been lazy?

When the self-examination is complete, some prayer, such as the following, may be said:

My God,
I am sorry for my sins with all my heart.
In choosing to do wrong
and failing to do good,
I have sinned against you
whom I should love above all things.
I firmly intend, with your help,
to do penance,
to sin no more,
and to avoid whatever leads me to sin.

Our Saviour Jesus Christ
suffered and died for us.
In his name, my God, have mercy.

Rite of Penance 1974 (5)

2 Confession

Greeting

The penitent kneels down at the place where the Sacrament of Penance is to be celebrated and makes the sign of the cross.

Penitent	In the name of the Father, and of the Son, and of the Holy Spirit. Amen.

The priest may bless the penitent and, using these or other words, invites the penitent to trust in God.

Jesus said, I have come to call not the righteous but sinners to repentance.
Luke 5:32

The penitent should indicate now how long it is since the last confession, and any other circumstances which might help the priest minister wisely.

The priest may read or recite a short passage of Scripture, proclaiming God's mercy and inviting repentance.

Confession

The penitent, speaking informally and frankly, confesses all his or her sins, perhaps introducing and concluding what is to be said with these words:

I confess to almighty God,
in the presence of blessed Mary and all the saints,
and you my father,
that I have sinned exceedingly
in thought, word and deed,
through my own grievous fault,
especially since my last confession.

Therefore I ask blessed Mary and all the saints
to pray to the Lord for me
and you, father, to give me counsel and penance,
and pronounce absolution of my sins.

The priest may ask the penitent to make an act of contrition.
The penitent may use these or other words:

My God, I am very sorry for all the sins by which I have offended you, and I resolve by the help of your grace not to sin again.

The priest gives advice and counsel and prescribes a penance. The penance – often a prayer to be said or a passage of Scripture to be read – is a small token of sorrow and takes the place of what were once quite substantial acts of punishment and restoration.

Absolution is then pronounced:

God, the Father of mercies,
through the death and resurrection of his Son
has reconciled the world to himself
and sent the Holy Spirit among us
for the forgiveness of sins;
through the ministry of the Church,
may God give you pardon and peace.
And I absolve you from your sins
in the name of the Father, and of the Son, and of the Holy Spirit.

Penitent   Amen.

The priest may then say:

May the Passion of our Lord Jesus,
the intercession of the Blessed Virgin Mary and of all the saints,
whatever good you do and suffering you endure,
heal your sins,
help you grow in holiness,
and reward you with eternal life.

The Lord has freed you from your sins.
Go in peace and pray for me a sinner too.

3 Thanksgiving

The penance is completed either immediately afterwards or as soon as possible. The following may be helpful:

From Psalm 145

1 I will exalt you, O God my King, *
    and bless your name for ever and ever.
2 Every day will I bless you *
    and praise your name for ever and ever.
3 The Lord is gracious and merciful, *
    long-suffering and of great goodness.
4 The Lord is loving to everyone *
    and his mercy is over all his creatures.

5 The Lord is sure in all his words *
    and faithful in all his deeds.
6 The Lord upholds all those who fall *
    and lifts up all those who are bowed down.
7 The eyes of all wait upon you, O Lord, *
    and you give them their food in due season.
8 You open wide your hand *
    and fill all things living with plenty.
9 The Lord is righteous in all his ways *
    and loving in all his works.
10 The Lord is near to those who call upon him *
    to all who call upon him faithfully.
11 He fulfils the desire of those who fear him; *
    he hears their cry and saves them.
12 My mouth shall speak the praise of the Lord, *
    and let all flesh bless his holy name for ever and ever.

   Glory . . .

Psalm 145:1–2, 8–9, 14–20, 22

For the whole of Psalm 145, see page 551.

Grant Lord, that I may not, for one moment, admit willingly into my soul any thought contrary to your love.

*Edward Bouverie Pusey**

Prayers for the Sick

Prayer for the Sick

Litany of Healing

Additional petitions, including names, may be included.

God the Father, your will for all people is health and salvation.
We praise and bless you, Lord.

God the Son, you came that we might have life,
and might have it more abundantly.
We praise and bless you, Lord.

God the Holy Spirit, you make our bodies the temple of your presence.
We praise and bless you, Lord.

Holy Trinity, one God, in you we live and move and have our being.
We praise and bless you, Lord.

Lord, grant your healing grace to all who are sick, injured or disabled,
that they may be made whole.
Hear us, Lord of life.

Grant to all who are lonely, anxious or depressed
a knowledge of your will and an awareness of your presence.
Hear us, Lord of life.

Grant to all who minister to those who are suffering
wisdom and skill, sympathy and patience.
Hear us, Lord of life.

Mend broken relationships, and restore to those in distress
soundness of mind and serenity of spirit.
Hear us, Lord of life.

Sustain and support those who seek your guidance,
and lift up all who are brought low by the trials of this life.
Hear us, Lord of life.

Grant to the dying peace and a holy death,
and uphold by the grace and consolation of your Holy Spirit
those who are bereaved.
Hear us, Lord of life.

Restore to wholeness whatever is broken by human sin,
in our lives, in our nation, and in the world.
Hear us, Lord of life.

You are the Lord, who does mighty wonders.
You have declared your power among the peoples.

With you, Lord, is the well of life.
And in your light do we see light.

Hear us, Lord of life.
Heal us, and make us whole.

Let us pray.

A period of silence follows.

O Lord our God, accept the fervent prayers of your people;
in the multitude of your mercies look with compassion
upon us and all who turn to you for help;
for you are gracious, O lover of souls,
and to you we give glory, Father, Son and Holy Spirit,
now and for ever.

Common Worship (1)

Other Prayers

Christ be with me, Christ within me,
Christ behind me, Christ before me,
Christ beside me, Christ to win me,
Christ to comfort and restore me.

Christ beneath me, Christ above me,
Christ in quiet, Christ in danger,
Christ in hearts of all that love me,
Christ in mouth of friends and stranger.

Saint Patrick's Breastplate

From Psalm 20

1 May the Lord hear you in the day of trouble, *
    the name of the God of Jacob defend you;
2 Send you help from his sanctuary *
    and strengthen you out of Zion;
3 Grant you your heart's desire *
    and fulfil all your mind.
4 May we rejoice in your salvation
    and triumph in the name of our God; *
    may the Lord perform all your petitions.

Psalm 20:1–2, 4–5

For a person or persons

Our Lord Jesus Christ,
present with us now in his risen power,
enter into your body and spirit,
take from you all that harms and hinders you,
and fill you with his healing and his peace.

Common Worship (1)

For a place

Visit, Lord, we pray, this place
and drive far from it all the snares of the enemy.
Let your holy angels dwell here to keep us in peace,
and may your blessing be upon it evermore;
through Jesus Christ our Lord.

Common Worship (1)

For a person before sleep

May the cross of the Son of God,
which is mightier than all the hosts of Satan,
and more glorious than all the hosts of heaven,
abide with you in your going out and in your coming in.
By day and by night, at morning and at evening,
at all times and in all places may it protect and defend you.
From the wrath of evil doers, from the assaults of evil spirits,

from foes visible and invisible, from the snares of the devil,
from all passions that beguile the soul and body;
may it guard, protect and deliver you.

Christaraksha – An Indian Prayer
Common Worship (1)

Salve, Regina

Hail, holy Queen, mother of mercy,
our life, our sweetness, and our hope.
To you do we cry,
poor banished children of Eve.
To you do we send up our sighs,
mourning and weeping in this vale of tears.
Turn then, most gracious advocate,
your eyes of mercy towards us,
and after this exile
show to us the blessed fruit of your womb, Jesus.
O clement, O loving,
O sweet Virgin Mary.

Prayer for the Dying

De Profundis

1 Out of the depths have I cried to you, O Lord *
   Lord, hear my voice:
      let your ears consider well the voice of my supplication.
2 If you, Lord, were to mark what is done amiss, *
   O Lord, who could stand?
3 But there is forgiveness with you, *
   so that you shall be feared.
4 I wait for the Lord; my soul waits for him; *
   in his word is my hope.
5 My soul waits for the Lord,
   more than the night-watch for the morning, *
   more than the night-watch for the morning.
6 O Israel, wait for the Lord, *
   for with the Lord there is mercy;
7 With him is plenteous redemption *
   and he shall redeem Israel from all their sins.

   Glory . . .

Psalm 130

Commendation of the dying

Proficiscere anima christiana

Go forth upon thy journey, Christian soul!
Go from this world! Go, in the name of God,
the omnipotent Father, who created thee!
Go, in the name of Jesus Christ, our Lord,
Son of the living God, who bled for thee!
Go, in the name of the Holy Spirit, who
hath poured upon thee! Go, in the name
Of Angels and Archangels; in the name
Of Thrones and Dominions; in the name
Of Princedoms and of Powers; and in the name
Of Cherubim and Seraphim, go forth!
Go, in the name of Patriarchs and Prophets;
And of Apostles and Evangelists,
Of Martyrs and Confessors; in the name
Of holy Monks and Hermits; in the name
of holy Virgins; and all the Saints of God,
Both men and women, go! Go on thy course,
And may thy dwelling be the Holy Mount
Of Sion: – through the same, through Christ, our Lord.

The Dream of Gerontius
John Henry Newman

or

N, go forth upon your journey from this world:
in the name of God the Father almighty, who created you;
in the name of Jesus Christ, who suffered death for you;
in the name of the Holy Spirit, who strengthens you;
in communion with the blessed saints,
and aided by angels and archangels,
and all the armies of the heavenly host.
May your portion this day be in peace,
and your dwelling the heavenly Jerusalem.

Common Worship (1)

or

Into your hands, O merciful Saviour,
we commend your servant *N*.
Acknowledge, we pray, a sheep of your own fold,
a lamb of your own flock,
a sinner of your own redeeming.
Enfold *him/her* in the arms of your mercy,
in the blessed rest of everlasting peace,
and in the glorious company of the saints in light.

Common Worship (1)

IV THE EUCHARIST

Preparation for Mass

Prayer of Saint Ambrose

Lord Jesus Christ,
I approach your banquet table
in fear and trembling,
for I am a sinner,
and dare not rely on my own worth,
but only on your goodness and mercy.
I am defiled by many sins in body and soul,
and by my unguarded thoughts and words.

Gracious God of majesty and awe,
I seek your protection,
I look for your healing.
Poor troubled sinner that I am,
I appeal to you, the fountain of all mercy.
I cannot bear your judgement,
but I trust in your salvation.

Lord, I show my wounds to you
and uncover my shame before you.
I know my sins are many and great,
and they fill me with fear,
but I hope in your mercies,
for they cannot be numbered.

Lord Jesus Christ, eternal king, God and man,
crucified for mankind,
look upon me with mercy and hear my prayer,
for I trust in you.
Have mercy on me,

full of sorrow and sin,
for the depth of your compassion never ends.

Praise to you, saving sacrifice,
offered on the wood of the cross for me and for all mankind.
Praise to the noble and precious blood,
flowing from the wounds of my crucified Lord Jesus Christ
and washing away the sins of the whole world.
Remember, Lord, your creature,
whom you have redeemed with your blood.

I repent of my sins,
and I long to put right what I have done.
Merciful Father, take away all my offences and sins;
purify me in body and soul,
and make me worthy to taste the holy of holies.

May your body and blood,
which I intend to receive, although I am unworthy,
be for me the remission of my sins,
the washing away of my guilt,
the end of my evil thoughts,
and the rebirth of my better instincts.
May it incite me to do the works pleasing to you
and profitable to my health in body and soul,
and be a firm defence
against the wiles of my enemies.

ICEL (5)

Prayer of Saint Thomas Aquinas

Almighty, everlasting God,
I draw near to the sacrament of your only-begotten Son,
our Lord Jesus Christ.
I who am sick approach the physician of life.
I who am unclean come to the fountain of mercy;
blind, to the light of eternal brightness;
poor and needy, to the Lord of heaven and earth.
Therefore, I implore you, in your boundless mercy,
to heal my sickness, cleanse my defilement,

enlighten my blindness, enrich my poverty,
and clothe my nakedness.

Then shall I dare to receive the bread of angels,
the King of kings and Lord of lords,
with reverence and humility,
contrition and love,
purity and faith,
with the purpose and intention necessary
for the good of my soul.
Grant, I beseech you, that I may receive
not only the Body and Blood of the Lord,
but also the grace and power of the sacrament.
Most merciful God,
enable me so to receive the Body of your only-begotten Son,
our Lord Jesus Christ, which he took from the Virgin Mary,
that I may be found worthy to be incorporated
into his mystical Body, and counted among his members.

Most loving Father,
grant that I may one day see face to face
your beloved Son, whom I now intend to receive
under the veil of the sacrament,
and who with you and the Holy Spirit,
lives and reigns for ever,
one God, world without end.

Stanbrook Abbey (4)

Father,
make our consciences clean
by the work of your Holy Spirit.
When your Son Jesus Christ comes to us
  in this holy sacrament
may he find in us
a home ready and prepared for him,
who lives and reigns for ever and ever.

Conscientias nostras, tr. AB. (8)

Surely the Lord is in this place and this is none but the house of God and the gate of heaven. And into that gate they shall enter and in that house they shall dwell, where there shall be no cloud nor sun, no darkness nor dazzling, but one equal light; no noise nor silence, but one equal music; no fears nor hopes, but one equal possession; no foes nor friends, but one equal communion and identity; no ends nor beginnings, but one equal eternity.

John Donne: Sermon cxlvi

A Priest's Prayer to Our Lady

Mother of mercy and love,
blessed Virgin Mary,
I am a poor and unworthy sinner,
and I turn to you in confidence and love.
You stood by your Son
as he hung dying on the cross.
Stand also by me, a poor sinner,
and by all the priests
who are offering Mass today
here and throughout the world.
Help us to offer a perfect and acceptable sacrifice
in the sight of the holy and undivided Trinity,
our most high God.

ICEL (5)

The Priest's Declaration of Purpose before Mass

My purpose is to celebrate Mass and to consecrate the body and blood of our Lord Jesus Christ, according to the rite of the holy Catholic Church, to the praise of almighty God and of the whole Church triumphant in heaven, for my own welfare and that of the whole Church militant on earth, for all who in general and in particular have commended themselves to my prayers, and for the well-being of the holy Catholic Church.

May joy and peace,
amendment of life,
room for true penitence,
the grace and comfort of the Holy Spirit,
and steadfastness in good works
be granted us by the almighty and merciful Lord.

Divine Office (14)

The Mass

A Form of Preparation (Common Worship)

This form may be used in any of three ways.

It may be used by individuals as part of their preparation for Holy Communion.

It may be used corporately on suitable occasions within Holy Communion where it replaces the sections entitled 'Prayer of Preparation' and 'Prayers of Penitence'.

It may be used as a separate service of preparation. When used in this way, there should be added at the beginning a greeting and at the end the Peace and the Lord's Prayer. Hymns, psalms and other suitable liturgical material may also be included.

Hymn

Come, Holy Ghost (Veni Creator Spiritus)

Come, Holy Ghost, our souls inspire,
And lighten with celestial fire;
Thou the anointing Spirit art,
Who dost thy sevenfold gifts impart.

Thy blessed unction from above
Is comfort, life and fire of love;
Enable with perpetual light
The dullness of our blinded sight.

Anoint and cheer our soiled face
With the abundance of thy grace;
Keep far our foes, give peace at home;
Where thou art guide no ill can come.

Teach us to know the Father, Son,
And thee, of Both, to be but One;
That through the ages all along
This may be our endless song:

Praise to thy eternal merit,
Father, Son and Holy Spirit.
Amen.

Exhortation

As we gather at the Lord's table we must recall the promises and warnings given to us in the Scriptures and so examine ourselves and repent of our sins. We should give thanks to God for his redemption of the world through his Son Jesus Christ and, as we remember Christ's death for us and receive the pledge of his love, resolve to serve him in holiness and righteousness all the days of our life.

The Commandments

Hear the commandments which God has given to his people, and examine your hearts.

I am the Lord your God: you shall have no other gods but me.
Amen. Lord, have mercy.

You shall not make for yourself any idol.
Amen. Lord, have mercy.

You shall not dishonour the name of the Lord your God.
Amen. Lord, have mercy.

Remember the Sabbath and keep it holy.
Amen. Lord, have mercy.

Honour your father and your mother.
Amen. Lord, have mercy.

You shall not commit murder.
Amen. Lord, have mercy.

You shall not commit adultery.
Amen. Lord, have mercy.

You shall not steal.
Amen. Lord, have mercy.

You shall not bear false witness against your neighbour.
Amen. Lord, have mercy.

You shall not covet anything which belongs to your neighbour.
**Amen. Lord, have mercy upon us
and write all these your laws in our hearts.**

or

Summary of the Law

Our Lord Jesus Christ said,
The first commandment is this:
'Hear, O Israel, the Lord our God is the only Lord.
You shall love the Lord your God with all your heart,
with all your soul, with all your mind,
and with all your strength.'

The second is this: 'Love your neighbour as yourself.'
There is no other commandment greater than these.
On these two commandments hang all the law and the prophets.

Amen. Lord, have mercy.

or

The Comfortable Words

Hear the words of comfort our Saviour Christ says
to all who truly turn to him:

Come to me, all who labour and are heavy laden,
and I will give you rest.

Matthew 11:28

God so loved the world that he gave his only-begotten Son,
that whoever believes in him should not perish
but have eternal life.

John 3:16

Hear what Saint Paul says:

This saying is true, and worthy of full acceptance,
that Christ Jesus came into the world to save sinners.

1 Timothy 1:15

Hear what Saint John says:

If anyone sins, we have an advocate with the Father,
Jesus Christ the righteous;
and he is the propitiation for our sins.

1 John 2:1–2

or

The Beatitudes

Let us hear our Lord's blessing on those who follow him.

Blessed are the poor in spirit,
for theirs is the kingdom of heaven.

Blessed are those who mourn,
for they shall be comforted.

Blessed are the meek,
for they shall inherit the earth.

Blessed are those who hunger and thirst after righteousness,
for they shall be satisfied.

Blessed are the merciful,
for they shall obtain mercy.

Blessed are the pure in heart,
for they shall see God.

Blessed are the peacemakers,
for they shall be called children of God.

Blessed are those who suffer persecution for righteousness' sake,
for theirs is the kingdom of heaven.

Silence for reflection

Confession

Father eternal, giver of light and grace,
we have sinned against you and against our neighbour,
in what we have thought,
in what we have said and done,
through ignorance, through weakness,
through our own deliberate fault.
We have wounded your love,
and marred your image in us.
We are sorry and ashamed,
and repent of all our sins.
For the sake of your Son Jesus Christ,
who died for us,
forgive us all that is past,
and lead us out from darkness
to walk as children of light.
Amen.

or another authorized confession may be used.

Absolution

Almighty God, our heavenly Father,
who in his great mercy
has promised forgiveness of sins
to all those who with heartfelt repentance and true faith turn to him:
have mercy on *us*;
pardon and deliver *us* from all *our* sins;
confirm and strengthen *us* in all goodness;
and bring *us* to everlasting life;
through Jesus Christ our Lord.
Amen.

The Mass

Order One (Common Worship)

On entering church

We adore you, most holy Lord Jesus Christ,
here, and in all your churches throughout all the world;
and we bless you,
because by your holy cross,
you have redeemed the world.

Saint Francis
A Daily Office SSF (3)

Was ever another command so obeyed? For century after century, spreading slowly to every continent and country and among every race on earth, this action has been done, in every conceivable human circumstance, for every conceivable human need from infancy and before it to extreme old age and after it, from the pinnacles of earthly greatness to the refuge of fugitives in the caves and dens of the earth . . . And best of all, week by week and month by month, on a hundred thousand successive Sundays, faithfully, unfailingly,
across all the parishes of Christendom, the pastors have done this just to make . . . the holy common people of God.

Dom Gregory Dix (11)

The Gathering

At the entry of the ministers a hymn may be sung.

The president may say:

In the name of the Father,
and of the Son,

and of the Holy Spirit.
Amen.

The Greeting

The president greets the people:

The Lord be with you
and also with you.

or

Grace, mercy and peace
from God our Father
and the Lord Jesus Christ
be with you
and also with you.

From Easter Day to Pentecost this acclamation follows:

Alleluia. Christ is risen.
He is risen indeed. Alleluia.

Words of welcome or introduction may be said.

Prayer of Preparation

This prayer may be said:

Almighty God,
to whom all hearts are open,
all desires known,
and from whom no secrets are hidden:
cleanse the thoughts of our hearts
by the inspiration of your Holy Spirit,
that we may perfectly love you,
and worthily magnify your holy name;
through Christ our Lord.
Amen.

Prayers of Penitence

A seasonal invitation to confession or these or other suitable words are used:

God so loved the world
that he gave his only Son Jesus Christ
to save us from our sins,
to be our advocate in heaven,
and to bring us to eternal life.

Let us confess our sins in penitence and faith,
firmly resolved to keep God's commandments
and to live in love and peace with all.

Almighty God, our heavenly Father,
we have sinned against you,
through our own fault,
in thought, and word, and deed,
and in what we have left undone.
We are heartily sorry,
and repent of all our sins.
For your Son our Lord Jesus Christ's sake,
forgive us all that is past;
and grant that we may serve you in newness of life
to the glory of your name.
Amen.

or

Almighty God, our heavenly Father,
we have sinned against you
and against our neighbour
in thought and word and deed,
through negligence, through weakness,
through our own deliberate fault.
We are truly sorry
and repent of all our sins.
For the sake of your Son Jesus Christ,
who died for us,
forgive us all that is past,
and grant that we may serve you in newness of life

to the glory of your name.
Amen.

or

Most merciful God,
Father of our Lord Jesus Christ,
we confess that we have sinned
in thought, word and deed.
We have not loved you with our whole heart.
We have not loved our neighbours as ourselves.
In your mercy
forgive what we have been,
help us to amend what we are,
and direct what we shall be;
that we may do justly,
love mercy,
and walk humbly with you, our God.
Amen.

Or, with suitable penitential sentences, the Kyrie Eleison *may be used:*

Lord, have mercy.
Lord, have mercy.

Christ, have mercy.
Christ, have mercy.

Lord, have mercy.
Lord, have mercy.

If another confession has already been used, the Kyrie Eleison *may be used without interpolation here or after the absolution.*

The president says:

Almighty God,
who forgives all who truly repent,
have mercy upon *us*,
pardon and deliver *us* from all *our* sins,
confirm and strengthen *us* in all goodness,

and keep *us* in life eternal;
through Jesus Christ our Lord.
Amen.

or

May almighty God have mercy on *us*,
forgive *us our* sins,
and bring *us* to everlasting life.
Amen.

Gloria in Excelsis

Gloria in Excelsis *may be used:*

**Glory to God in the highest,
and peace to his people on earth.**

**Lord God, heavenly King,
almighty God and Father,
we worship you, we give you thanks,
we praise you for your glory.**

**Lord Jesus Christ, only Son of the Father,
Lord God, Lamb of God,
you take away the sin of the world:
have mercy on us;
you are seated at the right hand of the Father:
receive our prayer.**

**For you alone are the Holy One,
you alone are the Lord,
you alone are the Most High, Jesus Christ,
with the Holy Spirit,
in the glory of God the Father.
Amen.**

The Collect

The president introduces a period of silent prayer with the words 'Let us pray' or a more specific bidding.

The Collect is said, and all respond:
Amen.

The Liturgy of the Word

Readings

Either one or two readings from Scripture precede the Gospel reading.

At the end of each the reader may say:

This is the word of the Lord.
Thanks be to God.

The psalm or canticle follows the first reading; other hymns and songs may be used between the readings.

Gospel reading

An acclamation may herald the Gospel reading.

When the Gospel is announced the reader says:

The Lord be with you
and also with you.

Hear the Gospel of our Lord Jesus Christ according to *N*.
Glory to you, O Lord.

At the end:

This is the Gospel of the Lord.
Praise to you, O Christ.

Sermon

The Creed

On Sundays and principal holy days an authorized translation of the Nicene Creed is used, or on occasion the Apostles' Creed (see page 594) or another authorized affirmation of faith may be used.

We believe in one God,
the Father, the almighty,
maker of heaven and earth,

of all that is,
seen and unseen.

We believe in one Lord, Jesus Christ,
the only Son of God,
eternally begotten of the Father,
God from God, Light from Light,
true God from true God,
begotten, not made,
of one Being with the Father;
through him all things were made.
For us and for our salvation he came down from heaven,
he became incarnate from the Holy Spirit and the Virgin Mary
and was made man.
For our sake he was crucified under Pontius Pilate;
he suffered death and was buried.
On the third day he rose again
in accordance with the Scriptures;
he ascended into heaven
and is seated at the right hand of the Father.
He will come again in glory to judge the living and the dead,
and his kingdom will have no end.

We believe in the Holy Spirit,
the Lord, the giver of life,
who proceeds from the Father and the Son,
who with the Father and the Son is worshipped and glorified,
who has spoken through the prophets.
We believe in one holy catholic and apostolic Church.
We acknowledge one baptism for the forgiveness of sins.
We look for the resurrection of the dead,
and the life of the world to come.
Amen.

Prayers of intercession

The prayers usually include these concerns and may follow this sequence:

- *The Church of Christ*
- *Creation, human society, the Sovereign and those in authority*
- *The local community*

- *Those who suffer*
- *The communion of saints*

These responses may be used:

Lord, in your mercy
hear our prayer.

or

Lord, hear us.
Lord, graciously hear us.

And at the end:

Merciful Father,
**accept these prayers
for the sake of your Son,
our Saviour Jesus Christ.
Amen.**

The Liturgy of the Sacrament

The Peace

The president may introduce the Peace with a suitable sentence, and then says:

The peace of the Lord be always with you
and also with you.

These words may be added:

Let us offer one another a sign of peace.

All may exchange a sign of peace.

Preparation of the Table
Taking of the Bread and Wine

A hymn may be sung.

> ### The Cherubic Hymn
>
> Let us, who in a mystery represent the cherubim and sing the thrice-holy hymn to the life-giving Trinity, lay aside now every care of this life. For we are about to receive the King of all, invisibly escorted by the angelic hosts. [*omit in Lent:* Alleluia, alleluia, alleluia.]
>
> Liturgy of Saint John Chrysostom

The gifts of the people may be gathered and presented.

The altar is prepared and bread and wine are placed upon it.

The president takes the bread and wine.

Blessed are you, Lord God of all creation:
through your goodness we have this bread to set before you,
which earth has given and human hands have made.
It will become for us the bread of life.
Blessed be God for ever.

Blessed are you, Lord God of all creation:
through your goodness we have this wine to set before you,
fruit of the vine and work of human hands.
It will become for us the cup of salvation.
Blessed be God for ever.

> *The following may be said:*
>
> Pray, brethren, that my sacrifice and yours
> may be acceptable to God, the almighty Father.
> **May the Lord accept the sacrifice at your hands**
> **for the praise and glory of his name,**
> **for our good, and the good of all his Church.**
>
> ICEL (5)
>
> *The Prayer over the Gifts may follow.*

The Eucharistic Prayer

An authorized Eucharistic Prayer is used.

The full text of the Eucharistic Prayers may be found as follows:

Prayer A	page 134	Prayer E	page 143
Prayer B	page 137	Prayer F	page 145
Prayer C	page 138	Prayer G	page 148
Prayer D	page 141	Prayer H	page 150

Prayers B, C and E fit the following outline:

The Lord be with you   *or*   The Lord is here.
and also with you.   **His Spirit is with us.**

Lift up your hearts.
We lift them to the Lord.

Let us give thanks to the Lord our God.
It is right to give thanks and praise.

The president praises God for his mighty acts.

Sundays in Ordinary Time:

It is truly right and just, our duty and our salvation,
always and everywhere to give you thanks,
holy Father, almighty and eternal God.
From sunrise to sunset this day is holy,
for Christ has risen from the tomb
and scattered the darkness of death
with light that will not fade.
This day the risen Lord walks with your gathered people,
unfolds for us your word,
and makes himself known in the breaking of the bread.
And though the night will overtake this day
you summon us to live in endless light,
the never-ceasing Sabbath of the Lord.
And so, with choirs of angels
and with all the heavenly host,
we proclaim your glory
and join their unending song of praise:

All respond:

**Holy, holy, holy Lord,
God of power and might,
heaven and earth are full of your glory.
Hosanna in the highest.**

**[Blessed is he who comes in the name of the Lord.
Hosanna in the highest.]**

The president recalls the Last Supper.

Eucharistic Prayer B:

Lord, you are holy indeed, the source of all holiness;
grant that by the power of your Holy Spirit,
and according to your holy will,
these gifts of bread and wine
may be to us the body and blood of our Lord Jesus Christ;

who, in the same night that he was betrayed,
took bread and gave you thanks;
he broke it and gave it to his disciples, saying:
Take, eat; this is my body which is given for you;
do this in remembrance of me.

In the same way, after supper
he took the cup and gave you thanks;
he gave it to them, saying:
Drink this, all of you;
this is my blood of the new covenant,
which is shed for you and for many for the forgiveness of sins.
Do this, as often as you drink it,
in remembrance of me.

One of these four acclamations may be used:

[Great is the mystery of faith:]
**Christ has died:
Christ is risen:
Christ will come again.**

[Praise to you, Lord Jesus:]
**Dying you destroyed our death,
rising you restored our life:
Lord Jesus, come in glory.**

[Christ is the bread of life:]
**When we eat this bread
and drink this cup,
we proclaim your death,
Lord Jesus,
until you come in glory.**

[Jesus Christ is Lord:]
**Lord, by your cross and
resurrection
you have set us free.
You are the Saviour of the
world.**

The Prayer continues.

Eucharistic Prayer B:

And so, Father, calling to mind his death on the cross,
his perfect sacrifice made once for the sins of the whole world;
rejoicing in his mighty resurrection and glorious ascension,
and looking for his coming in glory,
we celebrate this memorial of our redemption.
As we offer you this our sacrifice of praise and thanksgiving,
we bring before you this bread and this cup
and we thank you for counting us worthy
to stand in your presence and serve you.

Send the Holy Spirit on your people
and gather into one in your kingdom
all who share this one bread and one cup,
so that we, in the company of (*N* and) all the saints,
may praise and glorify you for ever,
through Jesus Christ our Lord;

by whom, and with whom, and in whom,
in the unity of the Holy Spirit,
all honour and glory be yours, almighty Father,
for ever and ever.

The Prayer leads into the doxology, to which all respond boldly:

Amen.

The Lord's Prayer

As our Saviour taught us, so we pray:

Our Father in heaven,
hallowed be your name,
your kingdom come,
your will be done,
on earth as in heaven.
Give us today our daily bread.
Forgive us our sins
as we forgive those who sin against us.
Lead us not into temptation
but deliver us from evil.
For the kingdom, the power,
and the glory are yours
now and for ever.
Amen.

or

Let us pray with confidence as our Saviour has taught us:

Our Father, who art in heaven,
hallowed be thy name;
thy kingdom come;
thy will be done;
on earth as it is in heaven.
Give us this day our daily bread.
And forgive us our trespasses,
as we forgive those who trespass against us.
And lead us not into temptation;
but deliver us from evil.
For thine is the kingdom,
the power and the glory,
for ever and ever.
Amen.

Breaking of the Bread

The president breaks the consecrated bread.

We break this bread
to share in the body of Christ.
**Though we are many, we are one body,
because we all share in one bread.**

or

Every time we eat this bread
and drink this cup,
**we proclaim the Lord's death
until he comes.**

Agnus Dei *may be used as the bread is broken:*

**Lamb of God,
you take away the sin of the world,
   have mercy on us.**

**Lamb of God,
you take away the sin of the world,
have mercy on us.**

**Lamb of God,
you take away the sin of the world,
grant us peace.**

or

**Jesus, Lamb of God,
have mercy on us.**

**Jesus, bearer of our sins,
have mercy on us.**

**Jesus, redeemer of the world,
grant us peace.**

Giving of Communion

The president says the invitation to communion:

This* is the Lamb of God
who takes away the sin of the world.
Blessed are those who are called to his supper.
Lord, I am not worthy to receive you,
but only say the word, and I shall be healed.

or

God's holy gifts
for God's holy people.
Jesus Christ is holy,
Jesus Christ is Lord,
to the glory of God the Father.

or, from Easter Day to Pentecost

Alleluia. Christ our passover is sacrificed for us.
Therefore let us keep the feast. Alleluia.

One of these prayers may be said before the distribution:

We do not presume
to come to this your table, merciful Lord,
trusting in our own righteousness,
but in your manifold and great mercies.
We are not worthy
so much as to gather up the crumbs under your table.
But you are the same Lord
whose nature is always to have mercy.
Grant us, therefore, gracious Lord,
so to eat the flesh of your dear Son Jesus Christ
and to drink his blood,
that our sinful bodies may be made clean by his body
and our souls washed through his most precious blood,
and that we may evermore dwell in him, and he in us.
Amen.

*In Common Worship, Jesus is . . .

or

Most merciful Lord,
your love compels us to come in.
Our hands were unclean,
our hearts were unprepared;
we were not fit
even to eat the crumbs from under your table.
But you, Lord, are the God of our salvation,
and share your bread with sinners.
So cleanse and feed us
with the precious body and blood of your Son,
that he may live in us and we in him;
and that we, with the whole company of Christ,
may sit and eat in your kingdom.
Amen.

The president and people receive communion.
Authorized words of distribution are used, such as:

The body of Christ.	**Amen.**
The blood of Christ.	**Amen.**

During the distribution hymns and anthems may be sung.

Communion devotions

Before Communion

At your mystical supper, Son of God, receive me today
as a partaker. I will not speak of the mystery to your
enemies. I will not let my lips touch your body with the
kiss of Judas. Like the thief I will acknowledge you:
Remember me when you come into your kingdom.

Liturgy of St John Chrysostom

Jesus remember me, when you come into your kingdom.

Luke 23:42

Lord, to whom can we go?
You have the words of eternal life.
John 6:68

My Lord and my God.
John 20:28

O come to my heart Lord Jesus:
there is room in my heart for you.

Good Jesu, who gavest thyself for me,
give me of the fullness of thy love,
that for all thy love, with thy love, I may love thee.
Edward Bouverie Pusey

After receiving Communion

Anima Christi

Soul of Christ, sanctify me,
Body of Christ, save me,
Blood of Christ, inebriate me,
Water from the side of Christ, wash me,
Passion of Christ, strengthen me.
O good Jesus, hear me.
Within your wounds hide me,
let me not be separated from you,
from the malicious enemy defend me,
in the hour of my death call me
and bid me come to you,
that with your saints I may praise you
for ever and ever.

Prayer after Communion

Silence is kept.

The post-communion or another suitable prayer is said.

All may say one of these prayers:

**Almighty God,
we thank you for feeding us
with the body and blood of your Son Jesus Christ.**

**Through him we offer you our souls and bodies
to be a living sacrifice.
Send us out
in the power of your Spirit
to live and work
to your praise and glory.
Amen.**

or

**Father of all,
we give you thanks and praise,
that when we were still far off
you met us in your Son and brought us home.
Dying and living, he declared your love,
gave us grace, and opened the gate of glory.
May we who share Christ's body live his risen life;
we who drink his cup bring life to others;
we whom the Spirit lights give light to the world.
Keep us firm in the hope you have set before us,
so we and all your children shall be free,
and the whole earth live to praise your name;
through Christ our Lord.
Amen.**

The Dismissal

A hymn may be sung.

The Lord be with you
and also with you.

The president may use the seasonal blessing, or another suitable blessing:

or

The peace of God,
which passes all understanding,
keep your hearts and minds
in the knowledge and love of God,

and of his Son Jesus Christ our Lord;
and the blessing of God almighty,
the Father, the Son, and the Holy Spirit,
be among you and remain with you always.
Amen.

Go in the peace of Christ.
Thanks be to God.

or, from Easter Day to Pentecost:

Go in the peace of Christ. Alleluia, Alleluia.
Thanks be to God. Alleluia, Alleluia.

The ministers and people depart.

Before leaving church

You are Christians!
Then your Lord is one and the same
with Jesus on the throne of his glory,
with Jesus in his blessed Sacrament,
with Jesus received into your hearts in Communion,
with Jesus who is mystically with you as you pray,
and with Jesus enshrined in the hearts and bodies of his brothers and sisters
   up and down the world.

Now go out into the highways and hedges,
and look for Jesus in the ragged and naked,
in the oppressed and sweated,
in those who have lost hope,
and in those who are struggling to make good.
Look for Jesus in them;
and when you find him,
gird yourselves with his towel of fellowship,
and wash his feet in the person of his brethren.

Bishop Frank Weston

Lord Jesus Christ,
take all my freedom,
my memory, my understanding, and my will.

All that I have and cherish
you have given me.
I surrender it all to be guided by your will.
Your grace and your love are wealth enough for me.
Give me these, Lord Jesus,
and I ask for nothing more.

ICEL (5)

or

Grant, O Lord God, that what we have heard with our ears
and sung with our lips, we may believe in our hearts
and practise in our lives; for Jesus Christ's sake.

Eric Milner-White (16)

Eucharistic Prayers

For Order One (Common Worship)

Prayer A

Prayer A (like Prayers B, C and E) is 'Western' in shape. The prayer for the Holy Spirit to come on the congregation and gifts comes before the words of Jesus at the Last Supper. In the West it is believed that when the words of Jesus are recited in the Eucharistic Prayer the bread and wine become the body and blood of Christ, sacramentally present. Prayer A represents further development of two Eucharistic Prayers composed by the Church of England in the 1960s.

In Prayer A (as in Prayer E) the acclamation ('Christ has died . . .) comes correspondingly later than in Prayers B, C and G.

If a preface is used, it replaces all words between the opening dialogue and the Sanctus.

The Lord be with you   *or*   The Lord is here.
and also with you.   **His Spirit is with us.**

Lift up your hearts.
We lift them to the Lord.

Let us give thanks to the Lord our God.
It is right to give thanks and praise.

It is indeed right,
it is our duty and our joy,
at all times and in all places

to give you thanks and praise,
holy Father, heavenly King,
almighty and eternal God,
through Jesus Christ your Son our Lord.

The following may be omitted if a short proper preface is used:

For he is your living Word;
through him you have created all things from the beginning,
and formed us in your own image.
[To you be glory and praise for ever.]

Through him you have freed us from the slavery of sin,
giving him to be born of a woman and to die upon the cross;
you raised him from the dead
and exalted him to your right hand on high.
[To you be glory and praise for ever.]

Through him you have sent upon us
your holy and life-giving Spirit,
and made us a people for your own possession.
[To you be glory and praise for ever.]

Short proper preface, when appropriate.

Therefore with angels and archangels,
and with all the company of heaven,
we proclaim your great and glorious name,
for ever praising you and saying:

Holy, holy, holy Lord,
God of power and might,
heaven and earth are full of your glory.
Hosanna in the highest.

[Blessed is he who comes in the name of the Lord.
Hosanna in the highest.]

Accept our praises, heavenly Father,
through your Son our Saviour Jesus Christ,
and as we follow his example and obey his command,
grant that by the power of your Holy Spirit
these gifts of bread and wine
may be to us his body and his blood;

who, in the same night that he was betrayed,
took bread and gave you thanks;
he broke it and gave it to his disciples, saying:
Take, eat; this is my body which is given for you;
do this in remembrance of me.
[**To you be glory and praise for ever.**]

In the same way, after supper
he took the cup and gave you thanks;
he gave it to them, saying:
Drink this, all of you;
this is my blood of the new covenant,
which is shed for you and for many for the forgiveness of sins.
Do this, as often as you drink it,
in remembrance of me.
[**To you be glory and praise for ever.**]

Therefore, heavenly Father,
we remember his offering of himself
made once for all upon the cross;
we proclaim his mighty resurrection and glorious ascension;
we look for the coming of your kingdom,
and with this bread and this cup
we make the memorial of Christ your Son our Lord.

One of these four acclamations is used:

[Great is the mystery of faith:]
Christ has died:
Christ is risen:
Christ will come again.

[Praise to you, Lord Jesus:]
Dying you destroyed
  our death,
rising you restored our life:
Lord Jesus, come in glory.

[Christ is the bread of life:]
When we eat this bread
  and drink this cup,
we proclaim your death,
  Lord Jesus,
until you come in glory.

[Jesus Christ is Lord:]
Lord, by your cross and
  resurrection
you have set us free.
You are the Saviour of the
  world.

Eucharistic Prayers

Accept through him, our great high priest,
this our sacrifice of thanks and praise,
and as we eat and drink these holy gifts
in the presence of your divine majesty,
renew us by your Spirit,
inspire us with your love
and unite us in the body of your Son,
Jesus Christ our Lord.
[To you be glory and praise for ever.]

Through him, and with him, and in him,
in the unity of the Holy Spirit,
with all who stand before you in earth and heaven,
we worship you, Father almighty,
in songs of everlasting praise:

**Blessing and honour and glory and power
be yours for ever and ever.
Amen.**

The service continues with the Lord's Prayer on page 126.

Prayer B

Prayer B (like Prayers A, C and E) is 'Western' in shape; it is closest to the second Roman Catholic Eucharistic Prayer. Both are versions of the Prayer of Hippolytus, one of the earliest Eucharistic Prayers the Church has.

On Sundays and Holy Days an extended preface usually replaces all words between the opening dialogue and the Sanctus. *The preface below follows that of Hippolytus closely.*

The Lord be with you	*or*	The Lord is here.
and also with you.		**His Spirit is with us.**

Lift up your hearts.
We lift them to the Lord.

Let us give thanks to the Lord our God.
It is right to give thanks and praise.

Father, we give you thanks and praise
through your beloved Son Jesus Christ, your living Word,

through whom you have created all things;
who was sent by you in your great goodness to be our Saviour.

By the power of the Holy Spirit he took flesh;
as your Son, born of the blessed Virgin,
he lived on earth and went about among us;
he opened wide his arms for us on the cross;
he put an end to death by dying for us;
and revealed the resurrection by rising to new life;
so he fulfilled your will and won for you a holy people.

Short proper preface, when appropriate:

Therefore with angels and archangels,
and with all the company of heaven,
we proclaim your great and glorious name,
for ever praising you and saying:

**Holy, holy, holy Lord,
God of power and might,
heaven and earth are full of your glory.
Hosanna in the highest.**

**[Blessed is he who comes in the name of the Lord.
Hosanna in the highest.]**

Lord, you are holy indeed . . . *(see page 124)*

The service continues with the Lord's Prayer on page 126.

Prayer C

Prayer C (like Prayers A, B and E) is 'Western' in shape; it is closest to Cranmer in words. The combination of his Prayer of Consecration and Prayer of Oblation produces, arguably, the clearest expression of Catholic eucharistic theology.

On Sundays and Holy Days an extended preface usually replaces all words between the opening dialogue and the Sanctus.

Eucharistic Prayers

The Lord be with you	*or*	The Lord is here.
and also with you.		**His Spirit is with us.**

Lift up your hearts.
We lift them to the Lord.

Let us give thanks to the Lord our God.
It is right to give thanks and praise.

It is indeed right,
it is our duty and our joy,
at all times and in all places
to give you thanks and praise,
holy Father, heavenly King,
almighty and eternal God,
through Jesus Christ our Lord:

Short proper preface, when appropriate.

or, when there is no proper preface:

For he is our great high priest,
who has loosed us from our sins
and has made us to be a royal priesthood to you,
our God and Father.

Therefore with angels and archangels,
and with all the company of heaven,
we proclaim your great and glorious name,
for ever praising you and saying:

Holy, holy, holy Lord,
God of power and might,
heaven and earth are full of your glory.
Hosanna in the highest.

[Blessed is he who comes in the name of the Lord.
Hosanna in the highest.]

All glory be to you, our heavenly Father,
who, in your tender mercy,
gave your only Son our Saviour Jesus Christ
to suffer death upon the cross for our redemption;
who made there by his one oblation of himself once offered
a full, perfect and sufficient sacrifice, oblation and satisfaction

for the sins of the whole world;
he instituted, and in his holy gospel commanded us to continue,
a perpetual memory of his precious death until he comes again.

Hear us, merciful Father, we humbly pray,
and grant that, by the power of your Holy Spirit,
we receiving these gifts of your creation, this bread and this wine,
according to your Son our Saviour Jesus Christ's holy institution,
in remembrance of his death and passion,
may be partakers of his most blessed body and blood;

who, in the same night that he was betrayed,
took bread and gave you thanks;
he broke it and gave it to his disciples, saying:
Take, eat; this is my body which is given for you;
do this in remembrance of me.

In the same way, after supper
he took the cup and gave you thanks;
he gave it to them, saying:
Drink this, all of you;
this is my blood of the new covenant,
which is shed for you and for many for the forgiveness of sins.
Do this, as often as you drink it,
in remembrance of me.

One of these four acclamations is used:

[Great is the mystery of faith:]
Christ has died:
Christ is risen:
Christ will come again.

[Praise to you, Lord Jesus:]
Dying you destroyed
   our death,
rising you restored our life:
Lord Jesus, come in glory.

[Christ is the bread of life:]
When we eat this bread
   and drink this cup,
we proclaim your death,
   Lord Jesus,
until you come in glory.

[Jesus Christ is Lord:]
Lord, by your cross and
   resurrection
you have set us free.
You are the Saviour of the
   world.

Therefore, Lord and heavenly Father,
in remembrance of the precious death and passion,
the mighty resurrection and glorious ascension
of your dear Son Jesus Christ,
we offer you through him this our sacrifice of praise and thanksgiving.

Grant that by his merits and death,
and through faith in his blood,
we and all your Church may receive forgiveness of our sins
and all other benefits of his passion.
Although we are unworthy, through our manifold sins,
to offer you any sacrifice,
yet we pray that you will accept this
the duty and service that we owe.
Do not weigh our merits, but pardon our offences,
and fill us all who share in this holy communion
with your grace and heavenly blessing;

through Jesus Christ our Lord,
by whom, and with whom, and in whom,
in the unity of the Holy Spirit,
all honour and glory be yours, almighty Father,
for ever and ever.
Amen.

The service continues with the Lord's Prayer on page 126.

Prayer D

Prayer D (like Prayers F, G and H) is 'Eastern' in shape. The prayer for the Holy Spirit to come on the congregation and gifts is later in the prayer than the narrative of the Last Supper. The climax of Prayer D is the final doxology and the congregation saying 'Amen'. Prayer D is a new Prayer, designed not least to meet the needs of children.

The Lord be with you	*or*	The Lord is here.
and also with you.		**His Spirit is with us.**

Lift up your hearts.
We lift them to the Lord.

Let us give thanks to the Lord our God.
It is right to give thanks and praise.

Almighty God, good Father to us all,
your face is turned towards your world.
In love you gave us Jesus your Son
to rescue us from sin and death.
Your Word goes out to call us home
to the city where angels sing your praise.
We join with them in heaven's song:

Holy, holy, holy Lord,
God of power and might,
heaven and earth are full of your glory.
Hosanna in the highest.

[Blessed is he who comes in the name of the Lord.
Hosanna in the highest.]

Father of all, we give you thanks
for every gift that comes from heaven.

To the darkness Jesus came as your light.
With signs of faith and words of hope
he touched untouchables with love and washed the guilty clean.

This is his story.
This is our song:
Hosanna in the highest.

The crowds came out to see your Son,
yet at the end they turned on him.
On the night he was betrayed
he came to table with his friends
to celebrate the freedom of your people.

This is his story.
This is our song:
Hosanna in the highest.

Jesus blessed you, Father, for the food;
he took bread, gave thanks, broke it and said:
This is my body, given for you all.
Jesus then gave thanks for the wine;
he took the cup, gave it and said:
This is my blood, shed for you all for the forgiveness of sins.
Do this in remembrance of me.

This is our story.
This is our song:
Hosanna in the highest.

Therefore, Father, with this bread and this cup
we celebrate the cross
on which he died to set us free.
Defying death he rose again
and is alive with you to plead for us and all the world.

This is our story.
This is our song:
Hosanna in the highest.

Send your Spirit on us now
that by these gifts we may feed on Christ
with opened eyes and hearts on fire.

May we and all who share this food
offer ourselves to live for you
and be welcomed at your feast in heaven
where all creation worships you,
Father, Son and Holy Spirit:

Blessing and honour and glory and power
be yours for ever and ever.
Amen.

The service continues with the Lord's Prayer on page 126.

Prayer E

Prayer E (like Prayers A, B and C) is 'Western' in shape. It is a new Prayer, and, not least in its brevity (without an extended preface), suitable for weekday use and to meet the needs of young people.

In Prayer E (as in Prayer A) the acclamation ('Christ has died . . .') comes slightly later than in Prayers B, C and G.

On Sundays and Holy Days an extended preface usually replaces all words between the opening dialogue and the Sanctus.

The Lord be with you	*or*	The Lord is here.
and also with you.		**His Spirit is with us.**

Lift up your hearts.
We lift them to the Lord.

Let us give thanks to the Lord our God.
It is right to give thanks and praise.

Father, you made the world and love your creation.
You gave your Son Jesus Christ to be our Saviour.
His dying and rising have set us free from sin and death.
And so we gladly thank you,
with saints and angels praising you, and saying:

Holy, holy, holy Lord,
God of power and might,
heaven and earth are full of your glory.
Hosanna in the highest.

[Blessed is he who comes in the name of the Lord.
Hosanna in the highest.]

We praise and bless you, loving Father,
through Jesus Christ, our Lord;
and as we obey his command,
send your Holy Spirit,
that broken bread and wine outpoured
may be for us the body and blood of your dear Son.

On the night before he died he had supper with his friends
and, taking bread, he praised you.
He broke the bread, gave it to them and said:
Take, eat; this is my body which is given for you;
do this in remembrance of me.

When supper was ended he took the cup of wine.
Again he praised you, gave it to them and said:
Drink this, all of you;
this is my blood of the new covenant,
which is shed for you and for many for the forgiveness of sins.
Do this, as often as you drink it, in remembrance of me.

So, Father, we remember all that Jesus did,
in him we plead with confidence his sacrifice
made once for all upon the cross.

Bringing before you the bread of life and cup of salvation,
we proclaim his death and resurrection
until he comes in glory.

One of these four acclamations is used:

[Great is the mystery of faith:]
Christ has died:
Christ is risen:
Christ will come again.

[Praise to you, Lord Jesus:]
Dying you destroyed
   our death,
rising you restored our life:
Lord Jesus, come in glory.

[Christ is the bread of life:]
When we eat this bread
   and drink this cup,
we proclaim your death,
   Lord Jesus,
until you come in glory.

[Jesus Christ is Lord:]
Lord, by your cross and
   resurrection
you have set us free.
You are the Saviour of the
   world.

Lord of all life,
help us to work together for that day
when your kingdom comes
and justice and mercy will be seen in all the earth.

Look with favour on your people,
gather us in your loving arms
and bring us with (*N* and) all the saints
to feast at your table in heaven.

Through Christ, and with Christ, and in Christ,
in the unity of the Holy Spirit,
all honour and glory are yours, O loving Father,
for ever and ever.
Amen.

The service continues with the Lord's Prayer on page 126.

Prayer F

Prayer F (like Prayers D, G and H) is 'Eastern' in shape. Prayer F bears some resemblance to the ancient Alexandrian anaphora attributed to St Basil.

The Lord be with you   *or*   The Lord is here.
and also with you.   **His Spirit is with us.**

Lift up your hearts.
We lift them to the Lord.

Let us give thanks to the Lord our God.
It is right to give thanks and praise.

You are worthy of our thanks and praise
Lord God of truth,
for by the breath of your mouth
you have spoken your word,
and all things have come into being.

You fashioned us in your image
and placed us in the garden of your delight.
Though we chose the path of rebellion
you would not abandon your own.

Again and again you drew us into your covenant of grace.
You gave your people the law and taught us by your prophets
to look for your reign of justice, mercy and peace.

As we watch for the signs of your kingdom on earth,
we echo the song of the angels in heaven,
evermore praising you and saying:

Holy, holy, holy Lord,
God of power and might,
heaven and earth are full of your glory.
Hosanna in the highest.

[Blessed is he who comes in the name of the Lord.
Hosanna in the highest.]

Lord God, you are the most holy one,
enthroned in splendour and light,
yet in the coming of your Son Jesus Christ
you reveal the power of your love
made perfect in our human weakness.
[Amen. Lord, we believe.]

Embracing our humanity,
Jesus showed us the way of salvation;

loving us to the end,
he gave himself to death for us;
dying for his own,
he set us free from the bonds of sin,
that we might rise and reign with him in glory.
[Amen. Lord, we believe.]

On the night he gave up himself for us all
he took bread and gave you thanks;
he broke it and gave it to his disciples, saying:
Take, eat; this is my body which is given for you;
do this in remembrance of me.
[Amen. Lord, we believe.]

In the same way, after supper
he took the cup and gave you thanks;
he gave it to them, saying:
Drink this, all of you; this is my blood of the new covenant
which is shed for you and for many for the forgiveness of sins.
Do this, as often as you drink it, in remembrance of me.
[Amen. Lord, we believe.]

Therefore we proclaim the death that he suffered on the cross,
we celebrate his resurrection, his bursting from the tomb,
we rejoice that he reigns at your right hand on high
and we long for his coming in glory.
[Amen. Come, Lord Jesus.]

As we recall the one, perfect sacrifice of our redemption,
Father, by your Holy Spirit let these gifts of your creation
be to us the body and blood of our Lord Jesus Christ;
form us into the likeness of Christ
and make us a perfect offering in your sight.
[Amen. Come, Holy Spirit.]

Look with favour on your people
and in your mercy hear the cry of our hearts.
Bless the earth,
heal the sick,
let the oppressed go free
and fill your Church with power from on high.
[Amen. Come, Holy Spirit.]

Gather your people from the ends of the earth
to feast with (*N* and) all your saints
at the table in your kingdom,
where the new creation is brought to perfection
in Jesus Christ our Lord;

by whom, and with whom, and in whom,
in the unity of the Holy Spirit,
all honour and glory be yours, almighty Father,
for ever and ever.
Amen.

The service continues with the Lord's Prayer on page 126.

Prayer G

Prayer G (like Prayers D, F and H) is 'Eastern' in shape. The reference to 'mother' in the prayer is not a theological aberration but a simile (cf. Deuteronomy 32:11; Matthew 23:37).

The Lord be with you	*or*	The Lord is here.
and also with you.		**His Spirit is with us.**

Lift up your hearts.
We lift them to the Lord.

Let us give thanks to the Lord our God.
It is right to give thanks and praise.

Blessed are you, Lord God,
our light and our salvation;
to you be glory and praise for ever.

From the beginning you have created all things
and all your works echo the silent music of your praise.
In the fullness of time you made us in your image,
the crown of all creation.

You give us breath and speech, that with angels and archangels
and all the powers of heaven
we may find a voice to sing your praise:
Holy, holy, holy Lord,
God of power and might,

heaven and earth are full of your glory.
Hosanna in the highest.

[Blessed is he who comes in the name of the Lord.
Hosanna in the highest.]

How wonderful the work of your hands, O Lord.
As a mother tenderly gathers her children,
you embraced a people as your own.
When they turned away and rebelled
your love remained steadfast.

From them you raised up Jesus our Saviour, born of Mary,
to be the living bread,
in whom all our hungers are satisfied.

He offered his life for sinners,
and with a love stronger than death
he opened wide his arms on the cross.

On the night before he died,
he came to supper with his friends
and, taking bread, he gave you thanks.
He broke it and gave it to them, saying:
Take, eat; this is my body which is given for you;
do this in remembrance of me.

At the end of supper, taking the cup of wine,
he gave you thanks, and said:
Drink this, all of you; this is my blood of the new covenant,
which is shed for you and for many for the forgiveness of sins.
Do this, as often as you drink it, in remembrance of me.

One of these four acclamations is used:

[Great is the mystery of faith:]　　　　　　　[Praise to you, Lord Jesus:]
Christ has died:　　　　　　　　　　　　**Dying you destroyed**
Christ is risen:　　　　　　　　　　　　　**our death,**
Christ will come again.　　　　　　　　**rising you restored our life:**
　　　　　　　　　　　　　　　　　　　　　Lord Jesus, come in glory.

[Christ is the bread of life:]
**When we eat this bread
and drink this cup,
we proclaim your death,
Lord Jesus,
until you come in glory.**

[Jesus Christ is Lord:]
**Lord, by your cross and
resurrection
you have set us free.
You are the Saviour of the
world.**

Father, we plead with confidence
his sacrifice made once for all upon the cross;
we remember his dying and rising in glory,
and we rejoice that he intercedes for us at your right hand.

Pour out your Holy Spirit as we bring before you
these gifts of your creation;
may they be for us the body and blood of your dear Son.

As we eat and drink these holy things in your presence,
form us in the likeness of Christ,
and build us into a living temple to your glory.

[Remember, Lord, your Church in every land.
Reveal her unity, guard her faith,
and preserve her in peace ...]

Bring us at the last with (*N* and) all the saints
to the vision of that eternal splendour
for which you have created us;
through Jesus Christ, our Lord,
by whom, with whom, and in whom,
with all who stand before you in earth and heaven,
we worship you, Father almighty, in songs of everlasting praise:

**Blessing and honour and glory and power
be yours for ever and ever.
Amen.**

The service continues with the Lord's Prayer on page 126.

Prayer H

Prayer H (like Prayers D, F and G) is 'Eastern' in shape. The climax of Prayer H is the 'Holy, holy, holy' at the end. Prayer H, a new prayer, is designed to enable greater congregational participation in the saying of the Eucharistic Prayer.

The Lord be with you	*or*	The Lord is here.
and also with you.		**His Spirit is with us.**

Lift up your hearts.
We lift them to the Lord.

Let us give thanks to the Lord our God.
It is right to give thanks and praise.

It is right to praise you, Father, Lord of all creation;
in your love you made us for yourself.

When we turned away
you did not reject us,
but came to meet us in your Son.
**You embraced us as your children
and welcomed us to sit and eat with you.**

In Christ you shared our life
that we might live in him and he in us.
**He opened his arms of love upon the cross
and made for all the perfect sacrifice for sin.**

On the night he was betrayed,
at supper with his friends
he took bread, and gave you thanks;
he broke it and gave it to them, saying:
Take, eat; this is my body which is given for you;
do this in remembrance of me.
**Father, we do this in remembrance of him:
his body is the bread of life.**

At the end of supper, taking the cup of wine,
he gave you thanks, and said:
Drink this, all of you; this is my blood of the new covenant,
which is shed for you for the forgiveness of sins;
do this in remembrance of me.
**Father, we do this in remembrance of him:
his blood is shed for all.**

As we proclaim his death and celebrate his rising in glory,
send your Holy Spirit that this bread and this wine
may be to us the body and blood of your dear Son.
As we eat and drink these holy gifts
make us one in Christ, our risen Lord.

With your whole Church throughout the world
we offer you this sacrifice of praise
and lift our voice to join the eternal song of heaven:

Holy, holy, holy Lord,
God of power and might,
Heaven and earth are full of your glory.
Hosanna in the highest.

The service continues with the Lord's Prayer on page 126.

The Mass

Order One In Traditional Language (Common Worship)

> ### *On entering church*
>
> We adore you, most holy Lord Jesus Christ,
> here, and in all your churches throughout all the world;
> and we bless you,
> because by your holy cross,
> you have redeemed the world.
>
>

Saint Francis
A Daily Office SSF (3)

>
> Was ever another command so obeyed? For century after century, spreading slowly to every continent and country and among every race on earth, this action has been done, in every conceivable human circumstance, for every conceivable human need from infancy and before it to extreme old age and after it, from the pinnacles of earthly greatness to the refuge of fugitives in the caves and dens of the earth . . . And best of all, week by week and month by month, on a hundred thousand successive Sundays, faithfully, unfailingly, across all the parishes of Christendom, the pastors have done this just to make . . . the holy common people of God.
>
>

Dom Gregory Dix (11)

The Gathering

At the entry of the ministers a hymn may be sung.

The president may say:

In the name of the Father,
and of the Son,

and of the Holy Spirit.
Amen.

The Greeting

The president greets the people:

The Lord be with you
and with thy spirit.

or

Grace, mercy and peace
from God our Father
and the Lord Jesus Christ
be with you
and with thy spirit.

From Easter Day to Pentecost this acclamation follows:

Alleluia. Christ is risen.
He is risen indeed. Alleluia.

Words of welcome or introduction may be said.

Prayer of Preparation

This prayer may be said:

**Almighty God,
unto whom all hearts be open,
all desires known,
and from whom no secrets are hid:
cleanse the thoughts of our hearts
by the inspiration of thy Holy Spirit,
that we may perfectly love thee,
and worthily magnify thy holy name;
through Christ our Lord.
Amen.**

Prayers of Penitence

A seasonal invitation to confession or these or other suitable words are used:

God so loved the world
that he gave his only Son Jesus Christ
to save us from our sins,
to be our advocate in heaven,
and to bring us to eternal life.

Let us confess our sins in penitence and faith,
firmly resolved to keep God's commandments
and to live in love and peace with all.

**Almighty God, our heavenly Father,
we have sinned against thee
and against our neighbour,
in thought and word and deed,
through negligence, through weakness,
through our own deliberate fault.
We are heartily sorry
and repent of all our sins.
For the sake of thy Son Jesus Christ,
who died for us,
forgive us all that is past,
and grant that we may serve thee in newness of life
to the glory of thy name.
Amen.**

or

**Most merciful God,
Father of our Lord Jesus Christ,
we confess that we have sinned
in thought, word and deed.
We have not loved thee with our whole heart.
We have not loved our neighbours as ourselves.
In thy mercy
forgive what we have been,
help us to amend what we are,
and direct what we shall be;
that we may do justly,**

**love mercy,
and walk humbly with thee, our God.
Amen.**

Or, with suitable penitential sentences, the Kyrie Eleison *may be used:*

Lord, have mercy.
Lord, have mercy.

Christ, have mercy.
Christ, have mercy.

Lord, have mercy.
Lord, have mercy.

If another confession has already been used, the Kyrie Eleison *may be used without interpolation here or after the absolution.*

The president says:

Almighty God,
who forgives all who truly repent,
have mercy upon *us*,
pardon and deliver *us* from all *our* sins,
confirm and strengthen *us* in all goodness,
and keep *us* in life eternal;
through Jesus Christ our Lord.
Amen.

or

May almighty God have mercy on *us*,
forgive *us our* sins,
and bring *us* to everlasting life.
Amen.

Gloria in Excelsis

Gloria in Excelsis *may be used:*

**Glory be to God on high,
and in earth peace, goodwill towards men.**

We praise thee, we bless thee,
we worship thee, we glorify thee,
we give thanks to thee for thy great glory,
O Lord God, heavenly King,
God the Father almighty.

O Lord, the only-begotten Son, Jesus Christ:
O Lord God, Lamb of God, Son of the Father,
that takest away the sins of the world,
have mercy upon us.
Thou that takest away the sins of the world,
receive our prayer.
Thou that sittest at the right hand of God the Father,
have mercy upon us.

For thou only art holy;
thou only art the Lord;
thou only, O Christ,
with the Holy Ghost,
art the Most High,
in the glory of God the Father.
Amen.

The Collect

The president introduces a period of silent prayer with the words 'Let us pray' or a more specific bidding.

The collect is said, and all respond:

Amen.

The Liturgy of the Word

Readings

Either one or two readings from Scripture precede the Gospel reading.

At the end of each the reader may say:

This is the word of the Lord.
Thanks be to God.

The psalm or canticle follows the first reading; other hymns and songs may be used between the readings.

Gospel reading

An acclamation may herald the Gospel reading.

When the Gospel is announced, the reader says:

The Lord be with you
and with thy spirit.

Hear the Gospel of our Lord Jesus Christ according to *N*.
Glory be to thee, O Lord.

At the end:

This is the Gospel of the Lord.
Praise be to thee, O Christ.

Sermon

The Creed

On Sundays and principal holy days an authorized translation of the Nicene Creed is used, or on occasion the Apostles' Creed (see page 594) or another authorized affirmation of faith may be used.

**I believe in one God the Father almighty,
maker of heaven and earth,
and of all things
visible and invisible:**

**And in one Lord Jesus Christ,
the only-begotten Son of God,
begotten of his Father before all worlds,
God of God, Light of Light,
very God of very God,
begotten, not made,
being of one substance with the Father,
by whom all things were made;
who for us men and for our salvation
came down from heaven,**

and was incarnate by the Holy Ghost of the Virgin Mary,
and was made man,
and was crucified also for us under Pontius Pilate.
He suffered and was buried,
and the third day he rose again
according to the Scriptures,
and ascended into heaven,
and sitteth on the right hand of the Father.
And he shall come again with glory
to judge both the quick and the dead:
whose kingdom shall have no end.

And I believe in the Holy Ghost,
the Lord, the giver of life,
who proceedeth from the Father and the Son,
who with the Father and the Son together
is worshipped and glorified,
who spake by the prophets.
And I believe one holy catholic and apostolic Church.
I acknowledge one baptism for the remission of sins.
And I look for the resurrection of the dead,
and the life of the world to come.
Amen.

Prayers of intercession

The prayers usually include these concerns and may follow this sequence:

- *The Church of Christ*
- *Creation, human society, the Sovereign and those in authority*
- *The local community*
- *Those who suffer*
- *The communion of saints*

These responses may be used:

Lord, in thy mercy
hear our prayer.

or

Lord, hear us.
Lord, graciously hear us.

And at the end:

Merciful Father,
accept these prayers
for the sake of thy Son,
our Saviour Jesus Christ.
Amen.

The Liturgy of the Sacrament

The Peace

The president may introduce the Peace with a suitable sentence, and then says:

The peace of the Lord be always with you
and with thy spirit.

These words may be added:

Let us offer one another a sign of peace.

All may exchange a sign of peace.

Preparation of the Table
Taking of the Bread and Wine

A hymn may be sung.

The Cherubic Hymn

The president takes the bread and wine.

Let us, who in a mystery represent the cherubim and sing the thrice-holy hymn to the life-giving Trinity, lay aside now every care of this life. For we are about to receive the King of all, invisibly escorted by the angelic hosts. [*omit in Lent:* Alleluia, alleluia, alleluia.]

Liturgy of Saint John Chrysostom

The gifts of the people may be gathered and presented.

The altar is prepared and bread and wine are placed upon it.

The president takes the bread and wine.

Blessed art thou, O Lord God of all creation:
through thy goodness we have this bread to set before thee,
which earth has given and human hands have made.
It will become for us the bread of life.
Blessed be God for ever.

Blessed art thou, O Lord God of all creation:
through thy goodness we have this wine to set before thee,
fruit of the vine and work of human hands.
It will become for us the cup of salvation.
Blessed be God for ever.

The following may be said:

Pray, brethren, that my sacrifice and yours
may be acceptable to God, the almighty Father.
May the Lord accept the sacrifice at your hands
for the praise and glory of his name,
for our good, and the good of all his Church.

ICEL (5)

The Prayer over the Gifts may follow.

The Eucharistic Prayer

One of the following Eucharistic Prayers is used: Prayer A or Prayer C.

Prayer A

The Lord be with you   *or*   The Lord is here.
and with thy spirit.   **His Spirit is with us.**

Lift up your hearts.
We lift them up unto the Lord.

Let us give thanks to the Lord our God.
It is meet and right so to do.

It is very meet, right and our bounden duty,
that we should at all times and in all places give thanks unto thee,

O Lord, holy Father,
almighty, everlasting God,
through Jesus Christ thine only Son our Lord.

The following may be omitted if a short proper preface is used:

For he is thy living Word;
through him thou hast created all things from the beginning,
and fashioned us in thine own image.

Through him thou didst redeem us from the slavery of sin,
giving him to be born of a woman,
to die upon the cross,
and to rise again for us.

Through him thou hast made us a people for thine own possession,
exalting him to thy right hand on high,
and sending forth through him thy holy and life-giving Spirit.

Short proper preface, when appropriate.

Therefore with angels and archangels,
and with all the company of heaven,
we laud and magnify thy glorious name,
evermore praising thee and saying:

Holy, holy, holy, Lord God of hosts,
heaven and earth are full of thy glory.
Glory be to thee, O Lord most high.

[Blessed is he that cometh in the name of the Lord.
Hosanna in the highest.]

Accept our praises, heavenly Father,
through thy Son our Saviour Jesus Christ,
and as we follow his example and obey his command,
grant that by the power of thy Holy Spirit
these gifts of bread and wine
may be unto us his body and his blood;

who, in the same night that he was betrayed, took bread;
and when he had given thanks to thee,
he broke it and gave it to his disciples, saying:
Take, eat; this is my body which is given for you;
do this in remembrance of me.

Likewise after supper he took the cup;
and when he had given thanks to thee, he gave it to them, saying:
Drink ye all of this;
for this is my blood of the new covenant,
which is shed for you and for many for the forgiveness of sins.
Do this, as oft as ye shall drink it,
in remembrance of me.

Wherefore, O Lord and heavenly Father,
we remember his offering of himself
made once for all upon the cross;
we proclaim his mighty resurrection and glorious ascension;
we look for the coming of his kingdom
and with this bread and this cup
we make the memorial of Christ thy Son our Lord.

One of the following may be used:

[Great is the mystery of faith:]
Christ has died:
Christ is risen:
Christ will come again.

or

[Jesus Christ is Lord:]
O Saviour of the world,
who by thy cross and precious blood hast redeemed us,
save us, and help us, we humbly beseech thee, O Lord.

Accept through him, our great high priest,
this our sacrifice of thanks and praise,
and as we eat and drink these holy gifts
in the presence of thy divine majesty,
renew us by thy Holy Spirit,
inspire us with thy love,
and unite us in the body of thy Son,
Jesus Christ our Lord,

by whom, and with whom, and in whom,
in the unity of the Holy Spirit,
all honour and glory be unto thee,

O Father almighty,
world without end.
Amen.

The service continues with the Lord's Prayer on page 126.

Prayer C

The Lord be with you	*or*	The Lord is here.
and with thy spirit.		**His Spirit is with us.**

Lift up your hearts.
We lift them up unto the Lord.

Let us give thanks to the Lord our God.
It is meet and right so to do.

It is very meet, right and our bounden duty,
that we should at all times and in all places give thanks unto thee,
O Lord, holy Father,
almighty, everlasting God,
through Jesus Christ thine only Son our Lord.

Short proper preface, when appropriate:

or, when there is no proper preface:

For he is the great high priest,
who has loosed us from our sins
and has made us to be a royal priesthood unto thee,
our God and Father.

Therefore with angels and archangels,
and with all the company of heaven,
we laud and magnify thy glorious name,
evermore praising thee and saying:

Holy, holy, holy, Lord God of hosts,
heaven and earth are full of thy glory.
Glory be to thee, O Lord most high.

[Blessed is he that cometh in the name of the Lord.
Hosanna in the highest.]

All glory be to thee,
almighty God, our heavenly Father,
who, of thy tender mercy,

didst give thine only Son Jesus Christ
to suffer death upon the cross for our redemption;
who made there,
by his one oblation of himself once offered,
a full, perfect and sufficient sacrifice, oblation and satisfaction
for the sins of the whole world;
and did institute,
and in his holy gospel command us to continue,
a perpetual memory of that his precious death,
until his coming again.

Hear us, O merciful Father, we most humbly beseech thee,
and grant that, by the power of thy Holy Spirit,
we receiving these thy creatures of bread and wine,
according to thy Son our Saviour Jesus Christ's holy institution,
in remembrance of his death and passion,
may be partakers of his most blessed body and blood;

who, in the same night that he was betrayed, took bread;
and when he had given thanks to thee,
he broke it and gave it to his disciples, saying:
Take, eat; this is my body which is given for you;
do this in remembrance of me.

Likewise after supper he took the cup;
and when he had given thanks to thee, he gave it to them, saying:
Drink ye all of this;
for this is my blood of the new covenant,
which is shed for you and for many for the forgiveness of sins.
Do this, as oft as ye shall drink it,
in remembrance of me.

One of the following may be used:

[Great is the mystery of faith:]
Christ has died:
Christ is risen:
Christ will come again.

or

[Jesus Christ is Lord:]
O Saviour of the world,

**who by thy cross and precious blood hast redeemed us,
save us, and help us, we humbly beseech thee, O Lord.**

Wherefore, O Lord and heavenly Father,
we thy humble servants,
having in remembrance
the precious death and passion of thy dear Son,
his mighty resurrection and glorious ascension,
entirely desire thy fatherly goodness
mercifully to accept this our sacrifice
of praise and thanksgiving;
most humbly beseeching thee to grant that
by the merits and death of thy Son Jesus Christ,
and through faith in his blood,
we and all thy whole Church may obtain
remission of our sins,
and all other benefits of his passion.
And although we be unworthy, through our manifold sins,
to offer unto thee any sacrifice,
yet we beseech thee
to accept this our bounden duty and service,
not weighing our merits, but pardoning our offences;
and to grant that all we, who are partakers of this holy communion,
may be fulfilled with thy grace and heavenly benediction;

through Jesus Christ our Lord,
by whom, and with whom, and in whom,
in the unity of the Holy Spirit,
all honour and glory be unto thee,
O Father almighty,
world without end.
Amen.

The service continues with the Lord's Prayer.

The Lord's Prayer

Let us pray with confidence as our Saviour has taught us:

**Our Father, who art in heaven,
hallowed be thy name;**

thy kingdom come;
thy will be done;
on earth as it is in heaven.
Give us this day our daily bread.
And forgive us our trespasses,
as we forgive those who trespass against us.
And lead us not into temptation;
but deliver us from evil.
For thine is the kingdom,
the power and the glory,
for ever and ever.
Amen.

Breaking of the Bread

The president breaks the consecrated bread.

We break this bread
to share in the body of Christ.
Though we are many, we are one body,
because we all share in one bread.

or

Every time we eat this bread
and drink this cup,
we proclaim the Lord's death
until he comes.

Agnus Dei *may be used as the bread is broken:*

O Lamb of God,
that takest away the sins of the world,
have mercy upon us.

O Lamb of God,
that takest away the sins of the world,
have mercy upon us.

O Lamb of God,
that takest away the sins of the world,
grant us thy peace.

Giving of Communion

The president says the invitation to communion:

Behold* the Lamb of God
who takes away the sin of the world.
Blessed are those who are called to his supper.
Lord, I am not worthy that thou shouldest come under my roof,
but speak the word only and my soul shall be healed.

or

God's holy gifts
for God's holy people.
Jesus Christ is holy,
Jesus Christ is Lord,
to the glory of God the Father.

or, from Easter Day to Pentecost

Alleluia. Christ our passover is sacrificed for us.
Therefore let us keep the feast. Alleluia.

This prayer may be said before the distribution:

We do not presume
to come to this thy table, O merciful Lord,
trusting in our own righteousness,
but in thy manifold and great mercies.
We are not worthy
so much as to gather up the crumbs under thy table.
But thou art the same Lord
whose nature is always to have mercy.
Grant us, therefore, gracious Lord,
so to eat the flesh of thy dear Son Jesus Christ
and to drink his blood,
that our sinful bodies may be made clean by his body
and our souls washed through his most precious blood,
and that we may evermore dwell in him, and he in us.
Amen.

The president and people receive communion.

*In Common Worship, Jesus is . . .

Authorized words of distribution are used, such as:

The body of Christ. **Amen.**

The blood of Christ. **Amen.**

During the distribution hymns and anthems may be sung.

Communion devotions

Before Communion

At your mystical supper, Son of God, receive me today
as a partaker. I will not speak of the mystery to your
enemies. I will not let my lips touch your body with the
kiss of Judas. Like the thief I will acknowledge you:
Remember me when you come into your kingdom.

Liturgy of St John Chrysostom

Jesus remember me, when you come into your kingdom.

Luke 23:42

Lord, to whom can we go?
You have the words of eternal life.

John 6:68

My Lord and my God.

John 20:28

O come to my heart Lord Jesus:
there is room in my heart for you.

Good Jesu, who gavest thyself for me,
give me of the fullness of thy love,
that for all thy love, with thy love, I may love thee.

Edward Bouverie Pusey

After receiving Communion

Petitions to the Holy Redeemer

Soul of Christ, be my sanctification;
Body of Christ, be my salvation;

Blood of Christ, fill all my veins;
Water of Christ's side, wash out my stains;
Passion of Christ, my comfort be;
O good Jesu, listen to me;
In thy wounds I fain would hide,
Ne'er to be parted from thy side;
Guard me, should the foe assail me;
Call me when my life shall fail me;
Bid me come to thee above,
With thy saints to sing thy love,
World without end.

John Henry Newman
Anima Christi

Prayer after Communion

Silence is kept.

The post-communion, or this or another suitable prayer is said:

Almighty and everlasting God,
we most heartily thank thee,
for that thou dost vouchsafe to feed us,
who have duly received these holy mysteries,
with the spiritual food of the most precious body and blood of thy Son our
    Saviour Jesus Christ;
and dost assure us thereby of thy favour and goodness towards us;
and that we are very members incorporate in the mystical body of thy Son,
which is the blessed company of all faithful people,
and are also heirs through hope of thy everlasting kingdom,
by the merits of the most precious death and passion of thy dear Son.
And we most humbly beseech thee, O heavenly Father,
so to assist us with thy grace,
that we may continue in that holy fellowship,
and do all such good works
as thou hast prepared for us to walk in;
through Jesus Christ our Lord, to whom, with thee and the Holy Spirit,
be all honour and glory,
world without end.
Amen.

All may say this prayer:

**Almighty God,
we thank thee for feeding us
with the body and blood of thy Son Jesus Christ.
Through him we offer thee our souls and bodies
to be a living sacrifice.
Send us out
in the power of thy Spirit
to live and work
to thy praise and glory.
Amen.**

The Dismissal

A hymn may be sung.

The Lord be with you
and with thy spirit.

The president may use the seasonal blessing, or another suitable blessing.

or

The peace of God,
which passes all understanding,
keep your hearts and minds
in the knowledge and love of God,
and of his Son Jesus Christ our Lord;
and the blessing of God almighty,
the Father, the Son, and the Holy Spirit,
be among you and remain with you always.
Amen.

Go in the peace of Christ.
Thanks be to God.

or, from Easter Day to Pentecost:

Go in the peace of Christ. Alleluia, Alleluia.
Thanks be to God. Alleluia, Alleluia.

The ministers and people depart.

Before leaving church

You are Christians!
Then your Lord is one and the same
with Jesus on the throne of his glory,
with Jesus in his blessed Sacrament,
with Jesus received into your hearts in Communion,
with Jesus who is mystically with you as you pray,
and with Jesus enshrined in the hearts and bodies of his brothers and sisters
    up and down the world.

Now go out into the highways and hedges,
and look for Jesus in the ragged and naked,
in the oppressed and sweated,
in those who have lost hope,
and in those who are struggling to make good.
Look for Jesus in them;
and when you find him,
gird yourselves with his towel of fellowship,
and wash his feet in the person of his brethren.

Bishop Frank Weston

Lord Jesus Christ,
take all my freedom,
my memory, my understanding, and my will.
All that I have and cherish
you have given me.
I surrender it all to be guided by your will.
Your grace and your love are wealth enough for me.
Give me these, Lord Jesus,
and I ask for nothing more.

ICEL (5)

or

Grant, O Lord God, that what we have heard with our ears
and sung with our lips, we may believe in our hearts
and practise in our lives; for Jesus Christ's sake.

Eric Milner-White (16)

Thanksgiving After Mass

Thanksgiving After Mass

We thank you, heavenly Father, for your holy name,
which you have caused to dwell in our hearts.
We thank you for the knowledge, faith and immortality
which you have made known to us
through Jesus your servant.
To you be glory, now and for ever.

from Didache (tr.AB) (8)

Prayer of Saint Thomas Aquinas

I give you thanks,
Lord, holy Father, everlasting God.
In your great mercy,
and not because of my own merits,
you have fed me, a sinner and your unworthy servant,
with the precious Body and Blood of your Son,
our Lord Jesus Christ.
I pray that this holy communion
may not serve as my judgement and condemnation,
but as my forgiveness and salvation.
May it be my armour of faith
and shield of good purpose.
May it root out in me all vice and evil desires,
increase my love and patience,
humility and obedience,
and every virtue.
Make it a firm defence
against the wiles of all my enemies, seen and unseen,

while restraining all evil impulses of flesh and spirit.
May it help me to cleave to you, the one true God,
and bring me a blessed death when you call.
I beseech you to bring me, a sinner,
to that great feast where,
with your Son and the Holy Spirit,
you are the true light of your holy ones,
their flawless blessedness,
everlasting joy,
and perfect happiness.
Through Christ our Lord.

Sunday Missal (19)

O sacrum convivium

O sacred banquet in which Christ is received,
the memory of his passion is renewed,
our lives are filled with grace,
and a pledge of future glory is given!

tr. AB (8)

Strengthen for service, Lord,
the hands that have taken holy things;
may the ears which have heard your word
   be deaf to clamour and dispute;
may the tongues which have sung your praise
   be free from deceit;
may the eyes which have seen the tokens of your love
   shine with the light of hope;
and may the bodies which have been fed with your body
   be refreshed with the fullness of your life;
glory to you for ever.

Syrian,
Common Worship (1)
Eighth Sunday after Trinity
(Post-Communion)

Prayer to Christ Crucified

O kind and loving Jesus,
I kneel here before you,

Thanksgiving after Mass

asking you most fervently
to put into my heart
the virtues of faith, hope and charity,
with true contrition for my sins
and a firm purpose of amendment.
Help me to contemplate with sorrow
your five precious wounds,
while I remember David's prophecy:
They have pierced my hands and my feet;
they have counted all my bones.

Stanbrook Abbey (4)

The Prayer of Self-Dedication to Jesus Christ (see page 11) and the Universal Prayer attributed to Pope Clement XI (see page 318) may also be used.

V THE CHURCH'S YEAR

Calendar

This Calendar is ecumenical. It is a version of both the Common Worship Calendar and the Roman Catholic General Calendar, augmented by much of the Roman Catholic Calendar for England proposed in 1996.

The Calendar prescribes different degrees of celebration, distinguished by typography.

- **SOLEMNITIES**
  On solemnities (**BOLD CAPITALS**) the *Gloria in excelsis* and Creed are used at Mass. The Mass propers and the readings (of which there are three) are as appointed for the day.

- **Feasts**
  On feasts (**Bold Type**), the *Gloria in excelsis* is used. The Mass propers and the readings (of which there are two) are as appointed for the day.

- Memorias
  On memorias (Ordinary Type), the *Gloria in excelsis* is not used. The Mass propers of the day are used but the readings are often the normal weekday ones. In Lent the collect of the memoir replaces the collect of the Lent weekday but the remainder of the Mass is as for the Lent weekday.

- *Other Commemorations*
  Also included (*Italics*) are commemorations of holy men and women who have not been formally canonized but who will be remembered, for instance, in the prayers for their Christian example.

- *Special prayer*
  Some days (***Bold Italics***) are days of special prayer.

January

1   **THE NAMING AND CIRCUMCISION OF JESUS:**
    Solemnity of MARY, MOTHER OF GOD
    World Day of Prayer for Peace
2   Basil the Great & Gregory Nazianzus, Bishops, Teachers of the Faith, 379 and 389
    Seraphim, Monk of Sarov, Spiritual Guide, 1833
    Vedanayagam Samuel Azariah, Bishop in South India, Evangelist, 1945
3
4
5
6   **THE EPIPHANY**
7
8
9
10 *William Laud, Archbishop of Canterbury, 1645*
11 *Mary Slessor, Missionary in West Africa, 1915*
12 Aelred of Hexham, Abbot of Rievaulx, 1167
    Benedict Biscop, Abbot of Wearmouth, Scholar, 689
13 Hilary, Bishop of Poitiers, Teacher of the Faith, 367
    Kentigern (Mungo), Missionary Bishop in Strathclyde and Cumbria, 603
    George Fox, Founder of the Society of Friends (the Quakers), 1691
14 *Richard Meux Benson, Founder of the Society of St John the Evangelist, 1915*
15
16
17 Antony of Egypt, Hermit, Abbot, 356
    Charles Gore, Bishop, Teacher, Founder of the Community of the Resurrection, 1932
18–25 **Octave of Prayer for Christian Unity**
19 Wulfstan, Bishop of Worcester, 1095
20 *Richard Rolle of Hampole, Spiritual Writer, 1349*
21 Agnes, Child-Martyr at Rome, 304
22 Vincent of Saragossa, Deacon, first Martyr of Spain, 304
23
24 Francis de Sales, Bishop of Geneva, Teacher of the Faith, 1622

25	**The Conversion of Paul**
26	Timothy and Titus, Companions of Paul
27	
28	Thomas Aquinas, Priest, Teacher, 1274
29	
30	Charles, King and Martyr, 1649
31	John Bosco, Priest, Founder of the Salesian Teaching Order, 1888

Sunday after 6 January: **The Baptism of the Lord**

February

1	Brigid, Abbess of Kildare, c525
2	**The Presentation of Christ in the Temple (Candlemas)**
3	Anskar, Archbishop of Hamburg, Missionary in Denmark and Sweden, 865
4	Gilbert of Sempringham, Founder of the Gilbertine Order, 1189
5	Agatha, Martyr at Catania, 3rd cent.
6	Paul Miki and the Martyrs of Japan, 1597
7	
8	
9	
10	Scholastica, sister of Benedict, Abbess of Plombariola, c543
11	Our Lady of Lourdes **World Day for the Sick**
12	
13	
14	**Cyril & Methodius, Missionaries to the Slavs, Patrons of Europe, 869, 885** *Valentine, Martyr at Rome, c269*
15	Sigfrid, Bishop, Apostle of Sweden, 1045 *Thomas Bray, Priest, Missionary, Founder of the SPCK and the SPG, 1730*
16	
17	*Janani Luwum, Archbishop of Uganda, Martyr, 1977*
18	
19	
20	
21	
22	**The See of Peter the Apostle**
23	Polycarp, Bishop of Smyrna, Martyr, c155
24	
25	
26	
27	*George Herbert, Priest, Poet, 1633*
28	
29	

March

1	**David, Bishop of Menevia, Patron of Wales, c601**
2	Chad, Bishop of Lichfield, Missionary, 672
3	
4	
5	
6	
7	Perpetua, Felicity and their Companions, Martyrs at Carthage, 203
8	*Edward King, Bishop of Lincoln, 1910*
9	
10	
11	
12	
13	
14	
15	
16	
17	**Patrick, Bishop of Armagh, Missionary, Patron of Ireland, c460**
18	Cyril, Bishop of Jerusalem, Teacher of the Faith, 386
19	**JOSEPH OF NAZARETH**
20	Cuthbert, Bishop of Lindisfarne, Missionary, 687
21	*Thomas Cranmer, Archbishop of Canterbury, 1556*
22	
23	
24	*Oscar Romero, Archbishop of San Salvador, Martyr, 1980*
	Walter Hilton of Thurgarton, Augustinian Friar, Mystic, 1396
25	**THE ANNUNCIATION OF THE LORD (*Lady Day*)**
26	*Harriet Monsell, Founder of the Community of St John the Baptist, Clewer, 1883*
27	
28	
29	
30	
31	*John Donne, Priest, Poet, 1631*

April

1 *Frederick Denison Maurice, Priest, Teacher of the Faith, 1872*
2
3
4
5
6
7 John Baptist de la Salle, Educationalist, 1719
8
9 *Dietrich Bonhoeffer, Pastor, Teacher, Martyr, 1945*
10 *William of Ockham, Franciscan Friar, Philosopher, Teacher, 1347*
   William Law, Priest, Spiritual Writer, 1761
11 *George Augustus Selwyn, first Bishop of New Zealand, 1878*
12
13
14
15
16 *Isabella Gilmore, Deaconess, 1923*
17
18
19 Alphege, Archbishop of Canterbury, Martyr, 1012
20
21 Anselm, Abbot of Le Bec, Archbishop of Canterbury, Teacher of the Faith, 1109
22
23 **GEORGE, MARTYR, PATRON OF ENGLAND, c304**
24 Mellitus, Bishop of London, first Bishop at St Paul's, 624
25 **Mark the Evangelist**
26
27 *Christina Rossetti, Poet, 1895*
28 Peter Chanel, Religious, Missionary in the South Pacific, Martyr, 1841
29 **Catherine of Siena, Mystic, Teacher, Patron of Europe, 1380**
30 *Pandita Mary Ramabai, Translator of the Scriptures, 1922*

May

1 or 3	**Philip and James, Apostles**
2	Athanasius, Bishop of Alexandria, Teacher of the Faith, 373
4	**English Saints and Martyrs of the Reformation Era**
5	
6	John the Apostle in Eastertide (formerly St John *ante portam Latinam*)
7	
8	*Julian of Norwich, Mystic, Teacher, c1417*
9	
10	
11	
12	
13	
14	**Matthias the Apostle**
15	
16	*Caroline Chisholm, Social Reformer, 1877*
17	
18	
19	Dunstan, Archbishop of Canterbury, Restorer of Monastic Life, 988
20	Alcuin of York, Deacon, Abbot of Tours, 820
21	Helena, Protector of the Holy Places, 330
22	
23	Petroc, Abbot of Padstow, 6th century
24	*John and Charles Wesley, Priests, Evangelists, Hymn Writers, 1792 and 1788*
25	The Venerable Bede, Priest, Monk at Jarrow, Scholar, Historian, 735 Aldhelm, Abbot of Malmesbury, Bishop of Sherborne, 709
26	Philip Neri, Founder of the Oratorians, Spiritual Guide, 1595 *John Calvin, Reformer, 1564*
27	Augustine, first Archbishop of Canterbury, 605
28	*Lanfranc, Prior of Le Bec, Archbishop of Canterbury, 1089*
29	
30	Joan of Arc, Visionary, 1431 *Josephine Butler, Social Reformer, 1906* *Apolo Kivebulaya, Priest, Evangelist in Central Africa, 1933*

31   **The Visit of the Blessed Virgin Mary to Elizabeth**

First Sunday after Pentecost: **TRINITY SUNDAY**
Thursday after Trinity Sunday: **CORPUS CHRISTI**
Friday after Second Sunday after
  Pentecost: **SACRED HEART OF JESUS**

Saturday after Second Sunday
  after Pentecost: *Immaculate Heart of Mary*

June

1	Justin, Martyr at Rome, c165
2	
3	Charles Lwanga and the Martyrs of Uganda, 1886, 1978
4	
5	Boniface (Wynfrith) of Crediton, Archbishop of Mainz, Apostle of Germany, Martyr, 754
6	*Ini Kopuria, Founder of the Melanesian Brotherhood, 1945*
7	
8	*Thomas Ken, Bishop of Bath and Wells, Non-Juror, Hymn Writer, 1711*
9	Columba, Abbot of Iona, Missionary, 597
	Ephrem of Syria, Deacon, Hymn Writer, Teacher of the Faith, 373
10	
11	Barnabas the Apostle
12	
13	Anthony of Padua, Priest, Teacher of the Faith, 1231
14	*Richard Baxter, Puritan Divine, 1691*
15	*Evelyn Underhill, Spiritual Writer, 1941*
16	Richard, Bishop of Chichester, 1253
	Joseph Butler, Bishop of Durham, Philosopher, 1752
17	*Samuel and Henrietta Barnett, Social Reformers, 1913 and 1936*
18	*Bernard Mizeki, Apostle to the MaShona, Martyr, 1896*
19	*Sundar Singh of India, Sadhu (holy man), Evangelist, Teacher of the Faith, 1929*
20 or 22	
	Alban, first Martyr of Britain, c209
21	Aloysius Gonzaga, Religious, 1591
22 or 6 July	
	Thomas More, Scholar, and John Fisher, Bishop of Rochester, Martyrs, 1535
23	Etheldreda, Abbess of Ely, c678
24	**THE BIRTH OF JOHN THE BAPTIST**
25	
26	
27	Cyril, Bishop of Alexandria, Teacher of the Faith, 444
28	Irenaeus, Bishop of Lyons, Teacher, Martyr, c200
29	**PETER AND PAUL, APOSTLES**
30	

July

1	*Henry and John Venn, Priests, Evangelical Divines, 1797 and 1813*
	Oliver Plunket, Archbishop of Armagh, Martyr, 1681
2	
3	**Thomas the Apostle**
4	
5	
6 or 22 June	**Thomas More, Scholar, and John Fisher, Bishop of Rochester, Martyrs, 1535**
7	
8	
9	
10	
11	**Benedict of Nursia, Abbot of Monte Casino, Father of Western Monasticism, Patron of Europe, c550**
12	
13	
14	*John Keble, Priest, Tractarian, Poet, 1866*
15	Bonaventure, Friar, Bishop, Teacher of the Faith, 1274
	Swithun, Bishop of Winchester, c862
16	Osmund, Bishop of Salisbury, 1099
17	
18	*Elizabeth Ferard, first Deaconess of the Church of England, Founder of the Community of St Andrew, 1883*
19	Gregory, Bishop of Nyssa, and his sister Macrina, Deaconess, Teachers of the Faith, c394 and c379
20	Margaret of Antioch, Martyr, 4th cent.
	Bartolome de la Casas, Apostle to the Indies, 1566
21	
22	Mary Magdalene
23	**Bridget of Sweden, Abbess of Vadstena, Patron of Europe, 1373**
24	
25	**James the Apostle**
26	Anne and Joachim, Parents of the Blessed Virgin Mary
27	*Brooke Foss Westcott, Bishop of Durham, Teacher of the Faith, 1901*

28
29   Mary, Martha and Lazarus, Companions of the Lord
30   *William Wilberforce, Social Reformer, 1833*
31   Ignatius of Loyola, Founder of the Society of Jesus, 1556

August

1	Alphonsus Liguori, Teacher of the Faith, 1787
2	
3	
4	Jean-Baptist Vianney, *Curé d'Ars*, Spiritual Guide, 1859
5	Oswald, King of Northumbria, Martyr, 642
6	**The Transfiguration of the Lord**
7	*John Mason Neale, Priest, Hymn Writer, 1866*
8	Dominic, Founder of the Order of Preachers, 1221
9	**Teresa Benedicta of the Cross (Edith Stein), Nun, Martyr, Patron of Europe, 1942**
	Mary Sumner, Founder of the Mothers' Union, 1921
10	**Laurence, Deacon at Rome, Martyr, 258**
11	Clare of Assisi, Founder of the Minoresses (Poor Clares), 1253
	John Henry Newman, Priest, Teacher, Tractarian, 1890
12	
13	*Jeremy Taylor, Bishop of Down and Connor, Teacher of the Faith, 1667*
	Florence Nightingale, Nurse, Social Reformer, 1910
	Octavia Hill, Worker for the Poor, 1912
14	Maximilian Kolbe, Friar, Martyr, 1941
15	**THE ASSUMPTION OF THE BLESSED VIRGIN MARY**
16	
17	
18	
19	
20	Bernard, Abbot of Clairvaux, Teacher of the Faith, 1153
	William and Catherine Booth, Founders of the Salvation Army, 1912 and 1890
21	
22	Our Lady, Mother and Queen
23	
24	**Bartholomew the Apostle**
25	
26	Dominic Barberi, Priest, Religious, Missionary, 1849
27	Monica, Mother of Augustine of Hippo, 387

28	Augustine, Bishop of Hippo, Teacher of the Faith, 430
29	The Beheading of John the Baptist
30	Margaret Clitherow and Anne Line, Married Women, and Margaret Ward, Virgin, Martyrs, 1586, 1601, 1588
	John Bunyan, Spiritual Writer, 1688
31	Aidan, Bishop of Lindisfarne, Missionary, 651
	Cuthberga, Founding Abbess of Wimborne, c725

September

1	Giles of Provence, Hermit, c710
2	*The Martyrs of Papua New Guinea, 1942*
3	Gregory the Great, Bishop of Rome, Teacher of the Faith, 604
4	Cuthbert, Bishop of Lindisfarne, Missionary, 687
	Birinus, Bishop of Dorchester (Oxon), Apostle of Wessex, 650
5	
6	*Allen Gardiner, founder of the South American Missionary Society, 1851*
7	
8	**The Birth of the Blessed Virgin Mary**
9	*Charles Fuge Lowder, Priest, Founder of the Society of the Holy Cross, 1880*
10	
11	
12	
13	John Chrysostom, Bishop of Constantinople, Teacher of the Faith, 407
14	**Holy Cross Day**
15	Our Lady of Sorrows
15 or 16	
	Cyprian, Bishop of Carthage, Martyr, 258
16	Ninian, Bishop of Galloway, Apostle of the Picts, c432
	Edward Bouverie Pusey, Priest, Tractarian, 1882
17	*Hildegard, Abbess of Bingen, Visionary, 1179*
18	
19	Theodore of Tarsus, Archbishop of Canterbury, 690
20	Andrew Kim Taegon and the Martyrs of Korea and the Pacific
	John Coleridge Patteson, First Bishop of Melanesia, and his Companions, Martyrs, 1871
21	**Matthew, Apostle and Evangelist**
22	
23	
24	Our Lady of Walsingham

25	*Sergei of Radonezh, Russian Monastic Reformer, Teacher of the Faith, 1392*
	Lancelot Andrewes, Bishop of Winchester, Spiritual Writer, 1626
26	*Wilson Carlile, Priest, Founder of the Church Army, 1942*
27	Vincent de Paul, Founder of the Congregation of the Mission (Lazarists), 1660
28	
29	**Michael and All Angels**
30	Jerome, Translator of the Scriptures, Teacher of the Faith, 420

October

1	Therese of Lisieux, Carmelite Nun, Spiritual Writer, 1897
	Remigius, Bishop of Rheims, Apostle of the Franks, 533
	Anthony Ashley Cooper, Earl of Shaftesbury, Social Reformer, 1885
2	The Guardian Angels
3	
4	Francis of Assisi, Friar, Deacon, Founder of the Friars Minor, 1226
5	
6	*William Tyndale, Translator of the Scriptures, Martyr, 1536*
7	
8	
9	Denys, Bishop of Paris, and his Companions, Martyrs, c258
	Robert Grosseteste, Bishop of Lincoln, Philosopher, Scientist, 1253
10	Paulinus, Bishop of York, Missionary, 644
	Thomas Traherne, Poet, Spiritual Writer, 1674
11	Ethelburga, Abbess of Barking, 675
	James the Deacon, Companion of Paulinus, 7th cent.
12	Wilfrid of Ripon, Bishop, Missionary, 709
	Elizabeth Fry, Prison Reformer, 1845
	Edith Cavell, Nurse, 1915
13	Edward the Confessor, King of England, 1066
14	
15	Teresa of Avila, Teacher of the Faith, 1582
16	*Nicholas Ridley, Bishop of London, and Hugh Latimer, Bishop of Worcester, Martyrs, 1555*
17	Ignatius, Bishop of Antioch, Martyr, c107
18	**Luke the Evangelist**
19	Frideswide, Abbess, Patron Saint of the city and University of Oxford, c735
	Henry Martyn, Translator of the Scriptures, Missionary in India and Persia, 1812
20	
21	
22	
23	
24	
25	Crispin and Crispinian, Martyrs at Rome, c287
26	Cedd, Abbot of Lastingham, Bishop of the East Saxons, 664

27	*Alfred the Great, King of the West Saxons, Scholar, 899*
28	**Simon and Jude, Apostles**
29	*James Hannington, Bishop of Eastern Equatorial Africa, Martyr in Uganda, 1885*
30	*Martin Luther, Reformer, 1546*

November

1	**ALL SAINTS' DAY**
2	**ALL SOULS' DAY**
3	Martin de Porres, Friar, 1639
	Richard Hooker, Priest, Anglican Apologist, Teacher of the Faith, 1600
4	Charles Borromeo, Archbishop of Milan, Educationalist, Reformer, 1584
5	
6	Leonard, Hermit, 6th cent.
	William Temple, Archbishop of Canterbury, Teacher, 1944
7	Willibrord of York, Bishop, Apostle of Frisia, 739
8	The Saints and Martyrs of England
9–15	**Prisoners' Week**
9	*Margery Kempe, Mystic, c1440*
10	Leo the Great, Bishop of Rome, Teacher of the Faith, 461
11	Martin, Bishop of Tours, c397
12	Josaphat Kunsevich, Archbishop of Polotsk, Martyr, 1623
13	*Charles Simeon, Priest, Evangelical Divine, 1836*
14	*Samuel Seabury, First Anglican Bishop in North America, 1796*
15	
16	Margaret, Queen of Scotland, Philanthropist, Reformer of the Church, 1093
	Edmund Rich of Abingdon, Archbishop of Canterbury, 1240
17	Hugh, Bishop of Lincoln, 1200
18	Elizabeth of Hungary, Princess of Thuringia, Philanthropist, 1231
19	Hilda, Abbess of Whitby, 680
	Mechtild, Beguine of Magdeburg, Mystic, 1280
20	Edmund, King of the East Angles, Martyr, 870
	Priscilla Lydia Sellon, Restorer of the Religious Life in the Church of England, 1876
21	**The Presentation of the Blessed Virgin Mary**
22	Cecilia, Martyr at Rome, c230
23	Clement, Bishop of Rome, Martyr, c100
24	
25	Catherine of Alexandria, Martyr, 4th cent.
	Isaac Watts, Hymn Writer, 1748
26	

27
28
29 *Day of Intercession and Thanksgiving for the Missionary Work of the Church*
30 **Andrew the Apostle**

Last Sunday of the Church's Year: **CHRIST THE KING**

December

1	*Charles de Foucauld, Hermit, Servant of the Poor, 1916*
2	
3	Francis Xavier, Apostle of the Indies, Missionary, 1552
4	John of Damascus, Monk, Teacher of the Faith, c749
	Nicholas Ferrar, Deacon, Founder of the Little Gidding Community, 1637
5	
6	Nicholas, Bishop of Myra, c326
7	Ambrose, Bishop of Milan, Teacher of the Faith, 397
8	**IMMACULATE CONCEPTION OF THE BLESSED VIRGIN MARY**
9	
10	
11	
12	
13	Lucy, Martyr at Syracuse, 304
	Samuel Johnson, Moralist, 1784
14	John of the Cross, Poet, Teacher of the Faith, 1591
15	
16	
17	***O Sapientia***
	Eglantine Jebb, Social Reformer, Founder of 'Save the Children', 1928
18	
19	
20	
21	
22	
23	
24	Christmas Eve
25	**CHRISTMAS DAY**
26	**Stephen, Deacon, First Martyr**
27	**John, Apostle and Evangelist**
28	**The Holy Innocents**
29	Thomas Becket, Archbishop of Canterbury, Martyr, 1170
30	
31	*John Wyclif, Reformer, 1384*

Sunday within the Christmas Octave
or, if no Sunday available, 30 December: **The Holy Family**

Table of Moveable Feasts

Year	Ash Weds	Easter	Ascension	Pentecost	Monday after Pentecost
2001	28 February	15 April	24 May	3 June	4 June: Week 9
2002	13 February	31 March	9 May	19 May	20 May: Week 7
2003	5 March	20 April	29 May	8 June	9 June: Week 10
2004	25 February	11 April	20 May	30 May	31 May: Week 9
2005	9 February	27 March	5 May	15 May	16 May: Week 7
2006	1 March	16 April	25 May	4 June	5 June: Week 9
2007	21 February	8 April	17 May	27 May	28 May: Week 8
2008	6 February	23 March	1 May	11 May	12 May: Week 6
2009	25 February	12 April	21 May	31 May	1 June: Week 9
2010	17 February	4 April	13 May	23 May	24 May: Week 8
2011	9 March	24 April	2 June	12 June	13 June: Week 11
2012	22 February	8 April	17 May	27 May	28 May: Week 8
2013	13 February	31 March	9 May	19 May	20 May: Week 7
2014	5 March	20 April	29 May	8 June	9 June: Week 10
2015	18 February	5 April	14 May	24 May	25 May: Week 8
2016	10 February	27 March	5 May	15 May	16 May: Week 7
2017	1 March	16 April	25 May	4 June	5 June: Week 9
2018	14 February	1 April	10 May	20 May	21 May: Week 7
2019	6 March	21 April	30 May	9 June	10 June: Week 10
2020	26 February	12 April	21 May	31 May	1 June: Week 9
2021	17 February	4 April	13 May	23 May	24 May: Week 8
2022	2 March	17 April	26 May	5 June	6 June: Week 10
2023	22 February	9 April	18 May	28 May	29 May: Week 8
2024	14 February	31 March	9 May	19 May	20 May: Week 7
2025	5 March	20 April	29 May	8 June	9 June: Week 10

Table of Moveable Feasts

Year	Corpus Christi	First Sunday of Advent	Lectionary Years (beginning on First Sunday of Advent)		
			Year	Sunday	Weekday
2001	14 June	2 December	2001/2002	A	2
2002	6 June	1 December	2002/2003	B	1
2003	19 June	30 November	2003/2004	C	2
2004	10 June	28 November	2004/2005	A	1
2005	26 May	27 November	2005/2006	B	2
2006	15 June	3 December	2006/2007	C	1
2007	7 June	2 December	2007/2008	A	2
2008	22 May	30 November	2008/2009	B	1
2009	11 June	29 November	2009/2010	C	2
2010	3 June	28 November	2010/2011	A	1
2011	23 June	27 November	2011/2012	B	2
2012	7 June	2 December	2012/2013	C	1
2013	30 May	1 December	2013/2014	A	2
2014	19 June	30 November	2014/2015	B	1
2015	4 June	29 November	2015/2016	C	2
2016	26 May	27 November	2016/2017	A	1
2017	15 June	3 December	2017/2018	B	2
2018	31 May	2 December	2018/2019	C	1
2019	20 June	1 December	2019/2020	A	2
2020	11 June	29 November	2020/2021	B	1
2021	3 June	28 November	2021/2022	C	2
2022	16 June	27 November	2022/2023	A	1
2023	8 June	3 December	2023/2024	B	2
2024	30 May	1 December	2024/2025	C	1
2025	19 June	30 November	2025/2026	A	2

ADVENT

Propers and Readings

Office Hymn

Conditor alme siderum

Eternal God, who made the stars
And to the faithful give your light,
Redeemer of our fallen race,
Give ear, O Christ, to heartfelt prayer.

You came with healing power to save
A world that languished, self-condemned:
The wounds of sin were wide and deep,
The cure for guilt was your free gift.

To night-bound peoples of this earth
In love's redeeming grace you came;
The bridegroom promised from of old,
Now born of Mary, virgin pure.

Before your strong yet gentle power
Creation kneels in reverent awe;
All things in heaven and on earth
In willing homage bow their heads.

We call upon you, holy Lord,
For you will come to judge the world:
Protect your pilgrim people here,
Keep safe our souls from Satan's grasp.

All praise and honour, glory, power,
To God the Father and the Son,

And to the Spirit, bond of love,
Through time and in the life to come.

LM
Anon Ninth Century (35)
Hymns for Prayer and Praise 103

Psalms and Canticles

Use Week 1 Psalmody from **First Sunday of Advent.**

Alternative Canticle at Morning Prayer

A Song of God's Herald *(Canticle 12) – see page 565.*

Short Readings

In days to come the mountain of the Lord's house shall be established as the highest of mountains, and shall be raised above the hills; all the nations shall stream to it. Many peoples shall come and say, 'Come, let us go up to the mountain of the Lord, to the house of the God of Jacob; that he may teach us his ways and that we may walk in his paths.'

Isaiah 2:2–3

or

The days are surely coming, says the Lord, when I will raise up for David a righteous Branch, and he shall reign as king and deal wisely, and shall execute justice and righteousness in the land. In his days Judah will be saved and Israel will live in safety. And this is the name by which he will be called: 'The Lord is our righteousness.'

Jeremiah 23:5–6

or

May the God of peace himself sanctify you entirely; and may your spirit and soul and body be kept sound and blameless at the coming of our Lord Jesus Christ.

1 Thessalonians 5:23

Long Readings
ADVENT SUNDAY

Year A	Year B	Year C
Isaiah 2:1–5	Isaiah 64:1–9	Jeremiah 33:14–16
Romans 13:11–14	1 Corinthians 1:3–9	1 Thessalonians 3:9–13
Matthew 24:36–44	Mark 13:24–37	Luke 21:25–36

following ADVENT SUNDAY

M	Isaiah 2:1–5 or 4:2–6	Matthew 8:5–11
T	Isaiah 11:1–10	Luke 10:21–24
W	Isaiah 25:6–10a	Matthew 15:29–37
Th	Isaiah 26:1–6	Matthew 7:21, 24–27
F	Isaiah 29:17–end	Matthew 9:27–31
S	Isaiah 30:19–21, 23–26	Matthew 9:35–10: 1, 6–8

SECOND SUNDAY OF ADVENT

Year A	Year B	Year C
Isaiah 11:1–10	Isaiah 40:1–11	Baruch 5:1–9
Romans 15:4–13	2 Peter 3:8–15a	Philippians 1:3–11
Matthew 3:1–12	Mark 1:1–8	Luke 3:1–6

following SECOND SUNDAY OF ADVENT

M	Isaiah 35	Luke 5:17–26
T	Isaiah 40:1–11	Matthew 18:12–14
W	Isaiah 40:25–end	Matthew 11:28–end
Th	Isaiah 41:13–20	Matthew 11:11–15
F	Isaiah 45:17–19	Matthew 11:16–19
S	Ecclesiasticus 48:1–4, 9–11	Matthew 17:10–13

THIRD SUNDAY OF ADVENT

Year A	Year B	Year C
Isaiah 35:1–10	Isaiah 61:1–4, 8–11	Zephaniah 3:14–20
James 5:7–10	1 Thessalonians 5:16–24	Philippians 4:4–7
Matthew 11:2–11	John 1:6–8, 19–28	Luke 3:7–18

following **THIRD SUNDAY OF ADVENT**

M	Numbers 24:2–7, 15–17	Matthew 21:23–27
T	Zephaniah 3:1–2, 9–13	Matthew 21:28–32
W	Isaiah 45:5–8, 19, 21–end	Luke 7:19–23
Th	Isaiah 54:1–10	Luke 7:24–30
F	Isaiah 56:1–3, 6–8	John 5:33–36

FOURTH SUNDAY OF ADVENT

Year A	Year B	Year C
Isaiah 7:10–16	2 Samuel 7:1–11, 16	Micah 5:2–5a
Romans 1:1–7	Romans 16:25–27	Hebrews 10:5–10
Matthew 1:18–25	Luke 1:26–38	Luke 1:39–45[46–55]

From 17 December to the Saturday after Epiphany inclusive, readings (except on **FOURTH SUNDAY OF ADVENT***) are according to date:*

December

17	Genesis 49:2, 8–10	Matthew 1:1–17
18	Jeremiah 23:5–8	Matthew 1:18–24
19	Judges 13:2–7, 24–25	Luke 1:5–25
20	Isaiah 7:10–14	Luke 1:26–38
21	Song of Songs 2:8–14	Luke 1:39–45
22	1 Samuel 1:24–28	Luke 1:46–56
23	Malachi 3:1–4; 4: 5–6	Luke 1:57–66
24	2 Samuel 7:1–5, 8–11, 16	Luke 1:67–79

Responsory

V/ Now it is time to awake out of sleep,
R/ For the night is far spent and the day is at hand.
V/ Now is our salvation nearer than when we first believed,
R/ For the night is far spent.
V/ Let us therefore cast off the works of darkness
and put on the armour of light,
R/ For the day is at hand.
V/ Put on the Lord Jesus Christ and make no provision for the flesh,
R/ For the night is far spent and the day is at hand.

Antiphons/Refrains and Texts for Meditation

A shoot shall come out from the stock of Jesse, and a branch shall grow out of his roots.

Isaiah 11:1

Prepare the way of the Lord, make his paths straight, and all flesh shall see the salvation of God.

cf. Isaiah 40:3–5

The glory of the Lord shall be revealed, and all flesh shall see it together.

Isaiah 40:53 (RSV)

Repent, for the kingdom of heaven is at hand.

Matthew 3:2 (RSV)

When the Lord comes, he will bring to light things now hidden in darkness, and will disclose the purposes of the heart.

cf. I Corinthians 4:5

Rejoice in the Lord always; again I will say, Rejoice. Let your gentleness be known to everyone. The Lord is near.

Philippians 4:4–5

For 17–24 December, the Advent Antiphons are the Refrains for the Magnificat. See below page 210.

Collect

Almighty God,
give us grace to cast away the works of darkness
and to put on the armour of light,
now in the time of this mortal life,
in which your Son Jesus Christ
   came to us in great humility;
that on the last day,
when he shall come again in his glorious majesty
   to judge the living and the dead,
we may rise to the life immortal;
through him who is alive and reigns with you,
in the unity of the Holy Spirit,
one God, now and for ever.

First Sunday of Advent
Common Worship (1)

Other Prayers

O Lord,
raise up (we pray thee) thy power,
and come among us,
and with great might succour us;
that whereas, through our sins and wickedness,
we are sore let and hindered
in running the race that is set before us,
thy bountiful grace and mercy
may speedily help and deliver us;
through the satisfaction of thy Son our Lord,
to whom with thee and the Holy Ghost
be honour and glory,
world without end.

Fourth Sunday in Advent
Book of Common Prayer (2)

O Lord our God,
make us watchful and keep us faithful
as we await the coming of your Son our Lord;
that, when he shall appear,
he may not find us sleeping in sin
but active in his service
and joyful in his praise;
through Jesus Christ our Lord.

First Sunday of Advent
(Post-Communion)
Common Worship (1)

O Christ, King of the Peoples,
awaited and desired for centuries by mankind,
wounded and scattered by sin,
you who are the cornerstone upon which mankind can
　　reconstruct itself
and regain a definite and enlightening guide
　　for its path through history,
you who reunited the divided peoples by means of your
　　sacrificial gift to the Father,
come and save man.
He is pitiable and great,

he was made by you with 'dust of the earth',
and he bears your image and likeness in him!

Pope John Paul II (25)

Antiphons

Used with the Magnificat *at Vespers.*

O Sapientia (17 December)

O WISDOM, coming forth from the mouth of the Most High,
and reaching mightily from one end of the earth to the other,
ordering all things well:
Come and teach us the way of prudence.

O Adonai (18 December)

O ADONAI, and leader of the house of Israel,
who appeared to Moses in the fire of the burning bush
and gave him the law on Sinai:
Come and redeem us with an outstretched arm.

O Radix (19 December)

O ROOT of Jesse, standing as a sign to the people,
before whom kings shall shut their mouths
and whom the nations shall seek:
Come and deliver us and do not delay.

O Clavis (20 December)

O KEY of David, and sceptre of the house of Israel,
who opens and no one can shut,
who shuts and no one can open:
Come and bring the prisoners from the prison house,
those who dwell in darkness and the shadow of death.

O Oriens (21 December)

O DAYSPRING, splendour of light eternal
and sun of righteousness:
Come and enlighten those who dwell in darkness
and the shadow of death.

O Rex *(22 December)*

O KING of the nations, and their desire,
the cornerstone making both one:
Come and save us, whom you formed from the dust.

O Emmanuel *(23 December)*

O EMMANUEL, our King and Lawgiver,
the desire of all nations and their Saviour:
Come and save us, O Lord our God.

A Daily Office SSF (3)

Christmas and the Annunciation of the Lord

Propers and Readings

Office Hymn

Christe, redemptor omnium

O Christ, redeemer, Lord of all,
And God the Father's only Son,
In all-transcending mystery
Begotten from eternity.

In you we see the Father's light,
The unknown glory of his face;
Throughout the world we cry to you,
In mercy hear your people's prayer.

Remember now, salvation's Lord,
That once you took our human flesh,
And from the Virgin Mother's womb
Were born in fellowship with us.

Each year this festal day proclaims
To all on earth the solemn word;
We call to mind the Word who came
From God's high throne to set us free.

Sky, ocean, earth, the universe,
And every creature ever made,
In exultation praise our God
Who sent his Son to save the world.

And we, for whom your precious blood,
Has won redemption, life and peace,
In new and joyful songs unite
To celebrate this holy birth.

All praise to you, blest Trinity,
To Father and incarnate Word,
Both with the Holy Spirit, one
For time and all eternity.

LM
Anon Sixth Century (35)
Hymns for Prayer and Praise 113

Psalms and Canticles

CHRISTMAS   *25 December*
and **ANNUNCIATION** *25 March*

Evening Prayer I   113
                     147:13–21
                     The Song of Christ's Glory
                     (Canticle 36) see page 584

Morning Prayer   Sunday Week 1

Evening Prayer II   110
                     130
                     A Song of Redemption
                     (Canticle 37) see page 585.

During Christmas Octave:

Morning Prayer *of the various feasts:* Sunday Week 1

Evening Prayer II *of Christmas*

NAMING AND   *1 January*
CIRCUMCISION

Evening Prayer I   113
                     147:13–21
                     A Song of God's Grace
                     (Canticle 35) see page 583.

Morning Prayer	Sunday Week 1
Evening Prayer II	122
	127
	A Song of God's Grace
	(Canticle 35) see page 583

CHRISTMAS 2

Sunday Week 2

Alternative Canticle at Morning Prayer

A Song of God's Chosen One *(Canticle 7) – see page 562.*

Short Readings

The people who walked in darkness have seen a great light; those who lived in a land of deep darkness – on them light has shined. For a child has been born for us, a son given to us; authority rests upon his shoulders; and he is named Wonderful Counsellor, Mighty God, Everlasting Father, Prince of Peace. His authority shall grow continually, and there shall be endless peace for the throne of David and his kingdom. He will establish and uphold it with justice and with righteousness from this time onwards and for evermore. The zeal of the Lord of hosts will do this.

Isaiah 9:2,6–7

or

When the fullness of time had come, God sent his Son, born of a woman, born under the law, in order to redeem those who were under the law, so that we might receive adoption as children. And because you are children, God has sent the Spirit of his Son into our hearts, crying, 'Abba! Father!' So you are no longer a slave but a child, and if a child then also an heir, through God.

Galatians 4:4–7

or

Long ago God spoke to our ancestors in many and various ways by the prophets, but in these last days he has spoken to us by a Son, whom he appointed heir of all things, through whom he also created the worlds. He is the reflection of God's glory and the exact imprint of God's very being, and he sustains all things by his powerful word.

Hebrews 1:1–3a

or

We declare to you what was from the beginning, what we have heard, what we have seen with our eyes, what we have looked at and touched with our hands, concerning the word of life – this life was revealed, and we have seen it and testify to it, and declare to you the eternal life that was with the Father and was revealed to us – we declare to you what we have seen and heard so that you also may have fellowship with us; and truly our fellowship is with the Father and with his Son Jesus Christ.

John 1:1–3

Long Readings

CHRISTMAS DAY

Midnight	*Dawn*	*Day*
Isaiah 9:2–7	Isaiah 62:6–12	Isaiah 52:7–10
Titus 2:11–14	Titus 3:4–7	Hebrews 1:1–4[5–12]
Luke 2:1–14[15–20]	Luke 2:[1–7]8–20	John 1:1–14

SUNDAY AFTER CHRISTMAS
or HOLY FAMILY

Year A	*Year B*	*Year C*
Isaiah 63:7–9	Isaiah 61:10–62:3	1 Samuel 2:18–20, 26
or Ecclesiasticus 3:2–6, 12–14		
Hebrews 2:10–18	Galatians 4:4–7	Colossians 3:12–17
Matthew 2:13–23	Luke 2:15–21	Luke 2:41–52

December
29 1 John 2:3–11   Luke 2:22–35
30 1 John 2:12–17   Luke 2:36–40
31 1 John 2:18–21   John 1:1–18

NAMING AND CIRCUMCISION OF JESUS:
Solemnity of
MARY, MOTHER OF GOD

1 January

Numbers 6:22–27
Galatians 4:4–7
Luke 2:15–21

SECOND SUNDAY AFTER CHRISTMAS
(If there are two Sundays between 25 December and 6 January)

Ecclesiasticus 24:1–12
Ephesians 1:3–14
John 1:[1–9]10–18

January

2	1 John 2:22–28	John 1:19–28
3	1 John 2:29–3:6	John 1:29–34
4	1 John 3:7–10	John 1:35–42
5	1 John 3:11–21	John 1:43–end

ANNUNCIATION   25 March

Isaiah 7:10–14
Hebrews 10:4–10
Luke 1:26–38

Responsory

- **R/** The Word of Life which was from the beginning,
- **R/** We proclaim to you.
- **V/** The darkness is passing away and the true light is already shining:
- **R/** The Word of Life which was from the beginning.
- **V/** That which we heard, which we saw with our eyes
  and touched with our hands,
- **R/** We proclaim to you.
- **V/** For our fellowship is with the Father
  and with his Son, Jesus Christ our Lord.
- **R/** The Word of Life which was from the beginning,
  we proclaim to you.

Antiphons/Refrains and Texts for Meditation

Unto us a child is born, unto us a son is given, and his name shall be called the Prince of Peace.

cf. Isaiah 9:6

Mary shall bear a son, and you are to name him Jesus, for he will save his people from their sins.

Matthew 1:21

Behold, I bring you good tidings of a great joy; for to you is born in the city of David a Saviour who is Christ the Lord.

Luke 2:10,11 (RSV)

The Word became flesh and lived among us and we have seen his glory, the glory as of a father's only son, full of grace and truth.

John 1:14

The grace of God has dawned upon the world through our Saviour Jesus Christ who sacrificed himself for us to purify a people as his own.

cf. Titus 2:11–14

O wonderful exchange! The Creator of human nature took on a human body and was born of the Virgin. He became man without having a human father and has bestowed on us his divine nature.

Magnificat Antiphon, 1 January, Evening Prayer II
Divine Office (14)

Collect
Almighty God,
in the birth of your Son
you have poured on us the new light of your incarnate Word,
and shown us the fullness of your love:
help us to walk in his light and dwell in his love
that we may know the fullness of his joy;
who is alive and reigns with you,
in the unity of the Holy Spirit,
one God, now and for ever.

Second Sunday of Christmas
Common Worship (1)

Other Prayers

Good Jesu, born as at this time, a little child for love of us; be thou born in me, that I may be a little child in love of thee; and hang on thy love as on my mother's bosom, trustfully, lovingly, peacefully; hushing all my cares in love of thee.

Edward Bouverie Pusey

O sweet Child of Bethlehem, grant that we may share with all our hearts in this profound mystery of Christmas. Put into our hearts this peace for which we sometimes seek so desperately and which you alone can give us. Help us to know one another better, and to live as children of the same Father. Reveal to us also your beauty, holiness and purity. Awaken in our hearts love and gratitude for your infinite goodness. Join us altogether in your love. And give us your heavenly peace.

Pope John XXIII (22)

Epiphany and Feasts of the Lord

Propers and Readings

Office Hymn

All praise to Christ

All praise to Christ, our Lord and king divine,
Yielding your glory in your love's design,
That in our darkened hearts your grace may shine.
Alleluia.

You came to us in lowliness of thought;
By you the outcast and the poor were sought;
And by your death was our redemption bought.
Alleluia.

The mind of Christ is as our minds should be:
He was a servant that we might be free,
Humbling himself to death on Calvary.
Alleluia.

And so we see in God's great purpose, how
Christ has been raised above all creatures now;
And at his name shall every nation bow.
Alleluia.

Let every tongue confess with one accord,
In heaven and earth, that Jesus Christ is Lord,
And God the Father be by all adored.
Alleluia.

Francis Bland Tucker* (37)
Hymns for Prayer and Praise 187

Psalms and Canticles
EPIPHANY AND BAPTISM OF THE LORD

Evening Prayer I	135 A Song of Christ's Appearing *(Canticle 38) see page 585.*
Morning Prayer	Sunday Week 1
Evening Prayer II	110 112 A Song of Moses and the Lamb *(Canticle 43) see page 589*

Use Week 1 Psalmody from Monday,
the day after the Baptism of the Lord

CANDLEMAS   2 February

Evening Prayer I	113 147:13–21 The Song of Christ's Glory *(Canticle 36) see page 584.*
Morning Prayer	Sunday Week 1
Evening Prayer II	110 130 A Song of Redemption *(Canticle 37) see page 585.*

TRANSFIGURATION   6 August
OF THE LORD

Evening Prayer I	*(Sundays only)* 113 117 A Song of the Lamb *(Canticle 44) see page 589.*
Morning Prayer	Sunday Week 1
Evening Prayer II	110 121

A Song of Christ's Appearing
(Canticle 38) see page 585.

HOLY CROSS	*14 September*
Evening Prayer I	*(Sundays only)* 147 The Song of Christ's Glory *(Canticle 36) see page 584.*
Morning Prayer	Sunday Week 1
Evening Prayer II	110 116 A Song of Praise *(Canticle 40) see page 587.*

Alternative Canticle at Morning Prayer

A Song of the New Jerusalem *(Canticle 17) – see page 570.*

Short Readings

From the rising of the sun to its setting my name is great among the nations, and in every place incense is offered to my name, and a pure offering; for my name is great among the nations, says the Lord.

Malachi 1:11 (RSV)

or

When we cry, 'Abba! Father!' it is that very Spirit bearing witness with our spirit that we are children of God, and if children, then heirs, heirs of God and joint heirs with Christ – if, in fact, we suffer with him so that we may also be glorified with him.

Romans 8:15b-17

or

It is the God who said, 'Let light shine out of darkness', who has shone in our hearts to give the light of the knowledge of the glory of God in the face of Christ.

2 Corinthians 4:6 (RSV)

or

God saved us and called us with a holy calling, not according to our works but according to his own purpose and grace. This grace was given to us in Christ Jesus before the ages began, but it has now been revealed through the appearing of our Saviour Christ Jesus, who abolished death and brought life and immortality to light through the gospel.

2 Timothy 1:9–10

Long Readings

EPIPHANY 6 January

Isaiah 60:1–6
Ephesians 3:1–12
Matthew 2:1–12

January

7	1 John 3:22–4: 6	Matthew 4:12–17, 23–end
8	1 John 4:7–10	Mark 6:34–44
9	1 John 4:11–18	Mark 6:45–52
10	1 John 4:19–5: 4	Luke 4:14–22
11	1 John 5:5–13	Luke 5:12–16
12	1 John 5:14–end	John 3:22–30

BAPTISM OF THE LORD *(Sunday after the Epiphany)*

Year A	*Year B*	*Year C*
Isaiah 42:1–9	Genesis 1:1–5	Isaiah 43:1–7
Acts 10:34–43	Acts 19:1–7	Acts 8:14–17
Matthew 3:13–17	Mark 1:4–11	Luke 3:15–17, 21–22

CANDLEMAS 2 February

Malachi 3:1–5
Hebrews 2:14–18
Luke 2:22–40

TRANSFIGURATION 6 August

Daniel 7:9–10, 13–14

and/or 2 Peter 1:16–19
Luke 9:28–36

HOLY CROSS DAY   *14 September*

Numbers 21:4–9
and/or Philippians 2:6–11
John 3:13–17

Responsory

R/ O worship the Lord in the beauty of holiness,
R/ Let the whole earth stand in awe of him.
V/ Tell it out among the nations that the Lord is King,
R/ O worship the Lord in the beauty of holiness.
V/ God's salvation has been openly shown to all people.
R/ Let the whole earth stand in awe of him.
V/ Declare his glory among the nations
and his wonders among all peoples.
R/ O worship the Lord in the beauty of holiness,
let the whole earth stand in awe of him.

For the Transfiguration of the Lord and Holy Cross Day:

R/ We worship you, Christ, and we bless you.
R/ We worship you, Christ, and we bless you.
V/ By your holy cross you have redeemed the world.
R/ We worship you, Christ, and we bless you.
V/ Glory . . . Holy Spirit.
R/ We worship you, Christ, and we bless you.

Antiphons/Refrains and Texts for Meditation

Opening their treasure-chests, the wise men offered him gifts of gold, frankincense and myrrh. And having been warned in a dream not to return to Herod, they left for their own country by another road.

Matthew 2:12

Three wonders mark this day we celebrate: today the star led the Magi to the manger; today water was changed into wine at the marriage feast; today Christ desired to be baptized by John in the river Jordan to bring us salvation, alleluia.

Magnificat Antiphon, Epiphany Evening Prayer II
Divine Office (14)

Christ was revealed in flesh, vindicated by the Spirit, seen by angels, proclaimed among Gentiles, believed in throughout the world, taken up in glory.

1 Timothy 3:16

God's love was revealed among us in this way: God sent his only Son into the world that we might live through him.

1 John 4:9

Especially suitable for Candlemas

This child is the light to enlighten the nations, and the glory of your people Israel.

cf. Luke 2:32

I am the light of the world. Whoever follows me will never walk in darkness but will have the light of life.

John 8:12

Especially suitable for the Transfiguration of the Lord

Jesus took with him Peter and James and John, and led them up a high mountain apart, by themselves. And he was transfigured before them, and his clothes became dazzling white, such as no one on earth could bleach them.

Mark 9:2–3

A cloud overshadowed them, and from the cloud there came a voice, 'This is my Son, the Beloved; listen to him!'

Mark 9:7

Especially suitable for Holy Cross Day

We proclaim Christ crucified, a stumbling-block to Jews and foolishness to Gentiles, but to those who are called, both Jews and Greeks, Christ the power of God and the wisdom of God. For God's foolishness is wiser than human wisdom, and God's weakness is stronger than human strength.

1 Corinthians 1:23–25

Collect

Almighty God,
whose Son revealed in signs and miracles
the wonder of your saving presence:
renew your people with your heavenly grace,
and in all our weakness
sustain us by your mighty power;
through Jesus Christ your Son our Lord,
who is alive and reigns with you,
in the unity of the Holy Spirit,
one God, now and for ever.

Third Sunday of Epiphany
Common Worship (1)

Other Prayers

O God,
who by the leading of a star
didst manifest thy only-begotten Son to the Gentiles:
Mercifully grant,
that we, which know thee now by faith,
may after this life have the fruition of thy glorious Godhead;
through Jesus Christ our Lord.

Collect for the Epiphany
Book of Common Prayer (2)

Eternal Light, shine into our hearts;
eternal Goodness, deliver us from evil;
eternal Power, be our support;
eternal Wisdom, scatter the darkness of our ignorance;
eternal Pity, have mercy on us;
that with all our heart and mind and strength
we may seek your face
and be brought by your infinite mercy to your holy presence;
through Jesus Christ our Lord.

Alcuin (21)

Lord of all time and eternity,
you opened the heavens
   and revealed yourself as Father
in the baptism of Jesus your beloved Son:
by the power of your Spirit
complete the heavenly work of our rebirth
through the waters of the new creation;
through Jesus Christ our Lord.

The Baptism of Christ
(Post-Communion)
Common Worship (1)

Ordinary Time before Lent

Propers and Readings

In the Roman Calendar, Ordinary Time begins on the Monday following the feast of the Baptism of the Lord, itself the first Sunday after Epiphany.

In the Common Worship (1) Calendar, the Epiphany season extends until Candlemas (2 February). Ordinary Time begins the day after.

Ordinary Time before Lent ends on Shrove Tuesday.

Office Hymn

As set for Lauds page 20 and Vespers page 626

Psalms and Canticles

Use Week 1 Psalmody from Monday after the Baptism of the Lord.

Alternative Canticle at Morning Prayer

A Song in Praise of the Works of God *(Canticle 31) – see page 581.*

Short Readings

Thus says the Lord: heaven is my throne and the earth is my footstool; what is the house that you would build for me, and what is my resting place? All these things my hand has made, and so all these things are mine, says the Lord. But this is the one to whom I will look, to the humble and contrite in spirit, who trembles at my word.

Isaiah 66:1–2

or

O the depths of the riches and wisdom and knowledge of God! How unsearchable are his judgements and how inscrutable his ways! 'For who has known the mind of the Lord? or who has been his counsellor?' 'Or who has given a gift to him, to receive a gift in return?' For from him and through him and to him are all things. To him be the glory for ever. Amen.

Romans 11:33–36

Long Readings

Sundays between
THE BAPTISM OF THE LORD *AND* LENT:

use Sundays 2–8 of Ordinary Time, as required. Common Worship (1) readings for Sundays before Lent may be used. See below.

Week 1 of the Year 1
M	Hebrews 1:1–6	Mark 1:14–20
T	Hebrews 2:5–12	Mark 1:21–28
W	Hebrews 2:14–end	Mark 1:29–39
Th	Hebrews 3:7–14	Mark 1:40–end
F	Hebrews 4:1–5, 11	Mark 2:1–12
S	Hebrews 4:12–16	Mark 2:13–17

Week 1 of Year 2
M	1 Samuel 1:1–8	Mark 1:14–20
T	1 Samuel 1:9–20	Mark 1:21–28
W	1 Samuel 3:1–10, 19–20	Mark 1:29–39
Th	1 Samuel 4:1–11	Mark 1:40–end
F	1 Samuel 8:4–7, 10–end	Mark 2:1–12
S	1 Samuel 9:1–4, 17–19; 10:1	Mark 2:13–17

Sunday between 14–20 January inclusive
[SECOND SUNDAY OF EPIPHANY] *[Sunday 2 of Ordinary Time]*

Year A	*Year B*	*Year C*
Isaiah 49:1–7	1 Samuel 3:1–10 [11–20]	Isaiah 62:1–5
1 Corinthians 1:1–9	Revelation 5:1–10	1 Corinthians 12:1–11
John 1:29–42	John 1:43–51	John 2:1–11

Week 2 of Year 1
M	Hebrews 5:1–10	Mark 2:18–22
T	Hebrews 6:10–end	Mark 2:23–end
W	Hebrews 7:1–3, 15–17	Mark 3:1–6
Th	Hebrews 7:25–8:6	Mark 3:7–12
F	Hebrews 8:6–end	Mark 3:13–19
S	Hebrews 9:2–3, 11–14	Mark 3: 20–21

Week 2 of Year 2
M	1 Samuel 15:16–23	Mark 2:18–22
T	1 Samuel 16:1–13	Mark 2:23–end
W	1 Samuel 17:32–33, 37,40–51	Mark 3:1–6
Th	1 Samuel 18:6–9; 19:1–7	Mark 3:7–12
F	1 Samuel 24:3–22a	Mark 3:13–19
S	2 Samuel 1:1–4, 11–12, 17–19, 23–end	Mark 3:20–21

Sunday between 21–27 January inclusive
[THIRD SUNDAY OF EPIPHANY]   *[Sunday 3 of Ordinary Time]*

Year A	*Year B*	*Year C*
Isaiah 9:1–4	Genesis 14:17–20	Nehemiah 8:1–3, 5–6, 8–10
1 Corinthians 1:10–18	Revelation 19:6–10	1 Corinthians 12: 12–31a
Matthew 4:12–23	John 2:1–11	Luke 4:14–21

Week 3 of Year 1
M	Hebrews 9:15, 24–end	Mark 3:22–30
T	Hebrews 10:1–10	Mark 3:31–end
W	Hebrews 10:11–18	Mark 4:1–20
Th	Hebrews 10:19–25	Mark 4:21–25
F	Hebrews 10:32–end	Mark 4:26–34
S	Hebrews 11:1–2, 8–19	Mark 4:35–end

Week 3 of Year 2
M	2 Samuel 5:1–7, 10	Mark 3:22–30
T	2 Samuel 6:12–15, 17–19	Mark 3:31–end
W	2 Samuel 7:4–17	Mark 3:1–6
Th	2 Samuel 7:18–19, 24–end	Mark 4:21–25
F	2 Samuel 11:1–10, 13–17	Mark 4:26–34
S	2 Samuel 12:1–7, 10–17	Mark 4:35–end

Sunday between 28 January and 1 February inclusive
[FOURTH SUNDAY OF EPIPHANY] *[Sunday 4 of Ordinary Time]*

Year A	Year B	Year C
1 Kings 17:8–16	Deuteronomy 18: 15–20	Ezekiel 43:27–44:4
1 Corinthians 1:18–31	Revelation 12:1–5a	1 Corinthians 13:1–13
John 2:1–11	Mark 1:21–28	Luke 2:22–40

Week 4 of Year 1
M	Hebrews 11:32–end	Mark 5:1–20
T	Hebrews 12:1–4	Mark 5:21–end
W	Hebrews 12: 4–7, 11–15	Mark 6:1–6
Th	Hebrews 12:18–19, 21–24	Mark 6:7–13
F	Hebrews 13:1–8	Mark 6:14–29
S	Hebrews 13:15–17, 20–21	Mark 6:30–34

Week 4 of Year 2
M	2 Samuel 15:13–14, 30; 16:5–13	Mark 5:1–20
T	2 Samuel 18: 9–10, 14, 24–25, 30–19:3	Mark 5:21–end
W	2 Samuel 24:2, 9–17	Mark 6:1–6
Th	1 Kings 2:1–4, 10–12	Mark 6:7–13
F	Ecclesiasticus 47:2–11	Mark 6:14–29
S	1 Kings 3:4–13	Mark 6:30–34

Sunday between 3–9 February inclusive
[Proper 1 of CWPS] *[Sunday 5 of Ordinary Time]*

Year A	Year B	Year C
Isaiah 58:1–9a[b–12]	Isaiah 40:21–31	Isaiah 6:1–8[9–13]
1 Corinthians 2:1–12 [13–16]	1 Corinthians 9:16–23	1 Corinthians 15:1–11
Matthew 5:13–20	Mark 1:29–39	Luke 5:1–11

Week 5 of Year 1
M	Genesis 1:1–19	Mark 6:53–end
T	Genesis 1:20–2:4a	Mark 7:1–13
W	Genesis 2:4b–9, 15–17	Mark 7:14–23
Th	Genesis 2:8–end	Mark 7:24–30

Ordinary Time

F	Genesis 3:1–8	Mark 7:31–end
S	Genesis 3:9–end	Mark 8:1–10

Week 5 of Year 2

M	1 Kings 8:1–7, 9–13	Mark 6:53–end
T	1 Kings 8:22–23, 27–30	Mark 7:1–13
W	1 Kings 10:1–10	Mark 7:14–23
Th	1 Kings 11:4–13	Mark 7:24–30
F	1 Kings11:29–32; 12:19	Mark 7:31–end
S	1 Kings 12:26–32; 13:33–34	Mark 8:1–10

Sunday between 10–16 February inclusive
[Proper 2 of CWPS]   [Sunday 6 of Ordinary Time]

Year A	Year B	Year C
Ecclesiasticus 15:15–20	2 Kings 5:1–14	Jeremiah 17:5–10
1 Corinthians 3:1–9	1 Corinthians 9:24–27	1 Corinthians 15:12–20
Matthew 5:21–37	Mark 1:40–45	Luke 6:17–26

Week 6 of Year 1

M	Genesis 4:1–15, 25	Mark 8:11–13
T	Genesis 6:5–8; 7: 1-5, 10	Mark 8:14–21
W	Genesis 8:6–13, 20–end	Mark 8:22–26
Th	Genesis 9:1–13	Mark 8:27–33
F	Genesis 11:1–9	Mark 8:34–9:1
S	Hebrews 11:1–7	Mark 9:2–13

Week 6 of Year 2

M	James 1:1–11	Mark 8:11–13
T	James 1:12–18	Mark 8:14–21
W	James 1:19–end	Mark 8:22–26
Th	James 2:1–9	Mark 8:27–33
F	James 2:14–24, 26	Mark 8:34–9:1
S	James 3:1–10	Mark 9:2–13

Sunday between 17–23 February inclusive
[Proper 3 of CWPS]   [Sunday 7 of Ordinary Time]

Year A	Year B	Year C
Leviticus 19:1–2, 9–18	Isaiah 43:18–25	Genesis 45:3–11, 15
1 Corinthians 3:10–11, 16–23	2 Corinthians 1:18–22	1 Corinthians 15:35–38, 42–50
Matthew 5:38–48	Mark 2:1–12	Luke 6:27–38

Week 7 of Year 1
M   Ecclesiasticus 1:1–10   Mark 9:1–29
T   Ecclesiasticus 2:1–11   Mark 9:30–37
W   Ecclesiasticus 4:11–19   Mark 9:38–40
Th Ecclesiasticus 5:1–8   Mark 9:41–end
F   Ecclesiasticus 6:5–17   Mark 10:1–12
S   Ecclesiasticus 17:1–15   Mark 10:13–16

Week 7 of year 2
M   James 3:13–end   Mark 9:14–29
T   James 4:1–10   Mark 9:30–37
W   James 4:13–end   Mark 9:38–40
Th James 5:1–6   Mark 9:41–end
F   James 5:9–12   Mark 10:1–12
S   James 5:13–end   Mark 10:13–16

Sunday between 24 February and 1 March inclusive
                                                      [Sunday 8 of Ordinary Time]

Year A	*Year B*	*Year C*
* Isaiah 49:14–14	* Hosea 2:16–17, 21–22	* Ecclesiasticus 27:4–7
* 1 Corinthians 4:1–5	* 2 Corinthians 3:1–6	* 1 Corinthians 15: 54–58
* Matthew 6:24–34	* Mark 2:18–22	* Luke 6:39–45

Week 8 of Year 1
M   Ecclesiasticus 17:24–29   Mark 10:17–27
T   Ecclesiasticus 35:1–12   Mark 10: 28–31
W   Ecclesiasticus 36:1,4–5, 10–17   Mark 10: 32–45
Th Ecclesiasticus 42:15–end   Mark 10:46–end
F   Ecclesiasticus 44:1, 9–13   Mark 11:11–26
S   Ecclesiasticus 51:12–20   Mark 11:27–end

Week 8 of Year 2
M   1 Peter 1:3–9   Mark 10:17–27
T   1 Peter 1:10–16   Mark 10:28–31
W   1 Peter 1:18–end   Mark 10:32–45
Th 1 Peter 2:2–5, 9–12   Mark 10:46–end
F   1 Peter 4:7–13   Mark 11:11–26
S   Jude 17, 20–end   Mark 11:27–end

Ordinary Time

Sunday between 2 March and 8 March inclusive
[Proper 4 of CWPS]   *[Sunday 9 of Ordinary Time]*

Year A	*Year B*	*Year C*
Deuteronomy 11:18–21, 26–28	Deuteronomy 5:12–15	1 Kings 8:22–23, 41–43
Romans 1:16–17; 3:22b-28[29–31]	2 Corinthians 4:5–12	Galatians 1:1–12
Matthew 7:21–29	Mark 2:23–3:6	Luke 7:1–10

Week 9 of Year 1
- M Tobit 1:1–2; 2:1–8   Mark 12:1–12
- T Tobit 2: 9–14   Mark 12:13–17
- W Tobit 3:1–11, 16–17   Mark 12:18–27
- Th Tobit 6:9–11; 7:1–15; 8:4–8 Mark 12:28–34
- F Tobit 11:5–15   Mark 12:35–37
- S Tobit 12:1, 5–15, 20a   Mark 12:38 end

Week 9 of Year 2
- M 2 Peter 1:2–7   Mark 12:1–12
- T 2 Peter 3:11–15, 17–18   Mark 12:13–17
- W 2 Timothy 1:1–3, 6–12   Mark 12:18–27
- Th 2 Timothy 2:8–15   Mark 12:28–34
- F 2 Timothy 3:10–end   Mark 12:35–37
- S 2 Timothy 4:1–8   Mark 12:38–end

Common Worship readings for Sundays before Lent

SECOND SUNDAY BEFORE LENT

Year A	*Year B*	*Year C*
Genesis 1:1–2:3	Proverbs 8:1, 22–31	Genesis 2:4b-9,15–25
Romans 8:18–25	Colossians 1:15–20	Revelation 4
Matthew 6:25–34	John 1:1–14	Luke 8:22–25

SUNDAY NEXT BEFORE LENT

Year A	*Year B*	*Year C*
Exodus 24:12–18	2 Kings 2:1–12	Exodus 34:29–35
2 Peter 1:16–21	2 Corinthians 4:3–6	2 Corinthians 3: 12–4:2
Matthew 17:1–9	Mark 9:2–9	Luke 9:28–36 [37–43]

Responsory

Sundays

R/ You are the Christ, the Son of the living God. Have mercy on us.
R/ You are the Christ, the Son of the living God. Have mercy on us.
V/ You are seated at the right hand of the Father.
R/ You are the Christ, the Son of the living God. Have mercy on us.
V/ Glory . . .Holy Spirit.
R/ You are the Christ, the Son of the living God. Have mercy on us.

Divine Office (14)

Weekdays

R/ I call with my whole heart; answer me, O Lord.
R/ I call with my whole heart; answer me, O Lord.
V/ I will keep your commandments.
R/ I call with my whole heart; answer me, O Lord.
V/ Glory . . . Holy Spirit.
R/ I call with my whole heart; answer me, O Lord.

Psalm 119:145

Antiphons/Refrains and Texts for Meditation

In everything by prayer and supplication with thanksgiving let your requests be made known to God.

Philippians 4:6 (RSV)

See what love the Father has given us, that we should be called children of God; and that is what we are.

1 John 3:1a

Collect

Almighty God,
who alone can bring order
to the unruly wills and passions of sinful humanity:
give your people grace
so to love what you command
and to desire what you promise,

that, among the many changes of this world,
our hearts may surely there be fixed
where true joys are to be found;
through Jesus Christ your Son our Lord,
who is alive and reigns with you,
in the unity of the Holy Spirit,
one God, now and for ever.

Third Sunday before Lent
Common Worship (1)

Other Prayers

Go before us, Lord, in all we do
with your most gracious favour,
and guide us with your continual help,
that in all our works
begun, continued and ended in you,
we may glorify your holy name,
and finally by your mercy receive everlasting life;
through Jesus Christ our Lord.

Fourth Sunday before Lent
(Post-Communion)
Common Worship (1)

Almighty God, the fountain of all wisdom,
you know our needs before we ask,
and our ignorance in asking:
have compassion on our weakness,
and give us those things
which for our unworthiness we dare not,
and for our blindness we cannot ask,
for the sake of your Son Jesus Christ our Lord.

Common Worship (1)

Lent

Propers and Readings

Office Hymn

Deus, creator omnium

O God, creator of us all,
From whom we come, to whom we go,
You look with pity on our hearts:
The weakness of our wills you know.

Forgive us all the wrong we do,
And purify each sinful soul.
What we have darkened, heal with light,
And what we have destroyed, make whole.

The fast by law and prophets taught,
By you, O Christ, was sanctified:
Bless all our penance, give us strength
To share the cross on which you died.

O God of mercy, hear our prayer,
With Christ your Son, and Spirit blest,
Transcendent Trinity in whom
Created things all come to rest.

LM
Saint Ambrose
translation c 1974
Stanbrook Abbey (4)
Hymns for Prayer and Praise 133

Psalms and Canticles

From **ASH WEDNESDAY** *until Saturday after, use Week 4.*

Use Week 1 Psalmody from **FIRST SUNDAY OF LENT.**

Alternative Canticle at Morning Prayer

A Song of the Word of the Lord (Canticle 16) see page 569.

Short Readings

Wash yourselves; make yourselves clean; remove the evil of your doings from before my eyes; cease to do evil, learn to do good; seek justice, rescue the oppressed, defend the orphan, plead for the widow.

Isaiah 1:16–18

or

I hate, I despise your festivals, and I take no delight in your solemn assemblies. Even though you offer me your burnt offerings and grain offerings, I will not accept them; and the offerings of well-being of your fatted animals I will not look upon. Take away from me the noise of your songs; I will not listen to the melody of your harps. But let justice roll down like waters, and righteousness like an ever-flowing stream.

Amos 5:21–24

or

I will arise and go to my father, and I will say to him, Father, I have sinned against heaven, and before you; I am no longer worthy to be called your son.

Luke 15:18,19 (RSV)

or

If we say we have no sin, we deceive ourselves, and the truth is not in us. If we confess our sins, he is faithful and just, and will forgive our sins and cleanse us from all unrighteousness.

1 John 1:8,9 (RSV)

Long Readings

ASH WEDNESDAY
Joel 2:1–2, 12–17
or Isaiah 58:1–12
2 Corinthians 5:20b -6:10
Matthew 6:1–6, 16–21
or John 8:1–11

following ASH WEDNESDAY
Th	Deuteronomy 30:15–end	Luke 9:22–25
F	Isaiah 58:1–9a	Matthew 9:14–15
S	Isaiah 58:9b–end	Luke 5: 27–32

FIRST SUNDAY OF LENT

Year A	Year B	Year C
Genesis 2:15–17; 3:1–7	Genesis 9:8–17	Deuteronomy 26:1–11
Romans 5:12–19	1 Peter 3:18–22	Romans 10:8b-13
Matthew 4:1–11	Mark 1:9–15	Luke 4:1–13

following FIRST SUNDAY OF LENT
M	Leviticus 19:1–2, 11–18	Matthew 25:31–end
T	Isaiah 55:10–11	Matthew 6:7–15
W	Jonah 3	Luke 11:29–32
Th	Esther 14:1–5, 12–14	Matthew 7:7–12
F	Ezekiel 18:21–28	Matthew 5:20–26
S	Deuteronomy 26:16–end	Matthew 5:43–end

SECOND SUNDAY OF LENT

Year A	Year B	Year C
Genesis 12:1–4a	Genesis 17:1–7, 15–16	Genesis 15:1–12, 17–18
Romans 4:1–5, 13–17	Romans 4:13–25	Philippians 3:17–4:1
John 3:1–17	Mark 8:31–38	Luke 13:31–35

following SECOND SUNDAY OF LENT
M	Daniel 9:4–10	Luke 6:36–38
T	Isaiah 1:10, 16–20	Matthew 23:1–12
W	Jeremiah 18:18–20	Matthew 20:17–28
Th	Jeremiah 17:5–10	Luke 16:19–end
F	Genesis 37:3–4, 12–13, 17–28	Matthew 21:33–43, 45–46
S	Micah 7:14–15, 18–20	Luke 15:1–3, 11–end

THIRD SUNDAY OF LENT

Year A	*Year B*	*Year C*
Exodus 17:1–7	Exodus 20:1–17	Isaiah 55:1–9
Romans 5:1–11	1 Corinthians 1:18–25	1 Corinthians 10:1–13
John 4:5–42	John 2:13–22	Luke 13:1–9

following THIRD SUNDAY OF LENT

M	2 Kings 5:1–15	Luke 4:24–30
T	Daniel 3:28, 35–44 *(Apocrypha)*	Matthew 18:21–end
W	Deuteronomy 4:1, 5–9	Matthew 5:17–19
Th	Jeremiah 7:23–28	Luke 11:14–23
F	Hosea 14:2–10	Mark 12:28–34
S	Hosea 5:15–6:6	Luke 18:9–14

FOURTH SUNDAY OF LENT

Year A	*Year B*	*Year C*
1 Samuel 16:1–13	Numbers 21:4–9	Joshua 5:9–12
Ephesians 5:8–14	Ephesians 2:1–10	2 Corinthians 5:16–21
John 9:1–41	John 3:14–21	Luke 15:1–3, 11b–32

or

MOTHERING SUNDAY

Exodus 2:10
or 1 Samuel 1:20–28
2 Corinthians 1:3–7
or Colossians 3:12–17
Luke 2:33–35
or John 19:25–27

following FOURTH SUNDAY OF LENT

M	Isaiah 65:17–21	John 4:43–end
T	Ezekiel 47:1–9, 12	John 5:1–3, 5–16
W	Isaiah 49:8–15	John 5:17–30
Th	Exodus 32:7–14	John 5:31–47
F	Wisdom 2:1, 12–22	John 7:1–2, 10, 25–30
S	Jeremiah 11:18–20	John 7:40–52

For **FIFTH SUNDAY OF LENT,** *see PASSIONTIDE below.*

Responsory

- **R/** To you, O Lord, I lift up my soul;
  O my God, in you I trust.
- **R/** To you, O Lord, I lift up my soul;
  O my God, in you I trust.
- **V/** You are the God of my salvation,
  in you I hope all the day long.
- **R/** O my God, in you I trust.
- **V/** Glory to the Father, and to the Son,
  and to the Holy Spirit.
- **R/** To you, O Lord, I lift up my soul;
  O my God, in you I trust.

Antiphons/Refrains and Texts for Meditation

As I live, says the Lord God, I have no pleasure in the death of the wicked, but that the wicked turn from his way and live.

Ezekiel 33:11a (RSV)

Great are your judgements and hard to describe; therefore uninstructed souls have gone astray.

Wisdom 17:1

You are the salt of the earth; but if salt has lost its taste, how can its saltiness be restored?

Matthew 5:13a

You are the light of the world. Let your light shine before others, so that they may see your good works and give glory to your Father in heaven.

Matthew 5:14a, 16

Whenever you pray, go into your room and shut the door and pray to your Father who is in secret; and your Father who sees in secret will reward you.

Matthew 6:6

God proves his love for us in that while we still were sinners Christ died for us.

Romans 5:8

Do you not know that in a race the runners all compete, but only one receives the prize? Run in such a way that you may win it.

1 Corinthians 9:24

Collect

Almighty and everlasting God,
you hate nothing that you have made
and forgive the sins of all those who are penitent:
create and make in us new and contrite hearts
that we, worthily lamenting our sins
and acknowledging our wretchedness,
may receive from you, the God of all mercy,
perfect remission and forgiveness;
through Jesus Christ your Son our Lord,
who is alive and reigns with you,
in the unity of the Holy Spirit,
one God, now and for ever.

Ash Wednesday
Common Worship (1)

Other Prayers

Good Jesu,
too late have I loved thee,
nor ever yet have I wholly followed thee;
make me now at last wholly to love thee,
and out of the fullness of thine infinite love
give me all the love I might have had, had I always loved thee.
O dearest Lord, too late have I loved thee, too late have I loved thee,
too late is it always, not always to have loved thee wholly.
Now, too, I cannot love thee as I would.
O dearest Lord, who art love,
give me of thine own love,
that therewith I may wholly love thee.

Edward Bouverie Pusey

Almighty God,
we pray that through this season of Lent,
by prayer and study and self-discipline,
we may penetrate more deeply into the mystery of Christ's sufferings;
that, following in the way of his cross and passion,
we may come to share
in the glory and triumph of his resurrection;
through Jesus Christ our Lord.

Contemporary Parish Prayers (38)

Lord God,
whose blessed Son our Saviour
gave his back to the smiters
and did not hide his face from shame:
give us grace to endure the sufferings of this present time
with sure confidence in the glory that shall be revealed;
through Jesus Christ our Lord.

Fourth Sunday of Lent
(Post-Communion)
Common Worship (1)

Seven Penitential Psalms

Psalm 6

1 O Lord, rebuke me not in your wrath; *
 neither chasten me in your fierce anger.
2 Have mercy on me, Lord, for I am weak; *
 Lord, heal me, for my bones are racked.
3 My soul also shakes with terror; *
 how long, O Lord, how long?
4 Turn again, O Lord, and deliver my soul; *
 save me for your loving mercy's sake.
5 For in death no one remembers you; *
 and who can give you thanks in the grave?
6 I am weary with my groaning; *
 every night I drench my pillow
 and flood my bed with my tears.
7 My eyes are wasted with grief *
 and worn away because of all my enemies.

8 Depart from me, all you that do evil, *
 for the Lord has heard the voice of my weeping.
9 The Lord has heard my supplication; *
 the Lord will receive my prayer.
10 All my enemies shall be put to shame and confusion; *
 they shall suddenly turn back in their shame.

 Glory . . .

Psalm 32

1 Happy the one whose transgression is forgiven, *
 and whose sin is covered!
2 Happy is the one to whom the Lord imputes no guilt, *
 and in whose spirit there is no guile.
3 For I held my tongue; *
 my bones wasted away
 through my groaning all day long.
4 Your hand was heavy upon me day and night; *
 my moisture was dried up like the drought in summer.

5 Then I acknowledged my sin to you *
    and my iniquity I did not hide.
6 I said, 'I will confess my transgressions to the Lord,' *
    and you forgave the guilt of my sin.
7 Therefore let all the faithful make their prayers to you
    in time of trouble; *
    in the great water flood, it shall not reach them.
8 You are a place for me to hide in;
    you preserve me from trouble; *
    you surround me with songs of deliverance.

9 'I will instruct you and teach you
    in the way that you should go; *
    I will guide you with my eye.
10 'Be not like horse or mule which have no understanding; *
    whose mouths must be held with bit and bridle,
    or else they will not stay near you.'
11 Great tribulations remain for the wicked, *
    but mercy embraces those who trust in the Lord.
12 Be glad, you righteous, and rejoice in the Lord; *
    shout for joy, all who are true of heart.

   Glory . . .

Psalm 38

1 Rebuke me not, O Lord, in your anger; *
    neither chasten me in your heavy displeasure.
2 For your arrows have stuck fast in me *
    and your hand presses hard upon me.
3 There is no health in my flesh
    because of your indignation; *
    there is no peace in my bones because of my sin.
4 For my iniquities have gone over my head; *
    their weight is a burden too heavy to bear.
5 My wounds stink and fester *
    because of my foolishness.
6 I am utterly bowed down and brought very low; *
    I go about mourning all the day long.
7 My loins are filled with searing pain; *
    there is no health in my flesh.

8 I am feeble and utterly crushed; *
 I roar aloud because of the disquiet of my heart.
9 O Lord, you know all my desires *
 and my sighing is not hidden from you.
10 My heart is pounding, my strength has failed me; *
 the light of my eyes is gone from me.
11 My friends and companions stand apart from my affliction; *
 my neighbours stand afar off.
12 Those who seek after my life lay snares for me; *
 and those who would harm me whisper evil
 and mutter slander all the day long.
13 But I am like one who is deaf and hears not, *
 like one that is dumb, who does not open his mouth.
14 I have become like one who does not hear *
 and from whose mouth comes no retort.
15 For in you, Lord, have I put my trust *
 you will answer me, O Lord my God.
16 For I prayed, 'Let them not triumph over me, *
 those who exult over me when my foot slips.'
17 Truly, I am on the verge of falling *
 and my pain is ever with me.
18 I will confess my iniquity *
 and be sorry for my sin.
19 Those that are my enemies without any cause are mighty, *
 and those who hate me wrongfully are many in number.
20 Those who repay evil for good are against me, *
 because the good is what I seek.
21 Forsake me not, O Lord; *
 be not far from me, O my God.
22 Make haste to help me, *
 O Lord of my salvation.

 Glory . . .

Psalm 51

1 Have mercy on me, O God, in your great goodness; *
 according to the abundance of your compassion
 blot out my offences.
2 Wash me thoroughly from my wickedness *
 and cleanse me from my sin.

3 For I acknowledge my faults *
    and my sin is ever before me.
4 Against you only have I sinned *
    and done what is evil in your sight,
5 So that you are justified in your sentence *
    and righteous in your judgement.
6 I have been wicked even from my birth, *
    a sinner when my mother conceived me.
7 Behold, you desire truth deep within me *
    and shall make me understand wisdom
    in the depths of my heart.
8 Purge me with hyssop and I shall be clean; *
    wash me and I shall be whiter than snow.
9 Make me hear of joy and gladness, *
    that the bones you have broken may rejoice.
10 Turn your face from my sins *
    and blot out all my misdeeds.
11 Make me a clean heart, O God, *
    and renew a right spirit within me.
12 Cast me not away from your presence *
    and take not your holy spirit from me.
13 Give me again the joy of your salvation *
    and sustain me with your gracious spirit;
14 Then shall I teach your ways to the wicked *
    and sinners shall return to you.
15 Deliver me from my guilt, O God,
    the God of my salvation, *
    and my tongue shall sing of your righteousness.
16 O Lord, open my lips *
    and my mouth shall proclaim your praise.
17 For you desire no sacrifice, else I would give it; *
    for you take no delight in burnt offerings.
18 The sacrifice of God is a broken spirit; *
    a broken and contrite heart, O God, you will not despise.
19 O be favourable and gracious to Zion; *
    build up the walls of Jerusalem.
20 Then you will accept sacrifices offered in righteousness,
    the burnt offerings and oblations; *
    then shall they offer up bulls on your altar.

   Glory . . .

Psalm 102

1 O Lord, hear my prayer *
 and let my crying come before you.
2 Hide not your face from me *
 in the day of my distress.
3 Incline your ear to me; *
 when I call, make haste to answer me,
4 For my days are consumed in smoke *
 and my bones burn away as in a furnace.
5 My heart is smitten down and withered like grass, *
 so that I forget to eat my bread.
6 From the sound of my groaning *
 my bones cleave fast to my skin.
7 I am become like a vulture in the wilderness, *
 like an owl that haunts the ruins.
8 I keep watch and am become like a sparrow *
 solitary upon the housetop.
9 My enemies revile me all the day long, *
 and those who rage at me have sworn together against me.
10 I have eaten ashes for bread *
 and mingled my drink with weeping,
11 Because of your indignation and wrath, *
 for you have taken me up and cast me down.
12 My days fade away like a shadow, *
 and I am withered like grass.

13 But you, O Lord, shall endure for ever *
 and your name through all generations.
14 You will arise and have pity on Zion; *
 it is time to have mercy upon her;
 surely the time has come.
15 For your servants love her very stones *
 and feel compassion for her dust.
16 Then shall the nations fear your name, O Lord, *
 and all the kings of the earth your glory,
17 When the Lord has built up Zion *
 and shown himself in glory;
18 When he has turned to the prayer of the destitute *
 and has not despised their plea.
19 This shall be written for those that come after, *
 and a people yet unborn shall praise the Lord.

20 For he has looked down from his holy height; *
     from the heavens he beheld the earth,
21 That he might hear the sighings of the prisoner *
     and set free those condemned to die;
22 That the name of the Lord may be proclaimed in Zion *
     and his praises in Jerusalem,
23 When the peoples are gathered together *
     and their kingdoms also, to serve the Lord.

24 He has brought down my strength in my journey *
     and has shortened my days.
25 I pray, 'O my God; do not take me in the midst of my days; *
     your years endure throughout all generations.
26 'In the beginning you laid the foundations of the earth, *
     and the heavens are the work of your hands;
27 'They shall perish, but you will endure; *
     they all shall wear out like a garment.
28 'You change them like clothing, and they shall be changed; *
     but you are the same, and your years shall not fail.
29 'The children of your servants shall continue, *
     and their descendants shall be established in your sight.'

Glory . . .

Psalm 130

1 Out of the depths have I cried to you, O Lord;
    Lord, hear my voice; *
    let your ears consider well the voice of my supplication.
2 If you, Lord, were to mark what is done amiss, *
    O Lord, who could stand?
3 But there is forgiveness with you, *
    so that you shall be feared.
4 I wait for the Lord; my soul waits for him; *
    in his word is my hope.
5 My soul waits for the Lord,
    more than the night-watch for the morning, *
    more than the night-watch for the morning.

6 O Israel, wait for the Lord, *
    for with the Lord there is mercy;

7 With him is plenteous redemption *
    and he shall redeem Israel from all their sins.

Glory . . .

Psalm 143

1 Hear my prayer, O Lord,
    and in your faithfulness give ear to my supplications; *
    answer me in your righteousness.
2 Enter not into judgement with your servant, *
    for in your sight shall no one living be justified.
3 For the enemy has pursued me,
    crushing my life to the ground, *
    making me sit in darkness like those long dead.
4 My spirit faints within me; *
    my heart within me is desolate.
5 I remember the time past; I muse upon all your deeds; *
    I consider the works of your hands.
6 I stretch out my hands to you; *
    my soul gasps for you like a thirsty land.
7 O Lord, make haste to answer me; my spirit fails me; *
    hide not your face from me
    lest I be like those who go down to the Pit.
8 Let me hear of your loving-kindness in the morning,
    for in you I put my trust; *
    show me the way that I should walk in,
    for I lift up my soul to you.
9 Deliver me, O Lord, from my enemies, *
    for I flee to you for refuge.
10 Teach me to do what pleases you, for you are my God; *
    let your kindly spirit lead me on a level path.
11 Revive me, O Lord, for your name's sake; *
    for your righteousness' sake, bring me out of trouble.
12 In your faithfulness, slay my enemies,
    and destroy all the adversaries of my soul, *
    for truly I am your servant.

Glory . . .

Passiontide

Propers and Readings

Office Hymn

Vexilla regis prodeunt

The royal banners forward go,
The cross shines forth in mystic glow;
Where he in flesh, our flesh who made,
Our sentence bore, our ransom paid.

Where deep for us the spear was dyed,
Life's torrent rushing from his side,
To wash us in that precious flood,
Where mingled water flowed, and Blood.

Fulfilled is all that David told
In true prophetic song of old,
Amid the nations, God saith he
Hath reigned and triumphed from the tree.

O tree of beauty, tree of light,
O tree with royal purple dight,
Elect on whose triumphal breast
Those holy limbs should find their rest.

On whose dear arms, so widely flung,
The weight of this world's ransom hung,
The price which none but he could pay,
And spoil the spoiler of his prey.

O cross, our one reliance, hail!
So may this Passiontide avail
To give fresh merit to the saint
And pardon to the penitent.

To thee, eternal Three in One,
Let homage meet by all be done;
As by thy cross thou dost restore,
Preserve and govern evermore.

LM
Venantius Fortunatus
tr. John Mason Neale
Hymns for Prayer and Praise 145

Psalms and Canticles

From LENT 5 until the Saturday before Holy Week: use Week 1 psalmody.

HOLY WEEK: use Week 2 psalmody.

Easter Triduum

MAUNDY THURSDAY

Evening Prayer	*(for those who do not attend the Evening Mass)*
	72
	A Song of the Kingdom of our God
	(Canticle 42) see page 588.
Night Prayer	*Use Sunday Night Prayer II.*

GOOD FRIDAY

Morning Prayer	51
	A Prayer of Habakkuk
	(Canticle 24) see page 575.
	147:13–21
Evening Prayer	*(for those who do not attend the Afternoon Liturgy)*
	116
	143
	The Song of Christ's Glory
	(Canticle 36) see page 584.
Night Prayer	*Use Sunday Night Prayer II*

HOLY SATURDAY

Morning Prayer	64
	A Song of the Living
	(Canticle 11) see page 564.
	150
Evening Prayer	116
	143
	The Song of Christ's Glory
	(Canticle 36) see page 584.
Night Prayer	*(for those who do not attend the Easter Vigil)*
	Use Sunday Night Prayer II.

Alternative Canticle at Morning Prayer

A Song of Lamentation *(Canticle 22) – see page 573.*

Short Readings

I was led like a gentle lamb led to the slaughter. And I did not know it was against me that they devised schemes, saying, 'Let us destroy the tree with its fruit, let us cut him off from the land of the living, so that his name will no longer be remembered.'

Jeremiah 11:19

or

Since we are justified by faith, we have peace with God through our Lord Jesus Christ, through whom we have obtained access to this grace in which we stand; and we boast of our hope in sharing the glory of God.

Romans 5:1–2

or

Christ humbled himself and became obedient unto death, even death on a cross. Therefore God has highly exalted him and bestowed on him the name which is above every name.

Philippians 2:8–9 (RSV)

or

In the days of his flesh, Jesus offered up prayers and supplications, with loud cries and tears, to the one who was able to save him from death, and he was heard because of his reverent submission. Although he was a Son, he learned obedience through what he suffered; and having been made perfect, he became the source of eternal salvation for all who obey him.

Hebrews 5:7–9

Long Readings
FIFTH SUNDAY OF LENT

Year A	*Year B*	*Year C*
Ezekiel 37:1–14	Jeremiah 31:31–34	Isaiah 43:16–21
Romans 8:6–11	Hebrews 5:5–10	Philippians 3:4b-14
John 11:1–45	John 12:20–33	John 12:1–8

following FIFTH SUNDAY OF LENT

M	Susanna 1–9, 15–17, 19–30, 33–62 or 41–62	John 8:1–11 *or* John 8:12–20
T	Numbers 21:4–9	John 8:21–30
W	Daniel 3:14–20, 24–25, 28	John 8:31–42
Th	Genesis 17:3–9	John 8:51–end
F	Jeremiah 20:10–13	John 10:31–end
S	Ezekiel 37:21–end	John 11:45–end

PALM SUNDAY

Liturgy of the Palms:

Year A	*Year B*	*Year C*
Matthew 21:1–11	Mark 11:1–11 *or* John 12:12–16	Luke 19:28–40

Mass Readings:

Year A	*Year B*	*Year C*
Isaiah 50:4–9a	Isaiah 50:4–9a	Isaiah 50:4–9a
Philippians 2:5–11	Philippians 2:5–11	Philippians 2:5–11
Matthew 26:14–27:11–54 *or* 27:11–54	Mark 14:1–15:47 *or* 15:1–39[40–47]	Luke 22:14–23:56 *or* 23:1–49

In **HOLY WEEK**

M   Isaiah 42:1–7   John 12:1–11
T   Isaiah 49:1–6[7]   John 12:20–36
                                   or John 13:21–33, 36–38
W Isaiah 50:4–9   John 13:21–32
                                   or Matthew 26:14–25

MAUNDY THURSDAY

Exodus 12:1–4[5–10]
1 Corinthians 11:23–26
John 13:1–17, 31b-35

GOOD FRIDAY

Isaiah 52:13–53:12
Hebrews 10:16–25
or 4:14–16; 5:7–9
John 18:1–19:42

EASTER VIGIL

At least three Old Testament readings are used, including the reading from Exodus.

Old Testament
Genesis 1:1–2:4a
Genesis 7:1–5, 11–18; 8:6–18; 9:8–13
Genesis 22:1–18
Exodus 14:10–31; 15:20–21
Isaiah 55:1–11
Baruch 3:9–15, 32–4:4
Ezekiel 36:24–28
Ezekiel 37:1–14
Zephaniah 3:14–20

Epistle
Romans 6:3–11

Gospel

Year A	*Year B*	*Year C*
Matthew 28:1–10	Mark 16:1–8	Luke 24:1–12

Responsory (except during the Easter Triduum)

R/ To you, O Lord, I lift up my soul;
O my God, in you I trust.
R/ To you, O Lord, I lift up my soul;
O my God, in you I trust.
V/ You are the God of my salvation,
in you I hope all the day long.
R/ O my God, in you I trust.
V/ Glory . . . Holy Spirit.
R/ To you, O Lord, I lift up my soul;
O my God, in you I trust.

or

R/ He shall free me from the snare of the hunter,
R/ He shall free me from the snare of the hunter,
V/ And from the deadly curse.
R/ He shall free me from the snare of the hunter,
V/ Glory . . . Holy Spirit.
R/ He shall free me from the snare of the hunter.

Responsory (Easter Triduum)

Maundy Thursday, in place of the responsory:

Christ humbled himself for us, and, in obedience, accepted death.

Good Friday, in place of the responsory:

Christ humbled himself for us, and, in obedience, accepted death, even death on a cross.

Holy Saturday, in place of the responsory:

Christ humbled himself for us, and, in obedience, accepted death, even death on a cross.
Therefore God raised him to the heights and gave him the name which is above all other names.

Antiphons/Refrains and Texts for Meditation

If any want to become my followers, let them deny themselves and take up their cross and follow me.

Matthew 16:24

Just as Moses lifted up the serpent in the wilderness, so must the Son of Man be lifted up, that whoever believes in him may have eternal life.

John 3:14–15

The word of the cross is folly to those who are perishing, but to us who are being saved, it is the power of God.

1 Corinthians 1:18 (RSV)

Especially suitable for Palm Sunday

Hosanna to the Son of David! Blessed is the one who comes in the name of the Lord! Hosanna in the highest heaven!

Matthew 21:9

Especially suitable for Maundy Thursday

I give you a new commandment that you love one another as I have loved you.

John 13:34

Especially suitable for Good Friday

Christ himself bore our sins in his body on the tree, that we might die to sin and live to righteousness. By his wounds you have been healed.

1 Peter 2:24 (RSV)

Especially suitable for Easter Eve

We were buried with Christ by baptism into death, so that we might no longer be enslaved to sin.

Romans 6:4, 6 (RSV)

Collect

Most merciful God,
who by the death and resurrection of your Son Jesus Christ
delivered and saved the world:
grant that by faith in him who suffered on the cross
we may triumph in the power of his victory;
through Jesus Christ your Son our Lord,
who is alive and reigns with you,
in the unity of the Holy Spirit,
one God, now and for ever.

Fifth Sunday of Lent
Common Worship (1)

Other Prayers

We adore thee, O Christ, and we bless thee, because by thy holy Cross thou hast redeemed the world. O Saviour of the world: who by thy Cross and precious Blood hast redeemed us, save us and help us, we humbly beseech thee, O Lord.

1549 Prayer Book

O Lord Jesus Christ, Son of the living God, we pray thee to set thy passion, cross and death between thy judgement and our souls, now and in the hour of our death. Vouchsafe to grant mercy and grace to the living, rest to the dead, to thy holy Church peace and concord, and to us sinners everlasting life and glory; for thou art alive and reignest, with the Father and the Holy Spirit, one God for ever and ever.

Hours of the BVM before 14th cent.

O Jesus, we devoutly embrace that honoured cross where thou didst love us even unto death. In that death we place all our confidence. Henceforth let us live only for thee; and in dying for thee let us die loving thee, and in thy sacred arms.

Richard Challoner
Stations of the Cross

O Jesus, our adorable Saviour, behold us prostrate at thy feet, imploring thy mercy for ourselves and for the souls of all the faithful departed. Vouchsafe to apply to us the infinite merits of thy Passion, on which we are about to meditate. Grant that while we trace this path of sighs and tears, our hearts may be so touched with contrition and repentance that we may be ready to embrace with joy all the crosses and sufferings and humiliations of this our life and pilgrimage.

Richard Challoner
Stations of the Cross

Make me cheerful under every cross, for love of thy cross; take from me all which displeases thee, or hinders thy love in me, that I may deeply love thee. Melt me with thy love, that I may be all love, and with my whole being love thee.

Edward Bouverie Pusey

Lord God, our heavenly Father, regard, we pray, with your divine pity the pains of all your children; and grant that the passion of our Lord and his infinite love may make fruitful for good the tribulations of the innocent, the sufferings of the sick, and the sorrows of the bereaved; through him who suffered in our flesh and died for our sake, your Son our Saviour Jesus Christ our Lord.

For use during the 1914–1918 War* (1b)

Lord Jesus Christ,
you have taught us
that what we do for the least of our brothers and sisters
we do also for you:
give us the will to be the servant of others
as you were the servant of all,
and gave up your life and died for us,
but are alive and reign, now and for ever.

Fifth Sunday of Lent
(Post-Communion)
Common Worship (1)

Stations of the Cross

The Stations of the Cross is a devotion dating from the late Middle Ages, and encouraged by the Franciscans, yet it is only in the last two or three hundred years that the number and sequence of stations have become established. Nowadays it has become common for a fifteenth station – the Resurrection – to be added. Occasionally those stations not explicitly derived from the Passion story in the Gospels are omitted.

A variety of different approaches to the Stations of the Cross has developed. The Stations of the Cross may be a public service or a personal devotion. The series may be used as a whole on one occasion or one station may be used each day for meditation. Pictures or sculptures mounted on the walls of the church allow one to move from station to station, for public and personal use, but the devotion also works well at home, perhaps with the assistance of pictures.

The method of Saint Alphonsus Liguori

The traditional method of Saint Alphonsus Liguori retains its appeal: for Saint Alphonsus, those who stand accused are not the historical participants in the drama – the religious leaders of the day and the soldiers – but the individual sinner. This method is a walk with Jesus and Mary. As we contemplate the physical suffering of Jesus, we identify with the mental pain his Mother suffered, and are reminded of Simeon's warning to Mary:

A sword will pierce your own soul too. (Luke 2:35)

The pain of the Mother watching her Son go to his death is the theme of the hymn which is often used for the procession, Stabat Mater dolorosa.

I Jesus is condemned to death

Kneel and say:

We adore you, O Christ and we bless you.
Because by your holy cross you have redeemed the world.

Then stand and think about the meaning of the Station.

Then kneel for an act of sorrow and prayer, perhaps for a particular intention.

I love you Jesus, my Love, above all things.
I repent with my whole heart for having offended you.

Never permit me to separate myself from you again.
Grant that I may love you always
then do with me what you please.

Our Father.

Hail Mary.

Glory . . .

Then a verse of the Stabat Mater *may be sung:*

At the Cross her station keeping,
Stood the mournful Mother weeping,
Close to Jesus at the last.

II Jesus accepts the cross

Kneel and say:

We adore you, O Christ and we bless you.
Because by your holy cross you have redeemed the world.

Then stand and think about the meaning of the Station.

Then kneel for an act of sorrow and prayer, perhaps for a particular intention.

I love you Jesus, my Love, above all things.
I repent with my whole heart for having offended you.
Never permit me to separate myself from you again.
Grant that I may love you always
then do with me what you please.

Our Father.

Hail Mary.

Glory . . .

Then a verse of the Stabat Mater *may be sung:*

Through her soul, of joy bereaved,
Bowed with anguish, deeply grieved,
Now at length the sword hath passed.

III Jesus falls for the first time

Kneel and say:

We adore you, O Christ and we bless you.
Because by your holy cross you have redeemed the world.

Then stand and think about the meaning of the Station.

Then kneel for an act of sorrow and prayer, perhaps for a particular intention.

I love you Jesus, my Love, above all things.
I repent with my whole heart for having offended you.
Never permit me to separate myself from you again.
Grant that I may love you always
then do with me what you please.

Our Father.

Hail Mary.

Glory . . .

Then a verse of the Stabat Mater *may be sung:*

O that blessed one, grief-laden,
Blessed Mother, blessed Maiden,
Mother of the all-holy One;

IV Jesus meets his Mother

Kneel and say:

We adore you, O Christ and we bless you.
Because by your holy cross you have redeemed the world.

Then stand and think about the meaning of the Station.

Then kneel for an act of sorrow and prayer, perhaps for a particular intention.

I love you Jesus, my Love, above all things.
I repent with my whole heart for having offended you.
Never permit me to separate myself from you again.
Grant that I may love you always
then do with me what you please.

Our Father.

Hail Mary.

Glory . . .

Then a verse of the Stabat Mater *may be sung:*

O that silent, ceaseless mourning,
O those dim eyes, never turning
From that wondrous, suffering Son.

V Simon Cyrene is made to carry the cross

Kneel and say:

We adore you, O Christ and we bless you.
Because by your holy cross you have redeemed the world.

Then stand and think about the meaning of the Station.

Then kneel for an act of sorrow and prayer, perhaps for a particular intention.

I love you Jesus, my Love, above all things.
I repent with my whole heart for having offended you.
Never permit me to separate myself from you again.
Grant that I may love you always
then do with me what you please.

Our Father.

Hail Mary.

Glory . . .

Then a verse of the Stabat Mater *may be sung:*

Who on Christ's dear Mother gazing,
In her trouble so amazing,
Born of woman, would not weep?

VI Veronica wipes the face of Jesus

Kneel and say:

We adore you, O Christ and we bless you.
Because by your holy cross you have redeemed the world.

Then stand and think about the meaning of the Station.

Then kneel for an act of sorrow and prayer, perhaps for a particular intention.

I love you Jesus, my Love, above all things.
I repent with my whole heart for having offended you.
Never permit me to separate myself from you again.
Grant that I may love you always
then do with me what you please.

Our Father.

Hail Mary.

Glory . . .

Then a verse of the Stabat Mater *may be sung:*

Who on Christ's dear Mother thinking,
Such a cup of sorrow drinking,
Would not share her sorrow deep?

VII *Jesus falls a second time*

Kneel and say:

We adore you, O Christ and we bless you.
Because by your holy cross you have redeemed the world.

Then stand and think about the meaning of the Station.

Then kneel for an act of sorrow and prayer, perhaps for a particular intention.

I love you Jesus, my Love, above all things.
I repent with my whole heart for having offended you.
Never permit me to separate myself from you again.
Grant that I may love you always
then do with me what you please.

Our Father.

Hail Mary.

Glory . . .

Then a verse of the Stabat Mater *may be sung:*

For his people's sins, in anguish,
There she saw the victim languish,
Bleed in torments, bleed and die.

VIII The Women of Jerusalem weep for Jesus

Kneel and say:

We adore you, O Christ and we bless you.
Because by your holy cross you have redeemed the world.

Then stand and think about the meaning of the Station.

Then kneel for an act of sorrow and prayer, perhaps for a particular intention.

I love you Jesus, my Love, above all things.
I repent with my whole heart for having offended you.
Never permit me to separate myself from you again.
Grant that I may love you always
then do with me what you please.

Our Father.

Hail Mary.

Glory . . .

Then a verse of the Stabat Mater *may be sung:*

Saw the Lord's anointed taken;
Saw her child in death forsaken;
Heard his last expiring cry.

IX Jesus falls for a third time

Kneel and say:

We adore you, O Christ and we bless you.
Because by your holy cross you have redeemed the world.

Then stand and think about the meaning of the Station.

Then kneel for an act of sorrow and prayer, perhaps for a particular intention.

I love you Jesus, my Love, above all things.
I repent with my whole heart for having offended you.
Never permit me to separate myself from you again.
Grant that I may love you always
then do with me what you please.

Our Father.

Hail Mary.

Glory . . .

Then a verse of the Stabat Mater *may be sung:*

In the passion of my Maker,
Be my sinful soul partaker,
May I bear with her my part;

X Jesus is stripped of his garments

Kneel and say:

We adore you, O Christ and we bless you.
Because by your holy cross you have redeemed the world.

Then stand and think about the meaning of the Station.

Then kneel for an act of sorrow and prayer, perhaps for a particular intention.

I love you Jesus, my Love, above all things.
I repent with my whole heart for having offended you.
Never permit me to separate myself from you again.
Grant that I may love you always
then do with me what you please.

Our Father.

Hail Mary.

Glory . . .

Then a verse of the Stabat Mater *may be sung:*

Of his Passion bear the token,
In a spirit bowed and broken
Bear his death within my heart.

XI Jesus is nailed to the cross

Kneel and say:

We adore you, O Christ and we bless you.
Because by your holy cross you have redeemed the world.

Then stand and think about the meaning of the Station.

Then kneel for an act of sorrow and prayer, perhaps for a particular intention.

I love you Jesus, my Love, above all things.
I repent with my whole heart for having offended you.
Never permit me to separate myself from you again.
Grant that I may love you always
then do with me what you please.

Our Father.

Hail Mary.

Glory . . .

Then a verse of the Stabat Mater *may be sung:*

May his wounds both wound and heal me,
He enkindle, cleanse, anneal me,
Be his Cross my hope and stay.

XII Jesus dies on the cross

Kneel and say:

We adore you, O Christ and we bless you.
Because by your holy cross you have redeemed the world.

Then stand and think about the meaning of the Station.

Then kneel for an act of sorrow and prayer, perhaps for a particular intention.

I love you Jesus, my Love, above all things.
I repent with my whole heart for having offended you.
Never permit me to separate myself from you again.
Grant that I may love you always
then do with me what you please.

Our Father.

Hail Mary.

Glory . . .

Then a verse of the Stabat Mater *may be sung:*

May he, when the mountains quiver,
From that flame which burns for ever
Shield me on the judgement day.

XIII *The body of Jesus is taken down from the cross*

Kneel and say:

We adore you, O Christ and we bless you.
Because by your holy cross you have redeemed the world.

Then stand and think about the meaning of the Station.

Then kneel for an act of sorrow and prayer, perhaps for a particular intention.

I love you Jesus, my Love, above all things.
I repent with my whole heart for having offended you.
Never permit me to separate myself from you again.
Grant that I may love you always
then do with me what you please.

Our Father.

Hail Mary.

Glory . . .

Then a verse of the Stabat Mater *may be sung:*

Jesu, may thy Cross defend me,
And thy saving death befriend me,
Cherished by thy deathless grace:

XIV *The body of Jesus is laid in the tomb*

Kneel and say:

We adore you, O Christ and we bless you.
Because by your holy cross you have redeemed the world.

Then stand and think about the meaning of the Station.

Then kneel for an act of sorrow and prayer, perhaps for a particular intention.

I love you Jesus, my Love, above all things.
I repent with my whole heart for having offended you.

Never permit me to separate myself from you again.
Grant that I may love you always
then do with me what you please.

Our Father.

Hail Mary.

Glory . . .

Then a verse of the Stabat Mater *may be sung:*

When to dust my dust returneth,
Grant a soul that to thee yearneth
In thy Paradise a place.

Stabat Mater
Jacopone da Todi?
tr. Bishop Mant,
Aubrey de Vere
and Others
English Hymnal 115

XV Jesus is raised from the dead

Remain standing and say:

We adore you, O Christ and we bless you.
Because by your holy cross you have redeemed the world.

Our Father.

Hail Mary.

Glory . . .

From Psalm 118

1 Open to me the gates of righteousness, *
   that I may enter and give thanks to the Lord.
2 This is the gate of the Lord; *
   the righteous shall enter through it.
3 I will give thanks to you, for you have answered me *
   and have become my salvation.
4 The stone which the builders rejected *
   has become the chief cornerstone.

5 Come, O Lord, and save us we pray. *
   Come, Lord, send us now prosperity.
6 Blessed is he who comes in the name of the Lord; *
   we bless you from the house of the Lord.

Psalm 118:19–22,25–26

A Procession of Scripture and Prayers

At each station there is a reading, or perhaps two. A choice for each station is suggested below. Readings from the Old Testament, the Psalms, the Epistles and the Gospels provide four distinct routes as well as a variety of combinations. Possible uses include praying at home and a quiet walk through the Stations of the Cross, in a church or out of doors.

After the reading a prayer is said and one is suggested below for each station. Then the verse of the Stabat Mater, *or of another suitable hymn is sung, whilst moving to the next station.*

I Jesus is condemned to death

Wisdom 2:12–20

Psalmody

1 False witnesses rose up against me; *
   they charged me with things I knew not.
2 They rewarded me evil for good, *
   to the desolation of my soul.
3 I behaved as one who mourns for his mother, *
   bowed down and brought very low.
4 But when I stumbled, they gathered in delight;
   they gathered together against me; *
   as if they were strangers I did not know
   they tore at me without ceasing.

Psalm 35:11–12,15–16

Philippians 2:5–11

Matthew 27:22–31
or *John 19:5–16a*

Jesus, Master,
King of the Jews,
Lord of the universe:
though you were condemned
to suffer and to die,
do not condemn us
when you come to be our judge.

AB (8)

II Jesus accepts the cross

Isaiah 53:3–5

Psalmody

1 I am forgotten like one that is dead, out of mind; *
    I have become like a broken vessel.
2 For I have heard the whispering of the crowd;
    fear is on every side; *
    they scheme together against me,
    and plot to take my life.
3 But my trust is in you, O Lord. *
    I have said, 'You are my God.
4 'My times are in your hand; *
    deliver me from the hand of my enemies,
    and save me for your mercy's sake.'

Psalm 31:12–15

1 Corinthians 1:18,23–25

Mark 8:34–35
or *John 19:16b-17*

Despised and rejected,
a man of sorrows:
you accepted the cross
to bear our iniquity.
Teach us, Lord, to deny ourselves
and, taking up the cross,
find you for all eternity.

AB (8)

III Jesus falls for the first time

Genesis 3:1–7

Psalmody

1 When I was in trouble I called to the Lord; *
    I called to the Lord and he answered me.
2 Deliver me, O Lord, from lying lips *
    and from a deceitful tongue.
3 My soul has dwelt too long *
    with enemies of peace.
4 I am for making peace, *
    but when I speak of it, they make ready for war.

Psalm 120:1–2, 6–7

Romans 7:18–24

Mark 12:1b-8
or *John 12:23–25*

Lord,
I long for what is right
but I cannot do it
for sin keeps dragging me down.
Raise me up each time I fall
and hide my life in yours,
who are alive at the right hand of the Father.

AB (8)

IV Jesus meets his Mother

1 Samuel 2:1–10

Psalmody

1 O Lord, my heart is not proud; *
    my eyes are not raised in haughty looks.
2 I do not occupy myself with great matters, *
    with things that are too high for me.
3 But I have quieted and stilled my soul,
    like a weaned child on its mother's breast; *
    so my soul is quieted within me.

    4 O Israel, trust in the Lord, *
          from this time forth for evermore.

Psalm 131

1 John 4:7–9

Luke 2:33–35
or *John 19:25–27*

Lord Jesus Christ,
your mother's soul was pierced by a sword,
as Simeon foretold.
Comfort those who stand by helpless,
strengthen and rescue the victims of terror;
give hope and solace to orphans and widows,
and, to all in distress, give healing and succour,
for you are the Saviour of all who seek you.

AB (8)

V Simon Cyrene is made to carry the cross

Isaiah 53:6–8

Psalmody

    1 My footsteps hold fast in the ways of your commandments; *
          my feet have not stumbled in your paths.
    2 I call upon you, O God, for you will answer me; *
          incline your ear to me, and listen to my words.
    3 Show me your marvellous loving-kindness, *
          O Saviour of those who take refuge at your right hand
          from those who rise up against them.
    4 Keep me as the apple of your eye; *
          hide me under the shadow of your wings.

Psalm 17:5–8

Galatians 6:2–10

Matthew 27:32
or *John 8:12*

Help us, good Lord,
to bear one another's burdens
as Simon Cyrene bore the burden of your cross.
May we be tireless in doing good
and eager to work for others.
As we take up the cross and follow you
may we learn that your burden is light.

AB (8)

VI Veronica wipes the face of Jesus

Ecclesiasticus 7:32–36

Psalmody

1 In you, O Lord, do I seek refuge; *
    let me never be put to shame.
2 Be for me a stronghold to which I may ever resort; *
    send out to save me, for you are my rock and my fortress.
3 For you are my hope, O Lord God, *
    my confidence, even from my youth.
4 Upon you have I leaned from my birth,
    when you drew me from my mother's womb; *
    my praise shall be always of you.

Psalm 71:1,3,5–6

2 Corinthians 1:3–5

Matthew 25:34–40
or *John 12:1–3*

Lord, I seek your face,
and find its imprint
in the loving actions of those I meet.
Transfigure me by your Spirit
that others may see you
in my living and in all that I do
for your name's sake.

AB (8)

VII Jesus falls a second time

Lamentations 1:13–14

Psalmody

1 Truly, God is loving to Israel, *
    to those who are pure in heart.
2 Nevertheless, my feet were almost gone; *
    my steps had well-nigh slipped.
3 Yet I am always with you; *
    you hold me by my right hand.
4 You will guide me with your counsel *
    and afterwards receive me with glory.

Psalm 73:1–2,23–24

Hebrews 13:12–16

Mark 12:10–11
or *John 12:26–29*

The good that I seek remains undone.
The wrong that I loathe I find myself doing.
Keep my feet from falling, Lord,
and guard my soul from sinning.
May I walk the way of sorrow
with so much love and perseverance
that I share in the wonder of your kingdom.

AB (8)

VIII The Women of Jerusalem weep for Jesus

Lamentations 2:8–15

Psalmody

1 O God, make speed to save me; *
    O Lord, make haste to help me.
2 Let those who seek my life
    be put to shame and confusion; *
    let them be turned back and disgraced
    who wish me evil.

3 Let those who mock and deride me *
       turn back because of their shame.
  4 But let all who seek you rejoice and be glad in you; *
       let those who love your salvation say always,
       'Great is the Lord!'

Psalm 70:1–4

1 Peter 4:13–16

Luke 23:27–32
or *John 16:21–22*

Deepen my understanding
and enlarge my vision, Lord.
Seeing the cares of others
and the turmoil of their lives,
may I weep with the anguished
and support the afflicted,
in trouble and in danger.

AB (8)

IX Jesus falls for a third time

Isaiah 53:10–12

Psalmody

  1 I am feeble and utterly crushed; *
       I roar aloud because of the disquiet of my heart.
  2 O Lord, you know all my desires *
       and my sighing is not hidden from you.
  3 My heart is pounding, my strength has failed me; *
       the light of my eyes is gone from me.
  4 My friends and companions stand apart from my affliction: *
       my neighbours stand afar off.

Psalm 38:8–12

2 Corinthians 12:9–10

Luke 21:5–6
or *John 15:18–25*

When my pride takes a tumble
and my confidence falters,
remind me, loving Saviour,
that, having emptied yourself
of every vestige of glory,
you took the form of a slave,
and hung for us on a gibbet.

AB (8)

X Jesus is stripped of his garments

Isaiah 63:1–5

Psalmody

1 My God, my God, why have you forsaken me, *
   and are so far from my salvation,
   from the words of my distress?
2 They gape upon me with their mouths, *
   as it were a ramping and a roaring lion.
3 I am poured out like water;
   all my bones are out of joint; *
   my heart has become like wax
   melting in the depths of my body.
4 My mouth is dried up like a potsherd;
   my tongue cleaves to my gums; *
   you have laid me in the dust of death.

Psalm 22:1,13–15

Colossians 3:5–14

Mark 9:2–4
or *John 19:23–24*

Lord, they stripped away your clothes
and threw dice for your robe:
strip away our false pride,
our glitter, our glory.
Clothe us in meekness,
with spiritual jewels,
let justice serve as our robe.

AB (8)

XI Jesus is nailed to the cross

Numbers 21:6–9

Psalmody

1 All who see me laugh me to scorn; *
   they curl their lips and wag their heads, saying,
2 'He trusted in the Lord; let him deliver him; *
   let him deliver him, if he delights in him.'
3 They pierce my hands and my feet.
   I can count all my bones; *
   they stand staring and looking upon me.
4 They divide my garments among them; *
   they cast lots for my clothing.

Psalm 22:7–8, 16b-18

Romans 8:31b-39

Mark 15:25–33
or *John 3:14–21*

Fearing hardship in desert places,
we grumble and enlarge upon our sorrows.
We forget that you're our Saviour,
the deeds you have done for us these many years.
As you are lifted up for us,
like the bronze serpent in the wilderness,
teach us to believe in you and so find healing.

AB (8)

XII Jesus dies on the cross

Isaiah 52:13–53:2

Psalmody

1 My soul cleaves to the dust; *
   O give me life according to your word.
2 I have acknowledged my ways and you have answered me; *
   O teach me your statutes.

3 Make me understand the way of your commandments, *
   and so shall I meditate on your wondrous works.
4 My soul melts away in tears of sorrow; *
   raise me up according to your word.

Psalm 119:25–28

2 Corinthians 5:1–8

Matthew 27:45–54
or *John 19:28–30*

The centurion saw the earthquake
and called you 'Son of God'.
We wonder, as we ponder
the example of your patience.
We marvel at your obedience
and resolve to worship you.

AB (8)

XIII The body of Jesus is taken down from the cross

Zechariah 12:10

Psalmody

1 By the waters of Babylon we sat down and wept, *
   when we remembered Zion.
2 As for our lyres, we hung them up *
   on the willows that grow in that land.
3 For there our captors asked for a song,
   our tormentors called for mirth: *
   'Sing us one of the songs of Zion.'
4 How shall we sing the Lord's song *
   in a strange land?

Psalm 137:1–4

Romans 8:10–11

Matthew 27:57–58
or *John 19:31–37*

Lord Jesus Christ,
as your mother beheld you,
lying dead upon her lap,
so may you – and she –
behold all who weep,
all who are broken,
all who are lost,
all for whom you gave up your life.

AB (8)

XIV The body of Jesus is laid in the tomb

Isaiah 53:9–10

Psalmody

1 I am counted as one gone down to the Pit; *
   I am like one that has no strength.
2 Lost among the dead, *
   like the slain who lie in the grave.
3 Whom you remember no more, *
   for they are cut off from your hand.
4 You have laid me in the lowest pit, *
   in a place of darkness in the abyss.

Psalm 88:1–5

Romans 6:3–11

Matthew 27:59–66
or *John 19:38–42*

Though your body was laid in a tomb,
you did not rest, Lord of the Sabbath.
Breaking open hell,
you freed the dead from prison.
Release us, and all who have died in you,
from the dungeon of sin
and the torment of separation.

AB (8)

XV Jesus is raised from the dead

Song of Solomon 2:10–13

Psalmody

1 The Lord is my strength and my song, *
 and he has become my salvation.
2 Joyful shouts of salvation *
 sound from the tents of the righteous *
3 'The right hand of the Lord does mighty deeds;
 the right hand of the Lord raises up; *
 the right hand of the Lord does mighty deeds.'
4 I shall not die, but live *
 and declare the works of the Lord.

Psalm 118:14–17

Acts 4:8–12

Matthew 28:1–9
or *John 20:1–10*

We praise and we bless you, Lord God,
for raising your Son in high triumph.
Raise us also to life in him,
that we may seek what is above,
and set our affections on the imperishable,
your kingdom and your justice,
the food which endures to eternal life.

AB (8)

EASTER

Propers and Readings

Alternative Invitatory at Morning Prayer

The Easter Anthems (Canticle 34) – see page 583.

Office Hymn

Ad cenam Agni providi

Egypt is far behind, the Red Sea crossed,
And newly clothed in robes of gleaming white
We come to share the supper of the Lamb,
And sing to Christ, our shepherd and our king.

Burnt on the altar of the cross for us,
His body there became our daily food:
We drink the blood poured out on our behalf,
And by that food we live our life in God.

Signed with the saving blood we stand secure,
While God's avenging angel passes by;
From Pharaoh's galling yoke set free at last
We eat the paschal lamb with joyous hearts.

Christ is the paschal Lamb we eat today,
Whose sacrifice fulfils the ancient rite:
Unleavened bread of faithfulness and truth
Is now the offering of his flesh and blood.

Worthy the victim for so great an act:
The powers of hell lie broken in their pride,
The people once in bondage now goes free,
And life returns where death had ruled supreme.

Christ with the dawn arises from the tomb,
A victor, he returns from death's domain,
He binds the evil one with chains of bronze,
And opens wide the gates of Paradise.

Maker of all, we beg of you to grant
That during this our joyous paschal time
You guard from every sickness and from death
The people that your Son has now redeemed.

Glory is yours, O Christ our Lord and God,
Arisen from the dead to be our life,
With Father and the Holy Spirit one
From age to age beyond the bounds of time.

Saint Niceta of Remesiana (35)
Hymns for Prayer and Praise 157

Psalms and Canticles

EASTER DAY and throughout the EASTER OCTAVE (including Low Sunday): Sunday Week 1.

From the Monday after the Second Sunday of Easter, use Week 2 etc.

Alternative Canticle at Morning Prayer

The Song of Moses and Miriam *(Canticle 1) – see page 557.*

Short Readings

God raised Jesus on the third day and allowed him to appear, not to all the people but to us who were chosen by God as witnesses, and who ate and drank with him after he rose from the dead. He commanded us to preach to the people and to testify that he is the one ordained by God as judge of the living and the dead. All the prophets testify about him that everyone who believes in him receives forgiveness of sins through his name.

Acts 10:40–43

or

Christ our passover lamb has been sacrificed for us. Let us therefore rejoice by putting away all malice and evil and confessing our sins with a sincere and true heart.

cf. 1 Corinthians 5:7–8

or

If you have been raised with Christ, seek the things that are above, where Christ is, seated at the right hand of God. Set your minds on things that are above, not on things that are on earth, for you have died, and your life is hidden with Christ in God. When Christ who is your life is revealed, then you also will be revealed with him in glory.

Colossians 3:1–4

or

May the God of peace, who brought back from the dead our Lord Jesus, the great shepherd of the sheep, by the blood of the eternal covenant, make you complete in everything good so that you may do his will, working among us that which is pleasing in his sight, through Jesus Christ; to whom be the glory for ever and ever. Amen.

Hebrews 13:20–21

Long Readings

EASTER DAY

Year A	Year B	Year C
Acts 10:34–43	Acts 10:34–43	Acts 10:34–43
Colossians 3:1–4	1 Corinthians 15:1–11	1 Corinthians 15:19–26
Matthew 28:1–10	Mark 13:24–37	Luke 21:25–36

EASTER WEEK

M	Acts 2:14, 22–32	Matthew 28:8–15
T	Acts 2:36–41	John 20:11–18
W	Acts 3:1–10	Luke 24:13–35
Th	Acts 3:11–end	Luke 24:35–48
F	Acts 4:1–12	John 21:1–14
S	Acts 4:13–21	Mark 16: 9–15

SECOND SUNDAY OF EASTER

Year A	Year B	Year C
Acts 2:14a, 22–32	Acts 4:32–35	Acts 5:27–32
1 Peter 1:3–9	1 John 1:1–2:2	Revelation 1:4–8
John 20:19–31	John 20:19–31	John 20:19–31

following **SECOND SUNDAY OF EASTER**

M	Acts 4:23–31	John 3:1–8
T	Acts 4: 32–end	John 3:7–15
W	Acts 5:17–26	John 3:16–21
Th	Acts 5:27–33	John 3:31–end
F	Acts 5:34–end	John 6:1–15
S	Acts 6:1–7	John 6:16–21

THIRD SUNDAY OF EASTER

Year A	Year B	Year C
Acts 2:14a, 36–41	Acts 3:12–19	Acts 9:1–6[7–20]
1 Peter 1:17–23	1 John 3:1–7	Revelation 5:11–14
Luke 24:13–35	Luke 24:36b-48	John 21:1–19

following **THIRD SUNDAY OF EASTER**

M	Acts 6:8–end	John 6:22–29
T	Acts 7:51–8:1	John 6:30–35
W	Acts 8:1–8	John 6:35–40
Th	Acts 8:26–end	John 6:44–51
F	Acts 9:1–20	John 6:52–59
S	Acts 9:31–42	John 6:60–69

FOURTH SUNDAY OF EASTER

Year A	Year B	Year C
Acts 2:42–47	Acts 4:5–12	Acts 9:36–43
1 Peter 2:19–25	1 John 3:16–24	Revelation 7:9–17
John 10:1–10	John 10:11–18	John 10:22–30

following **FOURTH SUNDAY OF EASTER**

M	Acts 11:1–18	John 10:1–10 or 11–18
T	Acts 11:19–26	John 10:22–30
W	Acts 12:24–13:5	John 12:44–end
Th	Acts 13:13–25	John 13:16–20
F	Acts 13:26–33	John 14:1–6
S	Acts 13:44–end	John 14:7–12

FIFTH SUNDAY OF EASTER

Year A	*Year B*	*Year C*
Acts 7:55–60	Acts 8:26–40	Acts 11:1–18
1 Peter 2:2–10	1 John 4:7–21	Revelation 21:1–6
John 14:1–14	John 15:1–8	John 13:31–35

following FIFTH SUNDAY OF EASTER

M	Acts 14:5–18	John 14:21–26
T	Acts 14:19–end	John 14:27–end
W	Acts 15:1–6	John 15: 1-8
Th	Acts 15:7–21	John 15:9–11
F	Acts 15:22–31	John 15:12–17
S	Acts 16:1–10	John 15:18–21

SIXTH SUNDAY OF EASTER

Year A	*Year B*	*Year C*
Acts 17:22–31	Acts 10:44–48	Acts 16:9–15
1 Peter 3:13–22	1 John 5:1–6	Revelation 21:10, 22 - 22:5
John 14:15–21	John 15:9–17	John 14:23–29 *or* John 5:1–9

following SIXTH SUNDAY OF EASTER

M	Acts 16:11–15	John 15:26–16:4
T	Acts 16:22–34	John 16:5–11
W	Acts 17:15, 22–18:8	John 16:12–19

For **ASCENSION***, see below.*

Responsory

On Easter Day and throughout the Easter Octave (including Low Sunday), in place of the responsory

This is the day which was made by the Lord:
let us rejoice and be glad, alleluia.

From the Monday after the Second Sunday of Easter until Pentecost

- R/ Awake, O sleeper, and arise from the dead
- R/ And Christ shall give you light.
- V/ You have died,
  and your life is hid with Christ in God.
- R/ Awake, O sleeper, and arise from the dead.
- V/ Set your minds on things that are above,
  not on things that are on the earth.
- R/ And Christ shall give you light.
- V/ When Christ our life appears
  you will appear with him in glory.
- R/ Awake, O sleeper, and arise from the dead,
  and Christ shall give you light.

Antiphons/Refrains and Texts for Meditation

On the first day of the week, at early dawn, the women came to the tomb, taking the spices that they had prepared. They found the stone rolled away from the tomb, but when they went in, they did not find the body.

Luke 24:1–3

I am the way, and the truth, and the life. No one comes to the Father except through me.

John 14:6

When it was evening on that day, the first day of the week, Jesus came and stood among the disciples and said, 'Peace be with you'.

cf. John 20:19

Blessed be the God and Father of our Lord Jesus Christ! By his great mercy we have been born anew to a living hope through the resurrection of Jesus Christ from the dead.

1 Peter 1:3 (RSV)

I am the first and the last, and the living one; I died, and behold I am alive for evermore.

Revelation 1:17–18

Collect

Almighty God,
who through your only-begotten Son Jesus Christ
have overcome death and opened to us
   the gate of everlasting life:
grant that, as by your grace going before us
   you put into our minds good desires,
so by your continual help
we may bring them to good effect;
through Jesus Christ your Son our Lord,
who is alive and reigns with you,
in the unity of the Holy Spirit,
one God, now and for ever.

Fifth Sunday of Easter
Common Worship (1)

Other Prayers

*The **Decision** and **Profession of Faith** (see page 83) may be used in preparation for the Renewal of Baptismal Promises at Easter.*

Grant, O Lord, that in thy wounds we may find our safety, in thy stripes our cure, in thy pain our peace, in thy cross our victory, in thy resurrection our triumph: and a crown of righteousness in the glories of thy eternal kingdom.

Jeremy Taylor*

God of undying life,
by your mighty hand
you raised up Jesus from the grave
and appointed him judge of the living and the dead.

Bestow upon those baptized into his death
the power flowing from his resurrection,
that we may proclaim near and far
the pardon and peace you give us.

Grant this through our Lord Jesus Christ,
   first-born from the dead,
who lives with you now and always in the
   unity of the Holy Spirit,
God for ever and ever.

ICEL (5)

Merciful Father,
you gave your Son Jesus Christ to be the good shepherd,
and in his love for us to lay down his life and rise again:
keep us always under his protection,
and give us grace to follow in his steps;
through Jesus Christ our Lord.

Fourth Sunday of Easter
(Post-Communion)
Common Worship (1)

Concluding the Office from Easter Day and throughout the Easter Octave (including Low Sunday):

Go in the peace of Christ, alleluia, alleluia.
Thanks be to God, alleluia, alleluia.

Ascension and the Seventh Sunday of Easter

Propers and Readings

Office Hymn

Aeterne rex altissime

King of all ages, throned on high,
Yet saviour too of those with faith,
Death at your onslaught died in fear
And grace triumphant rules supreme.

Risen from death, the heavenly Christ
Receives from God the Father's hand
Power over all created things:
A gift he could not know on earth.

Grant us to find our joy in you,
Possess you in our heavenly home,
King of this passing world of time,
And source of truth and lasting joy.

Then, at your coming on the clouds
With shining strength to be our judge,
Cancel the debt we owe you still,
Give back the glory we have lost.

Glory to you, O Christ our Lord,
Exalted far beyond our sight,

Reigning in bliss for evermore,
With Father and with Paraclete.

LM
Anon Tenth Century (35)
Hymns for Prayer and Praise 167

Psalms and Canticles

ASCENSION DAY

Evening Prayer I	113
	117
	A Song of the Kingdom of our God *(Canticle 42) see page 588.*
Morning Prayer	Sunday Week 1
Evening Prayer II	110
	47
	A Song of the Kingdom of our God *(Canticle 42) see page 588.*

SEVENTH SUNDAY OF EASTER

Psalms and Canticles as for Week 3.

PENTECOST

Evening Prayer I	113
	147:1–12
	A Song of Moses and the Lamb *(Canticle 43) see page 589.*
Morning Prayer	Sunday Week 1
Evening Prayer II	110
	114
	A Song of the Lamb *(Canticle 44) see page 589.*

Alternative Canticle at Morning Prayer

A Song of God's Reign *(Canticle 25) – see page 576.*

Short Readings

Jesus came and said to them, All authority in heaven and on earth has been given to me. Go therefore and make disciples of all nations, baptizing them in the name of the Father and of the Son and of the Holy Spirit, and teaching them to obey everything that I have commanded you. And remember, I am with you always, to the end of the age.

Matthew 28:18–20

or

Since we have a great high priest who has passed through the heavens, Jesus, the Son of God, let us with confidence draw near to the throne of grace, that we may receive mercy and find grace to help in time of need.

Hebrews 4:14, 16 (RSV)

Long Readings
ASCENSION DAY

Acts 1:1–11
Ephesians 1:15–23
Luke 24:44–53

following ASCENSION DAY

F	Acts 18: 9–18	John 16:20–23
S	Acts 18:23–end	John 16:23–28

SEVENTH SUNDAY OF EASTER

Year A	*Year B*	*Year C*
Acts 1:6–14	Acts 1:15–17, 21–26	Acts 16:16–34
1 Peter 4:12–14; 5:6–11	1 John 5:9–13	Revelation 22:12–14, 16–17, 20–21
John 17:1–11	John 17:6–19	John 17:20–26

following SEVENTH SUNDAY OF EASTER

M	Acts 19:1–8	John 16:29–end
T	Acts 20:17–27	John 17:1–11
W	Acts 20:28–end	John 17:11–19
Th	Acts 22:30; 23:6–11	John 17:20–end
F	Acts 25:13–21	John 21:15–19
S	Acts 28:16–20, 30–31	John 21:20–25

Responsory

R/ Christ ascended on high, alleluia, alleluia.
R/ Christ ascended on high, alleluia, alleluia.
V/ He led captivity captive.
R/ Christ ascended on high, alleluia, alleluia.
V/ Glory . . . Holy Spirit.
R/ Christ ascended on high, alleluia, alleluia.

Antiphons/Refrains and Texts for Meditation

God has gone up with a merry noise, the Lord with the sound of the trumpet.

Psalm 47:5

Peace I leave with you; my peace I give to you. If you love me, rejoice because I am going to the Father.

cf. John 14:27–28

Men of Galilee, why do you stand looking up towards heaven? This Jesus, who has been taken up from you into heaven, will come in the same way as you saw him go into heaven.

Acts 1:11

When he ascended on high he made captivity itself a captive; he gave gifts to his people.

Ephesians 4:8

Collect

O God the king of glory,
you have exalted your only Son Jesus Christ
with great triumph to your kingdom in heaven:
we beseech you, leave us not comfortless,
but send your Holy Spirit to strengthen us
and exalt us to the place
   where our Saviour Christ is gone before,
who is alive and reigns with you,
in the unity of the Holy Spirit,
one God, now and for ever.

Seventh Sunday of Easter
Common Worship (1)

Other Prayers

Grant, we beseech thee, Almighty God,
that like as we do believe thy only-begotten Son our Lord Jesus Christ
to have ascended into the heavens;
so we may also in heart and mind thither ascend,
and with him continually dwell,
who liveth and reigneth
with thee and the Holy Ghost, one God,
world without end.

Collect for Ascension Day
Book of Common Prayer (2)

Eternal God, giver of life and power,
your Son Jesus Christ has sent us into all the world
to preach the gospel of his kingdom:
confirm us in this mission,
and help us to live the good news we proclaim;
through Jesus Christ our Lord.

Seventh Sunday of Easter
(Post-Communion)
Common Worship (1)

Pentecost

Propers and Readings

Pentecost is no longer celebrated as the week beginning with Whit Sunday and ending with Trinity Sunday. The texts here are for use on Pentecost Sunday and perhaps for a Novena of Prayer from the Friday after Ascension Day until Pentecost Sunday (see Acts 1:14).

Office Hymn

Veni, creator Spiritus

Come, breath of God's creating Word,
And visit those who bear your seal;
Rejoice the hearts that you have made,
And fill them with the Father's grace.

We turn to you, our advocate,
The uncreated gift of God,
The living water, flame of love,
Who consecrates us to the Son.

You are yourself the sevenfold gift,
The finger of our God's right hand,
The Father's promised advocate,
Enriching us with words of praise.

Shine from within through every sense,
And pour your love into our hearts;
Make strong the weakness of our flesh
With your unfailing, timeless power.

Drive Satan headlong from our midst,
And bring us true and lasting peace;
Go on before to show the way,
And keep us from all paths of sin.

Grant us by your own gifts to know
The Father and his only Son;
And may we trust you all our days,
O ever-present Spirit-breath.

All glory to our God and Lord,
And to his Son who conquered death;
All glory to the Paraclete,
Who reigns with them eternally.

LM
Rabanus Maurus (35)
Hymns for Prayer and Praise 167

Psalms and Canticles

Evening Prayer I	113
	147:1–12
	A Song of Moses and the Lamb
	(Canticle 43) see page 589.
Morning Prayer	Sunday Week 1
Evening Prayer II	110
	114
	A Song of the Lamb
	(Canticle 44) see page 589.

On Monday after Pentecost, Ordinary Time begins.
Resume psalmody as outlined on page 333.

Alternative Canticle at Morning Prayer

A Song of Ezekiel *(Canticle 23)* – see page 574.

Short Readings

The God of our ancestors raised up Jesus, whom you had killed by hanging him on a tree. God exalted him at his right hand as Leader and Saviour, so that he might give repentance to Israel and forgiveness of sins. And we are witnesses to these things, and so is the Holy Spirit whom God has given to those who obey him.

Acts 5:30–32

or

God saved us, not because of any works of righteousness that we had done, but according to his mercy, through the water of rebirth and renewal by the Holy Spirit. This Spirit he poured out on us richly through Jesus Christ our Saviour, so that, having been justified by his grace, we might become heirs according to the hope of eternal life.

Titus 3:5b-7

Long Readings

following **ASCENSION DAY**

F	Acts 18: 9–18	John 16:20–23
S	Acts 18:23–end	John 16:23–28

SEVENTH SUNDAY OF EASTER

Year A	Year B	Year C
Acts 1:6–14	Acts 1:15–17, 21–26	Acts 16:16–34
1 Peter 4:12–14; 5:6–11	1 John 5:9–13	Revelation 22:12–14, 16–17, 20–21
John 17:1–11	John 17:6–19	John 17:20–26

following **SEVENTH SUNDAY OF EASTER**

M	Acts 19:1–8	John 16:29–end
T	Acts 20:17–27	John 17:1–11
W	Acts 20:28–end	John 17:11–19
Th	Acts 22:30; 23:6–11	John 17:20–end
F	Acts 25:13–21	John 21:15–19
S	Acts 28:16–20, 30–31	John 21:20–25

PENTECOST SUNDAY

Year A	Year B	Year C
Acts 2:1–21	Acts 2:1–21	Acts 2:1–21
1 Corinthians 12:3b-13	Romans 8:22–27	Romans 8:14–17
John 20:19–23 or John 7:37–39	John 15:26–27; 16:4b-15	John 14:8–17[25–27]

Responsory

R/   Come, Holy Spirit, fill the hearts of your people,
R/   And kindle in us the fire of your love.
V/   All who are led by the Spirit of God
        are children of God and fellow-heirs with Christ;
R/   Come, Holy Spirit, fill the hearts of your people.
V/   Renew the face of your creation, Lord,
        pouring on us the gifts of your Spirit,
R/   And kindle in us the fire of your love.
V/   For the creation waits with eager longing
        for the glorious liberty of the children of God.
R/   Come, Holy Spirit, fill the hearts of your people
        and kindle in us the fire of your love.

Antiphons/Refrains and Texts for Meditation

God's love has been poured into our hearts through the Holy Spirit that has been given to us.

Romans 5:5

What God has prepared for those who love him, he has revealed to us through the Spirit; for the Spirit searches everything, even the depths of God.

1 Corinthians 2:9–10

The fruit of the Spirit is love, joy, peace, patience, kindness, generosity, faithfulness, gentleness, and self-control.

Galatians 5:22

Come, Holy Spirit, fill the hearts of your faithful and kindle in them the fire of your love.

Send forth your Spirit and they shall be made new and you will renew the face of the earth.

Collect

God, who as at this time
taught the hearts of your faithful people
by sending to them the light of your Holy Spirit:

grant us by the same Spirit
to have a right judgement in all things
and evermore to rejoice in his holy comfort;
through the merits of Christ Jesus our Saviour,
who is alive and reigns with you,
in the unity of the Holy Spirit,
one God, now and for ever.

Day of Pentecost
Common Worship (1)

Other Prayers

Prayer of Saint Bonaventure for the Seven Gifts of the Spirit

Lord Jesus, as God's Spirit came down and rested upon you,
may the same Spirit rest upon us,
bestowing his sevenfold gifts.
First, grant us the gift of understanding,
by which your precepts may enlighten our minds.
Second, grant us counsel, by which we may follow in your footsteps on the path of righteousness.
Third, grant us courage, by which we may ward off the Enemy's attacks.
Fourth, grant us knowledge, by which we can distinguish good from evil.
Fifth, grant us piety, by which we may acquire compassionate hearts.
Sixth, grant us fear, by which we may draw back from evil and submit to what is good.
Seventh, grant us wisdom, that we may taste fully the life-giving sweetness of your love.

(39)

Good Jesu, fountain of love:
fill me with thy love,
absorb me into thy love,
compass me with thy love,
that I may see all things in the light of thy love,
receive all things as tokens of thy love,
speak of all things in words breathing of thy love,
win through thy love others to thy love,
be kindled, day by day, with a new glow of thy love,

until I be fitted to enter into thine everlasting love,
to adore thy love and love to adore thee,
   my God and my all.
Even so, come, Lord Jesu!

Edward Bouverie Pusey

O God the Holy Ghost who art light unto thine elect,
evermore enlighten us.
Thou who art fire of love, evermore enkindle us.
Thou who art Lord and giver of life, evermore live in us.
Thou who bestowest sevenfold grace, evermore replenish us.
As the wind is thy symbol, so forward our goings.
As the dove, so launch us heavenwards.
As water, so purify our spirits.
As a cloud, so abate our temptations.
As dew, so revive our languor.
As fire, so purge out our dross.

Christina Rossetti

O Holy Spirit,
giver of light and life,
impart to us thoughts higher than our own thoughts,
and prayers better than our own prayers,
and powers beyond our own powers,
that we may spend and be spent in the ways of love and goodness,
after the perfect image of our Lord Jesus Christ.

G. W. Briggs (18)

Look graciously upon us, O Holy Spirit,
and give us for our hallowing
thoughts which pass into prayer,
prayers which pass into love,
and love which passes into life with you for ever.

Anonymous

Trinity Sunday

Propers and Readings

Office Hymn

Adesto, sancta Trinitas

Be with us holy Trinity,
Three persons like in majesty,
One only God sustaining all,
Creator, saviour, comforter.

The hosts of angels worship you,
Adore you, and proclaim you Lord;
And all creation's powers unite
To bless your name from age to age.

In supplication here we kneel,
Your worshippers, with love and awe,
Repeating in our humbler prayers
The praises of the heavenly choir.

With all things living we adore
The Alpha and the Omega,
And celebrate in threefold name,
The glory of the one true light.

All praise to you, blest Trinity,
To Father and incarnate Word,
Both with the Holy Spirit, one
For time and all eternity.

LM
Anon Tenth or Eleventh Century (35)
Hymns for Prayer and Praise 178

Psalms and Canticles

Evening Prayer I	113
	147:13–21
	A Song of God's Grace
	(Canticle 35) see page 583.
Morning Prayer	Sunday Week 1
Evening Prayer II	110
	114
	A Song of the Lamb
	(Canticle 44) see page 589.

Alternative Canticle at Morning Prayer

The Song of the Three *(Canticle 33)* – see page 582.

Short Readings

As I, Daniel, looked, thrones were placed and one that was ancient of days took his seat; his raiment was white as snow, and the hair of his head like pure wool; his throne was fiery flames, its wheels were burning fire. A stream of fire issued and came forth from before him; a thousand thousands served him and ten thousand times ten thousand stood before him.

Daniel 7:9–10

or

It is God who establishes us with you in Christ and has anointed us, by putting his seal on us and giving us his Spirit in our hearts as a first instalment.

2 Corinthians 1:21–22

Long Readings

TRINITY SUNDAY

Year A	*Year B*	*Year C*
Isaiah 40:12–17, 27–31	Isaiah 6:1–8	Proverbs 8:1–4, 22–31
2 Corinthians 13:11–13	Romans 8:12–17	Romans 5:1–5
Matthew 28:16–20	John 3:1–17	John 16:12–15

Responsory

Sundays

R/ You are the Christ, the Son of the living God. Have mercy on us.
R/ You are the Christ, the Son of the living God. Have mercy on us.
V/ You are seated at the right hand of the Father.
R/ You are the Christ, the Son of the living God. Have mercy on us.
V/ Glory . . . Holy Spirit.
R/ You are the Christ, the Son of the living God. Have mercy on us.

Divine Office (14)

Weekdays

R/ I call with my whole heart; answer me, O Lord.
R/ I call with my whole heart; answer me, O Lord.
V/ I will keep your commandments.
R/ I call with my whole heart; answer me, O Lord.
V/ Glory . . . Holy Spirit.
R/ I call with my whole heart; answer me, O Lord.

Psalm 119:145

Antiphons/Refrains and Texts for Meditation

The grace of the Lord Jesus Christ, the love of God, and the communion of the Holy Spirit be with all of you.

2 Corinthians 12:13

Rejoice always, pray without ceasing, give thanks in all circumstances; for this is the will of God in Christ Jesus for you. Do not quench the Spirit.

1 Thessalonians 5:16–19

Glory to the Father, and to the Son, and to the Holy Spirit, the God who was, and who is, and who is to come, the Almighty.

cf. Revelation 1:8

Round the throne of God, day and night they never cease to sing, 'Holy, holy, holy is the Lord God Almighty, who was and is and is to come!'

cf. Revelation 4:8

Collect

Almighty and everlasting God,
you have given us your servants grace,
by the confession of a true faith,
to acknowledge the glory of the eternal Trinity
and in the power of the divine majesty to worship the Unity:
keep us steadfast in this faith,
that we may evermore be defended from all adversities;
through Jesus Christ your Son our Lord,
who is alive and reigns with you,
in the unity of the Holy Spirit,
one God, now and for ever.

Trinity Sunday
Common Worship (1)

Other Prayers

O adorable Trinity! What hast thou done for me? Thou hast made me the end of all things, and all the end of me. I in all, and all in me. In every soul whom thou hast created, thou hast given me the similitude of thyself to enjoy! Could my desire have devised such sublime enjoyments? Oh! Thou hast done more for us than we could ask or think. I praise and admire, and rejoice in thee; who are infinitely infinite in all thy doings.

Thomas Traherne

Holy, holy, holy is the Lord,
Holy is the Lord God almighty!
Holy, holy, holy is the Lord,
Holy is the Lord God almighty!
Who was, and is, and is to come!
Holy, holy, holy is the Lord.

Traditional

Corpus Christi

Propers and Readings

Office Hymn

Pange, lingua, gloriosi corporis mysterium

Hail our Saviour's glorious body,
Which his Virgin Mother bore;
hail the blood which, shed for sinners
Did a broken world restore;
Hail the sacrament most holy,
Flesh and blood of Christ adore.

To the Virgin, for our healing,
His own Son the Father sends;
From the Father's love proceeding
Sower, seed and Word descends:
Wondrous life of Word incarnate
With his greatest wonder ends.

On the paschal evening see him
With the chosen twelve recline,
To the old law still obedient
In its feast of love divine;
Love divine, the new law giving,
Gives himself as bread and wine.

By his word the Word almighty
Makes of bread his flesh indeed;
Wine becomes his very life-blood:
faith God's living Word must heed.

Faith alone may safely guide us
Where the senses cannot lead.

Come, adore this wondrous presence;
Bow to Christ, the source of grace:
Here is kept the ancient promise
Of God's earthly dwelling-place.
Sight is blind before God's glory,
Faith alone may see his face.

Glory be to God the Father,
Praise to his co-equal Son,
Adoration to the Spirit,
Bond of love, in Godhead one;
Blest be God by all creation
Joyously while ages run.

James Quinn SJ (38)

Psalms and Canticles

Evening Prayer I	111
	147:13–21
	A Song of the Kingdom of our God
	(Canticle 42) see page 588.
Morning Prayer	Sunday Week 1
Evening Prayer II	110
	116
	A Song of the Lamb
	(Canticle 44) see page 589.

Short Readings

Moses took the book of the covenant, and read it in the hearing of the people; and they said, 'All that the Lord has spoken we will do, and we will be obedient.' Moses took the blood and dashed it on the people, and said, 'See the blood of the covenant that the Lord has made with you in accordance with all these words.'

Exodus 24:7–8

or

You gave your people food of angels, and without their toil you supplied them from heaven with bread ready to eat, providing every pleasure and suited to every taste.

Wisdom 16:20–21

or

I received from the Lord what I also handed on to you, that the Lord Jesus on the night when he was betrayed took a loaf of bread, and when he had given thanks, he broke it and said, 'This is my body that is for you. Do this in remembrance of me.' In the same way he took the cup also, after supper, saying, 'This cup is the new covenant in my blood. Do this, as often as you drink it, in remembrance of me.' For as often as you eat this bread and drink the cup, you proclaim the Lord's death until he comes.

1 Corinthians 11:23–26

Long Readings

CORPUS CHRISTI

Genesis 14:18–20
1 Corinthians 11:23–26
John 6:51–58

or

Year A	*Year B*	*Year C*
* Deuteronomy 8:2–3, 14–16	* Exodus 24:3–8	* Genesis 14:18–20
* 1 Corinthians 10:16–17	* Hebrews 9:11–15	* 1 Corinthians 11: 23–26
* John 6:51–58	* Mark 14:12–16, 22–26	* Luke 9:11–17

Responsory

R/ Whoever comes to me will never be hungry.
R/ Lord, you give life to the world.
V/ The bread of God comes down from heaven.
R/ Whoever comes to me will never be hungry.

V/ Those who believe have eternal life.
R/ Lord, you give life to the world.
V/ Give us this bread, Lord, always.
R/ Whoever comes to me will never be hungry.
Lord, you give life to the world.

Antiphons/Refrains and Texts for Meditation

Wisdom says, 'Come, eat of my bread and drink of the wine I have mixed.'
Proverbs 9:4–5

Those who eat my flesh and drink my blood abide in me, and I in them.
John 6:56

The cup of blessing that we bless, is it not a sharing in the blood of Christ? The bread that we break, is it not a sharing in the body of Christ?
1 Corinthians 10:16

O sacred banquet in which Christ is received, the memory of his passion is renewed, our lives are filled with grace, and a pledge of future glory is given!
tr. AB (8)

Collect

Lord Jesus Christ,
we thank you that in this wonderful sacrament
you have given us the memorial of your passion:
grant us so to reverence the sacred mysteries
   of your body and blood
that we may know within ourselves
and show forth in our lives
the fruits of your redemption;
for you are alive and reign with the Father
in the unity of the Holy Spirit,
one God, now and for ever.

Corpus Christi
Common Worship (1)

Other Prayers

Lord, this is thy feast, prepared by thy longing, spread at thy command, attended at thine invitation, blessed by thine own Word, distributed by thine own hand, the undying memorial of thy sacrifice upon the cross, the full gift of thine everlasting love, and its perpetuation till time shall end. Lord, this is Bread of heaven, Bread of life, that, those who eat it never shall hunger more. And this the cup of pardon, healing, gladness, strength, that those who drink it, never thirst again.

Eric Milner-White (17)

O sacrum convivium

We praise and thank you, O Christ, for this sacred feast:
for here we receive you,
here the memory of your passion is renewed,
here our minds are filled with grace,
and here a pledge of future glory is given,
when we shall feast at that table where you reign
with all your saints for ever.

Eighteenth Sunday after Trinity
(Post-Communion)
Common Worship (1)

Visit to the Blessed Sacrament

Remind yourself of the abiding presence of Christ.

Remember, I am with you always, to the end of the age.

Matthew 28:20

Behold, the dwelling of God is with men. He will dwell with them, and they shall be his people, and God himself will be with them.

Revelation 21:3b (RSV)

I am the vine, you are the branches. Those who abide in me and I in them bear much fruit, because apart from me you can do nothing.

John 15:5

Spend some minutes in silence reflecting on one of these, or other, biblical verses. Psalms and readings etc. for Corpus Christi (see above) may be used.

Preparation before Mass (see page 109) or Thanksgiving after Mass (see page 173) might be appropriate.

Conclude with one or more of the devotions or prayers below:

O sacrum convivium

O sacred banquet in which Christ is received,
the memory of his passion is renewed,
our lives are filled with grace,
and a pledge of future glory is given!

tr. AB (8)

Adoro te

Godhead here in hiding, whom I do adore
Masked by these bare shadows, shape and nothing more,
See, Lord, at thy service low lies here a heart
Lost, all lost in wonder at the God thou art.

Seeing, touching, tasting are in thee deceived;
How says trusty hearing? That shall be believed;
What God's Son has told me, take for truth I do;
Truth himself speaks truly or there's nothing true.

On the cross thy godhead made no sign to men;
Here thy very manhood steals from human ken:
Both are my confession, both are my belief,
And I pray the prayer of the dying thief.

O thou our reminder of Christ crucified,
Living Bread, the life of us for whom he died,
Lend this life to me then: feed and feast my mind,
There be thou the sweetness man was meant to find.

Jesus whom I look at shrouded here below,
I beseech thee send me what I thirst for so,
Some day to gaze on thee face to face in light
And be blest for ever with thy glory's sight.

Gerard Manley Hopkins

Ave verum corpus

Hail, true Body, born of the Virgin Mary;
truly you suffered,
impaled on the cross for the sins of the world.
From your pierced side flowed blood and water.
In my last agony,
grant me a foretaste of your presence.
O sweet Jesus,
O gracious Jesus,
son of Mary,
have mercy on me.

tr. AB (8)

Prayer of Self-Dedication to Jesus Christ

Lord Jesus Christ,
take all my freedom,
my memory, my understanding, and my will.
All that I have and cherish
you have given me.
I surrender it all to be guided by your will.
Your grace and your love are wealth enough for me.
Give me these, Lord Jesus,
and I ask for nothing more.

ICEL (5)

Universal Prayer attributed to Pope Clement XI

Lord, I believe in you; O give me firmer faith.
I hope in you, give me surer hope.
I love you, make me love you more and more.
I am sorry to have failed you; make me sorrier yet.

I adore you as my first beginning, and long for you as my last end;
praise you as my constant benefactor, and call upon you as my gracious protector.

Guide me by your wisdom,
restrain me by your justice,
comfort me by your mercy,
defend me by your power.

I offer you, Lord, my thoughts, to be fixed on you;
my words, to have you for their theme;
my actions, to be done according to your will;
my hardships, to be endured for your sake.

My will is that your will be done,
in the manner you will,
and for as long as you will,
because it is your will.

I pray you, Lord, enlighten my understanding,
inflame my will,
purify my heart,
and sanctify my soul.

Help me to deplore my past offences and to resist temptation in future,
to subdue my evil inclinations and to cultivate the virtues proper for my state.
God of all goodness, fill me with love of you and hatred of myself,
with zeal for my neighbour and contempt of worldly things.

Teach me to be obedient to my superiors,
helpful to my subordinates,
faithful to friends,
forgiving to foes.

Let me vanquish pleasure by self-denial,
avarice by generosity,
anger by meekness,

and lukewarmness by fervour.
Make me prudent in planning,
courageous in taking risks;
in affliction, patient;
in prosperity, unassuming.

Lord, make me attentive at prayers,
moderate when I eat and drink,
diligent in my occupation,
and constant in good resolutions.

Let my conscience be clear,
my demeanour modest,
my talk blameless,
my life well-ordered.
Let me always be alert to keep nature in check,
to cherish your grace,
to keep your law,
and to earn salvation.

Teach me how petty is this world,
how immense your heaven;
time, how short;
eternity, how long.
Give me grace to prepare for death,
to dread your judgement,
to escape hell,
and to win a place in heaven:
through Christ our Lord.

Divine Office (14)

May the divine assistance remain with us always.

Benediction

O salutaris hostia

O saving victim, opening wide
The gate of heaven to man below;
Our foes press hard on every side,
Thine aid supply, thy strength bestow.

All praise and thanks to thee ascend
For evermore blest One in Three;
O grant us life that shall not end
In our true native land with thee.

or

O Priest and Victim, Word of Life,
Throw wide the gates of Paradise.
We face our foes in mortal strife;
You are our strength! O heed our cries.

To Father, Son and Spirit blest,
One only God, be ceaseless praise.
May you in goodness grant us rest
In heaven, our home, for endless days.

LM
James Quinn SJ (38)

Tantum ergo

Therefore we before him bending
This great sacrament revere;
Types and shadows have their ending,
For the newer rite is here;
Faith, our outward sense befriending,
Makes the inward vision clear.

Glory let us give and blessing
To the Father and the Son;
Honour, might and praise addressing,
While eternal ages run;
Ever too his love confessing,
Who from both, with both, is one.

or

Come, adore this wondrous presence;
Bow to Christ, the source of grace:
Here is kept the ancient promise
Of God's earthly dwelling-place.
Sight is blind before God's glory,
Faith alone may see his face.

Glory be to God the Father,
Praise to his co-equal Son,
Adoration to the Spirit,
Bond of love, in Godhead one;
Blest be God by all creation
Joyously while ages run.

James Quinn SJ (38)

Let us pray.

Lord Jesus Christ,
you gave us the eucharist
as the memorial of your suffering and death.
May our worship of this sacrament of your body and blood
help us to experience the salvation you won for us
and the peace of the kingdom
where you live with the Father and the Holy Spirit,
one God, for ever and ever.

ICEL (5)

The Divine Praises

Blessed be God.
Blessed be his holy name.
Blessed be Jesus Christ, true God and true man.
Blessed be the name of Jesus.
Blessed be his most sacred heart.
Blessed be his most precious blood.
Blessed be Jesus in the most holy sacrament of the altar.
Blessed be the Holy Spirit the Paraclete.
Blessed be the great Mother of God, Mary most holy.
Blessed be her holy and immaculate conception.
Blessed be her glorious assumption.

Blessed be the name of Mary, Virgin and mother.
Blessed be Saint Joseph, her spouse most chaste.
Blessed be God in his angels and in his saints.

Louis Felici SJ

Blessed and praised be Jesus Christ in the most holy sacrament.
Hosanna, hosanna, hosanna in excelsis.

Adoration of Christ in the Blessed Sacrament

Blessed, hallowed and adored
be Jesus Christ on his throne of glory
and in the most holy sacrament of the altar.
[Alleluia. Alleluia.] Amen.

Sacred Heart

Propers and Readings

Office Hymn

Summi parentis Filio

To Christ, the prince of peace,
And Son of God most high,
The Father of the world to come,
Sing we with holy joy.

Deep in his heart for us
The wound of love he bore;
That love wherewith he still inflames
The hearts that him adore.

O Jesu, victim blest,
What else but love divine
Could thee constrain to open thus
That sacred heart of thine?

O fount of endless life,
O spring of water clear,
O flame celestial, cleansing all
Who unto thee draw near.

Hide us in thy dear heart,
For thither do we fly;
There seek thy grace through life, in death
Thine immortality.

Praise to the Father be,
And sole-begotten Son;

Praise, holy Paraclete, to thee
While endless ages run.

tr. Edward Caswall
Anon Ninth Century
Hymns for Prayer and Praise 186

Psalms and Canticles

Evening Prayer I	113
	146
	A Song of Praise
	(Canticle 40) see page 587.
Morning Prayer	Sunday Week 1
Evening Prayer II	110
	111
	The Song of Christ's Glory
	(Canticle 36) see page 584.

Alternative Canticle at Morning Prayer

A Song of Ezekiel *(Canticle 23) – see page 574.*

Short Readings

Thus says the Lord: The people who survived the sword found grace in the wilderness; when Israel sought for rest, the Lord appeared to him from far away. I have loved you with an everlasting love; therefore I have continued my faithfulness to you. Again I will build you, and you shall be built.

Jeremiah 31:2–4

or

Who will separate us from the love of Christ? Will hardship, or distress, or persecution, or famine, or nakedness, or peril, or sword? As it is written, 'For your sake we are killed all day long; we are accounted as sheep to be slaughtered.' No, in all these things we are more than conquerors through him who loved us. For I am convinced that neither death, nor life, nor angels, nor rulers, nor things to come, nor powers, nor height, nor depth, nor anything else in all creation, will be able to separate us from the love of God in Christ Jesus our Lord.

Romans 8:35–39

Long Readings

SACRED HEART

Year A	Year B	Year C
* Deuteronomy 7:6–11	* Isaiah 12:2–6	* Ezekiel 34:11–16
* 1 John 4:7–16	* Ephesians 3:8–12, 14–19	* Romans 5:5–11
* Matthew 11:25–30	* John 19:31–37	* Luke 15:3–7

Responsory

R/ Take my yoke upon you, and learn from me
R/ For I am gentle and humble in heart.
V/ You will find rest for your souls.
R/ Take my yoke upon you, and learn from me.
V/ My yoke is easy and my burden is light
R/ For I am gentle and humble in heart
V/ Glory . . . Holy Spirit.
R/ Take my yoke upon you, and learn from me
   For I am gentle and humble in heart.

Antiphons/Refrains and Texts for Meditation

I will make an everlasting covenant with them, never to draw back from doing good to them.

Jeremiah 32:40

Come to me, all who labour and are heavy-laden, and I will give you rest.

Matthew 11:28 (RSV)

God, out of the great love with which he loved us, made us alive together with Christ.

Ephesians 2:4–5

Christ loved the church and gave himself up for her.

Ephesians 5:25b

Collect

God of life and love,
from the pierced heart of your Son
flowed water and blood,
cleansing the world
and giving birth to your Church.

Renew within your people
the love poured out on us in baptism,
and through the blessing-cup we share
keep us always faithful
to your life-giving covenant.

We make our prayer through our Lord Jesus
    Christ, your Son,
who lives and reigns with you in the unity of
    the Holy Spirit,
God for ever and ever.

ICEL (5)

Other Prayers

Almighty God, whose Son, our Lord and Saviour Jesus Christ, was moved with compassion for all who had gone astray and with indignation for all who had suffered wrong: inflame our hearts with the burning fire of your love, that we may seek out the lost, have mercy on the fallen and stand fast for truth and righteousness; through Jesus Christ your Son our Lord, who is alive and reigns with you, in the unity of the Holy Spirit, one God, now and for ever.

The Divine Compassion of Christ (3)

Love of the heart of Jesus, inflame my heart,
Charity of the heart of Jesus, flow into my heart.
Strength of the heart of Jesus, support my heart.
Mercy of the heart of Jesus, pardon my heart.
Patience of the heart of Jesus, grow not weary of my heart.
Kingdom of the heart of Jesus, be in my heart.
Wisdom of the heart of Jesus, teach my heart.
Will of the heart of Jesus, guide my heart.
Zeal of the heart of Jesus, consume my heart.
Immaculate Virgin Mary, pray for me to the heart of Jesus

Elizabeth Ruth Obbard (40)

Act of Consecration to the Sacred Heart of Jesus

I, *N*, give myself and consecrate to the Sacred Heart of our Lord Jesus Christ, my person and my life, my actions, pains and sufferings, so that I may be unwilling to make use of any part of my being save to honour, love, and glorify the Sacred Heart. This is my unchanging purpose, namely, to be all his, and to do all things for the love of him at the same time renouncing with all my heart whatever is displeasing to him. I therefore take you, O Sacred Heart, to be the only object of my love, the guardian of my life, my assurance of salvation, the remedy of my weakness and inconstancy, the atonement for all the faults of my life, and my sure refuge at the hour of death. Be then, O Heart of goodness, my justification before God our Father, and turn away from me his justified anger. O Heart of love, I put all my confidence in you, for I fear everything from my own wickedness and frailty, but I hope for all things from your goodness and bounty. Consume in me all that displeases you or resists your holy will; let your pure love imprint itself so deeply on my heart, that I shall never be able to forget or to be separated from you. May I obtain from your loving kindness the grace of having my name written on your heart, for in you I desire to place all my happiness and all my glory, living and dying in your true service.

Saint Margaret Mary Alacoque (20)

Litany of the Sacred Heart

Lord, have mercy.
Lord, have mercy.

Christ, have mercy.
Christ, have mercy.

Lord, have mercy.
Lord, have mercy.

Christ hear us.
Christ graciously hear us.

God the Father of heaven, have mercy on us.
God the Son, redeemer of the world, have mercy on us.
God the Holy Spirit, have mercy on us.
Holy Trinity, one God, have mercy on us.

Heart of Jesus, Son of the eternal Father, have mercy on us.
Heart of Jesus, formed by the Holy Spirit in the womb of the Virgin Mother, have mercy on us.
Heart of Jesus, united hypostatically to the Word of God, have mercy on us.
Heart of Jesus, infinite in majesty, have mercy on us.
Heart of Jesus, holy temple of God, have mercy on us.
Heart of Jesus, tabernacle of the Most High, have mercy on us.
Heart of Jesus, house of God and gate of heaven, have mercy on us.

Heart of Jesus, glowing furnace of charity, have mercy on us.
Heart of Jesus, abode of justice and love, have mercy on us.
Heart of Jesus, full of kindness and love, have mercy on us.
Heart of Jesus, abyss of all virtues, have mercy on us.
Heart of Jesus, most worthy of all praise, have mercy on us.
Heart of Jesus, King and centre of all hearts, have mercy on us.
Heart of Jesus, wherein are all the treasures of wisdom and knowledge, have mercy on us.
Heart of Jesus, wherein abides the fullness of the Godhead, have mercy on us.
Heart of Jesus, in which the Father was well-pleased, have mercy on us.
Heart of Jesus, of whose fullness we have all received, have mercy on us.
Heart of Jesus, desire of the eternal hills, have mercy on us.
Heart of Jesus, patient and abounding in mercy, have mercy on us.

Heart of Jesus, rich to all that call upon you, have mercy on us.
Heart of Jesus, source of life and holiness, have mercy on us.

Heart of Jesus, atonement for our iniquities, have mercy on us.
Heart of Jesus, glutted with reproaches, have mercy on us.
Heart of Jesus, bruised for our sins, have mercy on us.
Heart of Jesus, made obedient unto death, have mercy on us.
Heart of Jesus, pierced by the lance, have mercy on us.
Heart of Jesus, source of all consolation, have mercy on us.
Heart of Jesus, our life and resurrection, have mercy on us.
Heart of Jesus, our peace and reconciliation, have mercy on us.
Heart of Jesus, victim of sin, have mercy on us.
Heart of Jesus, salvation of all who trust in you, have mercy on us.
Heart of Jesus, hope of all who die in you, have mercy on us.
Heart of Jesus, delight of all the saints, have mercy on us.

Lamb of God, you take away the sins of the world,
spare us O Lord.

Lamb of God, you take away the sins of the world,
graciously hear us O Lord.

Lamb of God, you take away the sins of the world,
have mercy on us.

Jesus, meek and humble of heart,
make our hearts like your Heart.

Let us pray.

Almighty and everlasting God, look upon the Heart of your well-beloved Son, and upon the praise and satisfaction which he rendered to you on behalf of all sinners; and, being thus appeased, grant them the pardon which they seek from your mercy, in the name of Jesus Christ your Son, who lives and reigns with you for ever and ever.

A Book of Hours 1998 (41)

Ordinary Time: Monday after Pentecost until the end of October

Propers and Readings

Office Hymns

As set for Lauds page 20 and Vespers page 626.

or

Firmly I believe and truly

Firmly I believe and truly
God is three and God is one;
And I next acknowledge duly
Manhood taken by the Son.

And I trust and hope most fully
In that manhood crucified;
And each thought and deed unruly
Do to death, as he has died.

Simply to his grace and wholly
Light and life and strength belong,
And I love supremely, solely,
Him the holy, him the strong.

And I hold in veneration,
For the love of him alone,
Holy Church as his creation,
And her teachings as his own.

Adoration aye be given,
With and through the angelic host,
To the God of earth and heaven,
Father, Son, and Holy Ghost.

John Henry Newman
The Dream of Gerontius

or

Praise to the holiest

Praise to the holiest in the height,
And in the depth be praise,
In all his words most wonderful,
Most sure in all his ways.

O loving wisdom of our God!
When all was sin and shame,
A second Adam to the fight
And to the rescue came.

O wisest love! that flesh and blood
Which did in Adam fail,
Should strive afresh against their foe,
Should strive and should prevail;

And that a higher gift than grace
Should flesh and blood refine,
God's presence and his very self,
And essence all-divine.

O generous love! that he who smote
In Man for man the foe,
The double agony in Man
For man should undergo;

And in the garden secretly,
And on the cross on high,
Should teach his brethren, and inspire
To suffer and to die.

Praise to the holiest in the height,
And in the depth be praise,

In all his words most wonderful,
Most sure in all his ways.

John Henry Newman
The Dream of Gerontius

Psalms and Canticles

On Monday After Pentecost, Ordinary Time begins.
Resume psalmody as follows:

Year	Date of Monday after Pentecost	Week of Psalmody	Office Psalmody resumes with:
2001	4 June	Week 9	Week 1
2002	20 May	Week 7	Week 3
2003	9 June	Week 10	Week 2
2004	31 May	Week 9	Week 1
2005	16 May	Week 7	Week 3
2006	5 June	Week 9	Week 1
2007	28 May	Week 8	Week 4
2008	12 May	Week 6	Week 2
2009	1 June	Week 9	Week 1
2010	24 May	Week 8	Week 4
2011	13 June	Week 11	Week 3
2012	28 May	Week 8	Week 4
2013	20 May	Week 7	Week 3
2014	9 June	Week 10	Week 2
2015	25 May	Week 8	Week 4
2016	16 May	Week 7	Week 3
2017	5 June	Week 9	Week 1
2018	21 May	Week 7	Week 3
2019	10 June	Week 10	Week 2
2020	1 June	Week 9	Week 1
2021	24 May	Week 8	Week 4
2022	6 June	Week 10	Week 2
2023	29 May	Week 8	Week 4
2024	20 May	Week 7	Week 3
2025	9 June	Week 10	Week 2

Alternative Canticle at Morning Prayer

A Song of the Covenant (Canticle 13) – see page 566.

Short Readings

If there is among you anyone in need, a member of your community in any of your towns within the land that the Lord your God is giving you, do not be hard-hearted or tight-fisted towards your needy neighbour. You should rather open your hand, willingly lending enough to meet the need, whatever it may be.

Deuteronomy 15:7–8

or

We have not ceased praying for you and asking that you may be filled with the knowledge of God's will in all spiritual wisdom and understanding, so that you may lead lives worthy of the Lord, fully pleasing to him, as you bear fruit in every good work and as you grow in the knowledge of God. May you be made strong with all the strength that comes from his glorious power, and may you be prepared to endure everything with patience.

Colossians 1:9b-11

or

Even when we were with you, we gave you this command: Anyone unwilling to work should not eat. For we hear that some of you are living in idleness, mere busybodies, not doing any work. Now such persons we command and exhort in the Lord Jesus Christ to do their work quietly and to earn their own living. Brothers and sisters, do not be weary in doing what is right.

2 Thessalonians 3:10b-13

or

Remember Jesus Christ, raised from the dead, a descendant of David – that is my gospel. The saying is sure: If we have died with him, we will also live with him; if we endure, we will also reign with him; if we deny him, he will also deny us; if we are faithless, he remains faithful – for he cannot deny himself.

2 Timothy 2:8,11–13

Long Readings

ORDINARY TIME AFTER PENTECOST

Sunday between 22 and 28 May inclusive
[Sunday 8 of Ordinary Time]

Year A	Year B	Year C
* Isaiah 49:14–14	* Hosea 2:16–17, 21–22	* Ecclesiasticus 27:4–7
* 1 Corinthians 4:1–5	* 2 Corinthians 3:1–6	* 1 Corinthians 15: 54–58
* Matthew 6:24–34	* Mark 2:18–22	* Luke 6:39–45

Week 8 of Year 1
M   Ecclesiasticus 17:24–29   Mark 10:17–27
T   Ecclesiasticus 35:1–12   Mark 10: 28–31
W   Ecclesiasticus 36:1,4–5,10–17 Mark 10: 32–45
Th Ecclesiasticus 42:15–end   Mark 10:46–end
F   Ecclesiasticus 44:1, 9–13   Mark 11:11–26
S   Ecclesiasticus 51:12–20   Mark 11:27–end

Week 8 of Year 2
M   1 Peter 1:3–9   Mark 10:17–27
T   1 Peter 1:10–16   Mark 10:28–31
W   1 Peter 1:18–end   Mark 10:32–45
Th 1 Peter 2:2–5, 9–12   Mark 10:46–end
F   1 Peter 4:7–13   Mark 11:11–26
S   Jude 17, 20–end   Mark 11:27–end

Sunday between 29 May and 4 June inclusive
[Proper 4 of CWPS]   [Sunday 9 of Ordinary Time]

Year A	Year B	Year C
Deuteronomy 11:18–21, 26–28	Deuteronomy 5:12–15	1 Kings 8:22–23, 41–43
Romans 1:16–17; 3:22b-28[29–31]	2 Corinthians 4:5–12	Galatians 1:1–12
Matthew 7:21–29	Mark 2:23–3:6	Luke 7:1–10

Week 9 of Year 1
M   Tobit 1:1–2; 2:1–8   Mark 12:1–12
T   Tobit 2: 9–14   Mark 12:13–17

W	Tobit 3:1–11, 16–17	Mark 12:18–27
Th	Tobit 6:9–11; 7:1–15; 8:4–8	Mark 12:28–34
F	Tobit 11:5–15	Mark 12:35–37
S	Tobit 12:1, 5–15, 20a	Mark 12:38–end

Week 9 of Year 2

M	2 Peter 1:2–7	Mark 12:1–12
T	2 Peter 3:11–15, 17–18	Mark 12:13–17
W	2 Timothy 1:1–3, 6–12	Mark 12:18–27
Th	2 Timothy 2:8–15	Mark 12:28–34
F	2 Timothy 3:10–end	Mark 12:35–37:
S	2 Timothy 4:1–8	Mark 12:38–end

Sunday between 5–11 June inclusive
[Proper 5 of CWPS]   [Sunday 10 of Ordinary Time]

Year A	Year B	Year C
Hosea 5:15–6:6	Genesis 3:8–15	1 Kings 17:17–24
Romans 4:13–25	2 Corinthians 4:13–5:1	Galatians 1:11–24
Matthew 9:9–13,18–26	Mark 3:20–35	Luke 7:11–17

Week 10 of Year 1

M	2 Corinthians 1:1–7	Matthew 5:1–12
T	2 Corinthians 1:18–22	Matthew 5:13–16
W	2 Corinthians 3:4–11	Matthew 5:17–19
Th	2 Corinthians 3:15–4:1, 3–6	Matthew 5:20–26
F	2 Corinthians 4:7–15	Matthew 5:27–32
S	2 Corinthians 5:14–end	Matthew 5:33–37

Week 10 of Year 2

M	1 Kings 17:1–6	Matthew 5:1–12
T	1 Kings 17:7–16	Matthew 5:13–16
W	1 Kings 18:20–39	Matthew 5:17–19
Th	1 Kings 18:41–end	Matthew 5:20–26
F	1 Kings 19:9, 11–16	Matthew 5:27–32
S	1 Kings 19:19–end	Matthew 5:33–37

Sunday between 12–18 June inclusive
[Proper 6 of CWPS]　　　　　*[Sunday 11 of Ordinary Time]*

Year A	Year B	Year C
Exodus 19:2–8a	Ezekiel 17:22–24	2 Samuel 11:26–12:10, 13–15

Romans 5:1–8	2 Corinthians 5:6–10, [11–13]14–17	Galatians 2:15–21

Matthew 9:35–10:8 [9–23]	Mark 4:26–34	Luke 7:36–8:3

Week 11 of Year 1
M　2 Corinthians 6:1–10　　　　　Matthew 5:38–42
T　2 Corinthians 8: 1-9　　　　　Matthew 5:43–end
W　2 Corinthians 9:6–11　　　　　Matthew 6:1–6, 16–18
Th　2 Corinthians 11:1–11　　　　Matthew 6:7–15
F　2 Corinthians 11:18, 21a-30　　Matthew 6:19–23
S　2 Corinthians 12:1–10　　　　 Matthew 6:24–end

Week 11 of Year 2
M　1 Kings 21:1–16　　　　　　　Matthew 5:38–42
T　1 Kings 21:17–end　　　　　　Matthew 5:43–end
W　2 Kings 2:1, 6–14　　　　　　 Matthew 6:1–6, 16–18
Th　Ecclesiasticus 48:1–14　　　　Matthew 6:7–15
F　2 Kings 11:1–4, 9–18, 20　　　 Matthew 6:19–23
S　2 Chronicles 24:17–25　　　　 Matthew 6:24–end

Sunday between 19–25 June inclusive
[Proper 7 of CWPS]　　　　　*[Sunday 12 of Ordinary Time]*

Year A	Year B	Year C
Jeremiah 20:7–13	Job 38:1–11	Isaiah 65:1–9
Romans 6:1b-11	2 Corinthians 6:1–13	Galatians 3:23–29
Matthew 10:24–39	Mark 4:35–41	Luke 8:26–39

Week 12 of Year 1
M　Genesis 12:1–9　　　　　　　Matthew 7:1–5
T　Genesis 13:2, 5–end　　　　　 Matthew 7:6, 12–14
W　Genesis 15:1–12, 17–18　　　　Matthew 7:15–20
Th　Genesis 16:1–12, 15–16　　　 Matthew 7:21–end
F　Genesis 17:1, 9–10, 15–22　　　Matthew 8:1–4
S　Genesis 18:1–15　　　　　　　Matthew 8:5–17

Week 12 of Year 2
M 2 Kings 17:5–8, 13–15, 18   Matthew 7:1–5
T 2 Kings 19:9–11, 14–21a,   Matthew 7:6, 12–14
      31–36
W 2 Kings 22:8–13; 23:1–3   Matthew 7:15–20
Th 2 Kings 24:8–17   Matthew 7:21–end
F 2 Kings 25:1–12   Matthew 8:1–4
S Lamentations 2:2,10–14,18–19   Matthew 8:5–17

Sunday between 26 June and 2 July inclusive
[Proper 8 of CWPS]   *[Sunday 13 of Ordinary Time]*

Year A	Year B	Year C
Jeremiah 28:5–9	Wisdom 1:13–15; 2:23–24	1 Kings 19:15–16
Romans 6:12–23	2 Corinthians 8:7–15	Galatians 5:1,13–25
Matthew 10:40–42	Mark 5:21–43	Luke 9:51–62

Week 13 of Year 1
M Genesis 18:16–end   Matthew 8:18–22
T Genesis 19:15–29   Matthew 8:23–27
W Genesis 21:5, 8–20   Matthew 8:28–end
Th Genesis 22:1–19   Matthew 9:1–8
F Genesis 23:1–4, 19;   Matthew 9:9–13
      24: 1–8, 62–end
S Genesis 27:1–5a, 15–29   Matthew 9:14–17

Week 13 of Year 2
M Amos 2:6–10, 13–end   Matthew 8:18–22
T Amos 3:1–8; 4:11–12   Matthew 8:23–27
W Amos 5:14–15, 21–24   Matthew 8:28–end
Th Amos 7:10–end   Matthew 9:1–8
F Amos 8:4–6, 9–12   Matthew 9:9–13
S Amos 9:11–end   Matthew 9:14–17

Sunday between 3–9 July inclusive
[Proper 9 of CWPS]   *[Sunday 14 of Ordinary Time]*

Year A	Year B	Year C
Zechariah 9:9–12	Ezekiel 2:1–5	Isaiah 66:10–14
Romans 7:15–25a	2 Corinthians 12:2–10	Galatians 6:[1–6]7–16
Matthew 11:16–19, 25–30	Mark 6:1–13	Luke 10:1–11,16–20

Week 14 of Year 1

M	Genesis 28:10–end	Matthew 9:18–26
T	Genesis 32:22–end	Matthew 9:32–end
W	Genesis 41:55–end; 42: 5–7, 17–end	Matthew 10:1–7
Th	Genesis 44:18–21, 23–29; 45:1–5	Matthew 10:7–15
F	Genesis 46:1–7, 28–30	Matthew 10:16–23
S	Genesis 49:29–end; 50:15–25	Matthew 10:24–33

Week 14 of Year 2

M	Hosea 2:16–18, 21–22	Matthew 9:18–26
T	Hosea 8:4–7, 11–13	Matthew 9:32–end
W	Hosea 10:1–3, 7–8, 12	Matthew 10:1–7
Th	Hosea 11:1, 3–4, 8–9	Matthew 10:7–15
F	Hosea 14:2–end	Matthew 10:16–23
S	Isaiah 6:1–8	Matthew 10:24–33

Sunday between 10–16 July inclusive
[Proper 10 of CWPS]   [Sunday 15 of Ordinary Time]

Year A	*Year B*	*Year C*
Isaiah 55:10–13	Amos 7:7–15	Deuteronomy 30:9–14
Romans 8:1–11	Ephesians 1:3–14	Colossians 1:1–14
Matthew 13:1–9,18–23	Mark 6:14–29	Luke 10:25–37

Week 15 of Year 1

M	Exodus 1:8–14, 22	Matthew 10:34–11:1
T	Exodus 2:1–15	Matthew 11:20–24
W	Exodus 3:1–6, 9–12	Matthew 11:25–27
Th	Exodus 3:13–20	Matthew 11:28–end
F	Exodus 11:10–12:14	Matthew 12:1–8
S	Exodus 12:37–42	Matthew 12: 14–21

Week 15 of Year 2

M	Isaiah 1:11–17	Matthew 10:34–11:1
T	Isaiah 7:1–9	Matthew 11:20–24
W	Isaiah 10:5–7, 13–16	Matthew 11:25–27
Th	Isaiah 26:7–9, 16–19	Matthew 11:28–end
F	Isaiah 38:1–6, 21–22, 7–8	Matthew 12:1–8
S	Micah 2:1–5	Matthew 12:14–21

Sunday between 17–23 July inclusive
[Proper 11 of CWPS]   *[Sunday 16 of Ordinary Time]*

Year A
Wisdom 12:13,16–19
Romans 8:12–25
Matthew 13:24–30, 36–43

Year B
Jeremiah 23:1–6
Ephesians 2:11–22
Mark 6:30–34, 53–56

Year C
Genesis 18:1–10a
Colossians 1:15–28
Luke 10:38–42

Week 16 of Year 1
M Exodus 14:5–18   Matthew 12:38–42
T Exodus 14:21–15:1   Matthew 12:46–end
W Exodus 16:1–5, 9–15   Matthew 13:1–9
Th Exodus 19:1–2, 9–11, 16–20   Matthew 13:10–17
F Exodus 20:1–17   Matthew 13:18–23
S Exodus 24:3–8   Matthew 13:24–30

Week 16 of Year 2
M Micah 6:1–4, 6–8   Matthew 12:38–42
T Micah 7:14–15, 18–end   Matthew 12:46–end
W Jeremiah 1:1, 4–10   Matthew 13:1–9
Th Jeremiah 2:1–3, 7–8, 12–13   Matthew 13:10–17
F Jeremiah 3:14–17   Matthew 13:18–23
S Jeremiah 7:1–11   Matthew 13:24–30

Sunday between 24–30 July inclusive
[Proper 12 of CWPS]   *[Sunday 17 of Ordinary Time]*

Year A
1 Kings 3:5–12
Romans 8:26–39

Matthew 13:31–33, 44–52

Year B
2 Kings 4:42–44
Ephesians 3:14–21

John 6:1–21

Year C
Genesis 18:20–32
Colossians 2:6–15 [16–19]

Luke 11:1–13

Week 17 of Year 1
M Exodus 32:15–24, 30–34   Matthew 13:31–35
T Exodus 33: 7–11; 34:5–9, 28   Matthew 13:36–43
W Exodus 34:29–end   Matthew 13:44–46
Th Exodus 40:16–21, 34–end   Matthew 13:47–53
F Leviticus 23:1, 4–11, 15–16, 27, 34–37   Matthew 13:54–end
S Leviticus 25:1, 8–17   Matthew 14:1–12

Week 17 of Year 2
M   Jeremiah 13:1–11   Matthew 13:31–35
T   Jeremiah 14:17–end   Matthew 13:36–43
W   Jeremiah 15:10, 16–end   Matthew 13:44–46
Th Jeremiah 18:1–6   Matthew 13:47–53
F   Jeremiah 26:1–9   Matthew 13:54–end
S   Jeremiah 26:11–16, 24   Matthew 14:1–12

Sunday between 31 July and 6 August inclusive
[Proper 13 of CWPS]   *[Sunday 18 of Ordinary Time]*

Year A	*Year B*	*Year C*
Isaiah 55:1–5	Exodus 16:2–4, 9–15	Ecclesiastes 1:2, 12–14; 2:18–23
Romans 9:1–5	Ephesians 4:1–16	Colossians 3:1–11
Matthew 14:13–21	John 6:24–35	Luke 12:13–21

Week 18 of Year 1
M   Numbers 11:4–15   Matthew 14:13–21 or 14:22–end
T   Numbers 12:1–13   Matthew 14:22–end or 15:1–2, 10–14
W   Numbers 13:1, 2, 25–14:1, 26–35   Matthew 15:21–28
Th Numbers 20:1–13   Matthew 16:13–23
F   Deuteronomy 4:32–40   Matthew 16:24–end
S   Deuteronomy 6:4–13   Matthew 17:14–20

Week 18 of Year 2
M   Jeremiah 28   Matthew 14:13–21 or 14:22–end
T   Jeremiah 30:1–2, 12–15, 18–22   Matthew 14:22–end or 15:1–2, 10–14
W   Jeremiah 31:1–7   Matthew 15:21–28
Th Jeremiah 31:31–34   Matthew 16:13–23
F   Nahum 2:1, 3; 3:1–3, 6–7   Matthew 16:24–end
S   Habakkuk 1:12–2:4   Matthew 17:14–20

Sunday between 7–13 August inclusive
[Proper 14 of CWPS]   *[Sunday 19 of Ordinary Time]*

Year A	*Year B*	*Year C*
1 Kings 19:9–18	1 Kings 19:4–8	Genesis 15:1–6
Romans 10:5–15	Ephesians 4:25–5:2	Hebrews 11:1–3, 8–16

Matthew 14:22–33 John 6:35, 41–51 Luke 12:32–40

Week 19 of Year 1
M Deuteronomy 10:12–end   Matthew 17:22–end
T Deuteronomy 31:1–8   Matthew 18:1–5, 10, 12–14
W Deuteronomy 34   Matthew 18:15–20
Th Joshua 3:7–11, 13–17   Matthew 18:21–19:1
F Joshua 24:1–13   Matthew 19:3–12
S Joshua 24:14–29   Matthew 19:13–15

Week 19 of Year 2
M Ezekiel 1:2–5, 24–end   Matthew 17:22–end
T Ezekiel 2:8–3:4   Matthew 18:1–5, 10, 12–14
W Ezekiel 9:1–7; 10:18–22   Matthew 18:15–20
Th Ezekiel 12:1–12   Matthew 18:21–19:1
F Ezekiel 16:1–15, 60–end   Matthew 19:3–12
S Ezekiel 18:1–10, 13, 30, 32   Matthew 19:13–15

Sunday between 14–20 August inclusive
[Proper 15 of CWPS]   [Sunday 20 of Ordinary Time]

Year A	Year B	Year C
Isaiah 56:1, 6–8	Proverbs 9:1–6	Jeremiah 23:23–29
Romans 11:1–2a, 29–32	Ephesians 5:15–20	Hebrews 11:29–12:2
Matthew 15:[10–20] 21–28	John 6:51–58	Luke 12:49–56

Week 20 of Year 1
M Judges 2:11–19   Matthew 19:16–22
T Judges 6:11–24   Matthew 19:23–end
W Judges 9:6–15   Matthew 20:1–16
Th Judges 11:29–end   Matthew 22:1–14
F Ruth 1:1, 3–6, 14–16, 22   Matthew 22:34–40
S Ruth 2:1–3, 8–11; 4:13–17   Matthew 23:1–12

Week 20 of Year 2
M Ezekiel 24:15–24   Matthew 19:16–22
T Ezekiel 28:1–10   Matthew 19:23–end
W Ezekiel 34:1–11   Matthew 20:1–16
Th Ezekiel 36:23–28   Matthew 22:1–14
F Ezekiel 37:1–14   Matthew 22:34–40
S Ezekiel 43:1–7   Matthew 23:1–12

Sunday between 21–27 August inclusive

Ordinary Time

[Proper 16 of CWPS]   *[Sunday 21 of Ordinary Time]*

Year A	Year B	Year C
Isaiah 51:1–6	Joshua 24:1–2a, 14–18	Isaiah 58:9b-14
Romans 12:1–8	Ephesians 6:10–20	Hebrews 12:18–29
Matthew 16:13–20	John 6:56–69	Luke 13:10–17

Week 21 of Year 1
- M 1 Thessalonians 1:2–5, 8–10   Matthew 23:13–22
- T 1 Thessalonians 2:1–8   Matthew 23:23–26
- W 1 Thessalonians 2:9–13   Matthew 23:27–32
- Th 1 Thessalonians 3:7–end   Matthew 24:42–end
- F 1 Thessalonians 4:1–8   Matthew 25:1–13
- S 1 Thessalonians 4:9–12   Matthew 25:14–30

Week 21 of Year 2
- M 2 Thessalonians 1:1–5, 11–12   Matthew 23:13–22
- T 2 Thessalonians 2:1–3a, 14–17   Matthew 23:23–26
- W 2 Thessalonians 3:6–10,16–end   Matthew 23:27–32
- Th 1 Corinthians 1:1–9   Matthew 24:42–end
- F 1 Corinthians 1:17–25   Matthew 25:1–13
- S 1 Corinthians 1:26–end   Matthew 25:14–30

Sunday between 28 August and 3 September inclusive
[Proper 17 of CWPS]   *[Sunday 22 of Ordinary Time]*

Year A	Year B	Year C
Jeremiah 15:15–21	Deuteronomy 4:1–2, 6–9	Ecclesiasticus 10:12–18
Romans 12:9–21	James 1:17–27	Hebrews 13:1–8, 15–16
Matthew 16:21–28	Mark 7:1–8, 14–15, 21–23	Luke 14:1, 7–14

Week 22 of Year 1
- M 1 Thessalonians 4:13–end   Luke 4:16–30
- T 1 Thessalonians 5:1–6, 9–11   Luke 4:31–37
- W Colossians 1:1–8   Luke 4:38–end
- Th Colossians 1:9–14   Luke 5:1–11
- F Colossians 1:15–20   Luke 5:33–end
- S Colossians 1:21–23   Luke 6:1–5

Week 22 of Year 2

M	1 Corinthians 2:1–5	Luke 4:16–30
T	1 Corinthians 2:10–end	Luke 4:31–37
W	1 Corinthians 3:1–9	Luke 4:38–end
Th	1 Corinthians 3:18–end	Luke 5:1–11
F	1 Corinthians 4:1–5	Luke 5:33–end
S	1 Corinthians 4:6–15	Luke 6:1–5

Sunday between 4–10 September inclusive
[Proper 18 of CWPS]   [Sunday 23 of Ordinary Time]

Year A	*Year B*	*Year C*
Ezekiel 33:7–11	Isaiah 35:4–7a	Deuteronomy 30:15–20
Romans 13:8–14	James 2:1–10 [11–13], 14–17	Philemon 1–21
Matthew 18:15–20	Mark 7:24–37	Luke 14:25–33

Week 23 of Year 1

M	Colossians 1:24–2:3	Luke 6:6–11
T	Colossians 2:6–15	Luke 6:12–19
W	Colossians 3:1–11	Luke 6:20–26
Th	Colossians 3:12–17	Luke 6:27–38
F	1 Timothy 1:1–2, 12–14	Luke 6:39–42
S	1 Timothy 1:15–17	Luke 6:43–end

Week 23 of Year 2

M	1 Corinthians 5:1–8	Luke 6:6–11
T	1 Corinthians 6:1–11	Luke 6:12–19
W	1 Corinthians 7:25–31	Luke 6:20–26
Th	1 Corinthians 8:1–7, 11–end	Luke 6:27–38
F	1 Corinthians 9:16–19, 22–end	Luke 6:39–42
S	1 Corinthians 10:14–22	Luke 6:43–end

Sunday between 11–17 September inclusive
[Proper 19 of CWPS]   [Sunday 24 of Ordinary Time]

Year A	*Year B*	*Year C*
Genesis 50:15–21	Isaiah 50:4–9a	Exodus 32:7–14
Romans 14:1–12	James 3:1–12	1 Timothy 1:12–17
Matthew 18:21–35	Mark 8:27–38	Luke 15:1–10

Ordinary Time

Week 24 of Year 1
M   1 Timothy 2:1–8   Luke 7:1–10
T   1 Timothy 3:1–13   Luke 7:11–17
W   1 Timothy 3:14–end   Luke 7:31–35
Th 1 Timothy 4:12–end   Luke 7:36–end
F   1 Timothy 6:2–12   Luke 8:1–3
S   1 Timothy 6:13–16   Luke 8:4–15

Week 24 of Year 2
M   1 Corinthians 11:17–26, 33   Luke 7:1–10
T   1 Corinthians 12:12–14, 27–end   Luke 7:11–17
W   1 Corinthians 12:31–13:13   Luke 7:31–35
Th 1 Corinthians 15:1–11   Luke 7:36–end
F   1 Corinthians 15:12–20   Luke 8:1–3
S   1 Corinthians 15:35–37, 42–49   Luke 8:4–15

Sunday between 18–24 September inclusive
[Proper 20 of CWPS]   *[Sunday 25 of Ordinary Time]*

Year A	*Year B*	*Year C*
Jonah 3:10–4:11	Wisdom 1:16–2:1, 12–22	Amos 8:4–7
Philippians 1:21–30	James 3:13–4:3, 7–8a	1 Timothy 2:1–7
Matthew 20:1–16	Mark 9:30–37	Luke 16:1–13

Week 25 of Year 1
M   Ezra 1:1–6   Luke 8:16–18
T   Ezra 6:7–8, 12, 14–20   Luke 8:19–21
W   Ezra 9:5–9   Luke 9:1–6
Th Haggai 1:1–8   Luke 9:7–9
F   Haggai 1:15b–2:9   Luke 9:18–22
S   Zechariah 2:1–5, 10–11   Luke 9:43–45

Week 25 of Year 2
M   Proverbs 3:27–34   Luke 8:16–18
T   Proverbs 21:1–6, 10–13   Luke 8:19–21
W   Proverbs 30:5–9   Luke 9:1–6
Th Ecclesiastes 1:2–11   Luke 9:7–9
F   Ecclesiastes 3:1–11   Luke 9:18–22
S   Ecclesiastes 11:9–12:8   Luke 9:43–45

Sunday between 25 September and 1 October inclusive
[Proper 21 of CWPS]   *[Sunday 26 of Ordinary Time]*

Year A	Year B	Year C
Ezekiel 18:1–4, 25–32	Numbers 11:4–6, 10–16, 24–29	Amos 6:1a, 4–7
Philippians 2:1–13	James 5:13–20	1 Timothy 6:6–19
Matthew 21:23–32	Mark 9:38–50	Luke 16:19–31

Week 26 of Year 1
M Zechariah 8:1–8   Luke 9:46–50
T Zechariah 8:20–end   Luke 9:51–56
W Nehemiah 2:1–8   Luke 9:57–end
Th Nehemiah 8:1–12   Luke 10:1–12
F Baruch 1:15–end   Luke 10:13–16
S Baruch 4:5–12, 27–29   Luke 10:17–24

Week 26 of Year 2
M Job 1:6–end   Luke 9:46–50
T Job 3:1–3, 11–17, 20–23   Luke 9:51–56
W Job 9:1–12, 14–16   Luke 9:57–end
Th Job 19:21–27a   Luke 10:1–12
F Job 38:1, 12–21; 40:3–5   Luke 10:13–16
S Job 42:1–3, 6, 12–end   Luke 10:17–24

Sunday between 2–8 October inclusive
[Proper 22 of CWPS]   *[Sunday 27 of Ordinary Time]*

Year A	Year B	Year C
Isaiah 5:1–7	Genesis 2:18–24	Habakkuk 1:1–4; 2:1–4
Philippians 3:4b–14	Hebrews 1:1–4; 2:5–12	2 Timothy 1:1–14
Matthew 21:33–46	Mark 10:2–16	Luke 17:5–10

Week 27 of Year 1
M Jonah 1:1–2:1–2, 10   Luke 10:25–37
T Jonah 3   Luke 10:38–end
W Jonah 4   Luke 11:1–4
Th Malachi 3:13–4: 2a   Luke 11:5–13
F Joel 1:13–15; 2:1–2   Luke 11:15–26
S Joel 3:12–21   Luke 11:27–28

Week 27 of Year 2
M Galatians 1:6–12   Luke 10:25–37
T Galatians 1:13–end   Luke 10:38–end
W Galatians 2:1–2, 7–14   Luke 11:1–4
Th Galatians 3:1–5   Luke 11:5–13
F Galatians 3:7–14   Luke 11:15–26
S Galatians 3:22–end   Luke 11:27–28

Sunday between 9–15 October inclusive
[Proper 23 of CWPS]   *[Sunday 28 of Ordinary Time]*
Year A   *Year B*   *Year C*
Isaiah 25:1–9   Amos 5:6–7, 10–15   2 Kings 5:1–3, 7–15c
Philippians 4:1–9   Hebrews 4:12–16   2 Timothy 2:8–15
Matthew 22:1–14   Mark 10:17–31   Luke 17:11–19

Week 28 of Year 1
M Romans 1:1–7   Luke 11:29–32
T Romans 1:16–25   Luke 11:37–41
W Romans 2:1–11   Luke 11:42–46
Th Romans 3:21–30   Luke 11:47–end
F Romans 4:1–8   Luke 12:1–7
S Romans 4:13, 16–18   Luke 12:8–12

Week 28 of Year 2
M Galatians 4:21–24, 26–27, 31; 5:1   Luke 11:29–32
T Galatians 5:1–6   Luke 11:37–41
W Galatians 5:18–end   Luke 11:42–46
Th Ephesians 1:1, 3–10   Luke 11:47–end
F Ephesians 1:11–14   Luke 12:1–7
S Ephesians 1:15–end   Luke 12:8–12

Sunday between 16–22 October inclusive
[Proper 24 of CWPS]   *[Sunday 29 of Ordinary Time]*

Year A   *Year B*   *Year C*
Isaiah 45:1–7   Isaiah 53:4–12   Genesis 32:22–31
1 Thessalonians 1:1–10   Hebrews 5:1–10   2 Timothy 3:14–4:5
Matthew 22:15–22   Mark 10:35–45   Luke 18:1–8

Week 29 of Year 1
M Romans 4:20–end   Luke 12:13–21
T Romans 5:12, 15, 17–end   Luke 12:35–38

W	Romans 6:12–18	Luke 12:39–48
Th	Romans 6:19–end	Luke 12:49–53
F	Romans 7:18–end	Luke 12:54–end
S	Romans 8:1–11	Luke 13:1–9

Week 29 of Year 2

M	Ephesians 2:1–10	Luke 12:13–21
T	Ephesians 2:12–end	Luke 12:35–38
W	Ephesians 3:2–12	Luke 12:39–48
Th	Ephesians 3:14–end	Luke 12:49–53
F	Ephesians 4:1–6	Luke 12:54–end
S	Ephesians 4:7–16	Luke 13:1–9

Sunday between 23–29 October inclusive
[Proper 25 of CWPS]　　　*[Sunday 30 of Ordinary Time]*

Year A	Year B	Year C
Leviticus 19:1–2, 15–18	Jeremiah 31:7–9	Ecclesiasticus 35:12–17
1 Thessalonians 2:1–8	Hebrews 7:23–28	2 Timothy 4:6–8, 16–18
Matthew 22:34–46	Mark 10:46–52	Luke 18:9–14

Week 30 of Year 1

M	Romans 8:12–17	Luke 13:10–17
T	Romans 8:18–25	Luke 13:18–21
W	Romans 8:26–30	Luke 13:22–30
Th	Romans 8:31–end	Luke 13:31–end
F	Romans 9:1–5	Luke 14:1–6
S	Romans 11:1–2, 11–12, 25–29	Luke 14:1, 7–11

Week 30 of Year 2

M	Ephesians 4:32–5:8	Luke 13:10–17
T	Ephesians 5:21–end	Luke 13:18–21
W	Ephesians 6:1–9	Luke 13:22–30
Th	Ephesians 6:10–20	Luke 13:31–end
F	Philippians 1:1–11	Luke 14:1–6
S	Philippians 1:18–26	Luke 14:1, 7–11

For Weeks 31–34, see below page 427.

Responsory

R/ You are the Christ, the Son of the living God. Have mercy on us.
R/ You are the Christ, the Son of the living God. Have mercy on us.
V/ You are seated at the right hand of the Father.
R/ You are the Christ, the Son of the living God. Have mercy on us.
V/ Glory . . . Holy Spirit.
R/ You are the Christ, the Son of the living God. Have mercy on us.

Antiphons/Refrains and Texts for Meditation

Speak, Lord, for your servant is listening. You have the words of eternal life.
1 Samuel 3:9, John 6:68

You shall receive power when the Holy Spirit has come upon you; and you shall be my witnesses.
Acts 1:8 (RSV)

If anyone is in Christ, there is a new creation; everything old has passed away.
2 Corinthians 5:17

The word of the Lord endures for ever. That word is the good news announced to you.
1 Peter 1:25

Collects

Lord, you have taught us
that all our doings without love are nothing worth:
send your Holy Spirit
and pour into our hearts that most excellent gift of love,
the true bond of peace and of all virtues,
without which whoever lives is counted dead before you.
Grant this for your only Son Jesus Christ's sake,
who is alive and reigns with you,
in the unity of the Holy Spirit,
one God, now and for ever.

Second Sunday after Trinity
Common Worship (1)

or

Merciful God,
you have prepared for those who love you
such good things as pass our understanding:
pour into our hearts such love toward you
that we, loving you in all things and above all things,
may obtain your promises,
which exceed all that we can desire;
through Jesus Christ your Son our Lord,
who is alive and reigns with you,
in the unity of the Holy Spirit,
one God, now and for ever.

Sixth Sunday after Trinity
Common Worship (1)

or

Lord of all power and might,
the author and giver of all good things:
graft in our hearts the love of your name,
increase in us true religion,
nourish us with all goodness,
and of your great mercy keep us in the same;
through Jesus Christ your Son our Lord,
who is alive and reigns with you,
in the unity of the Holy Spirit,
one God, now and for ever.

Seventh Sunday after Trinity
Common Worship (1)

or

Let your merciful ears, O Lord,
be open to the prayers of your humble servants;
and that they may obtain their petitions
make them to ask such things as shall please you;
through Jesus Christ your Son our Lord,
who is alive and reigns with you,
in the unity of the Holy Spirit,
one God, now and for ever.

Tenth Sunday after Trinity
Common Worship (1)

or

Almighty and everlasting God,
you are always more ready to hear than we to pray
and to give more than either we desire or deserve:
pour down upon us the abundance of your mercy,
forgiving us those things of which our conscience is afraid
and giving us those good things
   which we are not worthy to ask
but through the merits and mediation
of Jesus Christ your Son our Lord,
who is alive and reigns with you,
in the unity of the Holy Spirit,
one God, now and for ever.

Twelfth Sunday after Trinity
Common Worship (1)

or

O God, forasmuch as without you
we are not able to please you;
mercifully grant that your Holy Spirit
may in all things direct and rule our hearts;
through Jesus Christ your Son our Lord,
who is alive and reigns with you,
in the unity of the Holy Spirit,
one God, now and for ever.

Nineteenth Sunday after Trinity
Common Worship (1)

Other Prayers

O Almighty Lord, and everlasting God, vouchsafe, we beseech thee, to direct, sanctify, and govern both our hearts and bodies, in the ways of thy laws, and in the works of thy commandments; that through thy most mighty protection, both here and ever, we may be preserved in body and soul; through our Lord and Saviour Jesus Christ.

The Order of Confirmation
Book of Common Prayer (2)

Grant, O Lord God, that what we have heard with our ears and sung with our lips, we may believe in our hearts and practise in our lives; for Jesus Christ's sake.

Eric Milner-White (16)

Lord God, the source of truth and love,
keep us faithful to the apostles' teaching and fellowship,
united in prayer and the breaking of bread,
and one in joy and simplicity of heart,
in Jesus Christ our Lord.

Fourteenth Sunday after Trinity
(Post Communion)
Common Worship (1)

God of peace,
whose Son Jesus Christ proclaimed the kingdom
and restored the broken to wholeness of life:
look with compassion on the anguish of the world,
and by your healing power
make whole both people and nations;
through our Lord and Saviour Jesus Christ.

Third Sunday before Advent
(Post-Communion)
Common Worship (1)

Pilgrimage

Lord God, our Father,
keep from harm all those who travel
by land, sea, and air.
Look after us on our journey
and bring us safely to our destination.
May our journeyings bring us closer to you.

Father, all-holy,
of old you made yourself the guide and
way for your people
as they wandered in the desert;
be our protection as we begin this journey,
so that we may return home again in safety.
You have given us your only Son to be our way to you;
make us follow him faithfully and unswervingly.
You gave us Mary as the image and model for following Christ,
grant that through her example we may live a new life.
You guide your pilgrim Church on earth through the Holy Spirit;
may we seek you in all things
and walk always in the way of your commandments.
Lord, be with us as we travel,
and bring us back safely to the place where we long to be:
we ask this through Christ our Lord.

All-powerful God, you always show mercy toward those who love you
and you are never far away from those who seek you.
Remain with your servants on their holy pilgrimage
and guide their way in accord with your will.
Shelter them with your protection by day,
give them the light of your grace by night,
and, as their companion on the journey,
bring them to their destination in safety.
We ask this through Christ our Lord.

We turn to you for protection, holy Mother of God.
Listen to our prayers and help us in our needs.
Save us from every danger, glorious and blessed Virgin.
Saint Gregory the Great, pray for us.
Saint Augustine of Canterbury, pray for us.
Saint Thomas Becket of Canterbury, pray for us.

May the Lord grant that the journey we begin, relying on him,
will end happily through his protection.

(13)

Pilgrimage Psalms

Originally sung by pilgrims en route to Jerusalem.

Psalm 120

A Song of Ascents

1 When I was in trouble I called to the Lord; *
   I called to the Lord and he answered me.
2 Deliver me, O Lord, from lying lips *
   and from a deceitful tongue.
3 What shall be given to you? *
   What more shall be done to you, deceitful tongue?
4 The sharp arrows of a warrior, *
   tempered in burning coals!
5 Woe is me, that I must lodge in Meshech *
   and dwell among the tents of Kedar.
6 My soul has dwelt too long *
   with enemies of peace.
7 I am for making peace, *
   but when I speak of it, they make ready for war.

Glory . . .

Psalm 121

A Song of Ascents

1 I lift up my eyes to the hills; *
   from where is my help to come?
2 My help comes from the Lord, *
   the maker of heaven and earth.
3 He will not suffer your foot to stumble; *
   he who watches over you will not sleep.
4 Behold, he who keeps watch over Israel *
   shall neither slumber nor sleep;

5 The Lord himself watches over you; *
   the Lord is your shade at your right hand,
6 So that the sun shall not strike you by day, *
   neither the moon by night.
7 The Lord shall keep you from all evil; *
   it is he who shall keep your soul.
8 The Lord shall keep watch over your going out
      and your coming in, *
   from this time forth for evermore.

   Glory . . .

Psalm 122

A Song of Ascents

1 I was glad when they said to me, *
   'Let us go to the house of the Lord.'
2 And now our feet are standing *
   within your gates, O Jerusalem;
3 Jerusalem, built as a city *
   that is at unity in itself.
4 Thither the tribes go up, the tribes of the Lord, *
   as is decreed for Israel,
   to give thanks to the name of the Lord.
5 For there are set the thrones of judgement, *
   the thrones of the house of David.
6 O pray for the peace of Jerusalem: *
   'May they prosper who love you.
7 'Peace be within your walls *
   and tranquillity within your palaces.'
8 For my kindred and companions' sake, *
   I will pray that peace be with you.
9 For the sake of the house of the Lord our God, *
   I will seek to do you good.

   Glory . . .

Psalm 123

A Song of Ascents

1 To you I lift up my eyes, *
    to you that are enthroned in the heavens.
2 As the eyes of servants look to the hand of their master, *
    or the eyes of a maid to the hand of her mistress,
3 So our eyes wait upon the Lord our God, *
    until he have mercy upon us.
4 Have mercy upon us, O Lord, have mercy upon us, *
    for we have had more than enough of contempt.
5 Our soul has had more than enough of the scorn of the arrogant, *
    and of the contempt of the proud.

   Glory . . .

Psalm 124

A Song of Ascents

1 If the Lord himself had not been on our side, *
    now may Israel say;
2 If the Lord had not been on our side, *
    when enemies rose up against us;
3 Then would they have swallowed us alive *
    when their anger burned against us;
4 Then would the waters have overwhelmed us
    and the torrent gone over our soul; *
    over our soul would have swept the raging waters.
5 But blessed be the Lord *
    who has not given us over to be a prey for their teeth.
6 Our soul has escaped
    as a bird from the snare of the fowler; *
    the snare is broken and we are delivered.
7 Our help is in the name of the Lord, *
    who has made heaven and earth.

   Glory . . .

Psalm 125

A Song of Ascents

1 Those who trust in the Lord are like Mount Zion, *
    which cannot be moved, but stands fast for ever
2 As the hills stand about Jerusalem, *
    so the Lord stands round about his people,
    from this time forth for evermore.
3 The sceptre of wickedness shall not hold sway
    over the land allotted to the righteous, *
    lest the righteous turn their hands to evil.
4 Do good, O Lord, to those who are good, *
    and to those who are true of heart.
5 Those who turn aside to crooked ways
    the Lord shall take away with the evil-doers; *
    but let there be peace upon Israel.

   Glory . . .

Psalm 126

A Song of Ascents

1 When the Lord restored the fortunes of Zion, *
    then were we like those who dream.
2 Then was our mouth filled with laughter *
    and our tongue with songs of joy.
3 Then said they among the nations, *
    'The Lord has done great things for them.'
4 The Lord has indeed done great things for us, *
    and therefore we rejoiced.
5 Restore again our fortunes, O Lord, *
    as the river beds of the desert.
6 Those who sow in tears *
    shall reap with songs of joy.
7 Those who go out weeping, bearing the seed, *
    will come back with shouts of joy,
    bearing their sheaves with them.

   Glory . . .

Psalm 127

A Song of Ascents

1 Unless the Lord builds the house, *
 those who build it labour in vain.
2 Unless the Lord keeps the city, *
 the guard keeps watch in vain.
3 It is in vain that you hasten to rise up early
 and go so late to rest, eating the bread of toil, *
 for he gives his beloved sleep.
4 Children are a heritage from the Lord *
 and the fruit of the womb is his gift.
5 Like arrows in the hand of a warrior, *
 so are the children of one's youth.
6 Happy are those who have their quiver full of them: *
 they shall not be put to shame
 when they dispute with their enemies in the gate.

Glory . . .

Psalm 128

A Song of Ascents

1 Blessed are all those who fear the Lord, *
 and walk in his ways.
2 You shall eat the fruit of the toil of your hands; *
 it shall go well with you, and happy shall you be.
3 Your wife within your house
 shall be like a fruitful vine; *
 your children round your table,
 like fresh olive branches.
4 Thus shall the one be blest *
 who fears the Lord.
5 The Lord from out of Zion bless you, *
 that you may see Jerusalem in prosperity
 all the days of your life.
6 May you see your children's children, *
 and may there be peace upon Israel.

Glory . . .

Psalm 129

A Song of Ascents

1 'Many a time have they fought against me from my youth,' *
    may Israel now say;
2 'Many a time have they fought against me from my youth, *
    but they have not prevailed against me.'
3 The ploughers ploughed upon my back *
    and made their furrows long.
4 But the righteous Lord *
    has cut the cords of the wicked in pieces.

5 Let them be put to shame and turned backwards, *
    as many as are enemies of Zion.
6 Let them be like grass upon the housetops *
    which withers before it can grow,
7 So that no reaper can fill his hand, *
    nor a binder of sheaves his bosom;
8 And none who go by may say,
    'The blessing of the Lord be upon you. *
    We bless you in the name of the Lord.'

Glory . . .

Psalm 130

A Song of Ascents

Penitential Psalm

1 Out of the depths have I cried to you, O Lord;
    Lord, hear my voice; *
    let your ears consider well the voice of my supplication.
2 If you, Lord, were to mark what is done amiss, *
    O Lord, who could stand?
3 But there is forgiveness with you, *
    so that you shall be feared.
4 I wait for the Lord; my soul waits for him; *
    in his word is my hope.

5 My soul waits for the Lord,
  more than the night-watch for the morning, *
  more than the night-watch for the morning.

6 O Israel, wait for the Lord, *
  for with the Lord there is mercy;
7 With him is plenteous redemption *
  and he shall redeem Israel from all their sins.

  Glory . . .

Psalm 131

A Song of Ascents

1 O Lord, my heart is not proud; *
  my eyes are not raised in haughty looks.
2 I do not occupy myself with great matters, *
  with things that are too great for me.
3 But I have quieted and stilled my soul,
  like a weaned child on its mother's breast; *
  so my soul is quieted within me.
4 O Israel, trust in the Lord, *
  from this time forth for evermore.

  Glory . . .

Psalm 132

A Song of Ascents

1 Lord, remember for David *
  all the hardships he endured;
2 How he swore an oath to the Lord *
  and vowed a vow to the Mighty One of Jacob:
3 'I will not come within the shelter of my house, *
  nor climb up into my bed;
4 'I will not allow my eyes to sleep, *
  nor let my eyelids slumber;
5 'Until I find a place for the Lord, *
  a dwelling for the Mighty One of Jacob.'

6 Now, we heard of the ark in Ephrathah *
    and found it in the fields of Ja-ar
7 Let us enter his dwelling place *
    and fall low before his footstool.
8 Arise, O Lord, into your resting-place, *
    you and the ark of your strength.
9 Let your priests be clothed with righteousness *
    and your faithful ones sing with joy.
10 For your servant David's sake, *
    turn not away the face of your anointed.
11 The Lord has sworn an oath to David; *
    a promise from which he will not shrink:
12 'Of the fruit of your body *
    shall I set upon your throne.
13 'If your children keep my covenant
    and my testimonies that I shall teach them, *
    their children also shall sit upon your throne for evermore.'
14 For the Lord has chosen Zion for himself; *
    he has desired her for his habitation:
15 'This shall be my resting-place for ever; *
    here will I dwell, for I have longed for her.
16 'I will abundantly bless her provision; *
    her poor will I satisfy with bread.
17 'I will clothe her priests with salvation, *
    and her faithful ones shall rejoice and sing.
18 'There will I make a horn to spring up for David; *
    I will keep a lantern burning for my anointed.
19 'As for his enemies, I will clothe them with shame; *
    but on him shall his crown be bright.'

   Glory . . .

Psalm 133

A Song of Ascents

1 Behold how good and pleasant it is *
    to dwell together in unity.
2 It is like the precious oil upon the head, *
    running down upon the beard,

3 Even on Aaron's beard, *
    running down upon the collar of his clothing.
4 It is like the dew of Hermon *
    running down upon the hills of Zion.
5 For there the Lord has promised his blessing; *
    even life for evermore.

   Glory . . .

Psalm 134

A Song of Ascents

1 Come, bless the Lord,
    all you servants of the Lord, *
    you that by night stand in the house of the Lord.
2 Lift up your hands towards the sanctuary *
    and bless the Lord.
3 The Lord who made heaven and earth *
    give you blessing out of Zion.

   Glory. . .

Our Lady

Propers and Readings

Office Hymn

Ave, maris stella

Star of sea and ocean,
Gateway to Man's haven,
Mother of our Maker,
Hear our prayer, O maiden.

Welcoming the Ave
Of God's simple greeting,
You have borne a Saviour
Far beyond all dreaming.

Loose the bonds that hold us,
Bound in sin's own blindness,
That with eyes now opened,
God's own light may guide us.

Show yourself, our Mother:
He will hear your pleading,
Whom your womb has sheltered
And whose hand brings healing.

Gentlest of all virgins,
That our love be faithful,
Keep us from all evil,
Gentle, strong and grateful.

Guard us through life's dangers,
Never turn and leave us,
May our hope find harbour
In the calm of Jesus.

Sing to God our Father
Through the Son who saves us;
Joyful in the Spirit
Everlasting praises.

Ralph Wright OSB (42)
Hymns for Prayer and Praise 305

Psalms and Canticles

Evening Prayer I	113
	147:13–21
	A Song of God's Grace
	(Canticle 35) see page 583.
Morning Prayer	Sunday Week 1
Evening Prayer II	122
	127
	A Song of God's Grace
	(Canticle 35) see page 583.

Alternative Psalmody

From Psalm 45

1 Kings' daughters are among your honourable women; *
   at your right hand stands the queen in gold of Ophir.
2 Hear, O daughter; consider and incline your ear; *
   forget your own people and your father's house.
3 So shall the king have pleasure in your beauty; *
   he is your lord, so do him honour.
4 The people of Tyre shall bring you gifts; *
   the richest of the people shall seek your favour.
5 The king's daughter is all glorious within; *
   her clothing is embroidered cloth of gold.
6 She shall be brought to the king in raiment of needlework; *
   after her the virgins that are her companions.

7 With joy and gladness shall they be brought *
   and enter into the palace of the king.
8 'Instead of your fathers you shall have sons, *
   whom you shall make princes over all the earth.
9 'I will make your name to be remembered through all generations; *
   therefore shall the peoples praise you for ever and ever.'

   Glory . . .

Psalm 45:9–17

Short Readings

Sing and rejoice, O daughter of Zion; for lo, I come and I will dwell in the midst of you, says the Lord. And many nations shall join themselves to the Lord in that day, and shall be my people; and I will dwell in the midst of you, and you shall know that the Lord of hosts has sent me to you.

Zechariah 2:10–12a (RSV)

or

When Jesus saw his mother and the disciple whom he loved standing beside her, he said to his mother, 'Woman, here is your son.' Then he said to the disciple, 'Here is your mother'. And from that hour the disciple took her into his own home.

John 19:26–27

or

When the fullness of time had come, God sent his Son, born of a woman, born under the law, in order to redeem those who were under the law, so that we might receive adoption as children.

Galatians 4:4–5

or

A great portent appeared in heaven: a woman clothed with the sun, with the moon under her feet, and on her head a crown of twelve stars.

Revelation 12:1

Long Readings

NAMING AND   *1 January*
CIRCUMCISION OF JESUS:
SOLEMNITY OF MARY,
MOTHER OF GOD

See CHRISTMAS section

VISIT OF MARY TO ELIZABETH   *31 May*

Zephaniah 3:14–18
or Romans 12:9–16
Luke 1:39–49[50–56]

ASSUMPTION OF THE BLESSED   *15 August*
VIRGIN MARY

Isaiah 61:10–11
or * Revelation 11:19–12:6, 10
Galatians 4:4–7
or * 1 Corinthians 15:20–26
Luke 1:46–56

Birth of the Blessed Virgin Mary   *8 September*

Micah 5:1–4
or Romans 8:18–30
Luke 1:26–38

IMMACULATE CONCEPTION OF   *8 December*
THE BLESSED VIRGIN MARY

* Genesis 3:9–15
* Ephesians 1:3–6, 11–12
* Luke 1:26–38

Responsory

R/   Hail, favoured one, the Lord is with you.
R/   Blessed are you among women.
V/   Do not be afraid, Mary,
       for you have found favour with God.

R/	Hail, favoured one, the Lord is with you.
V/	You will conceive in your womb and bear a son, and you shall call his name Jesus.
R/	Blessed are you among women.
V/	He will be great, and will be called the Son of the Most High.
R/	Hail, favoured one, the Lord is with you. Blessed are you among women.

Antiphons/Refrains and Texts for Meditation

The Lord himself will give you a sign. Behold, a virgin shall conceive and bear a son, and shall call his name Emmanuel.

cf. Isaiah 7:14 (RSV)

I will greatly rejoice in the Lord, for he has clothed me with the garments of salvation.

cf. Isaiah 61:10

Behold I am the handmaid of the Lord; let it be to me according to your word.

Luke 1:38 (RSV)

Blessed are you among women and blessed is the fruit of your womb!

Luke 1:42

Mary kept all these things, pondering them in her heart.

Luke 2:19 (RSV)

A sword will pierce your own soul also.

Luke 2:35a

Collect

Almighty God,
who looked upon the lowliness of the Blessed Virgin Mary
and chose her to be the mother of your only Son:
grant that we who are redeemed by his blood
may share with her in the glory of your eternal kingdom;
through Jesus Christ your Son our Lord,
who is alive and reigns with you,
in the unity of the Holy Spirit,
one God, now and for ever.

The Blessed Virgin Mary
Common Worship (1)

Other Prayers

Seventeenth-Century Anglican Marian Devotion

And first O Lord I praise and magnify thy name
For the most holy Virgin-Mother of God, who is the highest of thy saints
The most glorious of all thy creatures
The most perfect of all thy works
The nearest unto thee, in the throne of God
Whom thou didst please to make
Daughter of the eternal Father
Mother of the eternal Son
Spouse of the eternal Spirit
Tabernacle of the most glorious Trinity
Mother of Jesus
Mother of the Messiah
Mother of him who was the Desire of all Nations
Mother of the Prince of Peace
Mother of the King of Heaven
Mother of our Creator
Mother and Virgin
Mirror of humility and obedience
Mirror of wisdom and devotion
Mirror of modesty and chastity
Mirror of sweetness and resignation
Mirror of sanctity
Mirror of all virtues
The most illustrious light in the Church, wearing over all her beauties the veil of humility to shine more resplendently in thy eternal Glory.

And yet this holy Virgin-Mother styled herself but the handmaid of the Lord, and falls down with all the glorious hosts of angels, and with the armies of saints, at the foot of thy throne, to worship and glorify thee for ever and ever.

I praise thee Lord with all the powers and faculties of my soul; for doing in her all thy merciful works for my sake, and the benefit of mankind. For uttering the glorious Word: yea rather blessed are they that hear the Word of God, and keep it. And for looking round about upon thy disciples and saying, Behold my mother and my brethren. For whosoever shall do the will of God, the same is my brother and my sister and mother. Yea for what thou wilt say, Inasmuch as ye have done it to the least of these, ye have done it unto me.

The most unworthy of all thy servants falleth down to worship thee for thine own excellencies; even thee O Lord, for thine own perfection, and for all those glorious graces, given and imparted to this holy Virgin, and to all thy saints.

Thomas Traherne

God most high,
from the first moment of her conception
you favoured the Virgin Mary with your grace,
that she might become the mother of the world's Redeemer.

As you blessed the daughter of Israel,
so grant us the grace
to be fully engaged in your service,
eager to do your will.
Hasten that day of gladness
when you will bring to completion your saving work,
through Jesus Christ our Lord,
who lives and reigns with you in the unity of the Holy Spirit,
God for ever and ever.

(8 December)
ICEL (5)

Faithful to your promise, O God,
you have lifted up the lowly,
clothing with heavenly splendour
the woman who bore Christ, our life and resurrection.

Grant that the Church, prefigured in Mary,
may bear Christ to the world
and come to share his triumph.

We ask this through our Lord Jesus Christ, your Son,
who lives and reigns with you in the unity of the Holy Spirit,
God for ever and ever.

(15 August)
ICEL (5)

Lord Jesus Christ,
help us to follow the example of Mary,
always ready to do your will.
At the message of an angel
she welcomed you, God's Son,

and, filled with the light of your Spirit,
she became your temple.
May her prayers for us take away our weakness.
May we grow in grace as we go forward in faith
and may we be united with you
and with Mary
in the joyful kingdom you have prepared for us.

(13)

Prayers to our Lady

Memorare

Remember, O most blessed Virgin Mary, that never was it known that anyone who fled to your protection, implored your aid or sought your intercession, was left unaided. Filled, therefore, with confidence in your goodness, I fly to you, Virgin of virgins, my mother. To you I come, before you I stand, sinful and sorrowful. O Mother of the Word incarnate, despise not my petition, but in your mercy hear and answer me.

Salve Regina

Hail, holy Queen, mother of mercy,
our life, our sweetness, and our hope.
To you do we cry,
poor banished children of Eve.
To you do we send up our sighs,
mourning and weeping in this vale of tears.
Turn then, most gracious advocate,
your eyes of mercy towards us,
and after this exile
show to us the blessed fruit of your womb, Jesus.
O clement, O loving,
O sweet Virgin Mary.

Sub Tuum Praesidium

We turn to you for protection,
holy Mother of God.
Listen to our prayers
and help us in our needs.
Save us from every danger,
glorious and blessed Virgin.

ICEL (5)

Mary, Help of Those in Need

Holy Mary,
help those in need,
give strength to the weak,

comfort the sorrowful,
pray for God's people,
assist the clergy,
intercede for religious.

May all who seek your help
experience your unfailing protection.

ICEL (5)

The Priest's Prayer to our Lady before Mass

O Mother of pity and loving kindness,
most blessed Virgin Mary,
I, a worthless and wretched sinner,
fly to you in heartfelt love and confidence,
entreating your compassion.
You who stood by your dear Son
when he hung upon the cross,
have pity and deign to stand by me too,
wretched sinner that I am,
and by all the priests who are offering Mass this day,
here and elsewhere throughout holy Church.
By the help of your favour enable us to offer a sacrifice
    that shall be worthy and acceptable
in the sight of the most high and undivided Trinity.

Divine Office (14)

Prayer of Saint Augustine of Canterbury to Mary, Mother of the Church

Gracious Lady, you are mother and virgin;
you are the mother of the body and soul
of our Head and Redeemer;
you are also truly mother of all the members
of Christ's Mystical Body.
For through your love,
you have co-operated in the begetting
of the faithful in the Church.
Unique among women,

you are mother and virgin;
mother of Christ and virgin of Christ.
You are the beauty and charm of earth, O Virgin.
You are forever the image of the holy Church.
Through a woman came death;
through a woman came life,
yes, through you,
O Mother of God!

(13)

Juxta crucem tecum stare

Today I have stood with you beneath the Cross
and felt more certainly than ever before,
that you became our Mother beneath the Cross.
How faithfully an earthly mother strives
to fulfil her dying son's last wish.
But you were the handmaid of the Lord.
Subduing wholly your own life and being
to the life and being of God incarnate.
You have taken your own to your heart
and with your heart bleeding from bitter sorrow
have purchased for each one of us new life.
You know us all, our wounds and our defacement.
But you know also the heavenly radiance
in which your Son's love eternally bathes us.
And so you carefully direct our footsteps.
You find no pain too great to bring us to our goal,
so those whom you have chosen for companions,
to stand beside you at the eternal throne
must stand beside you here beneath the Cross
and with hearts bleeding from bitter sorrow
purchase heavenly radiance for the precious souls
with whom the Son of God entrusted you.

Saint Teresa Benedicta of the Cross
(Edith Stein)
Good Friday 1938

Hail Mary, Mother of Christ and of the Church!
Hail, our life, our sweetness and our hope!
To your care I entrust all the necessities of all families,
the joys of children,
the desires of the young,
the worries of adults,
the pains of the sick,
the serene old age of senior citizens!
I entrust to you the fidelity and the abnegation of your Son's ministers,
the hope of all those preparing themselves for this ministry,
the joyous dedication of virgins in cloisters,
the prayer and concern of men and women religious,
the lives and the commitment of all those
  who work for Christ's reign on this earth.
In your hands, I set the fatigue and the sweat of those
  who work with their hands;
the noble dedication of those who transmit knowledge,
and the efforts of those who learn it;
the beautiful vocation of those who alleviate the pains of others
  through their science and their service;
the commitment of those who seek truth
  through their understanding and intelligence.
In your heart I leave the aspirations
  of those who uprightly seek the prosperity of their brethren through
    economic activities;
  of those who, in service to truth, inform and correctly form public opinion;
  of those who, in politics, in armies, in labour or trades unions, or in
    service to civic order,
  lend their honest collaboration in favour of just, peaceful and secure
    social life.
Come to the aid of those suffering misfortunes,
those suffering because of loneliness, of hunger, of lack of work.
Strengthen the weak in faith.
Blessed Virgin, increase our faith,
  strengthen our hope,
  reawaken our charity.

Pope John Paul II (25)

See also FINAL ANTHEMS TO THE BLESSED VIRGIN MARY (pages 668–670)

The Shrine of our Lady of Walsingham

Little Walsingham, Norfolk, is famous for the appearance of the Blessed Virgin Mary to the Lady Richeldis of the Manor of Walsingham in the eleventh century. The shrine was destroyed by order of King Henry VIII in 1538 and rebuilt during the first half of the twentieth century. Walsingham is a place noted for ecumenical co-operation and understanding, though Anglicans and Roman Catholics have separate shrines. Orthodox Christians also have places of pilgrimage in Walsingham. Anglicans have a modern shrine church, dedicated in 1938 and resembling a continental place of pilgrimage. Roman Catholics own the mediaeval Slipper Chapel, outside the village, and have built nearby the lovely Chapel of Reconciliation in the simple style of a Norfolk barn.

The Pilgrimage Psalms, see page 354, are especially suitable for use on pilgrimage to Walsingham.

Prayers for use at Walsingham

Prayer at the Feet of Our Lady of Walsingham

O Mary,
O glorious Mother of my Saviour,
behold me at my journey's end
kneeling within this holy place
where, through the centuries,
you have been the devotion and confidence of Christians.
In this place where your name is so great,
your protection so assured,
your intercession so loving,
I humbly claim a share in your prayers,
O Mary, Our Lady of Walsingham.

Pray, dear Mother,
that our Lord may make good
all that is imperfect in my requests
and obtain for me the crowning favour
of a heart completely surrendered to his will.

O Mary, recall the solemn moment
when Jesus, your divine Son,
dying on the cross,
confided us to your maternal care.
You are our Mother,
we desire ever to remain your devout children.
Let us therefore feel the effects of your powerful
    intercession with Jesus Christ.
Make your name again glorious in this place
once renowned throughout our land
by your visits, favours and many miracles.

Pray, O holy Mother of God
for the conversion of England,
restoration of the sick,
consolation for the afflicted,
repentance of sinners,
peace to the departed.

O blessed Mary, Mother of God,
our Lady of Walsingham,
intercede for us.

Pilgrim's Manual, Walsingham (43)

Erasmus' Prayer to Our Lady of Walsingham

What shall I call thee, O Full of Grace? *Heaven*, for of thee arose the Sun of Righteousness; *Paradise*, for thou hast budded forth the Flower of Immortality; *Virgin*, for thou didst hold in thy embrace the Son who is God of all: Pray thou to him that he will save our souls.

Mother of God, we fly to you, our shade and shelter on our pilgrim's way. Look kindly on our prayers, and turn not from us in our time of need. But free us from the dangers that beset us, radiant and holy Virgin.

O alone of all women, Mother and Virgin, Mother most happy, Virgin most pure, now we, impure as we are, come to see thee who art all-pure; we salute thee; we worship thee as how we may with our humble offerings. May thy Son grant us, that imitating thy most holy manners, we also, by the grace of the Holy Ghost, may deserve spiritually to conceive the Lord Jesus in our inmost soul, and, once conceived, never to lose him.

Pilgrim's Manual, Walsingham (43)

Erasmus' Vow to Our Lady of Walsingham, 1511

Hail, Jesus' Mother, blessed evermore. Alone of women, God-bearing and Virgin, others may offer to thee various gifts, this man gold, that man again his silver; a third adorns thy shrine with precious stones. But this poor soul ... bringing ..., asks in return for his most humble gift that greatest blessing, piety of heart, and free remission of his many sins.

Pilgrim's Manual, Walsingham (43)

At the End of a Pilgrimage

O Mary, Mother of Jesus,
I thank God, through your Son,
for the grace of a happy pilgrimage,
and for all that has happened to me
while I have been here.
Pray for all those I have met here
and for all my fellow-pilgrims.
Pray that I may have a safe and happy return home,
and that God may give me the grace to do at home
what you have taught me to do here.

Pilgrim's Manual, Walsingham (43)

Other Prayers and Devotions

The Litany of Our Lady of Walsingham

Our Lady of Walsingham; pray to the Lord for us.
Mary, conceived without sin; pray to the Lord for us.
Mary the Virgin; pray to the Lord for us.
Mary the Mother of God; pray to the Lord for us.
Mary taken up into heaven; pray to the Lord for us.

Mary at Bethlehem; pray for all mothers.
Mary at Nazareth; pray for all families.
Mary at Cana; pray for all married couples.
Mary who stood by the Cross; pray for all who suffer.
Mary in the Upper Room; pray for all who wait.
Mary, model of womanhood; pray for all women.
Women of faith; keep us in mind.

Woman of hope; keep us in mind.
Woman of charity; keep us in mind.
Woman of suffering; keep us in mind.
Woman of anxiety; keep us in mind.
Woman of humility; keep us in mind.
Woman of purity; keep us in mind.
Woman of obedience; keep us in mind.

Woman who wondered; remember us to God.
Woman who listened; remember us to God.
Woman who followed him; remember us to God.
Woman who longed for him; remember us to God.
Woman who loves him; remember us to God.

Mother of God; be our mother always.
Mother of the Church; be our mother always.
Mother of the World; be our mother always.
Mother whom we need; be our mother always.

Mother who went on believing; we thank God for you.
Mother who never lost hope; we thank God for you.
Mother who loved to the end; we thank God for you.

All holy and ever-living God,
in giving Jesus Christ to be our Saviour and Brother,
you gave us Mary, his Mother,
to be our Mother also;
grant, we pray you,
that we may be worthy of so great a brother
and so dear a mother.
May we come at last to you,
the Father of us all,
through Jesus Christ your Son,
who lives and reigns with you and the Holy Spirit,
for ever and ever.

O Holy Spirit, Lord and Giver of life,
as you overshadowed Mary that she might be the
    Mother of Jesus our Saviour,
so work silently in my heart,

to form within me the fullness of his redeemed
   and redeeming humanity.
Give me his loving heart,
to burn with love for God and love for my neighbour;
give me a share of his joy and sorrow,

his weakness and his strength,
his labour for the world's salvation.
May Mary, blessed among women,
Mother of our Saviour,
pray for me,
that Christ may be formed in me,
that I may live in union of heart and will
with Jesus Christ, her Son, our Lord and Saviour.

Blessed are you, Lord our God, King of the universe:
to you be glory and praise for ever!
In the greatness of your mercy
you chose the Virgin Mary to be the mother of your only Son.
In her obedience the day of our redemption dawned
when, by the overshadowing of your Holy Spirit,
he took our flesh and dwelt in the darkness of her womb.
In her your glory shines as in the burning bush,
and so we call her blessed with every generation.
With her we rejoice in your salvation
and ponder in our hearts the mystery of your love.
May we bear with her the piercing sword of sorrow
in hope that we like her may share the joy of heaven.
As now we join our praise with hers, blessed among all women,
create in us a heart of love obedient to your will,
for you are Lord and you are our God for ever.

Pilgrim's Manual, Walshingham (43)

The Rosary

Introduction

Holding the Crucifix, the Apostles' Creed:

I believe in God,
the Father almighty,
maker of heaven and earth.
And in Jesus Christ, his only Son, our Lord,
who was conceived by the Holy Ghost,
born of the Virgin Mary
suffered under Pontius Pilate,
was crucified, dead and buried.
He descended into hell.
The third day he rose again from the dead;
he ascended into heaven
and sitteth on the right hand of God the Father almighty.
From thence he shall come to judge the quick and the dead.
I believe in the Holy Ghost;
the holy catholic church,
the communion of saints,
the forgiveness of sins,
the resurrection of the body;
and the life everlasting.

Book of Common Prayer (2)

or

I believe in God,
the Father almighty,
creator of heaven and earth.

I believe in Jesus Christ, his only Son, our Lord,
He was conceived by the power of the Holy Spirit
and born of the Virgin Mary.
He suffered under Pontius Pilate,
was crucified, died and was buried.
He descended to the dead.
On the third day he rose again.
He ascended into heaven,
and is seated at the right hand of the Father.
He will come again to judge the living and the dead.

I believe in the Holy Spirit,
the holy catholic church,
the communion of saints,
the forgiveness of sins,
the resurrection of the body;
and the life everlasting.

ELLC (15)

On the first bead, a Pater Noster:

Our Father, who art in heaven,
hallowed be thy name;
Thy kingdom come,
Thy will be done, on earth as it is in heaven.
Give us this day our daily bread,
and forgive us our trespasses,
as we forgive those who trespass against us;
and lead us not into temptation,
but deliver us from evil.
For thine is the kingdom, the power and the glory,
for ever and ever.

On each of the first three beads, an Ave Maria:

Hail Mary, full of grace,
the Lord is with thee.
Blessed art thou among women
and blessed is the fruit of thy womb, Jesus.
Holy Mary, Mother of God,
pray for us sinners, now, and at the hour of our death.

On the single bead following a Gloria Patri:

Glory be to the Father and to the Son and to the Holy Spirit:
as it was in the beginning, is now and ever shall be,
world without end.

or

Glory to the Father, and to the Son, and to the Holy Spirit:
as it was in the beginning, is now, and shall be for ever.

Remain on this bead (the bead before the medal) to begin the first Our Father of the first Mystery.

For each Mystery say one Our Father, followed by ten Hail Marys, followed by the Glory . . . At the Glory . . ., remain on the bead for the first Our Father of the next Mystery.

If all three sets of Mysteries are to be used, the loop of the rosary is used three times.

Eventually the devotion becomes second nature and the fingers and lips can be left to maintain the pattern. The mind is then free to contemplate the Mysteries. A text or longer passage of Scripture (such as are suggested below) may be read at each Mystery, and the Mystery may be offered in intercession for some intention. An intention is suggested for each Mystery.

Joyful Mysteries

Mondays and Thursdays, and Sundays from Advent Sunday to Candlemas

The Annunciation

Behold I am the handmaid of the Lord; let it be to me according to your word.
Luke 1:38 (RSV)

Luke 1:26–38

The safety of unborn children.

The Visitation

Blessed are you among women and blessed is the fruit of your womb!
Luke 1:42

Luke 1:39–45

Mothers.

The Nativity

Mary kept all these things, pondering them in her heart.

Luke 2:19 (RSV)

Luke 2:1–21

The homeless.

The Presentation

A sword will pierce your own soul also.

Luke 2:35a

Luke 2:22–40

The newly-baptized.

The Finding in the Temple

Did you not know that I must be in my Father's house?

Luke 2:49b

Luke 2:41–52

Children's growth in the spiritual life.

Sorrowful Mysteries

Tuesdays and Fridays, and Sundays from Candlemas to Easter.

The Agony in the Garden

Father, if you are willing, remove this cup from me; yet, not my will, but yours be done.

Luke 22:42

Luke 22:39–53

The sick and the terminally ill.

The Scourging at the Pillar

Prophesy! Who is it that struck you?

Luke 22:64

Luke 22:54–65

Those imprisoned and tortured for their beliefs.

The Crowning with Thorns

Hail, King of the Jews!

John 19:3

John 19:1–16

Those who face martyrdom.

Jesus carries his Cross

If they do this when the wood is green, what will happen when it is dry?
Luke 23:31

Luke 23:26–32

Christian men and women throughout the world.

The Crucifixion

Father, forgive them; for they do not know what they are doing.

Luke 23:34

Luke 23:33–47

Addicts and those enslaved by abuse.

Glorious Mysteries

Wednesdays and Saturdays, and Sundays from Easter until Advent Sunday.

The Resurrection

Why do you look for the living among the dead? he is not here but has risen.
Luke 24:5b

Luke 24:1–12

Justice, peace and reconciliation.

The Ascension

Men of Galilee, why do you stand looking up towards heaven? This Jesus, who has been taken up from you into heaven, will come in the same way as you saw him go into heaven.
Acts 1:11

Acts 1:1–14

Governments and civil authorities.

Pentecost

How is it that we hear, each of us, in our own native language?

Acts 2:8

Acts 2:1–12

Preaching the gospel at home and abroad.

The Assumption of Our Lady

A great portent appeared in heaven: a woman clothed with the sun, with the moon under her feet, and on her head a crown of twelve stars.

Revelation 12:1

Revelation 12:1–6

The faithful departed.

The Crowning of Our Lady

His bride has made herself ready; to her it has been granted to be clothed with fine linen, bright and pure – for the fine linen is the righteous deeds of the saints.

Revelation 19:8

Revelation 19:6–9a

The coming of God's kingdom.

THE GLORIOUS MYSTERIES
V · The Coronation

At the end of the Rosary

Salve Regina

Hail, holy Queen, mother of mercy,
our life, our sweetness, and our hope.
To you do we cry,
poor banished children of Eve.
To you do we send up our sighs,
mourning and weeping in this vale of tears.
Turn then, most gracious advocate,
your eyes of mercy towards us,
and after this exile
show to us the blessed fruit of your womb, Jesus.
O clement, O loving,
O sweet Virgin Mary.

Litany of Loreto

Lord, have mercy.
Lord, have mercy.

Christ, have mercy.
Christ, have mercy.

Lord, have mercy.
Lord, have mercy.

Christ hear us.
Christ graciously hear us.

God the Father of heaven, have mercy on us.
God the Son, redeemer of the world, have mercy on us.
God the Holy Spirit, have mercy on us.
Holy Trinity, one God, have mercy on us.

Holy Mary, pray for us.
Holy mother of God, pray for us.
Holy Virgin of virgins, pray for us.
Mother of Christ, pray for us.
Mother most pure, pray for us.
Mother most chaste, pray for us.
Mother inviolate, pray for us.
Mother undefiled, pray for us.
Mother most lovable, pray for us.
Mother most admirable, pray for us.
Mother of good counsel, pray for us.
Mother of our Creator, pray for us.
Mother of our Saviour, pray for us.
Mother of the Church, pray for us.
Mother of the Family, pray for us.

Virgin most prudent, pray for us.
Virgin most venerable, pray for us.
Virgin most renowned, pray for us.
Virgin most powerful, pray for us.
Virgin most merciful, pray for us.
Virgin most faithful, pray for us.

Mirror of justice, pray for us.
Seat of wisdom, pray for us.
Cause of our joy, pray for us.
Spiritual vessel, pray for us.
Vessel of honour, pray for us.
Singular vessel of devotion, pray for us.
Mystical rose, pray for us.
Tower of David, pray for us.

Tower of ivory, pray for us.
House of gold, pray for us.
Ark of the covenant, pray for us.
Gate of heaven, pray for us.
Morning star, pray for us.
Health of the sick, pray for us.
Refuge of sinners, pray for us.
Comfort of the afflicted, pray for us.
Help of Christians, pray for us.

Queen of angels, pray for us.
Queen of patriarchs, pray for us.
Queen of prophets, pray for us.
Queen of apostles, pray for us.
Queen of martyrs, pray for us.
Queen of confessors, pray for us.
Queen of virgins, pray for us.
Queen of all saints, pray for us.
Queen conceived without original sin, pray for us.
Queen assumed into heaven, pray for us.
Queen of the most holy Rosary, pray for us.
Queen of peace, pray for us.

Lamb of God, you take away the sins of the world,
spare us O Lord.

Lamb of God, you take away the sins of the world,
graciously hear us O Lord.

Lamb of God, you take away the sins of the world,
have mercy on us.

Christ, hear us.
Christ, graciously hear us.
Pray for us, O holy Mother of God,
that we may be made worthy of the promises of Christ.

Let us pray.

Grant that we your servants, Lord, may enjoy unfailing health of mind and body and through the prayers of the ever-blessed Virgin Mary in her glory, free us from our sorrows in this world and give eternal happiness in the next. Through Christ our Lord.

The Saints

Propers and Readings

Office Hymn

Blest are the pure in heart

Blest are the pure in heart,
For they shall see our God,
The secret of the Lord is theirs,
Their soul is Christ's abode.

The Lord, who left the heavens
Our life and peace to bring,
To dwell in lowliness with men,
Their pattern and their king;

Still to the lowly soul
He doth himself impart ,
And for his dwelling and his throne
Chooseth the pure in heart.

Lord, we thy presence seek;
May ours this blessing be;
Give us a pure and lowly heart
A temple meet for thee.

SM
John Keble
Hymns for Prayer and Praise 331

Psalms and Canticles

JOSEPH *19 March*

Evening Prayer I	of Holy Men (*see below*).
Morning Prayer	Sunday Week 1
Evening Prayer II	*of Holy Men (see below).*

BIRTH OF JOHN THE BAPTIST *24 June*

Evening Prayer I	*of Holy Men (see below).*
Morning Prayer	Sunday Week 1
Evening Prayer II	*of Holy Men (see below).*

PETER AND PAUL *29 June*

Evening Prayer I	117 147:13–21 A Song of God's Grace *(Canticle 35) see page 583*
Morning Prayer	Sunday Week 1
Evening Prayer II	116 126 A Song of God's Grace *(Canticle 35) see page 583.*

MICHAELMAS *29 September*

Morning Prayer	Sunday Week 1
Evening Prayer	8 138 A Song of Redemption *(Canticle 37) see page 585.*

ALL SAINTS *1 November*

Evening Prayer I	113 147:13–21

	A Song of the Lamb *(Canticle 44) see page 589.*
Morning Prayer	Sunday Week 1
Evening Prayer II	110 116 A Song of Praise *(Canticle 40) see page 587.*

APOSTLES

Conversion of Paul	25 January
See of Peter	22 February
Mark	25 April
Philip and James	1 or 3 May
Matthias	14 May
Thomas	3 July
James	25 July
Bartholomew	24 August
Matthew	21 September
Luke	18 October
Simon and Jude	28 October
Andrew	30 November
John	27 December
Evening Prayer I	*(Feast of Title only)* 117 147:13–21 A Song of God's Grace *(Canticle 35) see page 583.*
Morning Prayer	Sunday Week 1
Evening Prayer II	116 126 A Song of God's Grace *(Canticle 35) see page 583.*

MARTYRS

Perpetua, Felicity and their Companions	7 March
George	23 April
English Saints and Martyrs of the Reformation Era	4 May
Thomas More and John Fisher	22 June or 6 July
Laurence	10 August
Stephen	26 December
Holy Innocents	28 December
Thomas Becket	29 December
Evening Prayer I	*(Feast of Title only)* 118 A Song of Christ the Servant *(Canticle 39) see page 586.*
Morning Prayer	Sunday Week 1
Evening Prayer II	116 A Song of Praise *(Canticle 40) see page 587.*

HOLY MEN

David	1 March
Patrick	17 March
Augustine of Canterbury	27 May
Evening Prayer I	*(Feast of Title only)* 113 146 A Song of God's Grace *(Canticle 35) see page 583.*

Morning Prayer	Sunday Week 1
Evening Prayer II	15
	112
	A Song of Moses and of the Lamb
	(Canticle 43) see page 589.

HOLY WOMEN

Catherine of Siena	29 April
Mary Magdalene	22 July
Teresa of Avila	15 October

Evening Prayer I	*(Feast of Title only)*
	113
	147:13–21
	A Song of God's Grace
	(Canticle 35) see page 583.
Morning Prayer	Sunday Week 1
Evening Prayer II	122
	127
	A Song of God's Grace
	(Canticle 35) see page 583.

Alternative Canticle at Evening Prayer

A Song of the Redeemed
(Canticle 41) – see page 587.

Short Readings

Since we are surrounded by so great a cloud of witnesses, let us also lay aside every weight and the sin that clings so closely, and let us run with perseverance the race that is set before us, looking to Jesus the pioneer and perfecter of our faith, who for the sake of the joy that was set before him endured the cross, disregarding its shame, and has taken his seat at the right hand of the throne of God.

Hebrews 12:1–2

or

I looked, and here was a great multitude that no one could count, from every nation, from all tribes and peoples and languages, standing before the throne and before the Lamb, robed in white, with palm branches in their hands.

Revelation 7:9

Long Readings

Conversion of Paul *25 January*

Acts 9:1–22
Matthew 19:27–30

See of Peter *22 February*

* 1 Peter 5:1–4
* Matthew 16:13–19

David *1 March*

* Philippians 3:8–14
* Matthew 5:13–16

Patrick *17 March*

*Acts 13:46–49
*Luke 10:1–12, 17–20

JOSEPH *19 March*

2 Samuel 7:4–16
Romans 4:13–18
Matthew 1:18–25

GEORGE *23 April*

Revelation 12:7–12
2 Timothy 2:3–13
John 15:18–21

Mark

25 April

Ephesians 4:7–16
Mark 13:5–13

Philip and James

1 or 3 May

Ephesians 1:3–10
John 14:1–14

English Saints and Martyrs of the Reformation Era

4 May

* Acts 7:55–60
 Matthew 10:16–22

Matthias

14 May

Acts 1:15–26
John 15:9–17

Augustine
of Canterbury

27 May

1 Thessalonians 2:2b-8
Matthew 13:31–33

Thomas More and John Fisher

22 June or 6 July

* 2 Maccabees 6:18, 21, 24–31
* Matthew 24:4–13

BIRTH OF JOHN THE BAPTIST

24 June

Isaiah 40:1–11
Acts 13:14b-26
or Galatians 3:23–29
Luke 1:57–66, 80

PETER AND PAUL *29 June*

Acts 12:1–11
2 Timothy 4:6–8, 17–18
Matthew 16:13–19

Thomas *3 July*

Ephesians 2:19–22
John 20:24–29

James *25 July*

Acts 11:27–12:2
or 2 Corinthians 4:7–15
Matthew 20:20–28

Laurence *10 August*

2 Corinthians 9:6–10
John 12:24–26

Bartholomew *24 August*

Acts 5:12–16
or 1 Corinthians 4:9–15
Luke 22:24–30

Matthew *21 September*

2 Corinthians 4:1–6
Matthew 9:9–13

Michael and All Angels *29 September*

Genesis 28:10–17
or Revelation 12:7–12
John 1:47–51

Luke *18 October*

2 Timothy 4:5–17
Luke 10:1–9

Simon and Jude   *28 October*

Ephesians 2:19–22
John 15:17–27

ALL SAINTS' DAY   *1 November*

Revelation 7:9–17   Wisdom 3:1–9   Daniel 7:1–3, 15–18
1 John 3:1–3   Revelation 21:1–6a   Ephesians 1:11–23
Matthew 5:1–12   John 11:32–44   Luke 6:20–31

Andrew   *30 November*

Romans 10:12–18
Matthew 4:18–22

Stephen   *26 December*

Acts 7:51–60
Matthew 23:34–39

John   *27 December*

1 John 1:1–4
John 21:19b-25

Holy Innocents   *28 December*

Jeremiah 31:15–17
Matthew 2:8–13

Thomas Becket   *29 December*

* Colossians 1:24–29
Matthew 10:28–33
or * Luke 22:24–30

Martyrs

Romans 8:35–39
John 15:18–21

Holy Men and Women

1 Corinthians 12:31–13:13
Matthew 25:31–46

Responsory

On feasts of Martyrs:

R/	By your blood, O Lord you redeemed us for God
R/	From every tribe and language, from every people and nation.
V/	There is a great multitude that no one could number!
R/	By your blood, O Lord you redeemed us for God.
V/	Blessing and honour and glory and might
R/	From every tribe and language, from every people and nation.
V/	Worthy is the Lamb that was slain!
R/	By your blood, O Lord you ransomed us for God from every tribe and language, from every people and nation.

or

On feasts of Holy Men and Women:

R/	I will sing for ever of your love, O Lord; my lips shall proclaim your faithfulness.
R/	I will sing for ever of your love, O Lord; my lips shall proclaim your faithfulness.
V/	The heavens bear witness to your wonders;
R/	My lips shall proclaim your faithfulness.
V/	The assembly of your saints proclaims your truth.
R/	I will sing for ever of your love, O Lord.
V/	Glory to the Father, and to the Son, and to the Holy Spirit.
R/	I will sing for ever of your love, O Lord; my lips shall proclaim your faithfulness.

or

On the feast of St Michael and All Angels:

- **R/** Praise the Lord you angels of his:
- **R/** You mighty ones who do his bidding.
- **V/** The Son of Man will come with his angels in the glory of his Father.
- **R/** Praise the Lord you angels of his.
- **V/** Let all God's angels worship him.
- **R/** You mighty ones who do his bidding.
- **V/** He shall give his angels charge over you.
- **R/** Praise the Lord you angels of his:
  You mighty ones who do his bidding

Antiphons/Refrains and Texts for Meditation

I have called you friends because I have made known to you everything that I have heard from my Father.

John 15:15

We are fellow-citizens with the saints and of the household of God, through Christ our Lord, who came and preached peace to those who were far off and those who were near.

cf. Ephesians 2:19,17

May the God of peace sanctify you: may he so strengthen your hearts in holiness that you may be blameless before him at the coming of our Lord Jesus with his saints.

cf. 1 Thessalonians 5:23;3:13

You are a chosen race, a royal priesthood, a holy nation, God's own people, called out of darkness into his marvellous light.

1 Peter 2:9

Collect

Almighty God,
you have knit together your elect
in one communion and fellowship
in the mystical body of your Son Christ our Lord:
grant us grace so to follow your blessed saints
in all virtuous and godly living
that we may come to those inexpressible joys

that you have prepared for those who truly love you;
through Jesus Christ your Son our Lord,
who is alive and reigns with you,
in the unity of the Holy Spirit,
one God, now and for ever.

All Saints
Common Worship (1)

Other Prayers

God, who hast brought us near to an innumerable company of angels, and to the spirits of the just made perfect: grant us during our earthly pilgrimage to abide in their fellowship, and in our heavenly country to become partakers of their joy; through Jesus Christ our Lord.

William Bright

Mary, Mother of God and Mother of the Church,
pray for us.
Saint Gregory the Great,
pray for us.
Saint Augustine of Canterbury,
pray for us.
Saint Thomas Becket,
pray for us.

(13)

Almighty God,
you enabled Saint Thomas Becket
to lay down his life with undaunted spirit
for the rights of your Church.
Let his prayer help us to deny ourselves
for Christ in this life
and so find true life in heaven.

(13)

We turn to you for protection, holy Mother of God.
Listen to our prayers and help us in our needs.
Save us from every danger, glorious and blessed Virgin.
Saint Gregory the Great, pray for us.
Saint Augustine of Canterbury, pray for us.
Saint Thomas Becket of Canterbury, pray for us.

(13)

Holy Michael, Archangel,
defend us in the day of battle;
be our safeguard against the wickedness
and snares of the devil.
May God rebuke him, we humbly pray:
and do thou, prince of the heavenly host,

by the power of God thrust down to hell
Satan, and all wicked spirits who wander through the world
for the ruin of souls.

Ampleforth (7)

Saints Peter and Paul, pray for us.

Lord, come to the aid of your people,
who rely on the help of your holy apostles;
protect us and be our defence for ever.
We ask this through Christ our Lord.

ICEL (5)

Prayers of Holy Men and Women

Prayer of Saint Augustine of Hippo (i)

Almighty God, in whom we live and move and have our being, you have made us for yourself, so that our hearts are restless till they rest in you; grant us purity of heart and strength of purpose, that no passion may hinder us from knowing your will, no weakness from doing it; but in your light may we see light clearly, and in your service find perfect freedom; through Jesus Christ our Lord.

(20)

Prayer of Saint Augustine of Hippo (ii)

Eternal God, the light of the minds that know you, the joy of the hearts that love you, the strength of the wills that serve you; grant us so to know you that we may truly love you, so to love you that we may fully serve you, whom to serve is perfect freedom; through Jesus Christ our Lord.

(20)

Prayer of Saint Benedict

Gracious and holy Father, give us wisdom to perceive you, intelligence to understand you, diligence to seek you, patience to wait for you, eyes to behold you, a heart to meditate on you, and a life to proclaim you; through the power of the Spirit of Jesus Christ our Lord.

(20)

Prayer of Saint Columba

Lord, be a bright flame before me,
be a guiding star above me,
be a smooth path below me,
be a kindly shepherd behind me,
today and for evermore.

(20)

Prayer of Saint Anselm

O Lord God, grant us grace
to desire you with our whole heart,

that so desiring you, we may seek and find you;
and so finding you we may love you;
and so loving you
we may hate those sins
from which you have redeemed us
for the sake of Jesus Christ.

Prayer attributed to Saint Francis

Lord, make me an instrument of your peace.
Where there is hatred, let me sow love;
   where there is injury, pardon;
   where there is discord, union;
   where there is doubt, faith;
   where there is despair, hope;
   where there is darkness, light;
   where there is sadness, joy,
   for your mercy and truth's sake.

O Divine Master, grant that I may not so much seek
   to be consoled as to console,
   to be understood as to understand,
   to be loved as to love,
for it is in giving that we receive,
it is in pardoning that we are pardoned,
it is in dying that we are born to eternal life.

Prayer of Saint Clare of Assisi

I pray you, O gentle Jesus,
having redeemed me by my baptism from original sin,
so now by your precious Blood,
which is offered and received throughout the world,
deliver me from all evils, past, present and to come.
By your most cruel death give me lively faith,
   a firm hope and perfect charity,
so that I may love you with all my soul and strength.
Make me firm and steadfast in good works
and grant me perseverance in your service
so that I may be able to please you always.

Prayer of Saint Richard of Chichester

Thanks be to you, Lord Jesus Christ,
for all the benefits which you have given me,
for all the pains and insults which you have borne for me.
Most merciful redeemer, friend and brother
   may I know you more clearly,
   love you more dearly,
   and follow you more nearly.

Prayer of Saint Ignatius Loyola (i)

Take, Lord, all my liberty.
Receive my memory, my understanding, and my whole will.
Whatever I have and possess, you have given me;
to you I restore it wholly
and to your will I utterly surrender it for my direction.
Give me the love of you only, with your grace,
and I am rich enough;
nor do I ask anything beside.

Prayer of Saint Ignatius Loyola (ii)

Teach us, good Lord, to serve you as you deserve;
to give and not to count the cost;
to fight and not to heed the wounds;
to toil, and not to seek for rest;
to labour and not to ask for any reward,
save that of knowing that we do your will;
through Jesus Christ our Lord.

Prayer of Saint Thomas More

Almighty God,
have mercy on *N* and *N*,
and on all that bear me evil will and would me harm,
and by their faults and mine together,
by such easy, tender, merciful means
as thine infinite wisdom best can devise;
vouchsafe to amend and redress
and make us saved souls in heaven together,

where we may ever live and love
together with thee and thy blessed saints,
O glorious Trinity,
for the bitter passion of our sweet Saviour.

(19)

Prayer of Saint John of the Cross

O flame of the Holy Spirit, you pierce the very substance of my soul
and cauterize it with your heat.
You love me so much,
that you have put into my heart
the hope and the knowledge of eternal life.
Earlier my prayers never reached your ears,
because my love was so weak and impure;
so, although I yearned for you,
and begged you to warm my cold heart,
you could not hear me.
But now you have chosen to come to me,
and my love burns with such passion
that I know you hear my every prayer.
I pray what you want me to pray;
I desire what you want me to desire;
I do what you want me to do.
You have freed me to be your slave.

(44)

Prayer of Saint Francis de Sales (i)

You made me for yourself, O Lord, so that I might rejoice forever in the immensity of your glory. When shall I be worthy of that glory? When shall I praise you as I ought? I offer you, my Creator, all my desires and hopes; give me your blessing so that I may put them into practice, through Jesus Christ your Son who shed his blood for me on the cross.

(20)

Prayer of Saint Francis de Sales (ii)

I have trampled on your blessings, Lord, misused your grace and ungratefully rejected your gifts. I will be faithful in prayer, receive the sacraments often, listen to your word, and do what you tell me to.

(20)

Prayer of Saint Jane Frances de Chantal

O my Lord, I am in a dry land, all dried up and cracked by the violence of the north wind and the cold; but as you see, I ask for nothing more; you will send me both dew and warmth when it pleases you.

(20)

Prayer of Lancelot Andrewes

O God, most glorious, most bountiful, accept, we humbly beseech thee, our praises and thanksgivings for thy holy Catholic Church, the mother of us all who bear the name of Christ; for the faith which it hath conveyed in safety to our time, and the mercies by which it hath enlarged and comforted the souls of men; for the virtues which it hath established upon earth, and the holy lives by which it glorifieth both the world and thee; to whom, O blessed Trinity, be ascribed all honour, might, majesty and dominion, now and for ever.

(16)

Prayer of Jean-Jacques Olier

O Jesus living in Mary,
Come and live in thy servants,
In the spirit of thy sanctity,
In the fullness of thy strength,
In the reality of thy virtues,
In the perfection of thy ways,
In the communion of thy mysteries,
Be Lord over every opposing power,
In thine own Spirit, to the glory of the Father.

(20)

Prayer of Saint Jean-Baptiste Marie Vianney

I love you, O my God, and my only desire is to love you until the last breath of my life. I love you, and I would rather die loving you, than live without loving you. I love you, Lord, and the only grace I ask is to love you eternally. My God, if my tongue cannot say in every moment that I love you, I want my heart to repeat it to you as often as I draw breath.

(20)

Litany of the Saints

Lord, have mercy.
Lord, have mercy.

Christ, have mercy.
Christ, have mercy.

Lord, have mercy.
Lord, have mercy.

Holy Mary, Mother of God, pray for us.
Saint Michael, pray for us.
Holy angels of God, pray for us.
Saint John the Baptist, pray for us.
Saint Joseph, pray for us.
Saint Peter and Saint Paul, pray for us.
Saint Andrew, pray for us.
Saint John, pray for us.
Saint Mary Magdalene, pray for us.
Saint Stephen, pray for us.
Saint Ignatius, pray for us.
Saint Lawrence, pray for us.
Saint John Fisher and Saint Thomas More, pray for us.
Saint Perpetua and Saint Felicity, pray for us.
Saint Agnes, pray for us.
Saint Gregory, pray for us.
Saint Ambrose, pray for us.
Saint Augustine, pray for us.
Saint Athanasius, pray for us.
Saint Basil, pray for us.
Saint Martin, pray for us.
Saint Benedict, pray for us.
Saint Augustine of Canterbury, pray for us.
Saint Francis and Saint Dominic, pray for us.
Saint Francis Xavier, pray for us.
Saint John Vianney, pray for us.
Saint Catherine, pray for us.
Saint Teresa, pray for us.
All holy men and women, pray for us.

Lord, be merciful.
Lord, save your people.

From all evil,
Lord, save your people.

From every sin,
Lord, save your people.

From everlasting death,
Lord, save your people.

By your coming as man,
Lord, save your people.

By your death and rising to new life,
Lord, save your people.

By your gift of the Holy Spirit,
Lord, save your people.

Be merciful to us sinners,
Lord, hear our prayer.

Jesus Son of the living God,
Lord, hear our prayer.

Christ, hear us.
Christ, hear us.

Lord Jesus, hear our prayer.
Lord Jesus, hear our prayer.

ICEL (5)

The Faithful Departed

Propers and Readings

Office Hymn

Remember those, O Lord

Remember those, O Lord,
Who in your peace have died,
Yet may not gain love's high reward
Till love is purified.

With you they faced death's night,
Sealed with your victory sign,
Soon may the splendour of your light
On them for ever shine.

Sweet is their pain, yet deep,
Till perfect love is born;
Their lone night-watch they gladly keep
Before your radiant morn.

Your love is their great joy,
Your will their one desire;
As finest gold without alloy
Refine them in love's fire.

For them we humbly pray,
Perfect them in your love;
O may we share eternal day
With them in heaven above.

James Quinn SJ (38)
Hymns for Prayer and Praise 343

Psalms and Canticles

Morning Prayer   51
A Song of the Living
(Canticle 11) see page 564.
146 or 150

Evening Prayer   121
130
The Song of Christ's Glory
(Canticle 36) see page 584.

Alternative Canticle at Morning Prayer

A Song of the Righteous *(Canticle 28)* – see page 578.

Short Readings

I know that my Redeemer lives, and that at the last he will stand upon the earth; and after my skin has been thus destroyed, then in my flesh I shall see God, whom I shall see on my side, and my eyes shall behold, and not another.
Job 19:25–27a

or

Christ has been raised from the dead, the first fruits of those who have fallen asleep. For as by a man came death, by a man has come also the resurrection of the dead. For as in Adam all die, so also in Christ shall all be made alive.
1 Corinthians 15:20–22

Long Readings

ALL SOULS' DAY   *2 November*
(and Office for the Dead)

Lamentations 3:17–26
or Wisdom 3:1–9
* *or* Isaiah 25:6–9
Romans 5:5–11
or 1 Peter 1:3–9
John 5:19–25
or John 6:37–40

Responsory

- **R/** My soul waits for the Lord,
- **R/** For with the Lord there is mercy.
- **V/** With him is plenteous redemption
- **R/** My soul waits for the Lord.
- **V/** He shall redeem us from all our sins
- **R/** For with Lord there is mercy.
- **V/** In his word is my hope.
- **R/** My soul waits for the Lord,
  for with the Lord there is mercy.

Antiphons/Refrains and Texts for Meditation

The righteous will be remembered for ever; the memory of the righteous is a blessing.
Psalm 112:6; Proverbs 10:7 (RSV)

The souls of the righteous are in the hand of God and no torment will ever touch them. In the eyes of the foolish they seem to have died, but they are at peace.
Wisdom 3:1–3 (RSV)

I am the resurrection and the life. Those who believe in me, even though they die, will live, and everyone who lives and believes in me will never die.
John 11:25–26

Since we believe that Jesus died and rose again, even so, through Jesus, God will bring with him those who have died.
1 Thessalonians 4:14

Collect

Eternal God, our maker and redeemer,
grant us [with *N*] with all the faithful departed,
the sure benefits of your Son's saving passion and glorious resurrection
that, in the last day,
when you gather up all things in Christ,
we may with them enjoy the fullness of your promises;

through Jesus Christ your Son our Lord,
who is alive and reigns with you,
in the unity of the Holy Spirit,
one God, now and for ever.

The Funeral Service
Common Worship (1)

Other Prayers

Lord Jesus, our Redeemer,
you willingly gave yourself up to death,
so that all might be saved and pass from death to life.
By dying you unlocked the gates of life
for all those who believe in you.
So we commend *N* into your arms of mercy
believing that, with sins forgiven,
he will share a place of happiness, light and peace
in the kingdom of your glory for ever.

The Funeral Service
Common Worship (1)

O God,
glory of believers and life of the just,
by the death and resurrection of your Son, we are redeemed:
have mercy on your servant *N*,
and make *him* worthy to share the joys of paradise,
for *he* believed in the resurrection of the dead.
We ask this through our Lord Jesus Christ, your Son,
who lives and reigns with you and the Holy Spirit,
one God, for ever and ever.

Order of Christian Funerals (23)

The King and the Kingdom
(Ordinary Time in November and Christ the King)

Propers and Readings

Office Hymn

Christ is Lord

Christ is Lord, in glory reigning,
Priest for ever, king of kings,
While to him all glad creation
Praise and humble worship brings.

He has paid our regal ransom,
Nailed against that bitter wood:
Now the symbol of his conquest,
Royal and victorious rood.

When he comes again in splendour,
Cross upheld in pierced right hand,
All the power of hell shall perish
And no evil dare to stand.

Father, Son and Holy Spirit,
Trinity sublime we praise;
May your kingdom come among us,
Bringing peace to all our days.

87 87
Stanbrook Abbey (4)
Hymns for Prayer and Praise 103

Psalms and Canticles

Fourth Week Before **Advent** *(Week 31)*

Week 3

Third Week Before **Advent** *(Week 32)*

Week 4

Second Week Before **Advent** *(Week 33)*

Week 1

CHRIST THE KING *(Sunday before Advent)*

Evening Prayer I	113
	117
	A Song of Praise
	(Canticle 40) see page 587.
Morning Prayer	Sunday Week 1
Evening Prayer II	110
	145
	A Song of the Lamb
	(Canticle 44) see page 589.

Last Week Before **Advent** *(Week 34)*

Week 2

Alternative Canticle at Morning Prayer

A Song of the Bride *(Canticle 18) – see page 570.*

Short Readings

Pilate had an inscription written and put on the cross. It read 'Jesus of Nazareth, the King of the Jews.' It was written in Hebrew, in Latin, and in Greek.

John 19:19–20

or

In Christ all things in heaven and on earth were created, things visible and invisible, whether thrones or dominions or rulers or powers – all things have been created through him and for him. He himself is before all things, and in him all things hold together. He is the head of the body, the church; he is the beginning, the firstborn from the dead, so that he might come to have first place in everything.

Colossians 1:16b-18

Long Readings

Sunday between 30 October and 5 November inclusive
if All Saints' Day is not celebrated on Sunday
Fourth Sunday Before Advent   [Sunday 31 of Ordinary Time]

Year A	*Year B*	*Year C*
Micah 3:5–12	Deuteronomy 6:1–9	Isaiah 1:10–18
1 Thessalonians 2:9–13	Hebrews 9:11–14	2 Thessalonians 1:1–12
Matthew 24:1–14	Mark 12:28–34	Luke 19:1–10

Week 31 of Year 1
M Romans 11:29–end   Luke 14:12–14
T   Romans 12:5–16   Luke 14:15–24
W Romans 13:8–10   Luke 14:25–33
Th Romans 14:7–12   Luke 15:1–10
F   Romans 15:14–21   Luke 16:1–8
S   Romans 16:3–9, 16, 22–end Luke 16:9–15

Week 31 of Year 2
M Philippians 2:1–4   Luke 14:12–14
T   Philippians 2:5–11   Luke 14:15–24
W Philippians 2:12–18   Luke 14:25–33
Th Philippians 3:3–8   Luke 15:1–10
F   Philippians 3:17–4:1   Luke 16:1–8
S   Philippians 4:10–19   Luke 16:9–15

Sunday between 6–12 November inclusive
Third Sunday Before Advent [Sunday 32 of Ordinary Time]

Year A	Year B	Year C
Wisdom of Solomon 6:12–16	Jonah 3:1–5, 10	Job 19:23–27a
1 Thessalonians 4:13–18	Hebrews 9:24–28	2 Thessalonians 2:1–5, 13–17
Matthew 25:1–13	Mark 1:14–20	Luke 20:27–38

Week 32 of Year 1
M   Wisdom 1:1–7   Luke 17:1–6
T   Wisdom 2:23–3:9   Luke 17:7–10
W   Wisdom 6:1–11   Luke 17:11–19
Th   Wisdom 7:22–8:1   Luke 17:20–25
F   Wisdom 13:1–9   Luke 17:26–end
S   Wisdom 18:14–16; 19:6–9   Luke 18:1–8

Week 32 of Year 2
M   Titus 1:1–9   Luke 17:1–6
T   Titus 2:1–8, 11–14   Luke 17:7–10
W   Titus 3:1–7   Luke 17:11–19
Th   Philemon 7–20   Luke 17:20–25
F   2 John 4–9   Luke 17:26–end
S   3 John 5–8   Luke 18:1–8

Sunday between 13–19 November inclusive
Second Sunday Before Advent   *[Sunday 33 of Ordinary Time]*

Year A	Year B	Year C
Zephaniah 1:7, 12–18	Daniel 12:1–3	Malachi 4:1–2a
1 Thessalonians 5:1–11	Hebrews 10:11–14, [15–18]19–25	2 Thessalonians 3:6–13
Matthew 25:14–30	Mark 13:1–8	Luke 21:5–19

Week 33 of Year 1
M   1 Maccabees 1:10–15, 41–43, 54–57, 62–64   Luke 18:35–end
T   2 Maccabees 6:18–end   Luke 19:1–10
W   2 Maccabees 7:1, 20–31   Luke 19:11–28
Th   1 Maccabees 2:15–29   Luke 19:41–44
F   1 Maccabees 4:36–37, 52–59   Luke 19:45–end
S   1 Maccabees 6:1–13   Luke 20:27–40

Week 33 of Year 2
M Revelation 1:1–4; 2:1–5   Luke 18:35–end
T Revelation 3:1–6, 14–end   Luke 19:1–10
W Revelation 4   Luke19:11–28
Th Revelation 5:1–10   Luke19:41–44
F Revelation 10:8–11   Luke19:45–end
S Revelation 11:4–12   Luke 20:27–40

CHRIST THE KING
Sunday between 20–26 November inclusive

Year A	*Year B*	*Year C*
Ezekiel 34:11–16, 20–24	Daniel 7:9–10, 13–14	Jeremiah 23:1–6
Ephesians 1:15–23	Revelation 1:4b-8	Colossians 1:11–20
Matthew 25:31–46	John 18:33–37	Luke 23:33–43

Week 34 of Year 1
M Daniel 1:1–6, 8–20   Luke 21:1–4
T Daniel 2:31–45   Luke 21:5–11
W Daniel 5:1–6, 13–14, 16–17, 23–28
Th Daniel 6:12–end   Luke 21:20–28
F Daniel 7:2–14   Luke 21:29–33
S Daniel 7:15–27   Luke 21:34–36

Week 34 of Year 2
M Revelation 14:1–5   Luke 21:1–4
T Revelation 14:14–19   Luke 21:5–11
W Revelation 15:1–4   Luke 21:12–19
Th Revelation 18:1–2, 21–23; 19:1–3, 9   Luke 21:20–28
F Revelation 20:1–4, 11–21:2   Luke 21:29–33
S Revelation 22:1–7   Luke 21:34–36

Responsory

R/ By your blood, O Lord you redeemed us for God
R/ from every tribe and language,
from every people and nation.
V/ There is a great multitude that no one could number!
R/ By your blood, O Lord you redeemed us for God.
V/ Blessing and honour and glory and might
R/ from every tribe and language,
from every people and nation.
V/ Worthy is the Lamb that was slain!
R/ By your blood, O Lord you ransomed us for God
from every tribe and language,
from every people and nation.

Antiphons/Refrains and Texts for Meditation

I am with you always, to the end of the age.

Matthew 28:20

The time is fulfilled, and the kingdom of God is at hand; repent, and believe in the gospel.

Mark 1:14 (RSV)

He will reign over the house of Jacob for ever, and of his kingdom there will be no end.

Luke 1:33

Blessed is the king who comes in the name of the Lord. Peace in heaven and glory in the highest heaven.

Luke 19:38

The kingdom of the world has become the kingdom of our Lord and of his Christ, and he shall reign for ever and ever.

Revelation 11:15b (RSV)

Collect

Eternal Father,
whose Son Jesus Christ ascended to the throne of heaven
　that he might rule over all things as Lord and King:
keep the Church in the unity of the Spirit
and in the bond of peace
and bring the whole created order to worship at his feet;
who is alive and reigns with you,
in the unity of the Holy Spirit,
one God, now and for ever.

Christ the King
Common Worship (1)

Last Week before Advent (Week 34)

Stir up, we beseech thee, O Lord, the wills of thy faithful people; that they, plenteously bringing forth the fruit of good works, may of thee be plenteously rewarded; through Jesus Christ our Lord.

Collect for the Last Sunday after Trinity
Book of Common Prayer (2)

Other Prayers

God of all grace,
your Son Jesus Christ fed the hungry
with the bread of his life
and the word of his kingdom:
renew your people with your heavenly grace,
and in all our weakness
sustain us by your true and living bread;
who is alive, and reigns, now and for ever.

Last Sunday after Trinity
(Post-Communion)
Common Worship (1)

Act of Dedication to Christ The King

Loving Jesus, Redeemer of the world,
we are yours, and yours we wish to be.
To bind ourselves to you even more closely
we kneel before you today
and offer ourselves to your most Sacred Heart.

Praise to you, our Saviour and our King.

Have mercy on all who have never known you
and on all who reject you and refuse to obey you:
gentle Lord, draw them to yourself.

Praise to you, our Saviour and our King.

Reign over the faithful who have never left you,
reign over those who have squandered their inheritance,
the prodigal children who now are starving;
bring them back to their Father's house.

Praise to you, our Saviour and our King.

Reign over those who are misled by error or divided by discord.
Hasten the day when we shall be one in faith and truth,
one flock with you, the one Shepherd.
Give to your Church freedom and peace,
and to all nations justice and order.
Make the earth resound from pole to pole with a single cry:
Praise to the Divine Heart that gained our salvation;
glory and honour be his for ever and ever.

Praise to you, our Saviour and our King.

Leo XIII (5)

IV PSALMS AND CANTICLES

Psalms

Psalm 4

1 Answer me when I call, O God of my righteousness; *
    you set me at liberty when I was in trouble;
    have mercy on me and hear my prayer.
2 How long will you nobles dishonour my glory; *
    how long will you love vain things and seek after falsehood?
3 But know that the Lord has shown me his marvellous kindness; *
    when I call upon the Lord, he will hear me.
4 Stand in awe, and sin not; *
    commune with your own heart upon your bed, and be still.
5 Offer the sacrifices of righteousness *
    and put your trust in the Lord.
6 There are many that say, 'Who will show us any good?' *
    Lord, lift up the light of your countenance upon us.
7 You have put gladness in my heart, *
    more than when their corn and wine and oil increase.
8 In peace I will lie down and sleep, *
    for it is you Lord, only, who make me dwell in safety.

  Glory . . .

Psalm 5

1 Give ear to my words, O Lord; *
    consider my lamentation.
2 Hearken to the voice of my crying, my King and my God,*
    for to you I make my prayer.
3 In the morning, Lord, you will hear my voice; *
    early in the morning I make my appeal to you,
    and look up.

4 For you are the God who takes no pleasure in wickedness;*
   no evil can dwell with you.
5 The boastful cannot stand in your sight; *
   you hate all those that work wickedness.
6 You destroy those who speak lies; *
   the bloodthirsty and deceitful the Lord will abhor.
7 But as for me, through the greatness of your mercy,
   I will come into your house; *
   I will bow down towards your holy temple in awe of you.
8 Lead me, Lord, in your righteousness,
   because of my enemies; *
   make your way straight before my face.
9 For there is no truth in their mouth,
   in their heart is destruction, *
   their throat is an open sepulchre,
   and they flatter with their tongue.
10 Punish them, O God; *
   let them fall through their own devices.
11 Because of their many transgressions cast them out, *
   for they have rebelled against you.
12 But let all who take refuge in you be glad; *
   let them sing out their joy for ever.
13 You will shelter them, *
   so that those who love your name may exult in you.
14 For you, O Lord, will bless the righteous; *
   and with your favour you will defend them as with a shield.

   Glory . . .

Psalm 6

Penitential Psalm

1 O Lord, rebuke me not in your wrath; *
   neither chasten me in your fierce anger.
2 Have mercy on me, Lord, for I am weak; *
   Lord, heal me, for my bones are racked.
3 My soul also shakes with terror; *
   how long, O Lord, how long?
4 Turn again, O Lord, and deliver my soul; *
   save me for your loving mercy's sake.

5 For in death no one remembers you; *
    and who can give you thanks in the grave?
6 I am weary with my groaning; *
    every night I drench my pillow
    and flood my bed with my tears.
7 My eyes are wasted with grief *
    and worn away because of all my enemies.

8 Depart from me, all you that do evil, *
    for the Lord has heard the voice of my weeping.
9 The Lord has heard my supplication; *
    the Lord will receive my prayer.
10 All my enemies shall be put to shame and confusion; *
    they shall suddenly turn back in their shame.

   Glory . . .

Psalm 7

1 O Lord my God, in you I take refuge; *
    save me from all who pursue me, and deliver me,
2 Lest they rend me like a lion and tear me in pieces *
    while there is no one to help me.
3 O Lord my God, if I have done these things; *
    if there is any wickedness in my hands,
4 If I have repaid my friend with evil, *
    or plundered my enemy without a cause,
5 Then let my enemy pursue me and overtake me, *
    trample my life to the ground,
    and lay my honour in the dust.
6 Rise up, O Lord, in your wrath;
    lift yourself up against the fury of my enemies. *
   Awaken, my God, the judgement that you have commanded.
7 Let the assembly of the peoples gather round you; *
    be seated high above them: O Lord, judge the nations.
8 Give judgement for me according to my righteousness, O Lord, *
    and according to the innocence that is in me.
9 Let the malice of the wicked come to an end,
    but establish the righteous; *
   for you test the mind and heart, O righteous God.

10 God is my shield that is over me; *
    he saves the true of heart.
11 God is a righteous judge; *
    he is provoked all day long.
12 If they will not repent, God will whet his sword; *
    he has bent his bow and made it ready.
13 He has prepared the weapons of death; *
    he makes his arrows shafts of fire.
14 Behold those who are in labour with wickedness, *
    who conceive evil and give birth to lies.
15 They dig a pit and make it deep *
    and fall into the hole that they have made for others.
16 Their mischief rebounds on their own head; *
    their violence falls on their own scalp.
17 I will give thanks to the Lord for his righteousness, *
    and I will make music to the name of the Lord Most High.

Glory . . .

Psalm 8

1 *O Lord our governor,* *
    how glorious is your name in all the world!
2 Your majesty above the heavens is praised *
    out of the mouths of babes at the breast.
3 You have founded a stronghold against your foes, *
    that you might still the enemy and the avenger.
4 When I consider your heavens, the work of your fingers, *
    the moon and the stars that you have ordained,
5 What is man, that you should be mindful of him; *
    the son of man, that you should seek him out?
6 You have made him little lower than the angels *
    and crown him with glory and honour.
7 You have given him dominion over the works of your hands *
    and put all things under his feet,
8 All sheep and oxen, *
    even the wild beasts of the field,
9 The birds of the air, the fish of the sea *
    and whatever moves in the paths of the sea.

10 *O Lord our governor,* *
   how glorious is your name in all the world!

   Glory . . .

Psalm 11

1 In the Lord have I taken refuge; *
      how then can you say to me,
      'Flee like a bird to the hills:
2 'For see how the wicked bend the bow
      and fit their arrows to the string, *
      to shoot from the shadows at the true of heart.
3 'When the foundations are destroyed, *
      what can the righteous do?'
4 The Lord is in his holy temple; *
      the Lord's throne is in heaven.
5 His eyes behold, *
      his eyelids try every mortal being.
6 The Lord tries the righteous as well as the wicked, *
      but those who delight in violence his soul abhors.
7 Upon the wicked he shall rain coals of fire
      and burning sulphur; *
      scorching wind shall be their portion to drink.
8 For the Lord is righteous;
      he loves righteous deeds, *
      and those who are upright shall behold his face.

   Glory . . .

Psalm 13

1 How long will you forget me, O Lord; for ever? *
      How long will you hide your face from me?
2 How long shall I have anguish in my soul
      and grief in my heart, day after day? *
      How long shall my enemy triumph over me?
3 Look upon me and answer, O Lord my God; *
      lighten my eyes, lest I sleep in death;
4 Lest my enemy say, 'I have prevailed against him,' *
      and my foes rejoice that I have fallen.

5 But I put my trust in your steadfast love; *
    my heart will rejoice in your salvation.
6 I will sing to the Lord, *
    for he has dealt so bountifully with me.

   Glory . . .

Psalm 14

1 The fool has said in his heart, 'There is no God.' *
    Corrupt are they, and abominable in their wickedness;
    there is no-one that does good.
2 The Lord has looked down from heaven
    upon the children of earth, *
    to see if there is anyone who is wise
    and seeks after God.
3 But every one has turned back;
    all alike have become corrupt. *
    there is none that does good; no, not one.
4 Have they no knowledge, those evildoers, *
    who eat up my people as if they ate bread
    and do not call upon the Lord?
5 There shall they be in great fear; *
    for God is in the company of the righteous.
6 Though they would confound the counsel of the poor, *
    yet the Lord shall be their refuge.
7 O that Israel's salvation would come out of Zion! *
    When the Lord restores the fortunes of his people,
    then will Jacob rejoice and Israel be glad.

   Glory . . .

Psalm 15

1 Lord, who may dwell in your tabernacle? *
    Who may rest upon your holy hill?
2 Whoever leads an uncorrupt life *
    and does the thing that is right;
3 Who speaks the truth from the heart *
    and bears no deceit on the tongue;

4 Who does no evil to a friend *
   and pours no scorn on a neighbour;
5 In whose sight the wicked are not esteemed, *
   but who honours those who fear the Lord.
6 Whoever has sworn to a neighbour *
   and never goes back on that word;
7 Who does not lend money in hope of gain, *
   nor takes a bribe against the innocent;
8 Whoever does these things *
   shall never fall.

   Glory . . .

Psalm 16

1 Preserve me, O God, for in you have I taken refuge; *
   I have said to the Lord, 'You are my Lord,
   all my good depends on you.'
2 All my delight is upon the godly that are in the land, *
   upon those who are noble in heart.
3 Though the idols are legion that many run after, *
   their drink offerings of blood I will not offer,
   neither make mention of their names upon my lips.
4 The Lord himself is my portion and my cup;*
   in your hands alone is my fortune.
5 My share has fallen in a fair land; *
   indeed, I have a goodly heritage.

6 I will bless the Lord who has given me counsel *
   and in the night watches he instructs my heart.
7 I have set the Lord always before me; *
   he is at my right hand; I shall not fall.
8 Wherefore my heart is glad and my spirit rejoices; *
   my flesh also shall rest secure.
9 For you will not abandon my soul to Death, *
   nor suffer your faithful one to see the Pit.
10 You will show me the path of life;
    in your presence is the fullness of joy *
    and in your right hand are pleasures for evermore.

   Glory . . .

Psalm 17

1 Hear my just cause, O Lord; consider my complaint; *
   listen to my prayer, which comes not from lying lips.
2 Let my vindication come forth from your presence; *
   let your eyes behold what is right.
3 Weigh my heart, examine me by night, *
   refine me, and you will find no impurity in me.
4 My mouth does not trespass for earthly rewards; *
   I have heeded the words of your lips.
5 My footsteps hold fast in the ways of your commandments; *
   my feet have not stumbled in your paths.
6 I call upon you, O God, for you will answer me; *
   incline your ear to me, and listen to my words.
7 Show me your marvellous loving-kindness, *
   O Saviour of those who take refuge at your right hand
   from those who rise up against them.
8 Keep me as the apple of your eye; *
   hide me under the shadow of your wings,
9 From the wicked who assault me, *
   from my enemies who surround me to take away my life.
10 They have closed their heart to pity *
   and their mouth speaks proud things.
11 They press me hard, they surround me on every side, *
   watching how they may cast me to the ground,
12 Like a lion that is greedy for its prey *
   like a young lion lurking in secret places.
13 Arise, Lord; confront them and cast them down: *
   deliver me from the wicked by your sword.
14 Deliver me, O Lord, by your hand *
   from those whose portion in life is unending,
15 Whose bellies you fill with your treasure, *
   who are well supplied with children
   and leave their wealth to their little ones.
16 As for me, I shall behold your face in righteousness: *
   when I awake and behold your likeness, I shall be satisfied.

   Glory . . .

Psalm 19 (part one)

1 The heavens are telling the glory of God *
   and the firmament proclaims his handiwork.
2 One day pours out its song to another *
   and one night unfolds knowledge to another.
3 They have neither speech nor language *
   and their voices are not heard,
4 Yet their sound has gone out into all lands *
   and their words to the ends of the world.
5 In them has he set a tabernacle for the sun, *
   that comes forth as a bridegroom out of his chamber
   and rejoices as a champion to run his course.
6 It goes forth from the end of the heavens
   and runs to the very end again, *
   and there is nothing hidden from its heat.

  Glory . . .

Psalm 19 (part two)

7 The law of the Lord is perfect, reviving the soul; *
   the testimony of the Lord is sure
   and gives wisdom to the simple.
8 The statutes of the Lord are right and rejoice the heart; *
   the commandment of the Lord is pure
   and gives light to the eyes.
9 The fear of the Lord is clean and endures for ever; *
   the judgements of the Lord are true
   and righteous altogether.
10 More to be desired are they than gold,
   more than much fine gold, *
   sweeter also than honey,
   dripping from the honey-comb.
11 By them also is your servant taught *
   and in keeping them there is great reward.
12 Who can tell how often they offend? *
   O cleanse me from my secret faults!

13 Keep your servant also from presumptuous sins
    lest they get dominion over me; *
    so shall I be undefiled,
    and innocent of great offence.
14 Let the words of my mouth and the meditation of my heart
    be acceptable in your sight, *
    O Lord, my strength and my redeemer.

    Glory . . .

Psalm 20

1 May the Lord hear you in the day of trouble, *
    the name of the God of Jacob defend you;
2 Send you help from his sanctuary *
    and strengthen you out of Zion;
3 Remember all your offerings *
    and accept your burnt sacrifice;
4 Grant you your heart's desire *
    and fulfil all your mind.
5 May we rejoice in your salvation
    and triumph in the name of our God; *
    may the Lord perform all your petitions.

6 Now I know that the Lord will save his anointed; *
    he will answer him from his holy heaven,
    with the mighty strength of his right hand.
7 Some put their trust in chariots and some in horses, *
    but we will call only on the name of the Lord our God.
8 They are brought down and fallen, *
    but we are risen and stand upright.
9 O Lord, save the king *
    and answer us when we call upon you.

    Glory . . .

Psalm 21:1–7, 13

1 The king shall rejoice in your strength, O Lord; *
    how greatly shall he rejoice in your salvation!
2 You have given him his heart's desire *
    and have not denied the request of his lips.

3 For you come to meet him with blessings of goodness *
    and set a crown of pure gold upon his head.
4 He asked of you life and you gave it him, *
    length of days, for ever and ever.
5 His honour is great because of your salvation; *
    glory and majesty have you laid upon him.
6 You have granted him everlasting felicity *
    and will make him glad with joy in your presence.
7 For the king puts his trust in the Lord; *
    because of the loving-kindness of the Most High,
    he shall not be overthrown.
13 Be exalted, O Lord, in your own might; *
    we will make music and sing of your power.

   Glory . . .

Psalm 22

1 My God, my God, why have you forsaken me, *
    and are so far from my salvation,
    from the words of my distress?
2 O my God, I cry in the daytime,
    but you do not answer; *
    and by night also, but I find no rest.
3 Yet you are the Holy One, *
    enthroned upon the praises of Israel.
4 Our forebears trusted in you; *
    they trusted, and you delivered them.
5 They cried out to you and were delivered; *
    they put their trust in you and were not confounded.
6 But as for me, I am a worm and no man, *
    scorned by all and despised by the people.
7 All who see me laugh me to scorn; *
    they curl their lips and wag their heads, saying,
8 'He trusted in the Lord; let him deliver him; *
    let him deliver him, if he delights in him.'
9 But it is you that took me out of the womb *
    and laid me safe upon my mother's breast.
10 On you was I cast ever since I was born; *
    you are my God even from my mother's womb.

11 Be not far from me, for trouble is near at hand *
    and there is none to help.
12 Mighty oxen come around me; *
    fat bulls of Bashan close me in on every side.
13 They gape upon me with their mouths, *
    as it were a ramping and a roaring lion.
14 I am poured out like water;
    all my bones are out of joint; *
    my heart has become like wax
    melting in the depths of my body.
15 My mouth is dried up like a potsherd;
    my tongue cleaves to my gums; *
    you have laid me in the dust of death.
16 For the hounds are all about me,
    the pack of evil-doers close in on me; *
    they pierce my hands and my feet.
17 I can count all my bones; *
    they stand staring and looking upon me.
18 They divide my garments among them; *
    they cast lots for my clothing.
19 Be not far from me, O Lord; *
    you are my strength; hasten to help me.
20 Deliver my soul from the sword, *
    my poor life from the power of the dog.
21 Save me from the lion's mouth,
    from the horns of wild oxen. *
    You have answered me!

22 I will tell of your name to my people; *
    in the midst of the congregation will I praise you.
23 Praise the Lord, you that fear him; *
    O seed of Jacob, glorify him;
    stand in awe of him, O seed of Israel.
24 For he has not despised nor abhorred the suffering of the poor;
    neither has he hidden his face from them; *
    but when they cried to him he heard them.
25 From you comes my praise in the great congregation; *
    I will perform my vows
    in the presence of those that fear you.

26 The poor shall eat and be satisfied; *
    those who seek the Lord shall praise him;
    their hearts shall live for ever.
27 All the ends of the earth
    shall remember and turn to the Lord, *
    and all the families of the nations shall bow before him.
28 For the kingdom is the Lord's *
    and he rules over the nations.
29 How can those who sleep in the earth
    bow down in worship, *
    or those who go down to the dust kneel before him?
30 He has saved my life for himself;
    my descendants shall serve him; *
    this shall be told of the Lord for generations to come.
31 They shall come and make known his salvation,
    to a people yet unborn, *
    declaring that he, the Lord, has done it.

   Glory . . .

Psalm 23

1 The Lord is my shepherd; *
    therefore can I lack nothing.
2 He makes me lie down in green pastures *
    and leads me beside still waters.
3 He shall refresh my soul *
    and guide me in the paths of righteousness for his name's sake.
4 Even though I walk through the valley of the shadow of death,
    I will fear no evil; *
    for you are with me;
    your rod and your staff, they comfort me.
5 You have spread a table before me
    in the presence of those who trouble me; *
    you have anointed my head with oil
    and my cup shall be full.
6 Surely, goodness and loving mercy shall follow me
    all the days of my life, *
    and I will dwell in the house of the Lord for ever.

   Glory . . .

Psalm 24

1 The earth is the Lord's and all that fills it, *
   the compass of the world and all who dwell therein.
2 For he has founded it upon the seas *
   and set it firm upon the rivers of the deep.

3 'Who shall ascend the hill of the Lord, *
   or who can rise up in his holy place?'
4 'Those who have clean hands and a pure heart, *
   who have not lifted up their soul to an idol,
   nor sworn an oath to a lie;
5 'They shall receive a blessing from the Lord, *
   a just reward from the God of their salvation.'
6 Such is the company of those who seek him, *
   who seek your face, O God of Jacob.

7 Lift up your heads, O gates;
   and be lifted up, you everlasting doors; *
   and the King of glory shall come in.
8 'Who is the King of glory?' *
   'The Lord, strong and mighty,
   the Lord who is mighty in battle.'
9 Lift up your heads, O gates;
   be lifted up, you everlasting doors; *
   and the King of glory shall come in.
10 'Who is this King of glory?' *
   'The Lord of hosts,
   he is the King of glory'.

Glory . . .

Psalm 25

1 To you, O Lord, I lift up my soul;
   O my God, in you I trust; *
   let me not be put to shame;
   let not my enemies triumph over me.
2 Let none who look to you be put to shame, *
   but let the treacherous be shamed and frustrated.

3 Make me to know your ways, O Lord, *
   and teach me your paths.
4 Lead me in your truth and teach me, *
   for you are the God of my salvation;
   for you have I hoped all the day long.
5 Remember, Lord, your compassion and love, *
   for they are from everlasting.
6 Remember not the sins of my youth
   or my transgressions, *
   but think on me in your goodness, O Lord,
   according to your steadfast love.
7 Gracious and upright is the Lord; *
   therefore shall he teach sinners in the way.
8 He will guide the humble in doing right *
   and teach his way to the lowly.
9 All the paths of the Lord are mercy and truth *
   to those who keep his covenant and his testimonies.
10 For your name's sake, O Lord, *
   be merciful to my sin, for it is great.
11 Who are those who fear the Lord? *
   Them will he teach in the way that they should choose.
12 Their soul shall dwell at ease *
   and their offspring shall inherit the land.
13 The hidden purpose of the Lord is for those
   who fear him *
   and he will show them his covenant.
14 My eyes are ever looking to the Lord, *
   for he shall pluck my feet out of the net.
15 Turn to me and be gracious to me, *
   for I am alone and brought very low.
16 The sorrows of my heart have increased; *
   O bring me out of my distress.
17 Look upon my adversity and misery *
   and forgive me all my sin.
18 Look upon my enemies, for they are many *
   and they bear a violent hatred against me.
19 O keep my soul and deliver me; *
   let me not be put to shame, for I have put my trust in you.
20 Let integrity and uprightness preserve me, *
   for my hope has been in you.

21 Deliver Israel, O God, *
   out of all his troubles.

   Glory . . .

Psalm 26

 1 Give judgement for me, O Lord,
       for I have walked with integrity; *
       I have trusted in the Lord and have not faltered.
 2 Test me, O Lord, and try me; *
       examine my heart and my mind.
 3 For your love is before my eyes; *
       I have walked in your truth.
 4 I have not joined the company of the false, *
       nor consorted with the deceitful.
 5 I hate the gathering of evil-doers *
       and I will not sit down with the wicked.
 6 I will wash my hands in innocence, O Lord, *
       that I may go about your altar,
 7 To make heard the voice of thanksgiving *
       and tell of all your wonderful deeds.
 8 Lord, I love the house of your habitation *
       and the place where your glory abides.
 9 Sweep me not away with sinners, *
       nor my life with the bloodthirsty,
10 Whose hands are full of wicked schemes *
       and their right hand full of bribes.
11 As for me, I will walk with integrity; *
       redeem me, Lord, and be merciful to me.
12 My foot stands firm; *
       in the great congregation I will bless the Lord.

   Glory . . .

Psalm 27

 1 The Lord is my light and my salvation;
       whom then shall I fear? *
       The Lord is the strength of my life;
       of whom then shall I be afraid?

2 When the wicked, even my enemies and my foes,
    came upon me to eat up my flesh, *
    they stumbled and fell.
3 Though a host encamp against me,
    my heart shall not be afraid, *
    and though there rise up war against me,
    yet will I put my trust in him.
4 One thing have I asked of the Lord
    and that alone I seek: *
    that I may dwell in the house of the Lord
    all the days of my life,
5 To behold the fair beauty of the Lord *
    and to seek his will in his temple.
6 For in the day of trouble
    he shall hide me in his shelter; *
    in the secret place of his dwelling shall he hide me
    and set me high upon a rock.
7 And now shall he lift up my head *
    above my enemies round about me;
8 Therefore will I offer in his dwelling an oblation
    with great gladness; *
    I will sing and make music to the Lord.
9 Hear my voice, O Lord, when I call; *
    have mercy upon me and answer me.
10 My heart tells of your word, 'Seek my face.'*
    Your face, Lord, will I seek.
11 Hide not your face from me, *
    nor cast your servant away in displeasure.
12 You have been my helper; *
    leave me not, neither forsake me, O God of my salvation.
13 Though my father and my mother forsake me, *
    the Lord will take me up.
14 Teach me your way, O Lord; *
    lead me on a level path,
    because of those who lie in wait for me.
15 Deliver me not into the will of my adversaries, *
    for false witnesses have risen up against me,
    and those who breathe out violence.
16 I believe that I shall see the goodness of the Lord *
    in the land of the living.

17 Wait for the Lord;
 be strong and he shall comfort your heart; *
 wait patiently for the Lord.

 Glory . . .

Psalm 28

1 To you I call, O Lord my rock;
 be not deaf to my cry, *
 lest, if you do not hear me,
 I become like those who go down to the Pit.
2 Hear the voice of my prayer when I cry out to you, *
 when I lift up my hands to your holy of holies.
3 Do not snatch me away with the wicked,
 with the evildoers, *
 who speak peaceably with their neighbours,
 while malice is in their hearts.
4 Repay them according to their deeds *
 and according to the wickedness of their devices.
5 Reward them according to the work of their hands *
 and pay them their just deserts.
6 They take no heed of the Lord's doings,
 nor of the works of his hands; *
 therefore shall he break them down
 and not build them up.

7 Blessed be the Lord, *
 for he has heard the voice of my prayer.
8 The Lord is my strength and my shield; *
 my heart has trusted in him and I am helped;
9 Therefore my heart dances for joy *
 and in my song will I praise him.
10 The Lord is the strength of his people, *
 a safe refuge for his anointed.
11 Save your people and bless your inheritance; *
 shepherd them and carry them for ever.

 Glory . . .

Psalm 29

1 Ascribe to the Lord, you powers of heaven, *
    ascribe to the Lord glory and strength.
2 Ascribe to the Lord the honour due to his name; *
    worship the Lord in the beauty of holiness.
3 The voice of the Lord is upon the waters;
    the God of glory thunders; *
    the Lord is upon the mighty waters.
4 The voice of the Lord is mighty in operation; *
    the voice of the Lord is a glorious voice.
5 The voice of the Lord breaks the cedar trees; *
    the Lord breaks the cedars of Lebanon;
6 He makes Lebanon skip like a calf *
    and Sirion like a young wild ox.
7 The voice of the Lord splits the flash of lightning;
    the voice of the Lord shakes the wilderness; *
    the Lord shakes the wilderness of Kadesh.
8 The voice of the Lord makes the oak trees writhe
    and strips the forests bare; *
    in his temple all cry, 'Glory!'
9 The Lord sits enthroned above the water flood; *
    the Lord sits enthroned as king for evermore.
10 The Lord shall give strength to his people; *
    the Lord shall give his people the blessing of peace.

   Glory . . .

Psalm 30

1 I will exalt you, O Lord,
    because you have raised me up *
    and have not let my foes triumph over me.
2 O Lord my God, I cried out to you *
    and you have healed me.
3 You brought me up, O Lord, from the dead; *
    you restored me to life from among those that go down to the Pit.
4 Sing to the Lord, you servants of his; *
    give thanks to his holy name.
5 For his wrath endures but the twinkling of an eye,
    his favour for a lifetime. *

> Heaviness may endure for a night,
> but joy comes in the morning.

6 In my prosperity I said,
> 'I shall never be moved. *
> You, Lord, of your goodness,
> have made my hill so strong.'
7 Then you hid your face from me *
> and I was utterly dismayed.
8 To you, O Lord, I cried; *
> to the Lord I made my supplication:
9 'What profit is there in my blood,
> if I go down to the Pit? *
> Will the dust praise you or declare your faithfulness?
10 'Hear, O Lord, and have mercy upon me; *
> O Lord, be my helper.'
11 You have turned my mourning into dancing; *
> you have put off my sackcloth and girded me with gladness;
12 Therefore my heart sings to you without ceasing; *
> O Lord my God, I will give you thanks for ever.

> Glory . . .

Psalm 31:1–5

1 In you, O Lord, have I taken refuge;
> let me never be put to shame; *
> deliver me in your righteousness.
2 Incline your ear to me; *
> make haste to deliver me.
3 Be my strong rock, a fortress to save me,
> for you are my rock and my stronghold; *
> guide me, and lead me for your name's sake.
4 Take me out of the net
> that they have laid secretly for me, *
> for you are my strength.
5 Into your hands I commend my spirit, *
> for you have redeemed me, O Lord God of truth.

> Glory . . .

Psalm 32

Penitential Psalm

1 Happy the one whose transgression is forgiven, *
   and whose sin is covered!
2 Happy is the one to whom the Lord imputes no guilt, *
   and in whose spirit there is no guile.
3 For I held my tongue; *
   my bones wasted away
   through my groaning all day long.
4 Your hand was heavy upon me day and night; *
   my moisture was dried up like the drought in summer.
5 Then I acknowledged my sin to you *
   and my iniquity I did not hide.
6 I said, 'I will confess my transgressions to the Lord,' *
   and you forgave the guilt of my sin.
7 Therefore let all the faithful make their prayers to you in time of trouble; *
   in the great water flood, it shall not reach them.
8 You are a place for me to hide in;
   you preserve me from trouble; *
   you surround me with songs of deliverance.

9 'I will instruct you and teach you
   in the way that you should go; *
   I will guide you with my eye.
10 'Be not like horse or mule which have no understanding; *
   whose mouths must be held with bit and bridle,
   or else they will not stay near you.'
11 Great tribulations remain for the wicked, *
   but mercy embraces those who trust in the Lord.
12 Be glad, you righteous, and rejoice in the Lord; *
   shout for joy, all who are true of heart.

   Glory . . .

Psalm 33

1 Rejoice in the Lord, O you righteous, *
   for it is good for the just to sing praises.
2 Praise the Lord with the lyre; *
   on the ten-stringed harp sing his praise.

3 Sing for him a new song; *
    play skilfully, with shouts of praise.
4 For the word of the Lord is true *
    and all his works are sure.
5 He loves righteousness and justice; *
    the earth is full of the loving-kindness of the Lord.
6 By the word of the Lord were the heavens made *
    and all their host by the breath of his mouth.
7 He gathers up the waters of the sea as in a waterskin *
    and lays up the deep in his treasury.
8 Let all the earth fear the Lord; *
    stand in awe of him, all who dwell in the world.
9 For he spoke, and it was done; *
    he commanded, and it stood fast.
10 The Lord brings the counsel of the nations to naught; *
    he frustrates the designs of the peoples.
11 But the counsel of the Lord shall endure for ever *
    and the designs of his heart from generation to generation.
12 Happy the nation whose God is the Lord *
    and the people he has chosen for his own.
13 The Lord looks down from heaven *
    and beholds all the children of earth.
14 From where he sits enthroned he turns his gaze *
    on all who dwell on the earth.
15 He fashions all the hearts of them *
    and understands all their works.
16 No king is saved by the might of his host; *
    no warrior delivered by his great strength.
17 A horse is a vain hope for deliverance; *
    for all its strength it cannot save.

18 Behold, the eye of the Lord
    is upon those who fear him, *
    on those who wait in hope for his steadfast love,
19 To deliver their soul from death *
    and to feed them in time of famine.
20 Our soul waits longingly for the Lord; *
    he is our help and our shield.
21 Indeed, our heart rejoices in him; *
    in his holy name have we put our trust.

22 Let your loving-kindness, O Lord, be upon us, *
    as we have set our hope on you.

Glory . . .

Psalm 34

1 I will bless the Lord at all times; *
    his praise shall ever be in my mouth.
2 My soul shall glory in the Lord; *
    let the humble hear and be glad.
3 O magnify the Lord with me; *
    let us exalt his name together.
4 I sought the Lord and he answered me *
    and delivered me from all my fears.
5 Look upon him and be radiant *
    and your faces shall not be ashamed.
6 This poor soul cried, and the Lord heard me *
    and saved me from all my troubles.
7 The angel of the Lord encamps around those who fear him *
    and delivers them.
8 O taste and see that the Lord is gracious; *
    blessed is the one who trusts in him.
9 Fear the Lord, all you his holy ones, *
    for those who fear him lack nothing.
10 Lions may lack and suffer hunger, *
    but those who seek the Lord
    lack nothing that is good.

11 Come, my children, and listen to me; *
    I will teach you the fear of the Lord.
12 Who is there who delights in life *
    and longs for days to enjoy good things?
13 Keep your tongue from evil *
    and your lips from lying words.
14 Turn from evil and do good; *
    seek peace and pursue it.
15 The eyes of the Lord are upon the righteous *
    and his ears are open to their cry.
16 The face of the Lord is against those who do evil, *
    to root out the remembrance of them from the earth.

17 The righteous cry and the Lord hears them *
   and delivers them out of all their troubles.
18 The Lord is near to the brokenhearted *
   and will save those who are crushed in spirit.
19 Many are the troubles of the righteous; *
   from them all will the Lord deliver them.
20 He keeps all their bones, *
   so that not one of them is broken.
21 But evil shall slay the wicked *
   and those who hate the righteous will be condemned.
22 The Lord ransoms the life of his servants *
   and will condemn none who seek refuge in him.

Glory . . .

Psalm 36

1 Sin whispers to the wicked, in the depths of their heart; *
   there is no fear of God before their eyes.
2 They flatter themselves in their own eyes *
   that their abominable sin will not be found out.
3 The words of their mouth are unrighteous and full of deceit; *
   they have ceased to act wisely and to do good.
4 They think out mischief upon their beds
   and have set themselves in no good way; *
   nor do they abhor that which is evil.

5 Your love, O Lord, reaches to the heavens *
   and your faithfulness to the clouds.
6 Your righteousness stands like the strong mountains,
   your justice like the great deep; *
   you Lord, shall save both man and beast.
7 How precious is your loving mercy, O God! *
   All mortal flesh shall take refuge
   under the shadow of your wings.
8 They shall be satisfied with the abundance of your house; *
   they shall drink from the river of your delights.
9 For with you is the well of life,
   and in your light shall we see light.
10 O continue your loving-kindness to those who know you *
   and your righteousness to those who are true of heart.

11 Let not the foot of pride come against me, *
    nor the hand of the ungodly thrust me away.
12 There are they fallen, all who work wickedness. *
    They are cast down and shall not be able to stand.

Glory . . .

Psalm 38

Penitential Psalm

1 Rebuke me not, O Lord, in your anger; *
    neither chasten me in your heavy displeasure.
2 For your arrows have stuck fast in me *
    and your hand presses hard upon me.
3 There is no health in my flesh
    because of your indignation; *
    there is no peace in my bones because of my sin.
4 For my iniquities have gone over my head; *
    their weight is a burden too heavy to bear.
5 My wounds stink and fester *
    because of my foolishness.
6 I am utterly bowed down and brought very low; *
    I go about mourning all the day long.
7 My loins are filled with searing pain; *
    there is no health in my flesh.
8 I am feeble and utterly crushed; *
    I roar aloud because of the disquiet of my heart.
9 O Lord, you know all my desires *
    and my sighing is not hidden from you.
10 My heart is pounding, my strength has failed me; *
    the light of my eyes is gone from me.
11 My friends and companions stand apart from my affliction; *
    my neighbours stand afar off.
12 Those who seek after my life lay snares for me; *
    and those who would harm me whisper evil
    and mutter slander all the day long.
13 But I am like one who is deaf and hears not, *
    like one that is dumb, who does not open his mouth.
14 I have become like one who does not hear *
    and from whose mouth comes no retort.

15 For in you, Lord, have I put my trust *
    you will answer me, O Lord my God.
16 For I prayed, 'Let them not triumph over me, *
    those who exult over me when my foot slips.'
17 Truly, I am on the verge of falling *
    and my pain is ever with me.
18 I will confess my iniquity *
    and be sorry for my sin.
19 Those that are my enemies without any cause are mighty, *
    and those who hate me wrongfully are many in number.
20 Those who repay evil for good are against me, *
    because the good is what I seek.
21 Forsake me not, O Lord; *
    be not far from me, O my God.
22 Make haste to help me, *
    O Lord of my salvation.

    Glory . . .

Psalm 40

1 I waited patiently for the Lord; *
    he inclined to me and heard my cry.
2 He brought me out of the roaring pit,
    out of the mire and clay; *
    he set my feet upon a rock and made my footing sure.
3 He has put a new song in my mouth,
    a song of praise to our God; *
    many shall see and fear
    and put their trust in the Lord.
4 Blessed is the one who trusts in the Lord, *
    who does not turn to the proud that follow a lie.
5 Great are the wonders you have done, O Lord my God.
    How great your designs for us! *
    There is none that can be compared with you.
6 If I were to proclaim them and tell of them *
    they would be more than I am able to express.

7 Sacrifice and offering you do not desire *
    but my ears you have opened;

8 Burnt offering and sacrifice for sin you have not required; *
      then said I , 'Lo, I come.
   9 'In the scroll of the book it is written of me
      that I should do your will, O my God; *
      I delight to do it: your law is within my heart.'
  10 I have declared your righteousness in the great congregation; *
      behold, I did not restrain my lips,
      and that, O Lord, you know.
  11 Your righteousness I have not hidden in my heart;
      I have spoken of your faithfulness and your salvation; *
      I have not concealed your loving-kindness and truth
      from the great congregation.
  12 Do not withhold your compassion from me, O Lord; *
      let your love and your faithfulness always preserve me,
  13 For innumerable troubles have come about me;
      my sins have overtaken me so that I cannot look up; *
      they are more in number than the hairs of my head,
      and my heart falls me.
  14 Be pleased, O Lord, to deliver me; *
      Lord, make haste to help me.
  15 Let them be ashamed and altogether dismayed
      who seek after my life to destroy it; *
      let them be driven back and put to shame
      who wish me evil.
  16 Let those who heap insults upon me *
      be desolate because of their shame.
  17 Let all who seek you rejoice in you and be glad; *
      let those who love your salvation say always,
      'The Lord is great.'
  18 Though I am poor and needy, *
      the Lord cares for me.
  19 You are my helper and my deliverer; *
      O my God, make no delay.

   Glory . . .

Psalm 41

   1 Blessed are those who consider the poor and needy; *
      the Lord will deliver them in the time of trouble.

2 The Lord preserves them and restores their life,
    that they may be happy in the land; *
    he will not hand them over to the will of their enemies.
3 The Lord sustains them on their sick-bed; *
    their sickness, Lord, you will remove.
4 And so I said, 'Lord, be merciful to me; *
    heal me, for I have sinned against you.'

5 My enemies speak evil about me, *
    asking when I shall die and my name perish.
6 If they come to see me, they utter empty words; *
    their heart gathers mischief;
    when they go out, they tell it abroad.
7 All my enemies whisper together against me, *
    against me they devise evil,
8 Saying that a deadly thing has laid hold on me, *
    and that I will not rise again from where I lie.
9 Even my bosom friend, whom I trusted,
    who ate of my bread, *
    has lifted up his heel against me.

10 But you, O Lord, be merciful to me *
    and raise me up, that I may reward them.
11 By this I know that you favour me, *
    that my enemy does not triumph over me.
12 Because of my integrity, you uphold me *
    and will set me before your face for ever.
13 Blessed be the Lord God of Israel, *
    from everlasting to everlasting. Amen and Amen.

   Glory . . .

Psalm 42

1 As the deer longs for the water-brooks, *
    so longs my soul for you, O God.
2 My soul is athirst for God, even for the living God; *
    when shall I come to behold the face of God?
3 My tears have been my bread day and night, *
    while all day long they say to me, 'Where is now your God?'

4 Now when I think on these things, I pour out my soul: *
    how I went with the multitude
    and led the procession to the house of God,
5 With the voice of praise and thanksgiving, *
    among those who kept holy day.
6 *Why are you so full of heaviness, O my soul, *
    and why are you so disquieted within me?*
7 *O put your trust in God *
    for I will yet give him thanks,
    who is the help of my countenance, and my God.*

8 My soul is heavy within me; *
    therefore I will remember you from the land of Jordan,
    and from Hermon and the hill of Mizar.
9 Deep calls to deep in the thunder of your waterfalls; *
    all your breakers and waves have gone over me.
10 The Lord will grant his loving-kindness in the daytime; *
    through the night his song will be with me,
    a prayer to the God of my life.
11 I say to God my rock,
    'Why have you forgotten me, *
    and why go I so heavily, while the enemy oppresses me?'
12 As they crush my bones, my enemies mock me; *
    while all day long they say to me, 'Where is now your God?'
13 *Why are you so full of heaviness, O my soul *
    and why are you so disquieted within me?*
14 *O put your trust in God *
    for I will yet give him thanks,
    who is the help of my countenance, and my God.*

   Glory . . .

Psalm 43

1 Give judgement for me, O God,
    and defend my cause against an ungodly people; *
    deliver me from the deceitful and the wicked.
2 For you are the God of my refuge;
    why have you cast me from you, *
    and why go I so heavily, while the enemy oppresses me?

3 O send out your light and your truth, that they may lead me, *
    and bring me to your holy hill and to your dwelling;
4 That I may go to the altar of God,
    to the God of my joy and gladness; *
    and on the lyre I will give thanks to you, O God my God.
5 *Why are you so full of heaviness, O my soul,* *
    and why are you so disquieted within me?
6 *O put your trust in God;* *
    for I will yet give him thanks,
    who is the help of my countenance, and my God.

Glory . . .

Psalm 45

1 My heart is astir with gracious words; *
    as I make my song for the king,
    my tongue is the pen of a ready writer.
2 You are the fairest of men; *
    full of grace are your lips,
    for God has blessed you for ever.
3 Gird your sword upon your thigh, O mighty one; *
    gird on your majesty and glory.
4 Ride on and prosper in the cause of truth *
    and for the sake of humility and righteousness.
5 Your right hand will teach you terrible things; *
    your arrows will be sharp in the heart of the king's enemies,
    so that peoples fall under you.
6 Your throne is God's throne, for ever; *
    the sceptre of your kingdom is the sceptre of righteousness.
7 You love righteousness and hate iniquity; *
    therefore God, your God, has anointed you
    with the oil of gladness above your fellows.
8 All your garments are fragrant with myrrh, aloes and cassia; *
    from ivory palaces the music of strings makes you glad.
9 Kings' daughters are among your honourable women; *
    at your right hand stands the queen in gold of Ophir.
10 Hear, O daughter; consider and incline your ear; *
    forget your own people and your father's house.

11 So shall the king have pleasure in your beauty; *
    he is your lord, so do him honour.
12 The people of Tyre shall bring you gifts; *
    the richest of the people shall seek your favour.
13 The king's daughter is all glorious within; *
    her clothing is embroidered cloth of gold.
14 She shall be brought to the king in raiment of needlework; *
    after her the virgins that are her companions.
15 With joy and gladness shall they be brought *
    and enter into the palace of the king.
16 'Instead of your fathers you shall have sons, *
    whom you shall make princes over all the earth.
17 'I will make your name to be remembered through all generations; *
    therefore shall the peoples praise you for ever and ever.'

   Glory . . .

Psalm 46

1 God is our refuge and strength, *
    a very present help in trouble;
2 Therefore we will not fear, though the earth be moved, *
    and though the mountains tremble in the heart of the sea;
3 Though the waters rage and swell, *
    and though the mountains quake at the towering seas:

4 There is a river whose streams make glad the city of God, *
    the holy place of the dwelling of the Most High.
5 God is in the midst of her;
    therefore shall she not be removed; *
    God shall help her at the break of day.
6 The nations are in uproar and the kingdoms are shaken, *
    but God utters his voice and the earth shall melt away.
7 *The Lord of hosts is with us; **
    the God of Jacob is our stronghold.

8 Come and behold the works of the Lord, *
    what destruction he has wrought upon the earth.
9 He makes wars to cease in all the world; *
    he shatters the bow and snaps the spear
    and burns the chariots in the fire.

10 'Be still, and know that I am God; *
     I will be exalted among the nations;
     I will be exalted in the earth.'
11 *The Lord of hosts is with us;* *
     the God of Jacob is our stronghold.

   Glory . . .

Psalm 47

1 Clap your hands together, all you peoples; *
    O sing unto God with shouts of joy.
2 For the Lord Most High is to be feared; *
    he is the great King over all the earth.
3 He subdued the peoples under us *
    and the nations under our feet.
4 He has chosen our heritage for us, *
    the pride of Jacob, whom he loves.
5 God has gone up with a merry noise, *
    the Lord with the sound of the trumpet.
6 O sing praises to God, sing praises; *
    sing praises to our King, sing praises.
7 For God is the King of all the earth; *
    sing praises with all your skill.
8 God reigns over the nations; *
    God has taken his seat upon his holy throne.
9 The nobles of the peoples are gathered together *
    with the people of the God of Abraham.
10 For the powers of the earth belong to God *
    and he is very highly exalted.

   Glory . . .

Psalm 48

1 Great is the Lord and highly to be praised, *
    in the city of our God.
2 His holy mountain is fair and lifted high, *
    the joy of all the earth;
3 On Mount Zion, the divine dwelling place, *
    stands the city of the great king.

4 In her palaces God has shown himself *
   to be a sure refuge.

5 For behold, the kings of the earth assembled *
   and swept forward together.
6 They saw, and were dumbfounded; *
   dismayed, they fled in terror.
7 Trembling seized them there;
   they writhed like a woman in labour, *
   as when the east wind shatters the ships of Tarshish.
8 As we had heard, so have we seen
   in the city of the Lord of hosts, the city of our God: *
   God has established her for ever.

9 We have waited on your loving-kindness, O God, *
   in the midst of your temple.
10 As with your name, O God,
   so your praise reaches to the ends of the earth; *
   your right hand is full of justice.
11 Let Mount Zion rejoice and the daughters of Judah be glad, *
   because of your judgements, O Lord.
12 Walk about Zion and go round about her;
   count all her towers; *
   consider well her bulwarks; pass through her citadels,
13 That you may tell those who come after
   that such is our God for ever and ever. *
   It is he that shall be our guide for evermore.

   Glory . . .

Psalm 49

1 Hear this, all you peoples; *
   listen, all you that dwell in the world,
2 You of low or high degree, *
   both rich and poor together.
3 My mouth shall speak of wisdom *
   and my heart shall meditate on understanding.
4 I will incline my ear to a parable; *
   I will unfold my riddle with the lyre.

5 Why should I fear in evil days, *
    when the malice of my foes surrounds me,
6 Such as trust in their goods *
    and glory in the abundance of their riches?
7 For no one can indeed ransom another *
    or pay to God the price of deliverance.
8 To ransom a soul is too costly; *
    there is no price one could pay for it,
9 So that they might live for ever, *
    and never see the grave.
10 For we see that the wise die also;
    with the foolish and ignorant they perish *
    and leave their riches to others.
11 Their tomb is their home for ever,
    their dwelling through all generations, *
    though they call their lands after their own names.
12 Those who have honour, but lack understanding, *
    are like the beasts that perish.
13 Such is the way of those who boast in themselves, *
    the end of those who delight in their own words.
14 Like a flock of sheep they are destined to die;
    death is their shepherd; *
    they go down straight to the Pit.
15 Their beauty shall waste away *
    and the land of the dead shall be their dwelling.
16 But God shall ransom my soul; *
    from the grasp of death will he take me.
17 Be not afraid if some grow rich *
    and the glory of their house increases,
18 For they will carry nothing away when they die, *
    nor will their glory follow after them.
19 Though they count themselves happy while they live *
    and praise you for your success,
20 They shall enter the company of their ancestors *
    who will nevermore see the light.
21 Those who have honour but lack understanding, *
    are like the beasts that perish.

   Glory . . .

Psalm 51

Penitential Psalm

1 Have mercy on me, O God, in your great goodness; *
   according to the abundance of your compassion
   blot out my offences.
2 Wash me thoroughly from my wickedness *
   and cleanse me from my sin.
3 For I acknowledge my faults *
   and my sin is ever before me.
4 Against you only have I sinned *
   and done what is evil in your sight,
5 So that you are justified in your sentence *
   and righteous in your judgement.
6 I have been wicked even from my birth, *
   a sinner when my mother conceived me.
7 Behold, you desire truth deep within me *
   and shall make me understand wisdom
   in the depths of my heart.
8 Purge me with hyssop and I shall be clean; *
   wash me and I shall be whiter than snow.
9 Make me hear of joy and gladness, *
   that the bones you have broken may rejoice.
10 Turn your face from my sins *
   and blot out all my misdeeds.
11 Make me a clean heart, O God, *
   and renew a right spirit within me.
12 Cast me not away from your presence *
   and take not your holy spirit from me.
13 Give me again the joy of your salvation *
   and sustain me with your gracious spirit;
14 Then shall I teach your ways to the wicked *
   and sinners shall return to you.
15 Deliver me from my guilt, O God,
   the God of my salvation, *
   and my tongue shall sing of your righteousness.
16 O Lord, open my lips *
   and my mouth shall proclaim your praise.

17 For you desire no sacrifice, else I would give it; *
　　for you take no delight in burnt offerings.
18 The sacrifice of God is a broken spirit; *
　　a broken and contrite heart, O God, you will not despise.
19 O be favourable and gracious to Zion; *
　　build up the walls of Jerusalem.
20 Then you will accept sacrifices offered in righteousness,
　　　the burnt offerings and oblations; *
　　then shall they offer up bulls on your altar.

　　Glory . . .

Psalm 53

1 The fool has said in his heart, 'There is no God.' *
　　Corrupt are they, and abominable in their wickedness;
　　there is no one that does good.
2 God has looked down from heaven upon the children of earth, *
　　to see if there is anyone who is wise and seeks after God.
3 They are all gone out of the way;
　　all alike have become corrupt; *
　　there is no one that does good, no not one.
4 Have they no knowledge, those evil-doers, *
　　who eat up my people as if they ate bread,
　　and do not call upon God?
5 There shall they be in great fear,
　　such fear as never was; *
　　for God will scatter the bones of the ungodly.
6 They will be put to shame, *
　　because God has rejected them.
7 O that Israel's salvation would come out of Zion! *
　　When God restores the fortunes of his people
　　then will Jacob rejoice and Israel be glad.

　　Glory . . .

Psalm 54

1 Save me, O God, by your name *
　　and vindicate me by your power.

2 Hear my prayer, O God; *
      give heed to the words of my mouth.
3 For strangers have risen up against me,
      and the ruthless seek after my life; *
      they have not set God before them.
4 Behold, God is my helper; *
      it is the Lord who upholds my life.
5 May evil rebound on those who lie in wait for me; *
      destroy them in your faithfulness.
6 An offering of a free heart will I give you *
      and praise your name, O Lord, for it is gracious.
7 For he has delivered me out of all my trouble, *
      and my eye has seen the downfall of my enemies.

Glory . . .

Psalm 55

1 Hear my prayer, O God; *
      hide not yourself from my petition.
2 Give heed to me and answer me; *
      I am restless in my complaining.
3 I am alarmed at the voice of the enemy *
      and at the clamour of the wicked;
4 For they would bring down evil upon me *
      and are set against me in fury.
5 My heart is disquieted within me, *
      and the terrors of death have fallen upon me.
6 Fearfulness and trembling are come upon me, *
      and a horrible dread has overwhelmed me.
7 And I said: 'O that I had wings like a dove, *
      for then would I fly away and be at rest.
8 'Then would I flee far away *
      and make my lodging in the wilderness.
9 'I would make haste to escape *
      from the stormy wind and tempest.'
10 Confuse their tongues, O Lord, and divide them, *
      for I have seen violence and strife in the city.
11 Day and night they go about on her walls; *
      mischief and trouble are in her midst.

12 Wickedness walks in her streets; *
    oppression and guile never leave her squares.
13 For it was not an open enemy that reviled me, *
    for then I could have borne it;
14 Nor was it my adversary that puffed himself up against me, *
    for then I would have hid myself from him.
15 But it was even you, one like myself, *
    my companion and my own familiar friend.
16 We took sweet counsel together *
    and walked with the multitude in the house of God.
17 Let death come suddenly upon them;
    let them go down alive to the Pit; *
    for wickedness inhabits their dwellings, their very hearts.

18 As for me, I will call upon God *
    and the Lord will deliver me.
19 In the evening and morning and at noonday
    I will pray and make my supplication, *
    and he shall hear my voice.
20 He shall redeem my soul in peace
    from the battle waged against me, *
    for many have come upon me.
21 God, who is enthroned of old,
    will hear and bring them down; *
    they will not repent, for they have no fear of God.
22 My companion stretched out his hands against his friend *
    and has broken his covenant;
23 His speech was softer than butter, though war was in his heart; *
    his words were smoother than oil, yet are they naked swords.
24 Cast your burden upon the Lord and he will sustain you, *
    and will not let the righteous fall for ever.
25 But those that are bloodthirsty and deceitful, O God, *
    you will bring down to the pit of destruction.
26 They shall not live out half their days, *
    but my trust shall be in you, O Lord.

    Glory . . .

Psalm 56

1 Have mercy on me, O God, for they trample over me; *
   all day long they assault and oppress me.
2 My adversaries trample over me all the day long; *
   many are they that make proud war against me.
3 In the day of my fear I put my trust in you, *
   in God whose word I praise.
4 In God I trust, and will not fear, *
   for what can flesh do to me?
5 All day long they wound me with words; *
   their every thought is to do me evil.
6 They stir up trouble; they lie in wait; *
   marking my steps, they seek my life.
7 Shall they escape for all their wickedness? *
   In anger, O God, cast the peoples down.
8 You have counted up my groaning;
   put my tears into your bottle; *
   are they not written in your book?
9 Then shall my enemies turn back
   on the day when I call upon you; *
   this I know, for God is on my side.
10 In God whose word I praise,
   in the Lord whose word I praise, *
   in God I trust and will not fear
   what can flesh do to me?
11 To you, O God, will I fulfil my vows; *
   to you will I present my offerings of thanks,
12 For you will deliver my soul from death
   and my feet from falling, *
   that I may walk before God in the light of the living.

   Glory . . .

Psalm 57

1 Be merciful to me, O God, be merciful to me, *
   for my soul takes refuge in you;
2 In the shadow of your wings will I take refuge *
   until the storm of destruction has passed by.

3 I will call upon the Most High God, *
    the God who fulfils his purpose for me.
4 He will send from heaven and save me
    and rebuke those that would trample upon me; *
    God will send forth his love and his faithfulness.
5 I lie in the midst of lions, *
    people whose teeth are spears and arrows,
    and their tongue a sharp sword.
6 *Be exalted, O God, above the heavens; ★*
    and your glory over all the earth.
7 They have laid a net for my feet;
    my soul is pressed down; *
    they have dug a pit before me
    and will fall into it themselves.

8 My heart is ready, O God, my heart is ready; *
    I will sing and give you praise.
9 Awake, my soul; awake, harp and lyre, *
    that I may awaken the dawn.
10 I will give you thanks, O Lord, among the peoples; *
    I will sing praise to you among the nations.
11 For your loving-kindness is as high as the heavens, *
    and your faithfulness reaches to the clouds.
12 *Be exalted, O God, above the heavens, ★*
    and your glory over all the earth.

   Glory . . .

Psalm 59

1 Rescue me from my enemies, O my God; *
    set me high above those that rise up against me.
2 Save me from the evil-doers, *
    and from murderous foes deliver me.
3 For see how they lie in wait for my soul *
    and the mighty stir up trouble against me.
4 Not for any fault or sin of mine, O Lord; *
    for no offence, they run and prepare themselves for war.
5 Rouse yourself, come to my aid and see; *
    for you are the Lord of hosts, the God of Israel.

6 Awake, and judge all the nations; *
　show no mercy to the evil traitors.
7 They return at nightfall and snarl like dogs *
　and prowl about the city.
8 They pour out evil words with their mouths;
　swords are on their lips; *
　'For who,' they say, 'can hear us?'
9 But you laugh at them, O Lord; *
　you hold all the nations in derision.
10 For you, O my strength, will I watch; *
　you, O God, are my strong tower.
11 My God in his steadfast love will come to me; *
　he will let me behold the downfall of my enemies.
12 Slay them not, lest my people forget; *
　send them reeling by your might
　and bring them down, O Lord our shield.
13 For the sins of their mouth, for the words of their lips, *
　let them be taken in their pride.
14 For the cursing and falsehood they have uttered, *
　consume them in wrath, consume them till they are no more.
15 And they shall know that God rules in Jacob, *
　and to the ends of the earth.
16 And still they return at nightfall and snarl like dogs *
　and prowl about the city.
17 Though they forage for something to devour, *
　and howl if they are not filled,
18 Yet will I sing of your strength *
　and every morning praise your steadfast love;
19 For you have been my stronghold, *
　my refuge in the day of my trouble.
20 To you, O my strength, will I sing; *
　for you, O God, are my refuge,
　my God of steadfast love.

　Glory . . .

Psalm 60

1 O God, you have cast us off and broken us; *
    you have been angry; restore us to yourself again.
2 You have shaken the earth and torn it apart; *
    heal its wounds, for it trembles.
3 You have made your people drink bitter things; *
    we reel from the deadly wine you have given us.
4 You have made those who fear you to flee, *
    to escape from the range of the bow.
5 That your beloved may be delivered, *
    save us by your right hand and answer us.

6 God has spoken in his holiness: *
    'I will triumph and divide Shechem,
    and share out the valley of Succoth.
7 'Gilead is mine and Manasseh is mine; *
    Ephraim is my helmet and Judah my sceptre.
8 'Moab shall be my washpot;
    over Edom will I cast my sandal; *
    across Philistia will I shout in triumph.'
9 Who will lead me into the strong city? *
    Who will bring me into Edom?
10 Have you not cast us off, O God? *
    Will you no longer go forth with our troops?
11 Grant us your help against the enemy, *
    for earthly help is in vain.
12 Through God will we do great acts, *
    for it is he that shall tread down our enemies.

   Glory . . .

Psalm 61

1 Hear my crying, O God, *
    and listen to my prayer.
2 From the end of the earth I call to you with fainting heart; *
    O set me on the rock that is higher than I.
3 For you are my refuge, *
    a strong tower against the enemy.

4 Let me dwell in your tent for ever *
    and take refuge under the cover of your wings.
5 For you, O God, will hear my vows; *
    you will grant the request of those who fear your name.
6 You will add length of days to the life of the king, *
    that his years may endure throughout all generations.
7 May he sit enthroned before God for ever; *
    may steadfast love and truth watch over him.
8 So will I always sing praise to your name, *
    and day by day fulfil my vows.

Glory . . .

Psalm 62

1 On God alone my soul in stillness waits; *
    from him comes my salvation.
2 He alone is my rock and my salvation, *
    my stronghold, so that I shall never be shaken.
3 How long will all of you assail me to destroy me, *
    as you would a tottering wall or a leaning fence?
4 They plot only to thrust me down from my place of honour;
    lies are their chief delight; *
    they bless with their mouth, but in their heart they curse.
5 Wait on God alone in stillness, O my soul; *
    for in him is my hope.
6 He alone is my rock and my salvation, *
    my stronghold, so that I shall not be shaken.
7 In God is my strength and my glory; *
    God is my strong rock; in him is my refuge.

8 Put your trust in him always, my people; *
    pour out your hearts before him, for God is our refuge.
9 The peoples are but a breath,
    the whole human race a deceit; *
    on the scales they are altogether lighter than air
10 Put no trust in oppression; in robbery take no empty pride; *
    though wealth increase, set not your heart upon it.
11 God spoke once, and twice have I heard the same, *
    that power belongs to God.

12 Steadfast love belongs to you, O Lord, *
   for you repay everyone according to their deeds.

   Glory . . .

Psalm 63: 1–9

1 O God, you are my God; eagerly I seek you; *
   my soul is athirst for you.
2 My flesh also faints for you, *
   as in a dry and thirsty land where there is no water.
3 So would I gaze upon you in your holy place, *
   that I might behold your power and your glory.
4 Your loving-kindness is better than life itself *
   and so my lips shall praise you
5 I will bless you as long as I live *
   and lift up my hands in your name.
6 My soul shall be satisfied, as with marrow and fatness, *
   and my mouth shall praise you with joyful lips,
7 When I remember you upon my bed *
   and meditate on you in the watches of the night.
8 For you have been my helper *
   and under the shadow of your wings will I rejoice.
9 My soul clings to you; *
   your right hand shall hold me fast.

   Glory . . .

Psalm 64

1 Hear my voice, O God, in my complaint; *
   preserve my life from fear of the enemy.
2 Hide me from the conspiracy of the wicked, *
   from the gathering of evil-doers.
3 They sharpen their tongue like a sword *
   and aim their bitter words like arrows,
4 That they may shoot at the blameless from hiding places; *
   suddenly they shoot, and are not seen.
5 They hold fast to their evil course; *
   they talk of laying snares, saying, 'Who will see us?'

6 They search out wickedness and lay a cunning trap, *
    for deep are the inward thoughts of the heart.

7 But God will shoot at them with his swift arrow, *
    and suddenly they shall be wounded.
8 Their own tongues shall make them fall, *
    and all who see them shall wag their heads in scorn.
9 All peoples shall fear and tell what God has done, *
    and they will ponder all his works.
10 The righteous shall rejoice in the Lord
    and put their trust in him, *
    and all that are true of heart shall exult.

   Glory . . .

Psalm 65

1 Praise is due to you, O God, in Zion; *
    to you that answer prayer shall vows be paid.
2 To you shall all flesh come to confess their sins; *
    when our misdeeds prevail against us,
    you will purge them away.
3 Happy are they whom you choose
    and draw to your courts to dwell there. *
    We shall be satisfied with the blessings of your house,
    even of your holy temple.
4 With wonders you will answer us in your righteousness,
    O God of our salvation, *
    O hope of all the ends of the earth
    and of the farthest seas.
5 In your strength you set fast the mountains *
    and are girded about with might.
6 You stilled the raging of the seas, *
    the roaring of their waves,
    and the clamour of the peoples.
7 Those who dwell at the ends of the earth
    tremble at your marvels; *
    the gates of the morning and evening sing your praise.
8 You visit the earth and water it; *
    you make it very plenteous.

9 The river of God is full of water; *
    you prepare grain for your people,
    for so you provide.
10 You drench the furrows and smooth out the ridges; *
    you soften the ground with showers and bless its increase.
11 You crown the year with your goodness, *
    and your paths overflow with plenty.
12 May the pastures of the wilderness flow with goodness *
    and the hills be girded with joy.
13 May the meadows be clothed with flocks of sheep *
    and the valleys stand so thick with corn
    that they shall laugh and sing.

   Glory . . .

Psalm 67

1 God be gracious to us and bless us *
    and make his face to shine upon us,
2 That your way may be known upon earth, *
    your saving power among all nations.
3 *Let the peoples praise you, O God;* *
    let all the peoples praise you.

4 O let the nations rejoice and be glad, *
    for you will judge the peoples righteously
    and govern the nations upon earth.
5 *Let the peoples praise you, O God;* *
    let all the peoples praise you.

6 Then shall the earth bring forth her increase, *
    and God, our own God, will bless us.
7 God will bless us, *
    and all the ends of the world shall fear him.

   Glory . . .

Psalm 70

1 O God, make speed to save me; *
    O Lord, make haste to help me.

2 Let those who seek my life
    be put to shame and confusion; *
    let them be turned back and disgraced
    who wish me evil.
3 Let those who mock and deride me *
    turn back because of their shame.
4 But let all who seek you rejoice and be glad in you; *
    let those who love your salvation say always, 'Great is the Lord!'
5 As for me, I am poor and needy; *
    come to me quickly, O God.
6 You are my help and my deliverer; *
    O Lord, do not delay.

Glory . . .

Psalm 71

1 In you, O Lord, do I seek refuge; *
    let me never be put to shame.
2 In your righteousness, deliver me and set me free; *
    incline your ear to me and save me.
3 Be for me a stronghold to which I may ever resort; *
    send out to save me, for you are my rock and my fortress.
4 Deliver me, my God, from the hand of the wicked, *
    from the grasp of the evil-doer and the oppressor.
5 For you are my hope, O Lord God, *
    my confidence, even from my youth.
6 Upon you have I leaned from my birth,
    when you drew me from my mother's womb; *
    my praise shall be always of you.
7 I have become a portent to many, *
    but you are my refuge and my strength.
8 Let my mouth be full of your praise *
    and your glory all the day long.
9 Do not cast me away in the time of old age; *
    forsake me not when my strength fails.
10 For my enemies are talking against me, *
    and those who lie in wait for my life take counsel together.
11 They say, 'God has forsaken him;
    pursue him and take him, *
    because there is none to deliver him.'

12 O God, be not far from me; *
    come quickly to help me, O my God.
13 Let those who are against me
    be put to shame and disgrace; *
    let those who seek to do me evil
    be covered with scorn and reproach.
14 But as for me I will hope continually, *
    and will praise you more and more.
15 My mouth shall tell of your righteousness
    and salvation all the day long, *
    for I know no end of the telling.
16 I will begin with the mighty works of the Lord God; *
    I will recall your righteousness, yours alone.
17 O God, you have taught me since I was young, *
    and to this day I tell of your wonderful works.
18 Forsake me not, O God,
    when I am old and grey-headed, *
    till I make known your deeds to the next generation
    and your power to all that are to come.
19 Your righteousness, O God, reaches to the heavens; *
    in the great things you have done, who is like you, O God?
20 What troubles and adversities you have shown me, *
    and yet you will turn and refresh me
    and bring me from the deep of the earth again.
21 Increase my honour; *
    turn again and comfort me.
22 Therefore will I praise you upon the harp
    for your faithfulness, O my God; *
    I will sing to you with the lyre, O Holy One of Israel.
23 My lips will sing out as I play to you, *
    and so will my soul, which you have redeemed.
24 My tongue also will tell of your righteousness all the day long, *
    for they shall be shamed and disgraced
    who sought to do me evil.

   Glory . . .

Psalm 72

1 Give the king your judgements, O God, *
    and your righteousness to the son of a king.
2 Then shall he judge your people righteously *
    and your poor with justice.
3 May the mountains bring forth peace, *
    and the little hills righteousness for the people.
4 May he defend the poor among the people, *
    deliver the children of the needy and crush the oppressor.
5 May he live as long as the sun and moon endure, *
    from one generation to another.
6 May he come down like rain upon the mown grass, *
    like the showers that water the earth.
7 In his time shall righteousness flourish, *
    and abundance of peace
    till the moon shall be no more.

8 May his dominion extend from sea to sea *
    and from the River to the ends of the earth.
9 May his foes kneel before him *
    and his enemies lick the dust.
10 The kings of Tarshish and of the isles shall pay tribute; *
    the kings of Sheba and Seba shall bring gifts.
11 All kings shall fall down before him; *
    all nations shall do him service.
12 For he shall deliver the poor that cry out, *
    the needy and those who have no helper.
13 He shall have pity on the weak and poor; *
    he shall preserve the lives of the needy.
14 He shall redeem their lives from oppression and violence, *
    and dear shall their blood be in his sight.
15 Long may he live;
    unto him may be given gold from Sheba; *
    may prayer be made for him continually
    and may they bless him all the day long.
16 May there be abundance of grain on the earth,
    standing thick upon the hilltops; *
    may its fruit flourish like Lebanon
    and its grain grow like the grass of the field.

17 May his name remain for ever
 and be established as long as the sun endures; *
 may all nations be blest in him
 and call him blessed.
18 Blessed be the Lord, the God of Israel, *
 who alone does wonderful things.
19 And blessed be his glorious name for ever. *
 May all the earth be filled with his glory.
 Amen. Amen.

   Glory . . .

Psalm 74

1 O God, why have you utterly disowned us? *
 Why does your anger burn
 against the sheep of your pasture?
2 Remember your congregation that you purchased of old, *
 the tribe you redeemed for your own possession,
 and Mount Zion where you dwelt.
3 Hasten your steps towards the endless ruins, *
 where the enemy has laid waste all your sanctuary.
4 Your adversaries roared in the place of your worship; *
 they set up their banners as tokens of victory.
5 Like men brandishing axes on high in a thicket of trees, *
 all her carved work they smashed down with hatchet and hammer.
6 They set fire to your holy place; *
 they defiled the dwelling place of your name
 and razed it to the ground.
7 They said in their heart, 'Let us make havoc of them altogether,' *
 and they burned down all the sanctuaries of God in the land.
8 There are no signs to see, not one prophet left, *
 not one among us who knows how long.
9 How long, O God, will the adversary scoff? *
 Shall the enemy blaspheme your name for ever?
10 Why have you withheld your hand *
 and hidden your right hand in your bosom?
11 Yet God is my king from of old, *
 who did deeds of salvation in the midst of the earth.

12 It was you that divided the sea by your might *
    and shattered the heads of the dragons on the waters;
13 You alone crushed the heads of Leviathan *
    and gave him to the beasts of the desert for food.
14 You cleft the rock for fountain and flood; *
    you dried up ever-flowing rivers.
15 Yours is the day, yours also the night; *
    you established the moon and the sun.
16 You set all the bounds of the earth; *
    you fashioned both summer and winter.
17 Remember now, Lord, how the enemy scoffed, *
    how a foolish people despised your name.
18 Do not give to wild beasts the soul of your turtle dove; *
    forget not the lives of your poor for ever.
19 Look upon your creation,
    for the earth is full of darkness, *
    full of the haunts of violence.
20 Let not the oppressed turn away ashamed, *
    but let the poor and needy praise your name.
21 Arise, O God, maintain your own cause; *
    remember how fools revile you all the day long.
22 Forget not the clamour of your adversaries, *
    the tumult of your enemies that ascends continually.

   Glory . . .

Psalm 75

1 We give you thanks, O God, we give you thanks, *
    for your name is near, as your wonderful deeds declare.
2 'I will seize the appointed time; *
    I, the Lord, will judge with equity.
3 'Though the earth reels and all that dwell in her, *
    it is I that hold her pillars steady.
4 'To the boasters I say, "Boast no longer;" *
    and to the wicked, "Do not lift up your horn.
5 "'Do not lift up your horn on high; *
    do not speak with a stiff neck."'
6 For neither from the east nor from the west, *
    nor yet from the wilderness comes exaltation.

7 But God alone is judge; *
    he puts down one and raises up another.
8 For in the hand of the Lord there is a cup, *
    well mixed and full of foaming wine.
9 He pours it out for all the wicked of the earth; *
    they shall drink it, and drain the dregs.
10 But I will rejoice for ever *
    and make music to the God of Jacob.
11 All the horns of the wicked will I break, *
    but the horns of the righteous shall be exalted.

   Glory . . .

Psalm 76

1 In Judah God is known; *
    his name is great in Israel.
2 At Salem is his tabernacle, *
    and his dwelling place in Zion.
3 There broke he the flashing arrows of the bow, *
    the shield, the sword and the weapons of war.
4 In the light of splendour you appeared, *
    glorious from the eternal mountains.
5 The boastful were plundered; they have slept their sleep; *
    none of the warriors can lift their hand.
6 At your rebuke, O God of Jacob, *
    both horse and chariot fell stunned.
7 Terrible are you in majesty; *
    who can stand before your face when you are angry?
8 You caused your judgement to be heard from heaven; *
    the earth trembled and was still,
9 When God arose to judgement, *
    to save all the meek upon earth.
10 You crushed the wrath of the peoples *
    and bridled the wrathful remnant.
11 Make a vow to the Lord your God and keep it; *
    let all who are round about him bring gifts
    to him that is worthy to be feared.
12 He breaks down the spirit of princes *
    and strikes terror in the kings of the earth.

   Glory . . .

Psalm 77

1 I cry aloud to God; *
  I cry aloud to God and he will hear me.
2 In the day of my trouble I have sought the Lord; *
  by night my hand is stretched out and does not tire;
  my soul refuses comfort.
3 I think upon God and I groan; *
  I ponder, and my spirit faints.
4 You will not let my eyelids close; *
  I am so troubled that I cannot speak.
5 I consider the days of old; *
  I remember the years long past;
6 I commune with my heart in the night; *
  my spirit searches for understanding.
7 Will the Lord cast us off for ever? *
  Will he no more show us his favour?
8 Has his loving mercy clean gone for ever? *
  Has his promise come to an end for evermore?
9 Has God forgotten to be gracious? *
  Has he shut up his compassion in displeasure?
10 And I said, 'My grief is this: *
  that the right hand of the Most High has lost its strength.'
11 I will remember the works of the Lord *
  and call to mind your wonders of old time.
12 I will meditate on all your works *
  and ponder your mighty deeds.
13 Your way, O God, is holy; *
  who is so great a god as our God?
14 You are the God who worked wonders *
  and declared your power among the peoples.
15 With a mighty arm you redeemed your people, *
  the children of Jacob and Joseph.
16 The waters saw you, O God;
  the waters saw you and were afraid; *
  the depths also were troubled.
17 The clouds poured out water; the skies thundered; *
  your arrows flashed on every side;
18 The voice of your thunder was in the whirlwind;
  your lightnings lit up the ground; *
  the earth trembled and shook.

19 Your way was in the sea, and your paths in the great waters, *
    but your footsteps were not known.
20 You led your people like sheep *
    by the hand of Moses and Aaron.

   Glory . . .

Psalm 79

1 O God, the heathen have come into your heritage; *
    your holy temple have they defiled
    and made Jerusalem a heap of stones.
2 The dead bodies of your servants they have given
        to be food for the birds of the air, *
    and the flesh of your faithful to the beasts of the field.
3 Their blood have they shed like water
        on every side of Jerusalem, *
    and there was no one to bury them.
4 We have become the taunt of our neighbours, *
    the scorn and derision of those that are round about us.
5 Lord, how long will you be angry, for ever? *
    How long will your jealous fury blaze like fire?
6 Pour out your wrath upon the nations that have not known you, *
    and upon the kingdoms that have not called upon your name.
7 For they have devoured Jacob *
    and laid waste his dwelling place.
8 Remember not against us our former sins; *
    let your compassion make haste to meet us,
    for we are brought very low.
9 Help us, O God of our salvation, for the glory of your name; *
    deliver us, and wipe away our sins for your name's sake.
10 Why should the heathen say, *
    'Where is now their God?'
11 Let vengeance for your servants' blood that is shed *
    be known among the nations in our sight.
12 Let the sorrowful sighing of the prisoners come before you, *
    and by your mighty arm
    preserve those who are condemned to die.
13 May the taunts with which our neighbours taunted you, Lord, *
    return sevenfold into their bosom.

14 But we that are your people and the sheep of your pasture
　　　will give you thanks for ever, *
　　　and tell of your praise from generation to generation.

　Glory . . .

Psalm 80

　1 Hear, O Shepherd of Israel, *
　　　you that led Joseph like a flock;
　2 Shine forth, you that are enthroned upon the cherubim, *
　　　before Ephraim, Benjamin and Manasseh.
　3 Stir up your mighty strength *
　　　and come to our salvation.
　4 *Turn us again, O God;* *
　　　show the light of your countenance, and we shall be saved.

　5 O Lord God of hosts, *
　　　how long will you be angry at your people's prayer?
　6 You feed them with the bread of tears; *
　　　you give them abundance of tears to drink.
　7 You have made us the derision of our neighbours, *
　　　and our enemies laugh us to scorn.
　8 *Turn us again, O God of hosts;* *
　　　show the light of your countenance, and we shall be saved.

　9 You brought a vine out of Egypt; *
　　　you drove out the nations and planted it.
10 You made room around it, *
　　　and when it had taken root, it filled the land.
11 The hills were covered with its shadow *
　　　and the cedars of God by its boughs.
12 It stretched out its branches to the Sea *
　　　and its tendrils to the River.
13 Why then have you broken down its wall, *
　　　so that all who pass by pluck off its grapes?
14 The wild boar out of the wood tears it off, *
　　　and all the insects of the field devour it.

15 Turn again, O God of hosts, *
　　　look down from heaven and behold;

16 Cherish this vine which your right hand has planted, *
 and the branch that you made so strong for yourself.
17 Let those who burnt it with fire, who cut it down, *
 perish at the rebuke of your countenance.
18 Let your hand be upon the man at your right hand, *
 the son of man you made so strong for yourself.
19 And so will we not go back from you; *
 give us life, and we shall call upon your name.
20 *Turn us again, O Lord God of hosts; *
 show the light of your countenance, and we shall be saved.*

 Glory . . .

Psalm 81

1 Sing merrily to God our strength, *
 shout for joy to the God of Jacob.
2 Take up the song and sound the timbrel, *
 the tuneful lyre with the harp.
3 Blow the trumpet at the new moon, *
 as at the full moon, upon our solemn feast day.
4 For this is a statute for Israel, *
 a law of the God of Jacob;
5 The charge he laid on the people of Joseph, *
 when they came out of the land of Egypt.
6 I heard a voice I did not know, that said: *
 'I eased their shoulder from the burden;
 their hands were set free from bearing the load.
7 'You called upon me in trouble and I delivered you; *
 I answered you from the secret place of thunder
 and proved you at the waters of Meribah.
8 'Hear, O my people, and I will admonish you: *
 O Israel, if you would but listen to me!
9 'There shall be no strange god among you; *
 you shall not worship a foreign god.
10 'I am the Lord your God,
 who brought you up from the land of Egypt; *
 open your mouth wide and I shall fill it.'

11 But my people would not hear my voice *
 and Israel would not obey me.

12 So I sent them away in the stubbornness of their hearts, *
    and let them walk after their own counsels.
13 O that my people would listen to me, *
    that Israel would walk in my ways!
14 Then I should soon put down their enemies *
    and turn my hand against their adversaries.
15 Those who hate the Lord would be humbled before him, *
    and their punishment would last for ever.
16 But Israel would I feed with the finest wheat *
    and with honey from the rock would I satisfy them.

Glory . . .

Psalm 82

1 God has taken his stand in the council of heaven; *
    in the midst of the gods he gives judgement;
2 'How long will you judge unjustly *
    and show such favour to the wicked?
3 'You were to judge the weak and the orphan; *
    defend the right of the humble and needy;
4 'Rescue the weak and the poor; *
    deliver them from the hand of the wicked.
5 'They have no knowledge or wisdom;
    they walk on still in darkness; *
    all the foundations of the earth are shaken.
6 'Therefore I say that though you are gods *
    and all of you children of the Most High,
7 'Nevertheless, you shall die like mortals *
    and fall like one of their princes.'
8 Arise, O God and judge the earth, *
    for it is you that shall take all nations for your possession.

Glory . . .

Psalm 84

1 How lovely is your dwelling place, O Lord of hosts! *
    My soul has a desire and longing to enter the courts of the Lord;
    my heart and my flesh rejoice in the living God.

2 The sparrow has found her a house
   and the swallow a nest where she may lay her young: *
   at your altars, O Lord of hosts, my King and my God.
3 Blessed are they who dwell in your house: *
   they will always be praising you.
4 Blessed are those whose strength is in you, *
   in whose heart are the highways to Zion,
5 Who going through the barren valley find there a spring, *
   and the early rains will clothe it with blessing.
6 They will go from strength to strength *
   and appear before God in Zion.

7 O Lord God of hosts, hear my prayer; *
   listen, O God of Jacob.
8 Behold our defender, O God, *
   and look upon the face of your anointed.
9 For one day in your courts *
   is better than a thousand.
10 I would rather be a door-keeper in the house of my God *
   than dwell in the tents of ungodliness.
11 For the Lord God is both sun and shield;
    he will give grace and glory; *
    no good thing shall he withhold
    from those who walk with integrity.
12 O Lord God of hosts *
    blessed are those who put their trust in you.

Glory . . .

Psalm 85

1 Lord, you were gracious to your land; *
   you restored the fortunes of Jacob.
2 You forgave the offence of your people *
   and covered all their sins.
3 You laid aside all your fury *
   and turned from your wrathful indignation.

4 Restore us again, O God our Saviour, *
   and let your anger cease from us.
5 Will you be displeased with us for ever? *
   Will you stretch out your wrath from one generation to another?

6 Will you not give us life again, *
    that your people may rejoice in you?
 7 Show us your mercy, O Lord, *
    and grant us your salvation.

 8 I will listen to what the Lord God will say, *
    for he shall speak peace to his people and to the faithful,
    that they turn not again to folly.
 9 Truly, his salvation is near to those who fear him, *
    that his glory may dwell in our land.
10 Mercy and truth are met together, *
    righteousness and peace have kissed each other;
11 Truth shall spring up from the earth *
    and righteousness look down from heaven.
12 The Lord will indeed give all that is good, *
    and our land will yield its increase.
13 Righteousness shall go before him *
    and direct his steps in the way.

   Glory . . .

Psalm 86

 1 Incline your ear, O Lord, and answer me, *
    for I am poor and in misery.
 2 Preserve my soul, for I am faithful; *
    save your servant, for I put my trust in you.
 3 Be merciful to me, O Lord, for you are my God; *
    I call upon you all the day long.
 4 Gladden the soul of your servant, *
    for to you, O Lord, I lift up my soul.
 5 For you, Lord, are good and forgiving, *
    abounding in steadfast love to all who call upon you.
 6 Give ear, O Lord, to my prayer *
    and listen to the voice of my supplication.
 7 In the day of my distress I will call upon you, *
    for you will answer me.
 8 Among the gods there is none like you, O Lord, *
    nor any works like yours.
 9 All nations you have made shall come and worship you, O Lord, *
    and shall glorify your name.

10 For you are great and do wonderful things; *
    you alone are God.
11 Teach me your way, O Lord, and I will walk in your truth; *
    knit my heart to you, that I may fear your name.
12 I will thank you, O Lord my God, with all my heart, *
    and glorify your name for evermore;
13 For great is your steadfast love towards me, *
    for you have delivered my soul from the depths of the grave.
14 O God, the proud rise up against me,
    and a ruthless horde seek after my life; *
    they have not set you before their eyes.
15 But you, O Lord, are gracious and full of compassion, *
    slow to anger and full of kindness and truth.
16 O turn to me and have mercy upon me; *
    give your strength to your servant
    and save the child of your handmaid.
17 Show me a token of your favour,
    that those who hate me may see it and be ashamed; *
    because you, O Lord, have helped me and comforted me.

    Glory . . .

Psalm 87

1 His foundation is on the holy mountains. *
    The Lord loves the gates of Zion
    more than all the dwellings of Jacob.
2 Glorious things are spoken of you, *
    Zion, city of our God.
3 I record Egypt and Babylon as those who know me; *
    behold Philistia, Tyre and Ethiopia;
    in Zion were they born.
4 And of Zion it shall be said, 'Each one was born in her, *
    and the Most High himself has established her.'
5 The Lord will record as he writes up the peoples, *
    'This one also was born there.'
6 And as they dance they shall sing: *
    'All my fresh springs are in you.'

    Glory . . .

Psalm 88

1 O Lord, God of my salvation, *
   I have cried day and night before you.
2 Let my prayer come into your presence; *
   incline your ear to my cry.
3 For my soul is full of troubles; *
   my life draws near to the land of death.
4 I am counted as one gone down to the Pit; *
   I am like one that has no strength,
5 Lost among the dead, *
   like the slain who lie in the grave,
6 Whom you remember no more, *
   for they are cut off from your hand.
7 You have laid me in the lowest pit, *
   in a place of darkness in the abyss.
8 Your anger lies heavy upon me, *
   and you have afflicted me with all your waves.
9 You have put my friends far from me *
   and made me to be abhorred by them.
10 I am so fast in prison that I cannot get free; *
   my eyes fail from all my trouble.
11 Lord, I have called daily upon you; *
   I have stretched out my hands to you.
12 Do you work wonders for the dead? *
   Will the shades stand up and praise you?
13 Shall your loving-kindness be declared in the grave, *
   your faithfulness in the land of destruction?
14 Shall your wonders be known in the dark *
   or your righteous deeds in the land where all is forgotten?
15 But as for me, O Lord, I will cry to you; *
   early in the morning my prayer shall come before you.
16 Lord, why have you rejected my soul? *
   Why have you hidden your face from me?
17 I have been wretched and at the point of death from my youth; *
   I suffer your terrors and am no more seen.
18 Your wrath sweeps over me; *
   your horrors are come to destroy me;
19 All day long they come about me like water; *
   they close me in on every side.

20 Lover and friend have you put far from me *
   and hid my companions out of my sight.

   Glory . . .

Psalm 90

1 Lord, you have been our refuge *
   from one generation to another.
2 Before the mountains were brought forth,
   or the earth and the world were formed, *
   from everlasting to everlasting you are God.
3 You turn us back to dust and say: *
   'Turn back, O children of earth.'
4 For a thousand years in your sight are but as yesterday, *
   which passes like a watch in the night.
5 You sweep them away like a dream; *
   they fade away suddenly like the grass.
6 In the morning it is green and flourishes; *
   in the evening it is dried up and withered.
7 For we consume away in your displeasure; *
   we are afraid at your wrathful indignation.
8 You have set our misdeeds before you *
   and our secret sins in the light of your countenance.
9 When you are angry, all our days are gone; *
   our years come to an end like a sigh.
10 The days of our life are three score years and ten,
   or if our strength endures, even four score; *
   yet the sum of them is but labour and sorrow,
   for they soon pass away and we are gone.
11 Who regards the power of your wrath *
   and your indignation like those who fear you?
12 So teach us to number our days *
   that we may apply our hearts to wisdom.
13 Turn again, O Lord; how long will you delay? *
   Have compassion on your servants.
14 Satisfy us with your loving-kindness in the morning, *
   that we may rejoice and be glad in all our days.
15 Give us gladness for the days you have afflicted us *
   and for the years in which we have seen adversity.

16 Show your servants your works, *
    and let your glory be over their children.
17 May the gracious favour of the Lord our God be upon us; *
    prosper our handiwork; O prosper the work of our hands.

Glory . . .

Psalm 91

1 Whoever dwells in the shelter of the Most High *
    and abides under the shadow of the Almighty,
2 Shall say to the Lord, 'My refuge and my stronghold, *
    my God, in whom I put my trust.'
3 For he shall deliver you from the snare of the fowler *
    and from the deadly pestilence.
4 He shall cover you with his wings
    and you shall be safe under his feathers; *
    his faithfulness shall be your shield and buckler.
5 You shall not be afraid of any terror by night, *
    nor of the arrow that flies by day;
6 Of the pestilence that stalks in darkness, *
    nor of the sickness that destroys at noonday.
7 Though a thousand fall at your side
    and ten thousand at your right hand, *
    yet it shall not come near you.
8 Your eyes have only to behold *
    to see the reward of the wicked.
9 Because you have made the Lord your refuge *
    and the Most High your stronghold,
10 There shall no evil happen to you, *
    neither shall any plague come near your tent.
11 For he shall give his angels charge over you, *
    to keep you in all your ways.
12 They shall bear you in their hands, *
    lest you dash your foot against a stone.
13 You shall tread upon the lion and adder; *
    the young lion and the serpent you shall trample underfoot.
14 Because they have set their love upon me,
    therefore will I deliver them; *
    I will lift them up, because they know my name.

15 They will call upon me and I will answer them; *
    I am with them in trouble,
    I will deliver them and bring them to honour.
16 With long life will I satisfy them *
    and show them my salvation.

   Glory...

Psalm 92

1 It is a good thing to give thanks to the Lord *
    and to sing praises to your name, O Most High.
2 To tell of your love early in the morning *
    and of your faithfulness in the night-time,
3 Upon the ten-stringed instrument, upon the harp, *
    and to the melody of the lyre.
4 For you, Lord, have made me glad by your acts, *
    and I sing aloud at the work of your hands.
5 O Lord, how glorious are your works! *
    Your thoughts are very deep.
6 The senseless does not know, *
    nor do fools understand,
7 That though the wicked sprout like grass *
    and all the workers of iniquity flourish,
8 It is only to be destroyed for ever; *
    but you, O Lord, shall be exalted for evermore.
9 For lo, your enemies, O Lord,
    lo, your enemies shall perish, *
    and all the workers of iniquity shall be scattered.
10 But my horn you have exalted
    like the horns of wild oxen; *
    I am anointed with fresh oil.
11 My eyes will look down on my foes; *
    my ears shall hear the ruin of the evil-doers
    who rise up against me.
12 The righteous shall flourish like a palm tree, *
    and shall spread abroad like a cedar of Lebanon.
13 Such as are planted in the house of the Lord *
    shall flourish in the courts of our God.
14 They shall still bear fruit in old age; *
    they shall be vigorous and in full leaf;

15 That they may show that the Lord is true; *
 he is my rock,
 and there is no unrighteousness in him.

Glory . . .

Psalm 93

1 The Lord is king and has put on glorious apparel; *
 the Lord has put on his glory
 and girded himself with strength.
2 He has made the whole world so sure *
 that it cannot be moved.
3 Your throne been established from of old; *
 you are from everlasting.
4 The floods have lifted up, O Lord,
 the floods have lifted up their voice *
 the floods lift up their pounding waves.
5 Mightier than the thunder of many waters,
 mightier than the breakers of the sea, *
 the Lord on high is mightier.
6 Your testimonies are very sure; *
 holiness adorns your house, O Lord, for ever.

Glory . . .

Psalm 94

1 Lord God to whom vengeance belongs, *
 O God to whom vengeance belongs, shine out in majesty.
2 Rise up, O Judge of the earth; *
 give the arrogant their just deserts.
3 Lord, how long shall the wicked, *
 how long shall the wicked triumph?
4 How long shall the evil-doers boast *
 and pour out such impudent words?
5 They crush your people, O Lord, *
 and afflict your heritage.
6 They murder the widow and the stranger; *
 the orphans they put to death.

7 And yet they say, 'The Lord will not see, *
   neither shall the God of Jacob regard it.'
8 Consider, most stupid of people; *
   you fools, when will you understand?
9 He that planted the ear, shall he not hear? *
   He that formed the eye, shall he not see?
10 He who corrects the nations, shall he not punish? *
   He who teaches the peoples, does he lack knowledge?
11 The Lord knows every human thought, *
   that they are but a breath.

12 Blessed are those whom you chasten, O Lord, *
   whom you instruct from your law;
13 That you may give them rest in days of adversity, *
   until a pit is dug for the wicked.
14 For the Lord will not fail his people, *
   neither will he forsake his inheritance.
15 For justice shall return to the righteous, *
   and all that are true of heart shall follow it.

16 Who will rise up for me against the wicked? *
   Who will take my part against the evil-doers?
17 If the Lord had not helped me, *
   my soul would soon have been put to silence.
18 And when I said, 'My foot has slipped,' *
   your loving mercy, O Lord, upheld me.
19 In the multitude of cares that troubled my heart, *
   your comforts have refreshed my soul.
20 Will you have anything to do with the throne of wickedness, *
   which fashions evil through its law?
21 They gather together against the life of the righteous *
   and condemn the innocent to death.
22 But the Lord has become my stronghold *
   and my God the rock of my trust.
23 He will turn against them their own wickedness
   and silence them through their own malice; *
   the Lord our God will put them to silence.

   Glory . . .

Psalm 95

Venite, exultemus Domino

1 O come, let us sing to the Lord; *
   let us heartily rejoice in the rock of our salvation.
2 Let us come into his presence with thanksgiving; *
   and be glad in him with psalms.
3 For the Lord is a great God; *
   and a great king above all gods.
4 In his hand are the depths of the earth; *
   and the heights of the mountains are his also.
5 The sea is his, for he made it, *
   and his hands have moulded the dry land.
6 Come, let us worship and bow down *
   and kneel before the Lord our Maker.
7 For he is our God; *
   we are the people of his pasture and the sheep of his hand.

8 O that today you would listen to his voice!, *
   'Harden not your hearts as at Meribah,
   on that day at Massah in the wilderness,
9 'When your forebears tested me, and put me to the proof, *
   though they had seen my works.
10 'Forty years long I detested that generation and said, *
   "This people are wayward in their hearts;
   they do not know my ways."
11 'So I swore in my wrath, *
   "They shall not enter into my rest."'

   Glory . . .

Psalm 96

1 Sing to the Lord a new song; *
   sing to the Lord, all the earth.
2 Sing to the Lord and bless his name; *
   tell out his salvation from day to day.
3 Declare his glory among the nations *
   and his wonders among all peoples.

4 For great is the Lord and greatly to be praised; *
   he is more to be feared than all gods.
5 For all the gods of the nations are but idols; *
   it is the Lord who made the heavens.
6 Honour and majesty are before him; *
   power and splendour are in his sanctuary.

7 Ascribe to the Lord, you families of the peoples; *
   ascribe to the Lord honour and strength.
8 Ascribe to the Lord the honour due to his name; *
   bring offerings and come into his courts.
9 O worship the Lord in the beauty of holiness; *
   let the whole earth tremble before him.
10 Tell it out among the nations that the Lord is king. *
   He has made the world so sure that it cannot be moved;
   he will judge the peoples with equity.

11 Let the heavens rejoice and let the earth be glad; *
   let the sea thunder and all that is in it;
12 Let the fields be joyful and all that is in them; *
   let all the trees of the wood shout for joy before the Lord.
13 For he comes, he comes to judge the earth; *
   with righteousness he will judge the world
   and the peoples with his truth.

   Glory . . .

Psalm 97

1 The Lord is king: let the earth rejoice; *
   let the multitude of the isles be glad.
2 Clouds and darkness are round about him; *
   righteousness and justice are the foundation of his throne.
3 Fire goes before him *
   and burns up his enemies on every side.

4 His lightnings lit up the world; *
   the earth saw it and trembled.
5 The mountains melted like wax at the presence of the Lord, *
   at the presence of the Lord of the whole earth.
6 The heavens declared his righteousness, *
   and all the peoples have seen his glory.

7 Confounded be all who worship carved images
     and delight in mere idols, *
   Bow down before him, all you gods.
 8 Zion heard and was glad, and the daughters of Judah rejoiced, *
     because of your judgements, O Lord.
 9 For you, Lord, are most high over all the earth; *
     you are exalted far above all gods.

10 The Lord loves those who hate evil; *
     he preserves the lives of his faithful
     and delivers them from the hand of the wicked.
11 Light has sprung up for the righteous *
     and joy for the true of heart.
12 Rejoice in the Lord, you righteous, *
     and give thanks to his holy name.

   Glory . . .

Psalm 98

 1 Sing to the Lord a new song, *
     for he has done marvellous things.
 2 His own right hand and his holy arm *
     have won for him the victory.
 3 The Lord has made known his salvation; *
     his deliverance has he openly shown in the sight of the nations.
 4 He has remembered his mercy and faithfulness
     towards the house of Israel, *
     and all the ends of the earth have seen the salvation of our God.

 5 Sound praises to the Lord, all the earth; *
     break into singing and make music.
 6 Make music to the Lord with the lyre, *
     with the lyre and the voice of melody.
 7 With trumpets and the sound of the horn *
     sound praises before the Lord, the King.

 8 Let the sea thunder and all that fills it, *
     the world and all that dwell upon it.
 9 Let the rivers clap their hands *
     and let the hills ring out together before the Lord,
     for he comes to judge the earth.

10 In righteousness shall he judge the world *
    and the peoples with equity.

   Glory . . .

Psalm 99

1 The Lord is king; let the peoples tremble; *
    he is enthroned above the cherubim: let the earth shake.
2 The Lord is great in Zion *
    and high above all peoples.
3 Let them praise your name, which is great and awesome; *
    the Lord our God is holy.
4 Mighty king, who loves justice,
    you have established equity; *
    you have executed justice and righteousness in Jacob.
5 *Exalt the Lord our God; *
    bow down before his footstool, for he is holy.*

6 Moses and Aaron among his priests
    and Samuel among those who call upon his name; *
    they called upon the Lord and he answered them.
7 He spoke to them out of the pillar of cloud; *
    they kept his testimonies and the law that he gave them.
8 You answered them, O Lord our God; *
    you were a God who forgave them
    and pardoned them for their offences.
9 *Exalt the Lord our God
    and worship him upon his holy hill, *
    for the Lord our God is holy.*

   Glory . . .

Psalm 100

Jubilate Deo

1 O be joyful in the Lord, all the earth; *
    serve the Lord with gladness
    and come before his presence with a song.

2 Know that the Lord is God; *
    it is he that has made us and we are his;
    we are his people and the sheep of his pasture.
3 Enter his gates with thanksgiving;
    and his courts with praise; *
    give thanks to him and bless his holy name.
4 For the Lord is gracious; his love is everlasting, *
    and his faithfulness endures from generation to generation.

Glory . . .

Psalm 101

1 I will sing of faithfulness and justice; *
    to you, O Lord, will I sing.
2 Let me be wise in the way that is perfect; *
    when will you come to me?
3 I will walk with purity of heart *
    within the walls of my house.
4 I will not set before my eyes *
    a counsel that is evil.
5 I abhor the deeds of unfaithfulness; *
    they shall not cling to me.
6 A crooked heart shall depart from me; *
    I will not know a wicked person.
7 One who slanders a neighbour in secret *
    I will quickly put to silence.
8 Haughty eyes and an arrogant heart *
    I will not endure.
9 My eyes are upon the faithful in the land, *
    that they might dwell with me.
10 One who walks in the way that is pure *
    shall be my servant.
11 There shall not dwell in my house *
    one that practises deceit.
12 One who utters falsehood *
    shall not continue in my sight.
13 Morning by morning will I put to silence *
    all the wicked in the land.

14 To cut off from the city of the Lord *
   all those who practise evil.

   Glory . . .

Psalm 102

Penitential Psalm

1 O Lord, hear my prayer *
   and let my crying come before you.
2 Hide not your face from me *
   in the day of my distress.
3 Incline your ear to me; *
   when I call, make haste to answer me,
4 For my days are consumed in smoke *
   and my bones burn away as in a furnace.
5 My heart is smitten down and withered like grass, *
   so that I forget to eat my bread.
6 From the sound of my groaning *
   my bones cleave fast to my skin.
7 I am become like a vulture in the wilderness, *
   like an owl that haunts the ruins.
8 I keep watch and am become like a sparrow *
   solitary upon the housetop.
9 My enemies revile me all the day long, *
   and those who rage at me have sworn together against me.
10 I have eaten ashes for bread *
   and mingled my drink with weeping,
11 Because of your indignation and wrath, *
   for you have taken me up and cast me down.
12 My days fade away like a shadow, *
   and I am withered like grass.

13 But you, O Lord, shall endure for ever *
   and your name through all generations.
14 You will arise and have pity on Zion; *
   it is time to have mercy upon her;
   surely the time has come.
15 For your servants love her very stones *
   and feel compassion for her dust.

16 Then shall the nations fear your name, O Lord, *
   and all the kings of the earth your glory,
17 When the Lord has built up Zion *
   and shown himself in glory;
18 When he has turned to the prayer of the destitute *
   and has not despised their plea.
19 This shall be written for those that come after, *
   and a people yet unborn shall praise the Lord.
20 For he has looked down from his holy height; *
   from the heavens he beheld the earth,
21 That he might hear the sighings of the prisoner *
   and set free those condemned to die;
22 That the name of the Lord may be proclaimed in Zion *
   and his praises in Jerusalem,
23 When the peoples are gathered together *
   and their kingdoms also, to serve the Lord.

24 He has brought down my strength in my journey *
   and has shortened my days.
25 I pray, 'O my God; do not take me in the midst of my days; *
   your years endure throughout all generations.
26 'In the beginning you laid the foundations of the earth, *
   and the heavens are the work of your hands;
27 'They shall perish, but you will endure; *
   they all shall wear out like a garment.
28 'You change them like clothing, and they shall be changed; *
   but you are the same, and your years shall not fail.
29 'The children of your servants shall continue, *
   and their descendants shall be established in your sight.'

   Glory . . .

Psalm 104

1 Bless the Lord, O my soul. *
   O Lord my God, how excellent is your greatness!
2 You are clothed with majesty and honour, *
   wrapped in light as in a garment.
3 You spread out the heavens like a curtain *
   and lay the beams of your dwelling-place in the waters above.

4 You make the clouds your chariot *
    and ride on the wings of the wind.
5 You make the winds your messengers *
    and flames of fire your servants.
6 You laid the foundations of the earth, *
    that it never should move at any time.
7 You covered it with the deep like a garment; *
    the waters stood high above the hills.
8 At your rebuke they fled; *
    at the voice of your thunder they hastened away.
9 They rose up to the hills and flowed down to the valleys beneath, *
    to the place which you had appointed for them.
10 You have set them their bounds that they should not pass, *
    nor turn again to cover the earth.
11 You send the springs into the brooks, *
    which run among the hills.
12 They give drink to every beast of the field, *
    and the wild asses quench their thirst.
13 Beside them the birds of the air make their nests *
    and sing among the branches.
14 You water the hills from your dwelling on high; *
    the earth is filled with the fruit of your works.
15 You make grass to grow for the cattle *
    and plants to meet our needs,
16 Bringing forth food from the earth *
    and wine to gladden our hearts,
17 Oil to give us a cheerful countenance *
    and bread to strengthen our hearts.
18 The trees of the Lord are full of sap, *
    the cedars of Lebanon which he planted,
19 In which the birds build their nests, *
    while the fir trees are a dwelling for the stork.
20 The mountains are a refuge for the wild goats *
    and the stony cliffs for the conies.
21 You appointed the moon to mark the seasons, *
    and the sun knows the time for its setting.
22 You make darkness that it may be night, *
    in which all the beasts of the forest creep forth.
23 The lions roar for their prey *
    and seek their food from God.

24 The sun rises and they are gone *
    to lay themselves down in their dens.
25 People go forth to their work *
    and to their labour until the evening.

26 O Lord, how manifold are your works! *
    In wisdom you have made them all;
    the earth is full of your creatures.
27 There is the sea, spread far and wide, *
    and there move creatures beyond number, both small and great.
28 There go the ships, and there is that Leviathan *
    which you have made to play in the deep.
29 All of these look to you *
    to give them their food in due season.
30 When you give it them, they gather it; *
    you open your hand and they are filled with good.
31 When you hide your face they are troubled; *
    when you take away their breath,
    they die and return again to the dust.
32 When you send forth your spirit, they are created, *
    and you renew the face of the earth.

33 May the glory of the Lord endure for ever; *
    may the Lord rejoice in his works.
34 He looks on the earth and it trembles; *
    he touches the mountains and they smoke.
35 I will sing to the Lord as long as I live; *
    I will make music to my God while I have my being.
36 So shall my song please him *
    while I rejoice in the Lord.
37 Let sinners be consumed out of the earth
    and the wicked be no more. *
    Bless the Lord, O my soul.
    Alleluia.

    Glory . . .

Psalm 105

1 O give thanks to the Lord and call upon his name; *
   make known his deeds among the peoples.
2 Sing to him, sing praises, *
   and tell of all his marvellous works.
3 Rejoice in the praise of his holy name; *
   let the hearts of them rejoice who seek the Lord.
4 Seek the Lord and his strength; *
   seek his face continually.
5 Remember the marvels he has done, *
   his wonders and the judgements of his mouth,
6 O seed of Abraham his servant, *
   O children of Jacob his chosen.
7 He is the Lord our God; *
   his judgements are in all the earth.
8 He has always been mindful of his covenant, *
   the promise that he made for a thousand generations:
9 The covenant he made with Abraham, *
   the oath that he swore to Isaac,
10 Which he established as a statute for Jacob, *
   an everlasting covenant for Israel.
11 Saying, 'To you will I give the land of Canaan, *
   to be the portion of your inheritance.'
12 When they were but few in number, *
   of little account, and sojourners in the land,
13 Wandering from nation to nation, *
   from one kingdom to another people,
14 He suffered no-one to do them wrong *
   and rebuked even kings for their sake,
15 Saying, 'Touch not my anointed *
   and do my prophets no harm.'

16 Then he called down famine over the land *
   and broke every staff of bread.
17 But he sent a man before them, *
   Joseph, who was sold as a slave.
18 They shackled his feet with fetters; *
   his neck was ringed with iron.
19 Until all he foretold came to pass, *
   the word of the Lord tested him.

20 The king sent and released him; *
    the ruler of peoples set him free.
21 He appointed him lord of his household *
    and ruler of all he possessed,
22 To instruct his princes as he willed *
    and to teach his counsellors wisdom.

23 Then Israel came into Egypt; *
    Jacob sojourned in the land of Ham.
24 And the Lord made his people exceedingly fruitful; *
    he made them too many for their adversaries,
25 Whose heart he turned, so that they hated his people *
    and dealt craftily with his servants.
26 Then sent he Moses his servant *
    and Aaron whom he had chosen.
27 He showed his signs through their word *
    and his wonders in the land of Ham.
28 He sent darkness and it grew dark; *
    yet they did not heed his words.
29 He turned their waters into blood *
    and slew all their fish.
30 Their land swarmed with frogs, *
    even in their kings' chambers.
31 He spoke the word, and there came clouds of flies, *
    swarms of gnats within all their borders.
32 He gave them hailstones for rain *
    and flames of lightning in their land.
33 He blasted their vines and their fig trees *
    and shattered trees across their country.
34 He spoke the word, and the grasshoppers came *
    and young locusts without number;
35 They ate every plant in their land *
    and devoured the fruit of their soil.
36 He smote all the firstborn in their land, *
    the first fruits of all their strength.

37 Then he brought them out with silver and gold; *
    there was not one among their tribes that stumbled.
38 Egypt was glad at their departing, *
    for a dread of them had fallen upon them.

39 He spread out a cloud for a covering *
    and a fire to light up the night.
40 They asked and he brought them quails; *
    he satisfied them with the bread of heaven.
41 He opened the rock, and the waters gushed out *
    and ran in the dry places like a river.
42 For he remembered his holy word *
    and Abraham, his servant.
43 So he brought forth his people with joy, *
    his chosen ones with singing.
44 He gave them the lands of the nations *
    and they took possession of the fruit of their toil,
45 That they might keep his statutes *
    and faithfully observe his laws.
    Alleluia.

    Glory . . .

Psalm 108

1 My heart is ready, O God, my heart is ready; *
    I will sing and give you praise.
2 Awake, my soul; awake, harp and lyre, *
    that I may awaken the dawn.
3 I will give you thanks, O Lord, among the peoples; *
    I will sing praise to you among the nations.
4 For your loving-kindness reaches to the heavens *
    and your faithfulness reaches to the clouds.
5 Be exalted, O God, above the heavens *
    and your glory over all the earth.
6 That your beloved may be delivered, *
    save with your right hand and answer me.

7 God has spoken in his holiness: *
    'I will triumph and divide Shechem,
    and share out the valley of Succoth.
8 'Gilead is mine and Manasseh is mine; *
    Ephraim is my helmet and Judah my sceptre.
9 'Moab shall be my wash-pot,
    over Edom will I cast my sandal, *
    across Philistia will I shout in triumph.'

10 Who will lead me into the strong city? *
   who will bring me into Edom?
11 Have you not cast us off, O God? *
   Will you no longer go forth with our troops?
12 O grant us your help against the enemy, *
   for earthly help is in vain.
13 Through God will we do great acts, *
   for it is he that shall tread down our enemies.

   Glory . . .

Psalm 110

1 The Lord said to my lord, 'Sit at my right hand, *
   until I make your enemies your footstool.'
2 May the Lord stretch forth the sceptre of your power; *
   rule from Zion in the midst of your enemies.
3 'Noble are you on this day of your birth; *
   on the holy mountain, from the womb of the dawn
   the dew of your new birth is upon you.'
4 The Lord has sworn and will not retract: *
   'You are a priest for ever after the order of Melchizedek.'
5 The king at your right hand, O Lord, *
   shall smite down kings in the day of his wrath.
6 In all his majesty, he shall judge among the nations, *
   smiting heads over all the wide earth.
7 He shall drink from the brook beside the way; *
   therefore shall he lift high his head.

   Glory . . .

Psalm 111

1 Alleluia.
   I will give thanks to the Lord with my whole heart, *
   in the company of the faithful and in the congregation.
2 The works of the Lord are great, *
   sought out by all who delight in them.
3 His work is full of majesty and honour, *
   and his righteousness endures for ever.

4 He appointed a memorial for his marvellous deeds; *
    the Lord is gracious and full of compassion.
5 He gave food to those who feared him; *
    he is ever mindful of his covenant.
6 He showed his people the power of his works *
    in giving them the heritage of the nations.
7 The works of his hands are truth and justice; *
    all his commandments are sure.
8 They stand fast for ever and ever; *
    they are done in truth and equity.
9 He sent redemption to his people;
    he commanded his covenant for ever; *
    holy and awesome is his name.
10 The fear of the Lord is the beginning of wisdom;
    a good understanding have those who live by it; *
    his praise endures for ever.

   Glory . . .

Psalm 112

1 Alleluia.
    Blessed are those who fear the Lord *
    and have great delight in his commandments.
2 Their descendants will be mighty in the land, *
    a generation of the faithful that will be blest.
3 Wealth and riches will be in their house, *
    and their righteousness endures for ever.
4 Light shines in the darkness for the upright; *
    gracious and full of compassion are the righteous.
5 It goes well with those who are generous in lending *
    and order their affairs with justice,
6 For they will never be shaken; *
    the righteous will be held in everlasting remembrance.
7 They will not be afraid of any evil tidings; *
    their heart is steadfast, trusting in the Lord.
8 Their heart is sustained and will not fear; *
    until they see the downfall of their foes.
9 They have given freely to the poor;
    their righteousness stands fast for ever; *
    their head will be exalted with honour.

10 The wicked shall see it and be angry;
   they shall gnash their teeth in despair; *
   the desire of the wicked shall perish.

Glory . . .

Psalm 113

1 Alleluia.
   Give praise, you servants of the Lord, *
   O praise the name of the Lord.
2 Blessed be the name of the Lord, *
   from this time forth and for evermore.
3 From the rising of the sun to its setting *
   let the name of the Lord be praised.
4 The Lord is high above all nations *
   and his glory above the heavens.
5 Who is like the Lord our God,
   that has his throne so high, *
   yet humbles himself to behold
   the things of heaven and earth?
6 He raises the poor from the dust *
   and lifts the needy from the ashes,
7 To set them with princes, *
   with the princes of his people.
8 He gives the barren woman a place in the house *
   and makes her a joyful mother of children.
   Alleluia.

Glory . . .

Psalm 114

1 When Israel came out of Egypt, *
   the house of Jacob from a people of a strange tongue,
2 Judah became his sanctuary, *
   Israel his dominion.
3 The sea saw that, and fled; *
   Jordan was driven back.
4 The mountains skipped like rams, *
   the little hills like young sheep.

5 What ailed you, O sea, that you fled? *
   O Jordan, that you were driven back?
6 You mountains, that you skipped like rams, *
   you little hills like young sheep?
7 Tremble, O earth, at the presence of the Lord, *
   at the presence of the God of Jacob,
8 Who turns the hard rock into a pool of water, *
   the flint-stone into a springing well.

   Glory . . .

Psalm 115

1 Not to us, Lord, not to us,
     but to your name give the glory, *
     for the sake of your loving mercy and truth.
2 Why should the heathen say, *
     'Where is now their God?'
3 As for our God, he is in heaven; *
     he does whatever he pleases.
4 Their idols are silver and gold, *
     the work of human hands.
5 They have mouths, but cannot speak; *
     eyes have they, but cannot see;
6 They have ears, but cannot hear; *
     noses have they, but cannot smell;
7 They have hands, but cannot feel;
     feet have they, but cannot walk; *
     not a whisper do they make from their throats.
8 Those who make them shall become like them *
     and so will all who put their trust in them.

9 But you, Israel, put your trust in the Lord; *
     he is their help and their shield.
10 House of Aaron, trust in the Lord; *
     he is their help and their shield.
11 You that fear the Lord, trust in the Lord; *
     he is their help and their shield.
12 The Lord has been mindful of us and he will bless us; *
     may he bless the house of Israel;
     may he bless the house of Aaron;

13 May he bless those who fear the Lord, *
   both small and great together.
14 May the Lord increase you more and more, *
   you and your children after you.
15 May you be blest by the Lord, *
   the maker of heaven and earth.
16 The heavens are the heavens of the Lord, *
   but the earth he has entrusted to his children.
17 The dead do not praise the Lord, *
   nor those gone down into silence;
18 But we will bless the Lord, *
   from this time forth for evermore.
   Alleluia.

   Glory . . .

Psalm 116

1 I love the Lord,
   for he has heard the voice of my supplication; *
   because he inclined his ear to me
   on the day I called to him.
2 The snares of death encompassed me;
   the pains of hell took hold of me; *
   by grief and sorrow was I held.
3 Then I called upon the name of the Lord; *
   'O Lord, I beg you, deliver my soul.'
4 Gracious is the Lord and righteous; *
   our God is full of compassion.
5 The Lord watches over the simple; *
   I was brought very low and he saved me.
6 Turn again to your rest, O my soul; *
   for the Lord has been gracious to you.
7 For you have delivered my soul from death, *
   my eyes from tears and my feet from falling.
8 I will walk before the Lord *
   in the land of the living.

9 I believed that I should perish
   for I was sorely troubled; *

and I said in my alarm,
   'Everyone is a liar.'
10 How shall I repay the Lord *
   for all the benefits he has given to me?
11 I will lift up the cup of salvation *
   and call upon the name of the Lord.
12 I will fulfil my vows to the Lord *
   in the presence of all his people.
13 Precious in the sight of the Lord *
   is the death of his faithful servants.
14 O Lord, I am your servant, *
   your servant, the child of your handmaid;
   you have freed me from my bonds.
15 I will offer to you a sacrifice of thanksgiving *
   and call upon the name of the Lord.
16 I will fulfil my vows to the Lord *
   in the presence of all his people,
17 In the courts of the house of the Lord, *
   in the midst of you, O Jerusalem.
   Alleluia.

   Glory . . .

Psalm 117

1 O praise the Lord, all you nations; *
   praise him, all you peoples.
2 For great is his steadfast love towards us, *
   and the faithfulness of the Lord endures for ever.
   Alleluia!

   Glory . . .

Psalm 118

1 O give thanks to the Lord, for he is good; *
   his mercy endures forever.
2 Let Israel now proclaim, *
   'His mercy endures forever'.
3 Let the house of Aaron now proclaim, *
   'His mercy endures forever.'

4 Let those who fear the Lord proclaim *
    'His mercy endures forever.'
5 In my constraint, I called to the Lord; *
    the Lord answered and set me free.
6 The Lord is at my side; I will not fear; *
    what can flesh do to me?
7 With the Lord at my side as my saviour, *
    I shall see the downfall of my enemies.
8 It is better to take refuge in the Lord *
    than to put any confidence in flesh.
9 It is better to take refuge in the Lord *
    than to put any confidence in princes.
10 All the nations encompassed me, *
    but by the name of the Lord I drove them back.
11 They hemmed me in, they hemmed me in on every side, *
    but by the name of the Lord I drove them back.
12 They swarmed about me like bees;
    they blazed like fire among thorns, *
    but by the name of the Lord I drove them back.

13 Surely, I was thrust to the brink, *
    but the Lord came to my help.
14 The Lord is my strength and my song, *
    and he has become my salvation.
15 Joyful shouts of salvation *
    sound from the tents of the righteous *
16 'The right hand of the Lord does mighty deeds;
    the right hand of the Lord raises up; *
    the right hand of the Lord does mighty deeds.'
17 I shall not die, but live *
    and declare the works of the Lord.
18 The Lord has punished me sorely, *
    but he has not given me over to death.
19 Open to me the gates of righteousness, *
    that I may enter and give thanks to the Lord.
20 This is the gate of the Lord; *
    the righteous shall enter through it.
21 I will give thanks to you, for you have answered me *
    and have become my salvation.
22 The stone which the builders rejected *
    has become the chief cornerstone.

23 This is the Lord's doing, *
    and it is marvellous in our eyes.
24 This is the day that the Lord has made; *
    we will rejoice and be glad in it.
25 Come, O Lord, and save us we pray. *
    Come, Lord, send us now prosperity.
26 Blessed is he who comes in the name of the Lord; *
    we bless you from the house of the Lord.
27 The Lord is God; he has given us light; *
    link the pilgrims with cords
    right to the horns of the altar.
28 You are my God and I will thank you; *
    you are my God and I will exalt you.
29 O give thanks to the Lord, for he is good; *
    his mercy endures for ever.

   Glory . . .

Psalm 119

1 Aleph

1 Blessed are those whose way is pure, *
    who walk in the law of the Lord.
2 Blessed are those who keep his testimonies *
    and seek him with all their whole heart,
3 Those who do no wickedness, *
    but walk in his ways.
4 You, O Lord, have charged *
    that we should diligently keep your commandments.
5 O that my ways were made so direct *
    that I might keep your statutes.
6 Then I should not be put to shame, *
    because I have regard for all your commandments.
7 I will thank you with an unfeigned heart, *
    when I have learned your righteous judgements.
8 I will keep your statutes; *
    O forsake me not utterly.

   Glory . . .

2 Beth

9 How shall young people cleanse their way *
  to keep themselves according to your word?
10 With my whole heart have I sought you; *
  O let me not go astray from your commandments.
11 Your words have I hidden within my heart, *
  that I should not sin against you.
12 Blessed are you, O Lord; *
  O teach me your statutes.
13 With my lips have I been telling *
  of all the judgements of your mouth.
14 I have taken greater delight in the way of your testimonies *
  than in all manner of riches.
15 I will meditate on your commandments *
  and contemplate your ways.
16 My delight shall be in your statutes *
  and I will not forget your word.

Glory . . .

3 Gimel

17 O do good to your servant that I may live, *
  and so shall I keep your word.
18 Open my eyes, that I may see *
  the wonders of your law.
19 I am a stranger upon earth; *
  hide not your commandments from me.
20 My soul is consumed at all times *
  with fervent longing for your judgements.
21 You have rebuked the arrogant; *
  cursed are those who stray from your commandments.
22 Turn from me shame and rebuke, *
  for I have kept your testimonies.
23 Rulers also sit and speak against me, *
  but your servant meditates on your statutes.
24 For your testimonies are my delight; *
  they are my faithful counsellors.

Glory . . .

4 Daleth

25 My soul cleaves to the dust; *
    O give me life according to your word.
26 I have acknowledged my ways and you have answered me; *
    O teach me your statutes.
27 Make me understand the way of your commandments, *
    and so shall I meditate on your wondrous works.
28 My soul melts away in tears of sorrow; *
    raise me up according to your word.
29 Take from me the way of falsehood; *
    be gracious to me through your law.
30 I have chosen the way of truth *
    and your judgements have I laid before me.
31 I hold fast to your testimonies; *
    O Lord, let me not be put to shame.
32 I will run the way of your commandments, *
    when you have set my heart at liberty.

    Glory . . .

5 He

33 Teach me, O Lord, the way of your statutes *
    and I shall keep it to the end.
34 Give me understanding and I shall keep your law; *
    I shall keep it with my whole heart.
35 Lead me in the path of your commandments, *
    for therein is my delight.
36 Incline my heart to your testimonies *
    and not to unjust gain.
37 Turn away my eyes lest they gaze on vanities; *
    O give me life in your way.
38 Confirm to your servant your promise, *
    which stands for all who fear you.
39 Turn away the reproach which I dread, *
    because your judgements are good.
40 Behold, I long for your commandments; *
    in your righteousness give me life.

    Glory . . .

6 *Waw*

41 Let your faithful love come unto me, O Lord, *
    even your salvation, according to your promise.
42 Then shall I answer those who taunt me, *
    for my trust is in your word.
43 O take not the word of truth utterly out of my mouth, *
    for my hope is in your judgements.
44 So shall I always keep your law; *
    I shall keep it for ever and ever.
45 I will walk at liberty, *
    because I study your commandments.
46 I will tell of your testimonies, even before kings, *
    and will not be ashamed.
47 My delight shall be in your commandments, *
    which I have greatly loved.
48 My hands will I lift up to your commandments,
        which I love, *
    and I will meditate on your statutes.

Glory . . .

7 *Zayin*

49 Remember your word to your servant, *
    on which you have built my hope.
50 This is my comfort in my trouble, *
    that your promise gives me life.
51 The proud have derided me cruelly, *
    but I have not turned aside from your law.
52 I have remembered your everlasting judgements, O Lord, *
    and have been comforted.
53 I am seized with indignation at the wicked, *
    for they have forsaken your law.
54 Your statutes have been like songs to me *
    in the house of my pilgrimage.
55 I have thought on your name in the night, O Lord, *
    and so have I kept your law.
56 These blessings have been mine, *
    for I have kept your commandments.

Glory . . .

8 *Heth*

57 You only are my portion. O Lord; *
   I have promised to keep your words.
58 I entreat you with all my heart, *
   be merciful to me according to your promise.
59 I have considered my ways *
   and turned my feet back to your testimonies.
60 I made haste and did not delay *
   to keep your commandments.
61 Though the cords of the wicked entangle me, *
   I do not forget your law.
62 At midnight I will rise to give you thanks, *
   because of your righteous judgements.
63 I am a companion of all those who fear you, *
   those who keep your commandments.
64 The earth, O Lord, is full of your faithful love; *
   instruct me in your statutes.

   Glory . . .

9 *Teth*

65 You have dealt graciously with your servant, *
   according to your word, O Lord.
66 O teach me true understanding and knowledge, *
   for I have trusted in your commandments.
67 Before I was afflicted I went astray; *
   but now I keep your word.
68 You are gracious and do good; *
   O Lord, teach me your statutes.
69 The proud have smeared me with lies, *
   but I will keep your commandments with my whole heart.
70 Their heart has become gross with fat, *
   but my delight is in your law.
71 It is good for me that I have been afflicted, *
   that I may learn your statutes.
72 The law of your mouth is dearer to me *
   than a hoard of gold and silver.

   Glory . . .

10 Yodh

73 Your hands have made me and fashioned me; *
    give me understanding, that I may learn your commandments.
74 Those who fear you will be glad when they see me, *
    because I have hoped in your word.
75 I know, O Lord, that your judgements are right, *
    and that in very faithfulness you caused me to be troubled.
76 Let your faithful love be my comfort, *
    according to your promise to your servant.
77 Let your tender mercies come to me, that I may live, *
    for your law is my delight.
78 Let the proud be put to shame, for they wrong me with lies; *
    but I will meditate on your commandments.
79 Let those who fear you turn to me, *
    even those who know your testimonies.
80 Let my heart be sound in your statutes, *
    that I may not be put to shame.

Glory . . .

11 Kaph

81 My soul is pining for your salvation; *
    I have hoped in your word.
82 My eyes fail with watching for your word, *
    while I say, 'O when will you comfort me?'
83 I have become like a wineskin in the smoke, *
    yet I do not forget your statutes.
84 How many are the days of your servants? *
    When will you bring judgement on those who persecute me?
85 The proud have dug pits for me *
    in defiance of your law.
86 All your commandments are true; *
    help me, for they persecute me with falsehood.
87 They had almost made an end of me on earth, *
    but I have not forsaken your commandments.
88 Give me life according to your loving-kindness; *
    so shall I keep the testimonies of your mouth.

Glory . . .

12 Lamedh

89 O Lord, your word is everlasting; *
   it ever stands firm in the heavens.
90 Your faithfulness also remains from one generation to another; *
   you have established the earth and it abides.
91 So also your judgements stand firm this day, *
   for all things are your servants.
92 If your law had not been my delight, *
   I should have perished in my trouble.
93 I will never forget your commandments, *
   for by them you have given me life.
94 I am yours, O save me! *
   for I have sought your commandments.
95 The wicked have waited for me to destroy me; *
   but I will meditate on your testimonies.
96 I have seen an end of all perfection, *
   but your commandment knows no bounds.

Glory . . .

13 Mem

97 Lord. how I love your law! *
   All the day long it is my study.
98 Your commandments have made me wiser than my enemies, *
   for they are ever with me.
99 I have more understanding than all my teachers, *
   for your testimonies are my meditation.
100 I am wiser than the aged, *
   because I keep your commandments.
101 I restrain my feet from every evil way, *
   that I may keep your word.
102 I have not turned aside from your judgements, *
   for you have been my teacher.
103 How sweet are your words on my tongue! *
   They are sweeter than honey to my mouth.
104 Through your commandments I get understanding; *
   therefore I hate all lying ways.

Glory . . .

14 Nun

105 Your word is a lantern to my feet *
    and a light upon my path.
106 I have sworn and will fulfil it, *
    to keep your righteous judgements.
107 I am troubled above measure; *
    give me life, O Lord, according to your word.
108 Accept the freewill offering of my mouth, O Lord, *
    and teach me your judgements.
109 My soul is ever in my hand, *
    yet I do not forget your law.
110 The wicked have laid a snare for me, *
    but I have not strayed from your commandments.
111 Your testimonies have I claimed as my heritage for ever; *
    for they are the very joy of my heart.
112 I have applied my heart to fulfil your statutes; *
    always, even to the end.

    Glory . . .

15 Samekh

113 I hate those who are double-minded, *
    but your law do I love.
114 You are my hiding place and my shield *
    and my hope is in your word.
115 Away from me, you wicked! *
    I will keep the commandments of my God.
116 Sustain me according to your promise, that I may live, *
    and let me not be disappointed in my hope.
117 Hold me up and I shall be saved, *
    and my delight shall be ever in your statutes.
118 You set at naught those who depart from your statutes, *
    for their deceiving is in vain.
119 You consider all the wicked as dross; *
    therefore I love your testimonies.
120 My flesh trembles for fear of you *
    and I am afraid of your judgements.

    Glory . . .

16 Ayin

121 I have done what is just and right; *
    O give me not over to my oppressors.
122 Stand surety for your servant's good; *
    let not the proud oppress me.
123 My eyes fail with watching for your salvation *
    and for your righteous promise.
124 O deal with your servant according to your faithful love *
    and teach me your statutes.
125 I am your servant; O grant me understanding, *
    that I may know your testimonies.
126 It is time for you to act, O Lord, *
    for they frustrate your law.
127 Therefore I love your commandments *
    above gold, even much fine gold.
128 Therefore I direct my steps by all your precepts, *
    and all false ways I utterly abhor.

    Glory . . .

17 Pe

129 Your testimonies are wonderful; *
    therefore my soul keeps them.
130 The opening of your word gives light; *
    it gives understanding to the simple.
131 I open my mouth and draw in my breath, *
    as I long for your commandments.
132 Turn to me and be gracious to me, *
    as is your way with those who love your name.
133 Order my steps by your word, *
    and let no wickedness have dominion over me.
134 Redeem me from earthly oppressors *
    so that I may keep your commandments.
135 Show the light of your countenance upon your servant *
    and teach me your statutes.
136 My eyes run down with streams of water, *
    because the wicked do not keep your law.

    Glory . . .

18 Tsadhe

137 Righteous are you, O Lord, *
    and true are your judgements.
138 You have ordered your decrees in righteousness, *
    and in great faithfulness.
139 My indignation destroys me, *
    because my adversaries forget your word.
140 Your word has been tried to the uttermost *
    and so your servant loves it.
141 I am small and of no reputation, *
    yet do I not forget your commandments.
142 Your righteousness is an everlasting righteousness *
    and your law is the truth.
143 Trouble and heaviness have taken hold upon me, *
    yet my delight is in your commandments.
144 The righteousness of your testimonies is everlasting; *
    O grant me understanding and I shall live.

    Glory . . .

19 Qoph

145 I call with my whole heart; *
    answer me, O Lord, that I may keep your statutes.
146 To you I call, O save me! *
    And I shall keep your testimonies.
147 Early in the morning I cry to you, *
    for in your word is my trust.
148 My eyes are open before the night watches, *
    that I may meditate on your word.
149 Hear my voice, O Lord, according to your faithful love; *
    according to your judgement, give me life.
150 They draw near that in malice persecute me, *
    who are far from your law.
151 You, O Lord, are near at hand, *
    and all your commandments are true.
152 Long have I known of your testimonies, *
    that you have founded them for ever.

    Glory . . .

20 Resh

153 O consider my affliction and deliver me, *
   for I do not forget your law,
154 Plead my cause and redeem me; *
   according to your promise, give me life.
155 Salvation is far from the wicked, *
   for they do not seek your statutes.
156 Great is your compassion, O Lord; *
   give me life, according to your judgements.
157 Many there are that persecute and oppress me, *
   yet do I not swerve from your testimonies.
158 It grieves me when I see the treacherous, *
   for they do not keep your word.
159 Consider, O Lord, how I love your commandments; *
   give me life according to your loving-kindness.
160 The sum of your word is truth, *
   and all your righteous judgements endure for evermore.

   Glory . . .

21 Shin

161 Princes have persecuted me without a cause, *
   but my heart stands in awe of your word.
162 I am as glad of your word *
   as one who finds great spoils.
163 As for lies, I hate and abhor them, *
   but your law do I love.
164 Seven times a day do I praise you, *
   because of your righteous judgements.
165 Great peace have they who love your law; *
   nothing shall make them stumble.
166 Lord, I have looked for your salvation *
   and I have fulfilled your commandments.
167 My soul has kept your testimonies *
   and greatly have I loved them.
168 I have kept your commandments and testimonies, *
   for all my ways are before you.

   Glory . . .

22 Taw

169 Let my cry come before you, O Lord; *
    give me understanding, according to your word.
170 Let my supplication come before you; *
    deliver me, according to your promise.
171 My lips shall pour forth your praise, *
    when you have taught me your statutes.
172 My tongue shall sing of your word, *
    for all your commandments are righteous.
173 Let your hand reach out to help me, *
    for I have chosen your commandments.
174 I have longed for your salvation, O Lord, *
    and your law is my delight.
175 Let my soul live and it shall praise you, *
    and let your judgements be my help.
176 I have gone astray like a sheep that is lost; *
    O seek your servant, for I do not forget your commandments.

Glory . . .

Psalm 120

A Song of Ascents

1 When I was in trouble I called to the Lord; *
    I called to the Lord and he answered me.
2 Deliver me, O Lord, from lying lips *
    and from a deceitful tongue.
3 What shall be given to you? *
    What more shall be done to you, deceitful tongue?
4 The sharp arrows of a warrior, *
    tempered in burning coals!
5 Woe is me, that I must lodge in Meshech *
    and dwell among the tents of Kedar.
6 My soul has dwelt too long *
    with enemies of peace.
7 I am for making peace, *
    but when I speak of it, they make ready for war.

Glory . . .

Psalm 121

A Song of Ascents

1 I lift up my eyes to the hills; *
   from where is my help to come?
2 My help comes from the Lord, *
   the maker of heaven and earth.
3 He will not suffer your foot to stumble; *
   he who watches over you will not sleep.
4 Behold, he who keeps watch over Israel *
   shall neither slumber nor sleep;
5 The Lord himself watches over you; *
   the Lord is your shade at your right hand,
6 So that the sun shall not strike you by day, *
   neither the moon by night.
7 The Lord shall keep you from all evil; *
   it is he who shall keep your soul.
8 The Lord shall keep watch over your going out
   and your coming in, *
   from this time forth for evermore.

   Glory . . .

Psalm 122

A Song of Ascents

1 I was glad when they said to me, *
   'Let us go to the house of the Lord.'
2 And now our feet are standing *
   within your gates, O Jerusalem;
3 Jerusalem, built as a city *
   that is at unity in itself.
4 Thither the tribes go up, the tribes of the Lord, *
   as is decreed for Israel,
   to give thanks to the name of the Lord.
5 For there are set the thrones of judgement, *
   the thrones of the house of David.
6 O pray for the peace of Jerusalem: *
   'May they prosper who love you.

7 'Peace be within your walls *
   and tranquillity within your palaces.'
8 For my kindred and companions' sake, *
   I will pray that peace be with you.
9 For the sake of the house of the Lord our God, *
   I will seek to do you good.

   Glory . . .

Psalm 123

A Song of Ascents

1 To you I lift up my eyes, *
   to you that are enthroned in the heavens.
2 As the eyes of servants look to the hand of their master, *
   or the eyes of a maid to the hand of her mistress,
3 So our eyes wait upon the Lord our God, *
   until he have mercy upon us.
4 Have mercy upon us, O Lord, have mercy upon us, *
   for we have had more than enough of contempt.
5 Our soul has had more than enough of the scorn of the arrogant, *
   and of the contempt of the proud.

   Glory . . .

Psalm 124

A Song of Ascents

1 If the Lord himself had not been on our side, *
   now may Israel say;
2 If the Lord had not been on our side, *
   when enemies rose up against us;
3 Then would they have swallowed us alive *
   when their anger burned against us;
4 Then would the waters have overwhelmed us
   and the torrent gone over our soul; *
   over our soul would have swept the raging waters.
5 But blessed be the Lord *
   who has not given us over to be a prey for their teeth.

6 Our soul has escaped
    as a bird from the snare of the fowler; *
    the snare is broken and we are delivered.
7 Our help is in the name of the Lord, *
    who has made heaven and earth.

   Glory . . .

Psalm 125

A Song of Ascents

1 Those who trust in the Lord are like Mount Zion, *
    which cannot be moved, but stands fast for ever.
2 As the hills stand about Jerusalem, *
    so the Lord stands round about his people,
    from this time forth for evermore.
3 The sceptre of wickedness shall not hold sway
    over the land allotted to the righteous, *
    lest the righteous turn their hands to evil.
4 Do good, O Lord, to those who are good, *
    and to those who are true of heart.
5 Those who turn aside to crooked ways
    the Lord shall take away with the evil-doers; *
    but let there be peace upon Israel.

   Glory . . .

Psalm 126

A Song of Ascents

1 When the Lord restored the fortunes of Zion, *
    then were we like those who dream.
2 Then was our mouth filled with laughter *
    and our tongue with songs of joy.
3 Then said they among the nations, *
    'The Lord has done great things for them.'
4 The Lord has indeed done great things for us, *
    and therefore we rejoiced.

5 Restore again our fortunes, O Lord, *
   as the river beds of the desert.
6 Those who sow in tears *
   shall reap with songs of joy.
7 Those who go out weeping, bearing the seed, *
   will come back with shouts of joy,
   bearing their sheaves with them.

   Glory . . .

Psalm 127

A Song of Ascents

1 Unless the Lord builds the house, *
   those who build it labour in vain.
2 Unless the Lord keeps the city, *
   the guard keeps watch in vain.
3 It is in vain that you hasten to rise up early
   and go so late to rest, eating the bread of toil, *
   for he gives his beloved sleep.

4 Children are a heritage from the Lord *
   and the fruit of the womb is his gift.
5 Like arrows in the hand of a warrior, *
   so are the children of one's youth.
6 Happy are those who have their quiver full of them: *
   they shall not be put to shame
   when they dispute with their enemies in the gate.

   Glory . . .

Psalm 128

A Song of Ascents

1 Blessed are all those who fear the Lord, *
   and walk in his ways.
2 You shall eat the fruit of the toil of your hands; *
   it shall go well with you, and happy shall you be.

3 Your wife within your house
   shall be like a fruitful vine; *
   your children round your table,
   like fresh olive branches.
4 Thus shall the one be blest *
   who fears the Lord.
5 The Lord from out of Zion bless you, *
   that you may see Jerusalem in prosperity
   all the days of your life.
6 May you see your children's children, *
   and may there be peace upon Israel.

   Glory . . .

Psalm 129

A Song of Ascents

1 'Many a time have they fought against me from my youth,' *
   may Israel now say;
2 'Many a time have they fought against me from my youth, *
   but they have not prevailed against me.'
3 The ploughers ploughed upon my back *
   and made their furrows long.
4 But the righteous Lord *
   has cut the cords of the wicked in pieces.

5 Let them be put to shame and turned backwards, *
   as many as are enemies of Zion.
6 Let them be like grass upon the housetops *
   which withers before it can grow,
7 So that no reaper can fill his hand, *
   nor a binder of sheaves his bosom;
8 And none who go by may say,
   'The blessing of the Lord be upon you. *
   We bless you in the name of the Lord.'

   Glory . . .

Psalm 130

A Song of Ascents

Penitential Psalm

1 Out of the depths have I cried to you, O Lord;
   Lord, hear my voice; *
   let your ears consider well the voice of my supplication.
2 If you, Lord, were to mark what is done amiss, *
   O Lord, who could stand?
3 But there is forgiveness with you, *
   so that you shall be feared.
4 I wait for the Lord; my soul waits for him; *
   in his word is my hope.
5 My soul waits for the Lord,
   more than the night-watch for the morning, *
   more than the night-watch for the morning.

6 O Israel, wait for the Lord, *
   for with the Lord there is mercy;
7 With him is plenteous redemption *
   and he shall redeem Israel from all their sins.

   Glory . . .

Psalm 131

A Song of Ascents

1 O Lord, my heart is not proud; *
   my eyes are not raised in haughty looks.
2 I do not occupy myself with great matters, *
   with things that are too great for me.
3 But I have quieted and stilled my soul,
   like a weaned child on its mother's breast; *
   so my soul is quieted within me.
4 O Israel, trust in the Lord, *
   from this time forth for evermore.

   Glory . . .

Psalm 132

A Song of Ascents

1 Lord, remember for David *
    all the hardships he endured;
2 How he swore an oath to the Lord *
    and vowed a vow to the Mighty One of Jacob:
3 'I will not come within the shelter of my house, *
    nor climb up into my bed;
4 'I will not allow my eyes to sleep, *
    nor let my eyelids slumber;
5 'Until I find a place for the Lord, *
    a dwelling for the Mighty One of Jacob.'

6 Now, we heard of the ark in Ephrathah *
    and found it in the fields of Ja-ar
7 Let us enter his dwelling place *
    and fall low before his footstool.
8 Arise, O Lord, into your resting-place, *
    you and the ark of your strength.
9 Let your priests be clothed with righteousness *
    and your faithful ones sing with joy.
10 For your servant David's sake, *
    turn not away the face of your anointed.

11 The Lord has sworn an oath to David; *
    a promise from which he will not shrink:
12 'Of the fruit of your body *
    shall I set upon your throne.
13 'If your children keep my covenant
    and my testimonies that I shall teach them, *
    their children also shall sit upon your throne for evermore.'
14 For the Lord has chosen Zion for himself; *
    he has desired her for his habitation:
15 'This shall be my resting-place for ever; *
    here will I dwell, for I have longed for her.

16 'I will abundantly bless her provision; *
    her poor will I satisfy with bread.
17 'I will clothe her priests with salvation, *
    and her faithful ones shall rejoice and sing.

18 'There will I make a horn to spring up for David; *
    I will keep a lantern burning for my anointed.
19 'As for his enemies, I will clothe them with shame; *
    but on him shall his crown be bright.'

   Glory . . .

Psalm 133

A Song of Ascents

1 Behold how good and pleasant it is *
   to dwell together in unity.
2 It is like the precious oil upon the head, *
   running down upon the beard,
3 Even on Aaron's beard, *
   running down upon the collar of his clothing.
4 It is like the dew of Hermon *
   running down upon the hills of Zion.
5 For there the Lord has promised his blessing; *
   even life for evermore.

   Glory . . .

Psalm 134

A Song of Ascents

1 Come, bless the Lord,
   all you servants of the Lord, *
   you that by night stand in the house of the Lord.
2 Lift up your hands towards the sanctuary *
   and bless the Lord.
3 The Lord who made heaven and earth *
   give you blessing out of Zion.

   Glory. . .

Psalm 135

1 Alleluia.
   Praise the name of the Lord; *
   give praise, you servants of the Lord,
2 You that stand in the house of the Lord, *
   in the courts of the house of our God.
3 Praise the Lord, for the Lord is good; *
   make music to his name, for it is lovely.
4 For the Lord has chosen Jacob for himself *
   and Israel for his own possession.

5 For I know that the Lord is great *
   and that our Lord is above all gods.
6 The Lord does whatever he pleases
   in heaven and on earth, *
   in the seas and in all the deeps.
7 He brings up the clouds from the ends of the earth; *
   he makes lightning with the rain
   and brings the winds out of his treasuries.
8 He smote the first-born of Egypt, *
   the first-born of man and beast.
9 He sent signs and wonders into your midst, O Egypt, *
   upon Pharaoh and all his servants.
10 He smote many nations *
   and slew mighty kings:
11 Sihon, king of the Amorites,
   and Og, the king of Bashan, *
   and all the kingdoms of Canaan.
12 He gave their land as a heritage, *
   a heritage for Israel his people.
13 Your name, O Lord, endures for ever *
   and shall be remembered through all generations.
14 For the Lord will vindicate his people *
   and have compassion on his servants.
15 The idols of the nations are but silver and gold, *
   the work of human hands.
16 They have mouths, but cannot speak; *
   eyes have they, but cannot see;
17 They have ears, but cannot hear; *
   neither is there any breath in their mouths.

18 Those who make them shall become like them, *
      and so will all who put their trust in them.
19 Bless the Lord, O house of Israel; *
      O house of Aaron, bless the Lord.
20 Bless the Lord, O house of Levi; *
      you who fear the Lord, bless the Lord.
21 Blessed be the Lord from Zion, *
      who dwells in Jerusalem.
      Alleluia.

   Glory . . .

Psalm 136

1 Give thanks to the Lord, for he is gracious, *
     for his mercy endures for ever
2 Give thanks to the God of gods, *
     for his mercy endures for ever
3 Give thanks to the Lord of lords, *
     for his mercy endures for ever;
4 Who alone does great wonders, *
     for his mercy endures for ever;
5 Who by wisdom made the heavens, *
     for his mercy endures for ever;
6 Who laid out the earth upon the waters, *
     for his mercy endures for ever;
7 Who made the great lights, *
     for his mercy endures for ever;
8 The sun to rule the day, *
     for his mercy endures for ever;
9 The moon and the stars to govern the night, *
     for his mercy endures for ever;
10 Who smote the first-born of Egypt, *
     for his mercy endures for ever;
11 And brought out Israel from among them, *
     for his mercy endures for ever;
12 With a mighty hand and outstretched arm, *
     for his mercy endures for ever;
13 Who divided the Red Sea in two, *
     for his mercy endures for ever;

14 And made Israel to pass through the midst of it, *
    for his mercy endures for ever;
15 But Pharaoh and his host he overthrew in the Red Sea, *
    for his mercy endures for ever;
16 Who led his people through the wilderness, *
    for his mercy endures for ever;
17 Who smote great kings, *
    for his mercy endures for ever;
18 And slew mighty kings, *
    for his mercy endures for ever;
19 Sihon, king of the Amorites, *
    for his mercy endures for ever;
20 And Og, the king of Bashan, *
    for his mercy endures for ever;
21 And gave away their land for a heritage, *
    for his mercy endures for ever;
22 A heritage for Israel his servant, *
    for his mercy endures for ever;

23 Who remembered us when we were in trouble, *
    for his mercy endures for ever;
24 And delivered us from our enemies, *
    for his mercy endures for ever;
25 Who gives food to all creatures, *
    for his mercy endures for ever.
26 Give thanks to the God of heaven, *
    for his mercy endures for ever.

   Glory . . .

Psalm 137:1–6

1 By the waters of Babylon we sat down and wept, *
    when we remembered Zion.
2 As for our harps, we hung them up *
    on the willows that grow in that land.
3 For there our captors asked for a song,
    our tormentors called for mirth: *
    'Sing us one of the songs of Zion.'
4 How shall we sing the Lord's song *
    in a strange land?

5 If I forget you, O Jerusalem, *
>   let my right hand forget its skill.
6 Let my tongue cleave to the roof of my mouth
>   if I do not remember you, *
>   if I set not Jerusalem above my highest joy.

> Glory . . .

Psalm 138

1 I will give thanks to you, O Lord, with my whole heart; *
>   before the gods will I sing praise to you.
2 I will bow down towards your holy temple
>   and praise your name,
>   because of your love and faithfulness; *
>   for you have glorified your name
>   and your word above all things.
3 In the day that I called to you, you answered me; *
>   you put new strength in my soul.
4 All the kings of the earth shall praise you, O Lord, *
>   for they have heard the words of your mouth.
5 They shall sing of the ways of the Lord, *
>   that great is the glory of the Lord.
6 Though the Lord be high, he watches over the lowly; *
>   as for the proud. he regards them from afar.
7 Though I walk in the midst of trouble,
>   you will preserve me; *
>   you will stretch forth your hand against the fury of my enemies;
>   your right hand will save me.
8 The Lord shall make good his purpose for me; *
>   your loving-kindness, O Lord, endures for ever;
>   forsake not the work of your hands.

>   Glory . . .

Psalm 139

1 O Lord, you have searched me out and known me; *
>   you know my sitting down and my rising up;
>   you discern my thoughts from afar.

2 You mark out my journeys and my resting place *
    and are acquainted with all my ways.
3 For there is not a word on my tongue, *
    but you, O Lord, know it altogether.
4 You encompass me behind and before *
    and lay your hand upon me.
5 Such knowledge is too wonderful for me, *
    so high that I cannot attain it.
6 Where can I go then from your spirit? *
    Or where can I flee from your presence?
7 If I climb up to heaven, you are there; *
    if I make the grave my bed, you are there also.
8 If I take the wings of the morning *
    and dwell in the uttermost parts of the sea,
9 Even there your hand shall lead me, *
    your right hand hold me fast.
10 If I say, 'Surely the darkness will cover me *
    and the light around me turn to night,'
11 Even darkness is no darkness with you;
    the night is as clear as the day; *
    darkness and light to you are both alike.

12 For you yourself created my inmost parts; *
    you knit me together in my mother's womb.
13 I thank you, for I am fearfully and wonderfully made; *
    marvellous are your works, my soul knows well.
14 My frame was not hidden from you, *
    when I was made in secret
    and woven in the depths of the earth.
15 Your eyes beheld my form, as yet unfinished; *
    already in your book were all my members written,
16 As day by day they were fashioned *
    when as yet there was none of them.
17 How deep are your counsels to me, O God! *
    How great is the sum of them!
18 If I count them, they are more in number than the sand, *
    and at the end, I am still in your presence.

19 O that you would slay the wicked, O God, *
    that the bloodthirsty might depart from me.

20 They speak against you with wicked intent; *
   your enemies take up your name for evil.
21 Do I not oppose those, O Lord, who oppose you? *
   Do I not abhor those who rise up against you?
22 I hate them with a perfect hatred; *
   they have become my own enemies also.

23 Search me out, O God, and know my heart; *
   try me and examine my thoughts.
24 See if there is any way of wickedness in me *
   and lead me in the way everlasting.

   Glory . . .

Psalm 140

1 Deliver me, O Lord, from evil-doers *
   and protect me from the violent,
2 Who devise evil in their hearts *
   and stir up strife all the day long.
3 They have sharpened their tongues like a serpent; *
   adder's poison is under their lips.
4 Keep me, O Lord, from the hands of the wicked; *
   protect me from the violent
   who seek to make me stumble.
5 The proud have laid a snare for me
   and spread out a net of cords; *
   they have set traps along my path.
6 I have said to the Lord, 'You are my God; *
   listen, O Lord, to the voice of my supplication.
7 'O Lord God, the strength of my salvation, *
   you have covered my head in the day of battle.
8 'Do not grant the desires of the wicked, O Lord, *
   do not prosper their wicked plans.
9 'Let not those who surround me lift up their heads; *
   let the evil of their own lips fall upon them.
10 'Let hot burning coals rain upon them; *
    let them be cast into the depths, that they rise not again.'
11 No slanderer shall prosper on the earth, *
    and evil shall hunt down the violent to overthrow them.

12 I know that the Lord will bring justice for the oppressed *
    and maintain the cause of the needy.
13 Surely, the righteous will give thanks to your name, *
    and the upright shall dwell in your presence.

   Glory . . .

Psalm 141

1 O Lord, I call to you; come to me quickly; *
    hear my voice when I cry to you.
2 Let my prayer rise before you as incense, *
    the lifting up of my hands as the evening sacrifice.
3 Set a watch before my mouth, O Lord, *
    and guard the door of my lips;
4 Let not my heart incline to any evil thing; *
    let me not be occupied in wickedness with evil-doers,
    nor taste the pleasures of their table.
5 Let the righteous smite me in friendly rebuke;
    but let not the oil of the unrighteous anoint my head; *
    for my prayer is continually against their wicked deeds.
6 Let their rulers be overthrown in stony places; *
    that they may know my words are sweet.
7 As when a plough turns over the earth in furrows, *
    let their bones be scattered at the mouth of the Pit.
8 But my eyes are turned to you, Lord God; *
    in you I take refuge; do not leave me defenceless.
9 Protect me from the snare which they have laid for me *
    and from the traps of the evil-doers.
10 Let the wicked fall into their own nets, *
    while I pass by in safety.

   Glory . . .

Psalm 142

1 I cry aloud to the Lord; *
    to the Lord I make my supplication.
2 I pour out my complaint before him *
    and tell him of my trouble.

3 When my spirit faints within me, you know my path; *
   in the way wherein I walk have they laid a snare for me.
4 I look to my right hand, and find no one who knows me; *
   I have no place to flee unto, and no one cares for my soul.
5 I cry out to you, O Lord, and say: *
   'You are my refuge, my portion in the land of the living.
6 'Listen to my cry, for I am brought very low; *
   save me from my persecutors, for they are too strong for me.
7 'Bring my soul out of prison,
   that I may give thanks to your name; *
   when you have dealt bountifully with me,
   then shall the righteous gather around me.'

Glory . . .

Psalm 143

Penitential Psalm

1 Hear my prayer, O Lord,
   and in your faithfulness give ear to my supplications; *
   answer me in your righteousness.
2 Enter not into judgement with your servant, *
   for in your sight shall no one living be justified.
3 For the enemy has pursued me,
   crushing my life to the ground, *
   making me sit in darkness like those long dead.
4 My spirit faints within me; *
   my heart within me is desolate.
5 I remember the time past; I muse upon all your deeds; *
   I consider the works of your hands.
6 I stretch out my hands to you; *
   my soul gasps for you like a thirsty land.
7 O Lord, make haste to answer me; my spirit fails me; *
   hide not your face from me
   lest I be like those who go down to the Pit.
8 Let me hear of your loving-kindness in the morning,
   for in you I put my trust; *
   show me the way that I should walk in,
   for I lift up my soul to you.

9 Deliver me, O Lord, from my enemies, *
>> for I flee to you for refuge.
10 Teach me to do what pleases you, for you are my God; *
>> let your kindly spirit lead me on a level path.
11 Revive me, O Lord, for your name's sake; *
>> for your righteousness' sake, bring me out of trouble.
12 In your faithfulness, slay my enemies,
>> and destroy all the adversaries of my soul, *
>> for truly I am your servant.

Glory . . .

Psalm 144

1 Blessed be the Lord my rock, *
>> who teaches my hands for war and my fingers for battle;
2 My steadfast help and my fortress,
>> my stronghold and my deliverer,
>> my shield in whom I trust, *
>> who subdues my people under me.
3 O Lord, what are mortals that you should consider them; *
>> mere human beings, that you should take thought for them?
4 They are like a breath of wind; *
>> their days pass away like a shadow.

5 Bow your heavens, O Lord, and come down; *
>> touch the mountains and they shall smoke.
6 Cast down your lightning and scatter them; *
>> shoot out your arrows and let thunder roar.
7 Reach down your hand from on high; *
>> deliver me and take me out of the great waters,
>> from the hand of foreign enemies,
8 Whose mouth speaks wickedness *
>> and whose right hand is the hand of falsehood.
9 O God, I will sing to you a new song; *
>> I will play to you on a ten-stringed harp.
10 You that give salvation to kings *
>> and have delivered David your servant.
11 Save me from the peril of the sword *
>> and deliver me from the hand of foreign enemies,

12 Whose mouth speaks wickedness *
   and whose right hand is the hand of falsehood;
13 So that our sons in their youth
   may be like well-nurtured plants, *
   and our daughters like pillars
   carved for the corners of the temple;
14 Our barns be filled with all manner of store; *
   our flocks bearing thousands,
   and ten thousands in our fields;
15 Our cattle be heavy with young : *
   may there be no miscarriage or untimely birth,
   no cry of distress in our streets.
16 Happy are the people whose blessing this is. *
   Happy are the people who have the Lord for their God.

   Glory . . .

Psalm 145

1 I will exalt you, O God my King, *
   and bless your name for ever and ever.
2 Every day will I bless you *
   and praise your name for ever and ever.
3 Great is the Lord and highly to be praised; *
   his greatness is beyond all searching out.
4 One generation shall praise your works to another *
   and declare your mighty acts.
5 They shall speak of the majesty of your glory, *
   and I will tell of all your wonderful deeds.
6 They shall speak of the majesty of your glory, *
   and I will also tell of your greatness.
7 They shall pour forth the story of your abundant kindness *
   and joyfully sing of your righteousness.
8 The Lord is gracious and merciful, *
   long-suffering and of great goodness.

9 The Lord is loving unto everyone *
   and his mercy is over all his creatures.
10 All your works praise you, O Lord, *
   and your faithful servants bless you.

11 They tell of the glory of your kingdom *
    and speak of your mighty power;
12 To make known to all peoples your mighty acts *
    and the glorious splendour of your kingdom.
13 Your kingdom is an everlasting kingdom; *
    your dominion endures throughout all ages.
14 The Lord is sure in all his words *
    and faithful in all his deeds.
15 The Lord upholds all those who fall *
    and lifts up all those who are bowed down.
16 The eyes of all wait upon you, O Lord, *
    and you give them their food in due season.
17 You open wide your hand *
    and fill all things living with plenty.
18 The Lord is righteous in all his ways *
    and loving in all his works.
19 The Lord is near to those who call upon him, *
    to all who call upon him faithfully.
20 He fulfils the desire of those who fear him; *
    he hears their cry and saves them.
21 The Lord watches over those who love him, *
    but all the wicked shall he destroy.
22 My mouth shall speak the praise of the Lord, *
    and let all flesh bless his holy name for ever and ever.

   Glory . . .

Psalm 146

1 Alleluia!
    Praise the Lord, O my soul:
    while I live will I praise the Lord; *
    as long as I have any being,
    I will sing praises to my God.
2 Put not your trust in princes,
    nor in any human power, *
    for there is no help in them.
3 When their breath goes out, they return to the earth; *
    on that day all their thoughts perish.

4 Happy are those who have the God of Jacob for their help, *
   whose hope is in the Lord their God;
5 Who made heaven and earth,
   the sea and all that is in them; *
   who keeps his promise for ever;
6 Who gives justice to those that suffer wrong *
   and bread to those who hunger.
7 The Lord looses those that are bound; *
   the Lord opens the eyes of the blind;
8 The Lord lifts up those who are bowed down; *
   the Lord loves the righteous;
9 The Lord watches over the stranger in the land;
   he upholds the orphan and widow; *
   but the way of the wicked he turns upside down.
10 The Lord shall reign for ever, *
   your God, O Zion, throughout all generations.
   Alleluia.

Glory . . .

Psalm 147 (part one)

1 Alleluia.
   How good it is to make music for our God, *
   how joyful to honour him with praise.
2 The Lord builds up Jerusalem *
   and gathers together the outcasts of Israel.
3 He heals the broken-hearted *
   and binds up all their wounds.
4 He counts the number of the stars *
   and calls them all by their names.
5 Great is our Lord and mighty in power; *
   his wisdom is beyond all telling.
6 The Lord lifts up the poor, *
   but casts down the wicked to the ground.
7 Sing to the Lord with thanksgiving; *
   make music to our God upon the lyre;
8 Who covers the heavens with clouds *
   and prepares rain for the earth;

9 Who makes grass to grow upon the mountains *
    and green plants to serve our needs.
10 He gives the beasts their food *
    and the young ravens when they cry.
11 He takes no pleasure in the power of a horse, *
    no delight in human strength.
12 But the Lord delights in those who fear him, *
    who put their trust in his steadfast love.

   Glory . . .

Psalm 147 (part two)

13 Sing praise to the Lord, O Jerusalem; *
    praise your God, O Zion;
14 For he has strengthened the bars of your gates *
    and has blest your children within you.
15 He has established peace in your borders *
    and satisfies you with the finest wheat.
16 He sends forth his command to the earth *
    and his word runs very swiftly.
17 He gives snow like wool *
    and scatters the hoarfrost like ashes.
18 He casts down his hailstones like morsels of bread; *
    who can endure his frost?
19 He sends forth his word and melts them; *
    he blows with his wind and the waters flow.
20 He declares his word to Jacob, *
    his statutes and judgements to Israel.
21 He has not dealt so with any other nation; *
    they do not know his laws.
    Alleluia.

   Glory . . .

Psalm 148

1 Alleluia.
    Praise the Lord from the heavens; *
    praise him in the heights.
2 Praise him, all you angels of his; *
    praise him, all his host.
3 Praise him, sun and moon; *
    praise him, all you stars of light.
4 Praise him, heaven of heavens, *
    and you waters above the heavens.
5 Let them praise the name of the Lord, *
    for he commanded and they were created.
6 He made them fast for ever and ever; *
    he gave them a law which shall not pass away.
7 Praise the Lord from the earth, *
    you sea monsters and all deeps;
8 Fire and hail, snow and mist, *
    tempestuous wind, fulfilling his word;
9 Mountains and all hills, *
    fruit trees and all cedars;
10 Wild beasts and all cattle, *
    creeping things and birds on the wing;
11 Kings of the earth and all peoples, *
    princes and all rulers of the world;
12 Young men and women,
    old and young together; *
    let them praise the name of the Lord.
13 For his name only is exalted, *
    his splendour above earth and heaven.
14 He has raised up the horn of his people
    and praise for all his faithful servants, *
    the children of Israel, a people who are near him.
    Alleluia.

    Glory . . .

Psalm 149

1 Alleluia.
   O sing to the Lord a new song; *
   sing his praise in the congregation of the faithful.
2 Let Israel rejoice in their maker; *
   let the children of Zion be joyful in their king.
3 Let them praise his name in the dance; *
   let them sing praise to him with timbrel and lyre
4 For the Lord has pleasure in his people *
   and adorns the poor with salvation.
5 Let the faithful be joyful in glory; *
   let them rejoice in their ranks;
6 With the praises of God in their mouths *
   and a two-edged sword in their hand;
7 To execute vengeance on the nations *
   and punishment on the peoples;
8 To bind their kings in chains *
   and their nobles with fetters of iron;
9 To execute on them the judgement decreed: *
   such honour have all his faithful servants.
   Alleluia.
   Glory . . .

Psalm 150

1 Alleluia.
   O praise God in his holiness; *
   praise him in the firmament of his power.
2 Praise him for his mighty acts; *
   praise him according to his excellent greatness.
3 Praise him with the blast of the trumpet; *
   praise him upon the harp and lyre.
4 Praise him with timbrel and dances; *
   praise him upon the strings and pipe.
5 Praise him with ringing cymbals; *
   praise him upon the clashing cymbals.
6 Let everything that has breath *
   praise the Lord.
   Alleluia.

  Glory . . .

Canticles

1 The Song of Moses and Miriam

Refrain: In your unfailing love, O Lord, *
        you lead the people whom you have redeemed.

1 I will sing to the Lord, who has triumphed gloriously, *
   the horse and his rider have been thrown into the sea.
2 The Lord is my strength and my song *
   and has become my salvation.
3 This is my God whom I will praise *
   the God of my forebears whom I will exalt.
4 The Lord is a warrior, *
   the Lord is his name.
5 Your right hand, O Lord, is glorious in power: *
   your right hand, O Lord, shatters the enemy.
6 At the blast of your nostrils, the sea covered them; *
   they sank as lead in the mighty waters.
7 In your unfailing love, O Lord, *
   you lead the people whom you have redeemed.
8 And by your invincible strength *
   you will guide them to your holy dwelling.
9 You will bring them in and plant them, O Lord, *
   in the sanctuary which your hands have established.

   Glory . . .

Refrain: In your unfailing love, O Lord, *
        you lead the people whom you have redeemed.

Exodus 15:1b-3,6,10,13,17
Common Worship (1)

2 A Song of the Rock

Refrain: I will proclaim the name of the Lord; *
    ascribe greatness to our God.

1 Give ear, O heavens, *
    and I will let the earth hear the words of my mouth.
2 May my teaching drop like the rain,
    my speech condense like the dew; *
    like gentle rain on grass,
    like showers on new growth.
3 For I will proclaim the name of the Lord;
    ascribe greatness to our God! *
    The Rock, his work is perfect,
    and all his ways are just.
4 A faithful God, without deceit,
    just and upright is he; *
    yet his degenerate children have dealt falsely with him,
    a perverse and crooked generation.
5 Do you thus repay the Lord,
    O foolish and senseless people? *
    Is not he your father, who created you,
    who made you and established you?
6 Remember the days of old,
    consider the years long past; *
    ask your father, and he will inform you; *
    your elders, and they will tell you.
7 When the Most High apportioned the nations,
    when he divided humankind, *
    he fixed the boundaries of the peoples
    according to the number of the gods;
8 The Lord's own portion was his people, *
    Jacob his allotted share.
9 He sustained him in a desert land,
    in a howling wilderness waste; *
    he shielded him, cared for him,
    guarded him as the apple of his eye.
10 As an eagle stirs up its nest,
    and hovers over its young; *
    as it spreads its wings, takes them up,
    and bears them aloft on its pinions,

11 The Lord alone guided him; *
   no foreign god was with him.

   Glory . . .

Refrain: I will proclaim the name of the Lord; *
   ascribe greatness to our God.

Deuteronomy 32:1–12 (RSV)

3 The Song of Hannah

Refrain: Blessed are those who believe, *
   for what God has promised will be fulfilled.

1 My heart exults in the Lord; *
   my strength is exalted in my God.
2 My mouth derides my enemies, *
   because I rejoice in your salvation.
3 There is no Holy One like you, O Lord, *
   nor any Rock like you, our God.
4 For you are a God of knowledge *
   and by you our actions are weighed.
5 The bows of the mighty are broken, *
   but the feeble gird on strength.
6 Those who were full now search for bread,*
   but those who were hungry are well fed.
7 The barren woman has borne sevenfold, *
   but she who has many children is forlorn.
8 Both the poor and the rich are of your making; *
   you bring low and you also exalt.
9 You raise up the poor from the dust, *
   and lift the needy from the ash heap.
10 You make them sit with the rulers *
   and inherit a place of honour.
11 For the pillars of the earth are yours *
   and on them you have set the world.

   Glory . . .

Refrain: Blessed are those who believe, *
   for what God has promised will be fulfilled.

1 Samuel 2:1–8
A Daily Office SSF (3)

4 A Song of David

Refrain: Splendour and majesty are yours, O God; *
  you are exalted as head over all.

1 Blessed are you, God of Israel, for ever and ever; *
  for yours is the greatness, the power,
  the glory, the splendour and the majesty.
2 Everything in heaven and on earth is yours; *
  yours is the kingdom, O Lord,
  and you are exalted as head over all.
3 Riches and honour come from you *
  and you rule over all.
4 In your hand are power and might; *
  yours it is to give power and strength to all.
5 And now we give you thanks, our God, *
  and praise your glorious name.
6 For all things come from you, *
  and of your own have we given you.

  Glory . . .

Refrain: Splendour and majesty are yours, O God; *
  you are exalted as head over all.

I Chronicles 29:10b-13,14b
Common Worship (1)

5 A Song of Solomon

Refrain: Many waters cannot quench love; *
  neither can the floods drown it.

1 Set me as a seal upon your heart, *
  as a seal upon your arm;
2 For love is strong as death
  passion fierce as the grave; *
  its flashes are flashes of fire,
  a raging flame.
3 Many waters cannot quench love, *
  neither can the floods drown it.

4 If all the wealth of our house
    were offered for love, *
      it would be utterly scorned.

  Glory . . .

Refrain: Many waters cannot quench love; *
    neither can the floods drown it.

Song of Solomon 8:7–8
A Daily Office SSF (3)

6 A Song of Peace

Refrain: Nation shall not lift up sword against nation, *
    neither shall they learn war any more.

1 Come, let us go up to the mountain of the Lord,
    to the house of the God of Jacob; *
    that he may teach us his ways
    and that we may walk in his paths.
2 For out of Zion shall go forth instruction, *
    and the word of the Lord from Jerusalem.
3 He shall judge between the nations, *
    and shall arbitrate for many peoples;
4 And they shall beat their swords into ploughshares, *
    and their spears into pruning hooks;
5 Nation shall not lift up sword against nation, *
    neither shall they learn war any more.
6 O house of Jacob, come, *
    let us walk in the light of the Lord!

  Glory . . .

Refrain: Nation shall not lift up sword against nation, *
    neither shall they learn war any more.

Isaiah 2:3–5

7 A Song of God's Chosen One

Refrain: The Spirit of the Lord shall rest upon him, *
  the spirit of wisdom and understanding.

1 There shall come forth a shoot from the stock of Jesse, *
  and a branch shall grow out of his roots.
2 And the Spirit of the Lord shall rest upon him, *
  the spirit of wisdom and understanding,
3 The spirit of counsel and might, *
  the spirit of knowledge and the fear of the Lord.
4 He shall not judge by what his eyes see, *
  or decide by what his ears hear,
5 But with righteousness he shall judge the poor, *
  and decide with equity for the meek of the earth.
6 The wolf shall dwell with the lamb, *
  and the leopard shall lie down with the kid.
7 The calf and the lion cub together, *
  with a little child to lead them.
8 They shall not hurt or destroy in all my holy mountain, *
  for the earth shall be full of the knowledge of the Lord
  as the waters cover the sea.

  Glory . . .

Refrain: The Spirit of the Lord shall rest upon him, *
  the spirit of wisdom and understanding.

Isaiah 11:1–4a, 6, 9
A Daily Office SSF (3)

8 A Song of Deliverance

Refrain: All the earth, shout and sing for joy, *
  for great in your midst is the Holy One.

1 'Behold, God is my salvation; *
  I will trust and will not be afraid;
2 'For the Lord God is my strength and my song, *
  and has become my salvation.'
3 With joy you will draw water *
  from the wells of salvation.
4 On that day you will say, *
  'Give thanks to the Lord, call upon his name;

5 'Make known his deeds among the nations, *
    proclaim that his name is exalted.
6 'Sing God's praises, who has triumphed gloriously; *
    let this be known in all the world.
7 'Shout and sing for joy, you that dwell in Zion, *
    for great in your midst is the Holy One of Israel.'

   Glory . . .

Refrain: All the earth, shout and sing for joy, *
    for great in your midst is the Holy One.

Isaiah 12:2–6
trans. A Daily Office SSF (3)

9 *A Song of Trust in the Lord*

Refrain: Trust in the Lord for ever, *
    for in the Lord God you have an everlasting rock.

1 We have a strong city;
    he sets up victory like walls and bulwarks. *
    Open the gates,
    so that the righteous nation that keeps faith may enter in.
2 Those of steadfast mind you keep in peace – *
    in peace because they trust in you.
3 Trust in the Lord for ever, *
    for in the Lord God you have an everlasting rock.
4 The way of the righteous is level; *
    O Just One, you make smooth the path of the righteous.
5 In the path of your judgements, O Lord,
    we wait for you; *
    your name and your renown are the soul's desire.
6 My soul yearns for you in the night, *
    my spirit within me earnestly seeks you.
7 For when your judgements are in the earth, *
    the inhabitants of the world learn righteousness.
8 O Lord, you will ordain peace for us, *
    for indeed, all that we have done,
    you have done for us.

   Glory . . .

Refrain: Trust in the Lord for ever, *
    for in the Lord God you have an everlasting rock.

Isaiah 26:1–4,7–9,12

10 A Song of the Might of the Lord

Refrain: Those who walk righteously and speak uprightly, *
    will dwell on the heights.

1 Hear, you who are far off,
    what I have done; *
    and you who are near,
    acknowledge my might.
2 The sinners in Zion are afraid;
    trembling has seized the godless: *
    'Who among us can dwell with the devouring fire?
    Who among us can dwell with everlasting flames?'
3 Those who walk righteously and speak uprightly, *
    who despise the gain of oppression,
    who wave away a bribe instead of accepting it,
4 Who stop their ears from hearing of bloodshed *
    and shut their eyes from looking on evil,
5 They will dwell on the heights;
    their refuge will be the fortresses of rocks; *
    their food will be supplied,
    their water assured.

  Glory . . .

Refrain: Those who walk righteously and speak uprightly, *
    will dwell on the heights.

Isaiah 33:13–16

11 A Song of the Living

Refrain: My eyes are weary with looking upward. *
    O Lord, I am oppressed; be my security!

1 I said, In the noontide of my days I must depart; *
    I am consigned to the gates of Sheol
    for the rest of my years.

2 I said, I shall not see the Lord
    in the land of the living; *
    I shall look upon mortals no more
    among the inhabitants of the world.
3 My dwelling is plucked up and removed from me
    like a shepherd's tent; *
    like a weaver I have rolled up my life;
    he cuts me off from the loom;
4 From day to night you bring me to an end;
    I cry for help until morning; *
    like a lion he breaks all my bones;
    from day to night you bring me to an end.
5 Like a swallow or a crane I clamour,
    I moan like a dove. *
    My eyes are weary with looking upward.
    O Lord, I am oppressed; be my security!
6 Surely it was for my welfare that I had great bitterness; *
    but you have held back my life from the pit of destruction,
    for you have cast all my sins behind your back.
7 For Sheol cannot thank you, death cannot praise you; *
    those who go down to the Pit cannot hope for your faithfulness.
8 The living, the living, they thank you, as I do this day; *
    fathers make known to children your faithfulness.
9 The Lord will save me, *
    and we will sing to stringed instruments
    all the days of our life, at the house of the Lord.

  Glory . . .

Refrain: My eyes are weary with looking upward. *
         O Lord, I am oppressed; be my security!

Isaiah 38:10–14, 17–20

12 *A Song of God's Herald*

Refrain: Lift up your voice with strength, *
         O herald of good tidings.

1 Go up to a high mountain,
    herald of good tidings to Zion; *
    lift up your voice with strength,
    herald of good tidings to Jerusalem.

2 Lift up your voice, fear not; *
   say to the cities of Judah, 'Behold your God!'
3 See the Lord God, coming with power, *
   coming to rule with his mighty arm.
4 He brings his reward for the people of God, *
   the recompense for those who are saved.
5 God will feed his flock like a shepherd, *
   and gather the lambs in his arms;
6 He will hold them to his breast, *
   and gently lead those that are with young.

   Glory . . .

Refrain: Lift up your voice with strength, *
   O herald of good tidings.

Isaiah 40:9–11
A Daily Office SSF (3)

13 A Song of the Covenant

Refrain: I have given you as a light to the nations, *
   and I have called you in righteousness.

1 Thus says God, who created the heavens, *
   who fashioned the earth and all that dwells in it;
2 Who gives breath to the people upon it *
   and spirit to those who walk in it,
3 'I am the Lord and I have called you in righteousness, *
   I have taken you by the hand and kept you;
4 'I have given you as a covenant to the people, *
   a light to the nations, to open the eyes that are blind,
5 'To bring out the captives from the dungeon, *
   from the prison, those who sit in darkness.
6 'I am the Lord, that is my name; *
   my glory I give to no other.'

   Glory . . .

Refrain: I have given you as a light to the nations, *
   and I have called you in righteousness.

Isaiah 42:5–8a
A Daily Office SSF (3)

14 A Song of the Lord's Salvation

Refrain: Sing to the Lord a new song, *
      his praise from the end of the earth!

1 Sing to the Lord a new song, *
    his praise from the end of the earth!
2 Let the sea roar and all that fills it, *
    the coastlands and their inhabitants.
3 Let the desert and its cities lift up their voice, *
    the villages that Kedar inhabits.
4 Let the inhabitants of Sela sing for joy, *
    let them shout from the top of the mountains.
5 Let them give glory to the Lord, *
    and declare his praise in the coastlands.
6 The Lord goes forth like a soldier,
    like a warrior he stirs up his fury; *
    he cries out, he shouts aloud,
    he shows himself mighty against his foes.
7 For a long time I have held my peace,
    I have kept still and restrained myself; *
    now I will cry out like a woman in labour,
    I will gasp and pant.
8 I will lay waste mountains and hills,
    and dry up all their herbage; *
    I will turn the rivers into islands,
    and dry up the pools.
9 I will lead the blind by a road they do not know, *
    by paths they have not known I will guide them.
10 I will turn the darkness before them into light, *
    the rough places into level ground.

    Glory . . .

Refrain: Sing to the Lord a new song, *
      his praise from the end of the earth!

Isaiah 42:10–16

15 A Song of God the Saviour

Refrain: Turn to me and be saved, all the ends of the earth! *
    For I am God, and there is no other.

1 Truly, you are a God who hides himself,
    O God of Israel, the Saviour. *
    All of them are put to shame and confounded,
    the makers of idols go in confusion together.
2 But Israel is saved by the Lord with everlasting salvation; *
    You shall not be put to shame or confounded to all eternity.
3 For thus says the Lord,
    who created the heavens (he is God!), *
    who formed the earth and made it (he established it;
    he did not create it a chaos, he formed it to be inhabited!):
    I am the Lord, and there is no other.
4 I did not speak in secret, in a land of darkness; *
    I did not say to the offspring of Jacob,
    'Seek me in chaos.'
5 I the Lord speak the truth, I declare what is right. *
    Assemble yourselves and come together,
    draw near, you survivors of the nations!
6 They have no knowledge – those who carry about their wooden idols, *
    and keep on praying to a god that cannot save.
7 Declare and present your case; let them take counsel together! *
    Who told this long ago? Who declared it of old?
    Was it not I, the Lord?
8 There is no other god besides me, *
    a righteous God and a Saviour;
    there is no one besides me.
9 Turn to me and be saved, all the ends of the earth! *
    For I am God, and there is no other.
10 By myself I have sworn,
    from my mouth has gone forth in righteousness *
    a word that shall not return:
    'To me every knee shall bow, every tongue shall swear.'
11 Only in the Lord, it shall be said of me, *
    are righteousness and strength;

12 All who were incensed against him
    shall come to him and be ashamed. *
    In the Lord all the offspring of Israel shall triumph and glory.

Glory . . .

Refrain: Turn to me and be saved, all the ends of the earth! *
    For I am God, and there is no other.

Isaiah 45:15–25

16 A Song of the Word of the Lord

Refrain: Return to the Lord, who will have mercy, *
    to our God, who will richly pardon.

1 Seek the Lord while he may be found, *
    call upon him while he is near;
2 Let the wicked abandon their ways, *
    and the unrighteous their thoughts;
3 Return to the Lord,
    who will have mercy; *
    to our God, who will richly pardon.
4 'For my thoughts are not your thoughts, *
    neither are your ways my ways,' says the Lord.
5 'For as the heavens are higher than the earth, *
    so are my ways higher than your ways
    and my thoughts than your thoughts.
6 'As the rain and the snow come down from above, *
    and return not again but water the earth,
7 'Bringing forth life and giving growth, *
    seed for sowing and bread to eat,
8 'So is my word that goes forth from my mouth; *
    it will not return to me fruitless,
9 'But it will accomplish that which I purpose, *
    and succeed in the task I gave it.'

Glory . . .

Refrain: Return to the Lord, who will have mercy, *
    to our God, who will richly pardon.

Isaiah 55:6–11
trans. A Daily Office SSF (3)

17 A Song of the New Jerusalem

Refrain: Nations will come to your light, *
    and kings to your dawning brightness.

1 Arise, shine out, for your light has come, *
    the glory of the Lord is rising upon you.
2 Though night still covers the earth, *
    and darkness the peoples;
3 Above you the Holy One arises, *
    and above you God's glory appears.
4 The nations will come to your light, *
    and kings to your dawning brightness.
5 Your gates will lie open continually, *
    shut neither by day nor by night.
6 The sound of violence shall be heard no longer in your land, *
    or ruin and devastation within your borders.
7 You will call your walls, Salvation, *
    and your gates, Praise.
8 No more will the sun give you daylight, *
    nor moonlight shine upon you;
9 But the Lord will be your everlasting light, *
    your God will be your splendour.
10 For you shall be called the city of God, *
    the dwelling of the Holy One of Israel.

Glory . . .

Refrain: Nations will come to your light, *
    and kings to your dawning brightness.

Isaiah 60:1–3,11a,18–19,14b
Common Worship (1)

18 A Song of the Bride

Refrain: God makes righteousness and praise *
    blossom before all the nations.

1 I will greatly rejoice in the Lord, *
    my soul shall exult in my God;
2 Who has clothed me with the garments of salvation, *
    and has covered me with the cloak of integrity,

3 As a bridegroom decks himself with a garland, *
   and as a bride adorns herself with her jewels.
4 For as the earth puts forth her blossom, *
   and as seeds in the garden spring up,
5 So shall God make righteousness and praise *
   blossom before all the nations.
6 For Zion's sake, I will not keep silent, *
   and for Jerusalem's sake, I will not rest,
7 Until her deliverance shines out like the dawn, *
   and her salvation as a burning torch.
8 The nations shall see your deliverance, *
   and all rulers shall see your glory;
9 Then you shall be called by a new name *
   which the mouth of God will give.
10 You shall be a crown of glory in the hand of the Lord, *
   a royal diadem in the hand of your God.

   Glory . . .

Refrain: God makes righteousness and praise *
   blossom before all the nations.

Isaiah 61:10–11; 62:1–3
trans. A Daily Office SSF (3)

19 A Song of Jerusalem our Mother

Refrain: As a mother comforts her child, so I will comfort you; *
   you shall be comforted in Jerusalem.

1 Rejoice with Jerusalem, and be glad for her,
   all you who love her; *
   rejoice with her in joy,
   all you who mourn over her –
2 That you may nurse and be satisfied from her consoling breasts; *
   that you may drink deeply with delight from the glorious bosom.
3 For thus says the Lord:
   'Behold, I will extend prosperity to her like a river, *
   and the wealth of the nations like an overflowing stream;
4 'And you shall nurse and be carried on her arm, *
   and dandled upon her knees.
5 'As a mother comforts her child, so I will comfort you; *
   you shall be comforted in Jerusalem.

6 'You shall see, and your heart shall rejoice; *
   your bodies shall flourish like the grass.'

Refrain: As a mother comforts her child, so I will comfort you; *
   you shall be comforted in Jerusalem.

Isaiah 66:10–14a

20 *A Song of Entreaty*

Refrain: We look for peace, but find no good; *
   for a time of healing, but there is terror instead.

1 Let my eyes run down night and day,
   and let them not cease, *
   for the virgin daughter – my people –
   is struck down with a crushing blow, with a very grievous wound.
2 If I go out into the field, look – those killed by the sword! *
   And if I enter the city, look – those sick with famine!
3 For both prophet and priest ply their trade throughout the land, *
   and have no knowledge.
4 Have you completely rejected Judah?
   Does your heart loathe Zion? *
   Why have you struck us down so that there is no healing for us?
5 We look for peace, but find no good; *
   for a time of healing, but there is terror instead.
6 We acknowledge our wickedness, O Lord, *
   the iniquity of our ancestors,
   for we have sinned against you.
7 Do not spurn us, for your name's sake;
   do not dishonour your glorious throne; *
   remember and do not break your covenant with us

Glory . . .

Refrain: We look for peace, but find no good; *
   for a time of healing, but there is terror instead.

trans. Jeremiah 14:17–21

21 *A Song of the Shepherd*

Refrain: I will turn their mourning into joy, *
    I will comfort them, and give them gladness for sorrow.

1 Hear the word of the Lord, O nations,
    and declare it in the coastlands far away; *
    say, 'He who scattered Israel will gather him,
    and will keep him as a shepherd a flock.'
2 For the Lord has ransomed Jacob, *
    and has redeemed him from hands too strong for him.
3 They shall come and sing aloud on the height of Zion, *
    and they shall be radiant over the goodness of the Lord,
4 Over the grain, the wine, and the oil,
    and over the young of the flock and the herd; *
    their life shall become like a watered garden,
    and they shall never languish again.
5 Then shall the young women rejoice in the dance, *
    and the young men and the old shall be merry.
6 I will turn their mourning into joy, *
    I will comfort them, and give them gladness for sorrow.
7 I will give the priests their fill of fatness, *
    and my people shall be satisfied with my bounty, says the Lord.

  Glory . . .

Refrain: I will turn their mourning into joy, *
    I will comfort them, and give them gladness for sorrow.
                                                    Jeremiah 31:10–14

22 *A Song of Lamentation*

1 Is it nothing to you, all you who pass by? *
    Look and see if there is any sorrow like my sorrow
2 Which was brought upon me, *
    which the Lord inflicted
    on the day of his fierce anger.
3 For these things I weep;
    my eyes flow with tears; *
    for a comforter is far from me,
    one to revive my courage.

4 The thought of my affliction is wormwood and gall! *
   My soul continually thinks of it
   and is bowed down within me.
5 But this I call to mind, *
   and therefore I have hope.
6 The steadfast love of the Lord never ceases:
   his mercies never come to an end; *
   They are new every morning;
   great is your faithfulness.
7 'The Lord is my portion,' says my soul, *
   'therefore I will hope in him.'
8 The Lord is good to those who wait for him, *
   to the soul that seeks him.
9 It is good that one should wait quietly *
   for the salvation of the Lord.
10 It is good for one to bear the yoke in youth, *
   to sit alone in silence
   when the Lord has imposed it,
11 To give one's cheek to the smiter, *
   and be filled with insults.
12 For the Lord will not reject for ever. *
   Although he causes grief, he will have compassion
   according to the abundance of his steadfast love.

   Glory . . .

Lamentation 1:12, 16; 3:19–28, 31–32

23 *A Song of Ezekiel*

Refrain: I will put a new spirit within you, *
   and you shall be my people.

1 I will take you from the nations, *
   and gather you from all the countries.
2 I will sprinkle clean water upon you, *
   and you shall be clean from all your uncleannesses.
3 A new heart I will give you, *
   and put a new spirit within you,
4 And I will remove from your body the heart of stone *
   and give you a heart of flesh.

5 You shall be my people, *
    and I will be your God.

Glory . . .

Refrain: I will put a new spirit within you, *
    and you shall be my people.

Ezekiel 36:24–26,28b
Common Worship (1)

24 A Prayer of Habakkuk

Refrain: I will rejoice in the Lord; *
    I will exult in the God of my salvation.

1 O Lord, I have heard of your renown; *
    and I stand in awe, O Lord, of your work.
2 In our own time revive it,
    in our own time make it known; *
    in wrath may you remember mercy.
3 God came from Teman, *
    the Holy One from Mount Paran.
4 His glory covered the heavens, *
    and the earth was full of his praise.
5 The brightness was like the sun; *
    rays came forth from his hand,
    where his power lay hidden.
6 You came forth to save your people, *
    to save your anointed.
7 You trampled the sea with your horses, *
    churning the mighty waters.
8 I hear, and I tremble within; *
    my lips quiver at the sound.
9 Rottenness enters into my bones, *
    and my steps tremble beneath me.
10 I wait quietly for the day of calamity *
    to come upon the people who attack us.
11 Though the fig tree does not blossom,
    and no fruit is on the vines; *
    though the produce of the olive fails
    and the fields yield no food;
12 Though the flock is cut off from the fold *

and there is no herd in the stalls,
13 Yet I will rejoice in the Lord; *
    I will exult in the God of my salvation.
14 God, the Lord, is my strength; *
    he makes my feet like the feet of a deer,
    and makes me tread upon the heights.

Glory . . .

Refrain: I will rejoice in the Lord; *
    I will exult in the God of my salvation.

Habakkuk 3:2–4, 13a, 15–19

25 A Song of God's Reign

Refrain: See what the Lord our God has done *
    and exalt him in the sight of the living.

1 Blessed be God, who lives for ever, *
    whose reign endures throughout all ages.
2 Declare God's praise before the nations, *
    you who are the children of Israel.
3 For if our God has scattered you among them, *
    there too has he shown you his greatness.
4 Exalt him in the sight of the living, *
    because he is our God and our Father for ever.
5 Though God punishes you for your wickedness, *
    mercy will be shown to you all.
6 God will gather you from every nation, *
    from wherever you have been scattered.
7 When you turn to the Lord
    with all your heart and soul, *
    God will hide his face from you no more.
8 See what the Lord has done for you *
    and give thanks with a loud voice.
9 Praise the Lord of righteousness *
    and exalt the King of the ages.

Glory . . .

Refrain: See what the Lord our God has done *
    and exalt him in the sight of the living.

Tobit 13:1–6
A Daily Office SSF (3)

26 A Song of Thanksgiving from a Liberated People

Refrain: How blessed are those who love you! *
 They will rejoice in your peace.

1 Let all men speak, *
 and give him thanks in Jerusalem.
2 O Jerusalem, the holy city,
 he will afflict you for the deeds of your sons, *
 but again he will show mercy to the sons of the righteous.
3 Give thanks worthily to the Lord,
 and praise the King of the ages, *
 that his tent may be raised for you again with joy.
4 May he cheer those within you who are captives, *
 and love those within you who are distressed,
 to all generations for ever.
5 Many nations will come from afar
 to the name of the Lord God, *
 bearing gifts in their hands,
 gifts for the King of heaven.
6 Generations of generations *
 will give you joyful praise.
7 Rejoice and be glad
 for the sons of the righteous; *
 for they will be gathered together,
 and will praise the Lord of the righteous.
8 How blessed are those who love you! *
 They will rejoice in your peace.
9 Blessed are those who grieved over all your afflictions; *
 for they will rejoice for you upon seeing all your glory,
10 And they will be made glad for ever. *
 Let my soul praise God the great King.

 Glory . . .

Refrain: How blessed are those who love you! *
 They will rejoice in your peace.

Tobit 13:8–11,13–15 (RSV)

27 A Song of God's Mercy

Refrain: O Lord, you are great and glorious, *
    wonderful in strength, invincible.

1 Begin a song to my God with tambourines, *
    sing to my Lord with cymbals.
2 Raise to him a new psalm; *
    exalt him and call upon his name.
3 For God is the Lord who crushes wars. *
    I will sing to my God a new song:
4 O Lord, you are great and glorious, *
    wonderful in strength, invincible.
5 Let all your creatures serve you, *
    for you spoke, and they were made.
6 You sent forth your spirit, and it formed them; *
    there is none that can resist your voice.
7 For the mountains shall be shaken to their foundations with the waters; *
    before your glance the rocks shall melt like wax,
8 But to those who fear you you show mercy. *
    Whoever fears the Lord is great forever.

   Glory . . .

Refrain: O Lord, you are great and glorious, *
    wonderful in strength, invincible.

Judith 16:2–3a, 13–16 (RSV)

28 A Song of the Righteous

Refrain: God has found the righteous worthy *
    and their hope is of immortality.

1 The souls of the righteous are in the hand of God *
    and no torment will ever touch them.
2 In the eyes of the foolish, they seem to have died; *
    but they are at peace.
3 For though, in the sight of others, they were punished, *
    their hope is of immortality.
4 Having been disciplined a little,
    they will receive great good, *
    because God tested them and found them worthy.

Canticles

5 Like gold in the furnace, God tried them *
   and, like a sacrificial burnt offering, accepted them.
6 In the time of their visitation, they will shine forth *
   and will run like sparks through the stubble.
7 They will govern nations and rule over peoples *
   and God will reign over them for ever.

   Glory . . .

Refrain: God has found the righteous worthy *
   and their hope is of immortality.

Wisdom 3:1–8
trans. A Daily Office SSF (3)

29 *A Song of the Knowledge of Wisdom*

Refrain: Send wisdom forth from the holy heavens, *
   and from the throne of your glory send her.

1 O God of my ancestors and Lord of mercy,
   who have made all things by your word, *
   and by your wisdom have formed humankind
2 To have dominion over the creatures you have made,
   and rule the world in holiness and righteousness, *
   and pronounce judgement in uprightness of soul,
3 Give me the wisdom that sits by your throne, *
   and do not reject me from among your servants.
4 For I am your servant
   the son of your serving girl, *
   a man who is weak and short-lived,
   with little understanding of judgement and laws;
5 For even one who is perfect among human beings *
   will be regarded as nothing
   without the wisdom that comes from you.
6 With you is wisdom,
   she who knows your works *
   and was present when you made the world;
7 She understands what is pleasing in your sight *
   and what is right according to your commandments.
8 Send her forth from the holy heavens, *
   and from the throne of your glory send her,

9 That she may labour at my side, *
   and that I may learn what is pleasing to you.
10 For she knows and understands all things, *
   and she will guide me wisely in my actions
   and guard me with her glory.

   Glory . . .

Refrain: Send wisdom forth from the holy heavens, *
   and from the throne of your glory send her.

Wisdom 9:1–6, 9–11

30 A Song of God's Servants

Refrain: Fill Zion with your majesty, *
   and your temple with your glory.

1 Have mercy, O Lord, on the people called by your name, *
   on Israel, whom you have named your first-born,
2 Have pity on the city of your sanctuary, *
   Jerusalem, the place of your dwelling.
3 Fill Zion with your majesty, *
   and your temple with your glory.
4 Bear witness to those whom you created in the beginning, *
   and fulfil the prophecies spoken in your name.
5 Reward those who wait for you *
   and let your prophets be found trustworthy.
6 Hear, O Lord, the prayer of your servants,
   according to your goodwill toward your people, *
   and all who are on the earth will know that you are the Lord,
   the God of the ages.

   Glory . . .

Refrain: Fill Zion with your majesty, *
   and your temple with your glory.

Ecclesiasticus 36:17–22

31 A Song in Praise of the Works of God

Refrain: Ascribe majesty to the name of the Most High; *
   let all creation give thanks with praise.

1 Listen to me, my faithful children, *
   and blossom like a rose
   growing by a stream of water.
2 Send out fragrance like incense
   and sing a hymn of praise, *
   bless our God for all creation.
3 Ascribe majesty to the name of the Most High, *
   give thanks with praise, with songs on your lips and with harps.
4 All your works are good, O God, *
   and whatever you command will be done.

Glory . . .

Refrain: Ascribe majesty to the name of the Most High; *
   let all creation give thanks with praise.

Ecclesiasticus 39:13–16
trans. A Daily Office SSF (3)

32 The Prayer of Azariah in the Furnace

1 Blessed are you, O Lord, God of our ancestors,
   and worthy of praise; *
   and glorious is your name forever!
2 For you are just in all you have done; *
   all your works are true and your ways right,
   and all your judgements are true.
3 For we have sinned and broken your law in turning away from you; *
   in all matters we have sinned grievously.
4 For your name's sake do not give us up forever,
   and do not annul your covenant. *
   Do not withdraw your mercy from us,
5 For the sake of Abraham your beloved
   and for the sake of your servant Isaac and Israel your holy one, *
   to whom you promised to multiply their descendants
   like the stars of heaven and like the sand on the shore of the sea.
6 For we, O Lord, have become fewer than any other nation, *
   and are brought low this day in all the world
   because of our sins.

7 In our day we have no ruler, or prophet, or leader, *
    no burnt offering, or sacrifice, or oblation, or incense,
    no place to make an offering before you and to find mercy.
8 Yet with a contrite heart and a humble spirit may we be accepted, *
    as though it were with burnt offerings of rams and bulls,
    or with tens of thousands of fat lambs.
9 Such may our sacrifice be in your sight today,
    and may we unreservedly follow you, *
    for no shame will come to those who trust in you.
10 And now with all our heart we follow you; *
    we fear you and seek your presence.

   Glory . . .

Daniel 3:3–4,6,11–18

33 The Song of the Three

Benedictus es

1 Blessed are you, the God of our ancestors, *
    worthy to be praised and exalted for ever.
2 Blessed is your holy and glorious name, *
    worthy to be praised and exalted for ever.
3 Blessed are you, in your holy and glorious temple, *
    worthy to be praised and exalted for ever.
4 Blessed are you who look into the depths, *
    worthy to be praised and exalted for ever.
5 Blessed are you, enthroned on the cherubim, *
    worthy to be praised and exalted for ever.
6 Blessed are you on the throne of your kingdom, *
    worthy to be praised and exalted for ever.
7 Blessed are you in the heights of heaven, *
    worthy to be praised and exalted for ever.

   Bless the Father, the Son and the Holy Spirit: *
   worthy to be praised and exalted for ever.

The Song of the Three 29–34
Common Worship (1)

34 The Easter Anthems

1 Christ our Passover has been sacrificed for us, *
   so let us celebrate the feast,
2 Not with the old leaven of corruption and wickedness: *
   but with the unleavened bread of sincerity and truth.
3 Christ once raised from the dead dies no more: *
   death has no more dominion over him.
4 In dying he died to sin once for all: *
   in living he lives to God.
5 See yourselves therefore as dead to sin: *
   and alive to God in Jesus Christ our Lord.
6 Christ has been raised from the dead: *
   the firstfruits of those who sleep.
7 For as by man came death: *
   by man has come also the resurrection of the dead;
8 For as in Adam all die: *
   even so in Christ shall all be made alive.

Glory . . .

From 1 Corinthians 5:7, Romans 6:9
and 1 Corinthians 15:20
Common Worship (1)

35 A Song of God's Grace

Refrain: The glorious grace of God *
        is freely bestowed on us in the Beloved.

1 Blessed are you,
   the God and Father of our Lord Jesus Christ, *
   for you have blest us in Christ Jesus
   with every spiritual blessing in the heavenly places.
2 You chose us to be yours in Christ
   before the foundation of the world, *
   that we should be holy and blameless before you.
3 In love you destined us to be your children,
   through Jesus Christ, *
   according to the purpose of your will,
4 To the praise of your glorious grace, *
   which you freely bestowed on us in the Beloved.

5 In you, we have redemption
    through the blood of Christ, *
    the forgiveness of our sins,
6 According to the riches of your grace, *
    which you have lavished upon us.
7 You have made known to us, in all wisdom and insight, *
    the mystery of your will,
8 According to your purpose
    which you set forth in Christ, *
    as a plan for the fullness of time,
9 To unite all things in Christ, *
    things in heaven and things on earth.

Glory . . .

Refrain: The glorious grace of God *
    is freely bestowed on us in the Beloved.

Ephesians 1:3–10
trans. A Daily Office SSF (3)

36 The Song of Christ's Glory

Refrain: At the name of Jesus every knee shall bow.

1 Christ Jesus was in the form of God, *
    but he did not cling to equality with God.
2 He emptied himself, taking the form of a servant, *
    and was born in our human likeness.
3 Being found in human form, he humbled himself, *
    and became obedient unto death, even death on a cross.
4 Therefore, God has highly exalted him, *
    and bestowed on him the name above every name,
5 That at the name of Jesus, every knee should bow, *
    in heaven and on earth and under the earth.
6 And every tongue confess that Jesus Christ is Lord, *
    to the glory of God the Father.

Glory . . .

Refrain: At the name of Jesus every knee shall bow.

Philippians 2:5b-11
Common Worship (1)

Canticles 585

37 A Song of Redemption

Refrain: Christ is the image of the invisible God, *
　　　　the first-born of all creation.

1 The Father has delivered us
　　from the dominion of darkness, *
　　and transferred us to the kingdom of his beloved Son;
2 In whom we have redemption, *
　　the forgiveness of our sins.
3 He is the image of the invisible God, *
　　the first-born of all creation.
4 For in him all things were created, *
　　in heaven and on earth, visible and invisible.
5 All things were created through him and for him, *
　　he is before all things
　　and in him all things hold together.
6 He is the head of the body, the Church, *
　　he is the beginning, the first-born from the dead.
7 For it pleased God that in him
　　all fullness should dwell, *
　　and through him all things be reconciled to himself.

　Glory . . .

Refrain: Christ is the image of the invisible God, *
　　　　the first-born of all creation.

Colossians 1:13–20
trans. A Daily Office SSF (3)

38 A Song of Christ's Appearing

Refrain: Christ was believed in throughout the world *
　　　　and taken up in glory.

1 Christ Jesus was revealed in the flesh *
　　and vindicated in the Spirit.
2 He was seen by angels *
　　and proclaimed among the nations.
3 Believed in throughout the world, *
　　he was taken up in glory.
4 This will be made manifest at the proper time *
　　by the blessed and only Sovereign,

5 Who alone has immortality, *
   and dwells in unapproachable light.

To the King of kings and Lord of lords
be honour and eternal dominion. Amen.

Refrain: Christ was believed in throughout the world *
        and taken up in glory.

1 Timothy 3:16; 6:16
trans. A Daily Office SSF (3)

39 A Song of Christ the Servant

Refrain: Christ committed no sin, *
        no guile was found on his lips.

1 Christ suffered for you, leaving you an example, *
   that you should follow in his steps.
2 He committed no sin, no guile was found on his lips, *
   when he was reviled, he did not revile in turn.
3 When he suffered, he did not threaten, *
   but he trusted in God who judges justly.
4 Christ himself bore our sins in his body on the tree, *
   that he might die to sin and live to righteousness.
5 By his wounds, you have been healed,
   for you were straying like sheep, *
   but have now returned
     to the Shepherd and Guardian of our souls.

Glory . . .

Refrain: Christ committed no sin, *
        no guile was found on his lips.

1 Peter 2:21–25
trans. A Daily Office SSF (3)

40 A Song of Praise

Refrain: You created all things, O God, *
and are worthy of our praise for ever.

1 You are worthy, our Lord and God, *
   to receive glory and honour and power.
2 For you have created all things, *
   and by your will they have their being.
3 You are worthy, O Lamb, for you were slain, *
   and by your blood you ransomed for God
   saints from every tribe and language and nation.
4 You have made them to be a kingdom and priests serving our God, *
   and they will reign with you on earth.

To the One who sits on the throne and to the Lamb *
be blessing and honour and glory and might,
for ever and ever. Amen.

Refrain: You created all things, O God, *
and are worthy of our praise for ever.

Revelation 4:11; 5:9b-10
trans. A Daily Office SSF (3)

41 A Song of the Redeemed

Refrain: Salvation belongs to our God, *
who will guide us to springs of living water.

1 Behold, a great multitude *
   which no one could number,
2 From every nation,
   from all tribes and peoples and tongues, *
   standing before the throne and the Lamb.
3 They were clothed in white robes
   and had palms in their hands, *
   and they cried with a loud voice, saying,
4 'Salvation belongs to our God *
   who sits on the throne,
   and to the Lamb.'
5 These are they
   who have come out of the great tribulation, *

     they have washed their robes
     and made them white in the blood of the Lamb;
6 Therefore they stand before the throne of God, *
     whom they serve day and night within the temple.
7 And the One who sits upon the throne *
     will shelter them with his presence.
8 They shall never again feel hunger or thirst, *
     the sun shall not strike them,
     nor any scorching heat.
9 For the Lamb at the heart of the throne *
     will be their Shepherd,
10 He will guide them to springs of living water, *
     and God will wipe away every tear from their eyes.

  To the One who sits on the throne and to the Lamb *
  be blessing and honour and glory and might,
     for ever and ever. Amen.

Refrain: Salvation belongs to our God *
     who will guide us to springs of living water.

Revelation 7:9–10, 14b-17
trans. A Daily Office SSF (3)

42 *A Song of the Kingdom of our God*

Refrain: Rejoice you heavens *
     and those who dwell in them!

1 We give you thanks, Lord God almighty,
     who are and who were, *
     for you have taken your great power and begun to reign.
2 The nations raged but your wrath has come, *
     and the time for judging the dead,
3 For rewarding your servants, the prophets and saints *
     and all who fear your name, both small and great.
4 Now have come the salvation and the power
     and the kingdom of God *
     and the authority of his Messiah,
5 For the accuser of our comrades has been thrown down, *
     who accuses them day and night before our God.
6 But they have conquered him by the blood of the Lamb *
     and by the word of their testimony,

7 For they did not cling to life even in the face of death. *
 Rejoice then, you heavens and those who dwell in them!

 To the One who sits on the throne and to the Lamb *
 be blessing and honour and glory and might,
 for ever and ever. Amen.

Refrain: Rejoice you heavens *
 and those who dwell in them!

Revelation 11:17–18;12:10b-12a

43 *A Song of Moses and of the Lamb*

Refrain: All nations shall come and worship you, *
 and share in the feast of your Kingdom, O Christ.

 1 Great and wonderful are your deeds, *
 Lord God the almighty.
 2 Just and true are your ways, *
 O Ruler of the nations.
 3 Who shall not revere you and praise your name, O Lord? *
 for you alone are holy.
 4 All nations shall come and worship in your presence, *
 for your just dealings have been revealed.

 To the One who sits on the throne and to the Lamb
 be blessing and honour and glory and might,
 for ever and ever. Amen.

Refrain: All nations shall come and worship you, *
 and share in the feast of your Kingdom, O Christ.

Revelation 15:3–4
trans. A Daily Office SSF (3)

44 *A Song of the Lamb*

Refrain: Let us rejoice and exult *
 and give glory and homage to our God.

 1 Salvation and glory and power belong to our God, *
 whose judgements are true and just.
 2 Praise our God, all you his servants, *
 all who fear him, both small and great.

3 The Lord our God, the Almighty, reigns: *
  let us rejoice and exult and give him the glory.
4 For the marriage of the Lamb has come *
  and his bride has made herself ready.
5 Blessed are those who are invited *
  to the wedding banquet of the Lamb.

  To the One who sits on the throne and to the Lamb *
  be blessing and honour and glory and might,
  for ever and ever. Amen.

Refrain: Let us rejoice and exult *
  and give glory and homage to our God.

Revelation 19: 1b, 5b, 6b-7, 9b
Common Worship (1)

VII PRAYER IN THE EVENING

Evening Prayers

Evening Prayers may begin with the Angelus *or* Regina Caeli *(see page 1) or conclude with one of the Final Anthems to the Blessed Virgin Mary (see page 668).*

In the name of the Father, and of the Son, and of the Holy Spirit.

Pater Noster

Our Father, who art in heaven,
hallowed be thy name;
Thy kingdom come,
Thy will be done, on earth as it is in heaven.
Give us this day our daily bread,
and forgive us our trespasses,
as we forgive those who trespass against us;
and lead us not into temptation,
but deliver us from evil.
For thine is the kingdom, the power and the glory,
for ever and ever.

Ave Maria

Hail Mary, full of grace,
the Lord is with thee.
Blessed art thou among women
and blessed is the fruit of thy womb, Jesus.
Holy Mary, Mother of God,
pray for us sinners, now, and at the hour of our death.

Gloria Patri

Glory be to the Father, and to the Son, and to the Holy Spirit:
as it was in the beginning, is now and ever shall be,
world without end.

or

Glory to the Father, and to the Son, and to the Holy Spirit:
as it was in the beginning, is now, and shall be for ever.

Apostles' Creed

I believe in God,
the Father almighty,
maker of heaven and earth.
And in Jesus Christ, his only Son, our Lord,
who was conceived by the Holy Ghost,
born of the Virgin Mary
suffered under Pontius Pilate,
was crucified, dead and buried.
He descended into hell.
The third day he rose again from the dead;
he ascended into heaven
and sitteth on the right hand of God the Father almighty.
From thence he shall come to judge the quick and the dead.
I believe in the Holy Ghost;
the holy catholic church,
the communion of saints,
the forgiveness of sins,
the resurrection of the body;
and the life everlasting.

Book of Common Prayer (2)

or

I believe in God,
the Father almighty,
creator of heaven and earth.

I believe in Jesus Christ, his only Son, our Lord.
He was conceived by the power of the Holy Spirit
and born of the Virgin Mary.
He suffered under Pontius Pilate,
was crucified, died and was buried.
He descended to the dead.
On the third day he rose again.
He ascended into heaven,
and is seated at the right hand of the Father.
He will come again to judge the living and the dead.

I believe in the Holy Spirit,
the holy catholic church,
the communion of saints,
the forgiveness of sins,
the resurrection of the body;
and the life everlasting.

ELLC (15)

As my evening prayer rises before you, O God,
so may your mercy come down upon me
   to cleanse my heart
and set me free to sing your praise,
now and for ever.

A Daily Office SSF* (3)

Summary of the Law

Our Lord Jesus Christ said, the first commandment is this:
'Hear, O Israel, the Lord our God is the only Lord.
You shall love the Lord your God with all your heart,
with all your soul, and with all your mind,
and with all your strength.'

The second is this: 'Love your neighbour as yourself.'
There is no other commandment greater than these.
On these two commandments hang all the law and the prophets.

Mark 12:29–31

Confession of sins

Almighty God,
long-suffering and of great goodness:
I confess to you,
I confess with my whole heart
my neglect and forgetfulness of your commandments,
my wrong doing, thinking, and speaking;
the hurts I have done to others,
and the good I have left undone.
O God, forgive me, for I have sinned against you;
and raise me to newness of life;
through Jesus Christ our Lord.

Common Worship (1)

or

My God, for love of you
I desire to hate and forsake all sins
by which I have ever displeased you;
and I resolve by the help of your grace
to commit them no more;
and to avoid all opportunities of sin.
Help long-suffering and of great goodness:
I confess to you,
I confess with my whole heart
my neglect and forgetfulness of your commandments,
my wrong doing, thinking, and speaking;
the hurts I have done to others,
and the good I have left undone.
O God, forgive me, for I have sinned against you;
and raise me to newness of life;
through Jesus Christ our Lord.

Common Worship (1)

May almighty God have mercy on us,
forgive us our sins,
and bring us to everlasting life,
through Jesus Christ our Lord.

Evening Prayers

Almighty and most merciful Father,
we have erred and strayed from thy ways like lost sheep,
we have followed too much the devices and desires of our own hearts,
we have offended against thy holy laws,
we have left undone those things which we ought to have done,
and we have done those things which we ought not to have done,
and there is no health in us:
but thou, O Lord, have mercy upon us miserable offenders;
spare thou them, O God, which confess their faults,
restore thou them that are penitent,
according to thy promises declared unto mankind
in Christ Jesu our Lord:
and grant, O most merciful Father, for his sake,
that we may hereafter
live a godly, righteous, and sober life,
to the glory of thy holy name.

Book of Common Prayer (2)

Grant, we beseech thee, merciful Lord, to thy faithful people pardon and peace; that they may be cleansed from all their sins, and serve thee with a quiet mind; through Jesus Christ our Lord.

Book of Common Prayer (2)

Prayer for growth in the Christian life

Eternal Light, shine in our hearts,
Eternal Goodness, deliver us from evil,
Eternal Power, be our support,
Eternal Wisdom, scatter the darkness of our ignorance,
Eternal Pity, have mercy upon us;
that with all our heart and mind and soul and strength
we may seek your face and be brought by your infinite mercy
to your holy presence; through Jesus Christ our Lord.

Alcuin
Eric Milner-White and G. W. Briggs (18)

Evening Prayer of Thanksgiving

Almighty Father, in your loving providence
every hair of our head is counted,
every tear is noted, and every prayer heard.

We thank you for your faithful goodness to us,
and ask for a peaceful evening, and blessed rest.

Ampleforth (7)

The Lord is everything to me.
   He is the strength of my heart,
   and the light of my mind.
He inclines my heart to everything good;
he strengthens it;
he also gives me good thoughts.
   He is my rest and my joy;
   he is my faith, hope and love.
He is my food and drink,
my raiment, my dwelling place.

Saint John of Kronstadt (10)

To become more like Jesus

God, our Father, you redeemed us
and made us your children in Christ.
Through him you have saved us from death
and given us your divine life of grace.
By becoming more like Jesus on earth,
may we come to share his glory in heaven.
Give us the peace of your kingdom,
which this world does not give.
By your loving care
protect the good you have given us.
Open our eyes to the wonders of your love
that we may serve you with a willing heart.

(13)

For faith in God's truths

Merciful Lord, hear our prayer.
May we who have received the gift of faith
share forever in the new life of Christ.
May the continuing work of the Redeemer
bring us eternal joy.
You have freed us from the darkness of error and sin.

Help us believe in your truths faithfully.
Grant that everything we do
may be led by the knowledge of your truth.

(13)

For God's guidance

Father in heaven, you made us your children.
Free us from darkness and keep us in the light of your truth.
The light of Jesus has scattered the darkness of hatred and sin.
Called to that light we ask for your guidance.
Form our lives in your truth.
Through the Holy Eucharist give us the power of your grace
that we may walk in the light of Jesus and serve him faithfully.

(13)

For forgiveness of sin

Heavenly Father, Creator of all,
may we serve you with all our hearts
and know your forgiveness in our lives.
Forgive our sins
and give us your life, your grace and your holiness.
Look upon us in our moments of need,
for you alone can give us true peace.
May we share in the peace of Christ
who offered his life in the service of all.
Help us with your kindness.
Make us strong through the Eucharist.
May we put into action
the saving mystery we celebrate in the Eucharist.
Protect us with your love
and prepare us for eternal happiness.

(13)

O my God,
whatever is nearer to me than thou,
things of this earth and things more naturally pleasing to me
will be sure to interrupt the sight of thee,
unless thy grace interfere.

Keep thou my eyes, my heart,
from any such miserable tyranny.
Break my bonds, raise my heart.
Keep my whole being fixed on thee.
Let me never lose sight of thee,
and while I gaze on thee,
let my love of thee grow more and more every day.

John Henry Newman

Longing for God

For those who love you, Lord,
you have prepared blessings which no eye has seen;
fill our hearts with longing for you,
that, loving you in all things and above all things,
we may obtain your promises,
which exceed every heart's desire.

ICEL (5)

God be in my head, and in my understanding;
God be in mine eyes, and in my looking;
God be in my mouth, and in my speaking;
God be in my heart, and in my thinking;
God be at mine end, and at my departing.

Sarum Primer 1514

Bring us, O Lord God, at our last awakening
into the house and gate of heaven,
to enter into that gate and dwell in that house,
where there shall be no darkness nor dazzling
   but one equal light,
no noise nor silence but one equal music,
no fears nor hopes but one equal possession,
no ends nor beginnings but one equal eternity,
in the habitations of thy majesty and thy glory,
world without end.

adapted from John Donne,
Eric Milner-White (16)

Abide with us, O most blessed and merciful Saviour, for it is toward evening and the day is far spent. As long as thou art present with us, we are in the light. When thou art present all is brightness, all is sweetness. We discourse with thee, watch with thee, live with thee and lie down with thee. Abide then with us, O thou whom our soul loveth, thou Sun of righteousness with healing under thy wings arise in our hearts; make thy light then to shine in darkness as a perfect day in the dead of night.

Henry Vaughan

O Lord support us all the day long,
till the shades lengthen and the evening comes,
and the busy world is hushed
and the fever of life is over
and our work is done.
Then in thy mercy give us a safe lodging
and a holy rest
and peace at the last.

John Henry Newman*

Lead, kindly Light, amid the encircling gloom,
Lead thou me on;
The night is dark, and I am far from home,
Lead thou me on.
Keep thou my feet; I do not ask to see
The distant scene; one step enough for me.

I was not ever thus, nor prayed that thou
Shouldest lead me on;
I loved to choose and see my path; but now
Lead thou me on.
I loved the garish day, and, spite of fears,
Pride ruled my will: remember not past years.

So long thy power hath blest me, sure it still
Will lead me on
O'er moor and fen, o'er crag and torrent, till
The night is gone,
And with the morn those angel faces smile,
Which I have loved long since, and lost awhile.

John Henry Newman

Into your hands, Lord and Father,
we commend our souls and our bodies,
our parents and our homes,
our friends and our neighbours,
our family and all who have done good to us,
our loved ones who have died,
all your people who faithfully believe
and all who need your pity and protection.
Enlighten us with your grace:
may we never be separated from you,
who are one God in Trinity,
God everlasting.

Saint Edmund of Abingdon*

Grant us, O Lord, the peace of claiming thee in death as our Father, because we have served thee in life as our God; for Jesus Christ's sake.

Eric Milner-White (17)

In preparation for Communion the next day

As watchmen wait for the morning, so do our souls long for you, O Christ. Come with the dawning of the day, and make yourselves known to us in the breaking of bread; for you are our God for ever and ever.

Mozarabic

Let us bless the Lord.
Thanks be to God.

May the Lord bless us, and keep us from all evil,
and bring us to everlasting life.

or

May the souls of the faithful departed,
through the mercy of God, rest in peace.

Intercessions

A General Intercession

O God, the creator and preserver of all mankind, we humbly beseech thee for all sorts and conditions of men; that thou wouldest be pleased to make thy ways known unto them, thy saving health unto all nations. More especially we pray for the good estate of the Catholic Church; that it may be so guided and governed by thy good Spirit, that all who profess and call themselves Christians may be led into the way of truth, and hold the faith in unity of spirit, in the bond of peace, and in righteousness of life. Finally we commend to thy fatherly goodness all those, who are any ways afflicted or distressed in mind, body, or estate; [*especially those for whom our prayers are desired*;] that it may please thee to comfort and relieve them, according to their several necessities, giving them patience under their sufferings, and a happy issue out of all their afflictions. And this we beg for Jesus Christ his sake.

Peter Gunning (2)

For a modern version of this prayer, see page 647.

1 The Church

For the Church

O God of unchangeable power and eternal light,
look favourably on your whole Church,
that wonderful and sacred mystery;
and by the operation of your providence,
carry out the work of human salvation;
and let the whole world feel and see
that things which were cast down are being raised up,
that those things which had grown old are being made new,

and that all things are returning to perfection,
through him from whom they took their origin,
Jesus Christ our Lord.

Gelasian Sacramentary

For the Church

Most gracious Father,
we pray for your holy catholic Church:
fill it with all truth,
and in all truth with all peace;
where it is corrupt, purge it;
where it is in error, direct it;
where anything is amiss, reform it;
where it is true, strengthen and confirm it;
where it is in want, furnish it.
where it is divided, heal it
   and unite it in your love;
through Jesus Christ our Lord.

Thomas Ken* (3)

For the Church

God our Shepherd, give to the Church a new vision and a new charity, new wisdom and fresh understanding, the revival of her brightness and the renewal of her unity; that the eternal message of thy Son, undefiled by the traditions of men, may be hailed as the good news of the new age; through him who maketh all things new, Jesus Christ our Lord.

Percy Dearmer

For the unity of the Church

Our God, amidst the deplorable division of your Church, let us never widen its breaches, but give us universal charity to all who are called by your name. Deliver us from the sins and errors, the schisms and heresies of the age. Give us grace daily to pray for the peace of your Church, and earnestly to seek it and to excite all we can to praise and to love you; through Jesus Christ, our one Saviour and Redeemer.

Thomas Ken*

For unity

O God, the Father of our Lord Jesus Christ, our only Saviour, the Prince of Peace: give us grace seriously to lay to heart the great dangers we are in by our unhappy divisions. Take away all hatred and prejudice, and whatsoever else may hinder us from godly union and concord: that, as there is but one Body, and one Spirit, and one hope of our calling, one Lord, one faith, one baptism, one God and Father of us all, so may we henceforth be all of one heart, and of one soul, united in one holy bond of truth and peace, of faith and charity, and may with one mind and one mouth glorify thee; through Jesus Christ our Lord.

Accession Service of King George I

For unity

Vouchsafe, we pray, almighty God, to grant to the whole Christian people unity, peace, and true concord, both visible and invisible, when you will and as you will; through Jesus Christ our Lord.

John Keble* (20)

For the Pope or Chief Bishop

O God, the shepherd and ruler of all the faithful,
look down favourably upon your servant *N*,
whom you have been pleased to appoint pastor over your Church;
grant, we beseech you, that he may benefit both by word and example
those over whom he is set,
and thus attain life eternal,
together with the flock committed to his care.
Through Christ our Lord.

For the Bishop

God, eternal shepherd,
you tend your Church in many ways,
and rule us with love.
Help your chosen servant *N*
as pastor for Christ,
to watch over your flock.
Help him to be a faithful teacher,
a wise administrator and a holy priest.
Though Christ our Lord.

For bishops and pastors

Almighty and everlasting God, who alone workest great marvels: Send down upon our bishops and other pastors, and all congregations committed to their charge, the healthful spirit of thy grace; and that they may truly please thee, pour upon them the continual dew of thy blessing. Grant this, O Lord, for the honour of our advocate and mediator, Jesus Christ.

Book of Common Prayer (2)

For bishops, priests and deacons

O God, who makest thine angels spirits and thy ministers a flame of fire, vouchsafe, we beseech thee, to stir up and confirm the sacred grace in all stewards of thy mysteries, that as ministering spirits they may gather out of thy kingdom all things that offend, and may kindle in the hearts of all, that fire which thou camest to send upon the earth; who with the Father and the Holy Ghost, livest and reignest, world without end.

Henry Parry Liddon

For the clergy

O Lord Jesus Christ,
who at your first coming
sent your messenger to prepare your way;
grant that the ministers and stewards of your mysteries
may likewise so make ready and prepare your way,
by turning the hearts of the disobedient to the wisdom of the just,
that at your second coming to judge the world,
we may be found an acceptable people in your sight;
you live and reign with the Father and the Holy Spirit,
ever one God, world without end.

John Cosin*

For the sacred ministry

Almighty God, look mercifully upon the world, which thou hast redeemed by the blood of thy dear Son, and incline the hearts of many to offer themselves for the sacred ministry of thy Church; so that by their labours thy light may shine in the darkness, and the coming of thy kingdom may be hastened by the perfecting of thine elect, through the same Jesus Christ our Lord.

Richard Meux Benson

For those in training for the sacred ministry

O thou true Light, that lightest every man that cometh into the world, do thou in thy mercy touch the hearts and lighten the understanding of all who are preparing for thy service, that they may readily acknowledge and cheerfully obey all that thou wouldst have them believe and practise to the benefit of thy people and their own salvation; who livest and reignest God for ever and ever.
Henry Parry Liddon

For the parish

Almighty and everlasting God, who dost govern all things in heaven and earth, mercifully hear the supplications of us thy servants; and grant to this parish all things needful for its spiritual welfare: schools wherein to bring up the young in thy faith and fear; ministers to labour in this portion of the vineyard; churches complete in the beauty of holiness. Strengthen and confirm the faithful, protect and guide the children; visit and relieve the sick and afflicted; turn and soften the wicked; rouse the careless; recover the fallen; restore the penitent; remove all hindrances to the advancement of thy truth; and bring all to be of one heart and mind within the fold of thy holy Church; to the honour and glory of thy blessed name, through Jesus Christ our Lord.
William John Butler

Prayer of the Confraternity of the Blessed Sacrament

Almighty God, look we pray, on the face of your beloved Son,
and for the sake of his merits
mercifully hear the prayers
which throughout our Confraternity
we continually offer to you;
and grant us unity, a true faith and a life agreeable to your will;
through Jesus Christ our Lord.

Prayer of the Society of the Holy Cross

We should glory in the cross of our Lord Jesus Christ,
for he is our salvation, our life and our resurrection.
Through him we are saved and made free.

Father, your Son showed the depth of this love
when, for our sake, he opened his arms on the cross;
and has commanded us to love one another.

Keep the brothers of our Society united in love and faith.
Through the power of the Cross
impressed inwardly upon our lives
and expressed outwardly in our work,
may we come to know your love and truth
through Christ our Lord.

Catholic League Prayer

Almighty God,
you gave us your only-begotten Son Jesus Christ
to be the way, the truth and the life;
we ask you to send your blessing upon all members of the Catholic League.
Inflame us with the love of the Sacred Heart
and deepen in us faith and penitence and zeal for your service.
By the prayers of the holy Virgin Mary, our patron,
grant peace and unity to your Church:
convert the hearts of all our people to our truth
and guide and prosper all we do in the League
to the glory of your name
and the extension of your kingdom.
We ask this through Christ our Lord.

For Forward in Faith

Father,
you sent Augustine to the people of England
to proclaim the faith delivered to Saint Peter
and the apostles.
May the work he began be renewed in this land
and continue to prosper.
Lord,
those who are divided you unite,
and those who are united you support.
Help us to live up to the call you have given us,
so that we may bear witness to the truth
and strive that all believers may be united
in the bond of peace and love.

For priestly vocations

O Lord, my God,
you renew the Church in every age
by raising up priests outstanding in holiness,
living witnesses of your unchanging love.
In your plan for our salvation
you provide shepherds for your people.
Fill the hearts of young men
with the spirit of courage and love
that they may answer your call generously.
Give parents the grace
to encourage vocations in their family
by prayer and good example.
Raise up worthy priests for your altars
and ardent but gentle servants of the Gospel.
Give the Church more priests
and keep them faithful in their love and service.
May many young men choose to serve you
by devoting themselves to the service of your people.

(13)

For vocations

Father, in your plan for our salvation
you provide shepherds for your people.
Fill your Church with the spirit of courage and love.
Raise up worthy ministers for your altars and
   ardent but true servants of the gospel.

ICEL (5)

For children in the Church

O Lord Jesus Christ, who didst take into thine arms the children brought to thee for blessing: bless always and in all places the children of thy Church, and thy Church in telling them of thee, that they may grow into thy likeness, keeping innocency, obedient to thy will and happy in thy house; for thy tender mercy's sake.

Eric Milner-White (16)

For a devoted laity in the Church

O Lord, our God,
you called us to be your Church.
As we gather together in your name,
may we love, honour, and follow your Son
to life eternal in the kingdom he promised.
Let our worship always be sincere,
and help us to find your saving love
in the Church and its sacraments.
Fill with the Spirit of Christ
we whom you call to live in the midst of the
world and its concerns.
Help us by our work on earth
to build up your eternal kingdom.
May we be effective witnesses
to the truth of the gospel
and make your Church a living presence
in the midst of the world.
Increase the gifts you have given your Church
that we may remain faithful
and continue to grow in holiness
in imitation of your beloved Son.

(13)

For those on retreat

O Lord Jesus Christ, who saidst to thy apostles, 'Come ye apart into a desert place and rest awhile,' for there were many coming and going: grant, we pray, to thy servants when they gather together in retreat, that they may rest awhile with thee. May they so seek thee, whom their souls desire to love, that they may both find thee and be found by thee. And grant such love and such wisdom to accompany the words which shall be spoken in thy name, that they may not fall to the ground, but may be helpful in leading us onward through the toils of our pilgrimage to that rest, which remaineth to the people of God; where, nevertheless, they rest not day and night from thy perfect service; who with the Father and the Holy Spirit art alive and reignest, one God, for ever and ever.

Richard Meux Benson

For perseverance

O Lord God, when thou givest to thy servants to endeavour any great matter, grant us also to know that it is not the beginning, but the continuing of the same unto the end, until it be thoroughly finished, which yieldeth the true glory; through him who for the finishing of thy work laid down his life, our Redeemer, Jesus Christ.

Sir Francis Drake (16)

For missionaries

Blessed Jesus, Lord of the harvest, send forth, we beseech thee, labourers into thy harvest, and by thy Holy Spirit, stir the hearts of many, that they may be ready to spend and be spent in thy service, and if it please thee, so to lose their life in this world, that they may gather fruit unto life eternal; Lord Jesus, lover of souls.

Robert Milman (20)

For perseverance in preaching the gospel

O blessed Jesus, our Lord and our Master, who wast pleased to thirst for our souls, grant that we may not be satisfied with the pleasures of this lower life, but even thirst for the salvation of the souls thou didst die to save, and, above all, to thirst for thee; grant this for thine own name's sake.

Edward King

For conversion of unbelievers

O God, who in the work of creation
commanded the light to shine out of darkness;
we pray that the light of the glorious gospel of Christ
may shine into the hearts of all your people,
dispelling the darkness of ignorance and unbelief,
and revealing to them the knowledge of your glory
in the face of Jesus Christ our Lord.

David Silk (21)

For conversion of unbelievers

O God of all the nations of the earth, remember the multitudes who, though created in your image, have not known you, nor the dying of your Son their

Saviour Jesus Christ; and grant that by the prayers and labours of your holy Church they may be delivered from all ignorance and unbelief, and brought to worship you; through him whom you have sent to be the Resurrection and the Life of all people, your Son Jesus Christ our Lord.

Saint Francis Xavier (20)

In penitence for Christian persecution of the Jews

O God, we are conscious that many centuries of blindness have blinded our eyes so that we no longer see the beauty of thy chosen people, nor recognize in their faces the features of our privileged brethren. We realize that the mark of Cain stands upon our foreheads. Across the centuries our brother Abel has lain in the blood which we drew or which we caused to be shed by forgetting thy love. Forgive us for the curse we falsely attached to their name as Jews. Forgive us for crucifying thee a second time in their flesh. For we knew not what we did.

Pope John XXIII (22)

2 The World

For the Queen

Almighty God, the fountain of all goodness, we humbly beseech thee to bless our Sovereign Lady, Queen Elizabeth, and all who are in authority under her; that they may order all things in wisdom, righteousness and peace, to the honour of thy holy name, and the good of thy Church and people; through Jesus Christ our Lord.

Book of Common Prayer (2)

For the Royal Family

Almighty God, the fountain of all goodness, we humbly beseech thee to bless Elizabeth the Queen Mother, Philip Duke of Edinburgh, Charles Prince of Wales, and all the Royal Family. Endue them with thy Holy Spirit; enrich them with thy heavenly grace; prosper them with all happiness; and bring them to thine everlasting kingdom; through Jesus Christ our Lord.

Book of Common Prayer (2)

For peace

Almighty God, from whom all thoughts of truth and peace proceed: kindle, we pray thee, in the hearts of all men the true love of peace, and guide with thy pure and peaceable wisdom those who take counsel for the nations of the earth; that in tranquillity thy kingdom may go forward, till the earth is filled with the knowledge of thy love; through Jesus Christ our Lord.

Francis Paget

For justice

O God, the King of righteousness, lead us, we pray, in the ways of justice and of peace. Inspire us to break down all oppression and wrong, to gain for every one their due reward, and from every one their due service; that each may live for all, and all may care for each, in the name of Jesus Christ our Lord.

William Temple (20)

For justice

Heavenly Father, in your word you have given us a vision of that holy City to which the nations of the world bring their glory: behold and visit, we pray, the cities of the earth. Renew the ties of mutual regard which form our civic life. Send us honest and able leaders. Enable us to eliminate poverty, prejudice, and oppression, that peace may prevail with righteousness, and justice with order, and that men and women from different cultures and with differing talents may find with one another the fulfilment of their humanity; through Jesus Christ our Lord.

Book of Common Prayer 1979, ECUSA (28)

For social justice and responsibility

Eternal God,
in whose perfect realm
no sword is drawn but the sword of righteousness,
and no strength known but the strength of love:
so guide and inspire the work of those who seek your kingdom
that all your people may find their security
in that love which casts out fear
and in the fellowship revealed to us
in Jesus Christ our Saviour.

Common Worship (1)

For those engaged in commerce and industry

Almighty God and Father,
you have so ordered our life
   that we are dependent on one another:
prosper those engaged in commerce and industry
and direct their minds and hands
that they may rightly use your gifts in the service of others;
through Jesus Christ our Lord.

Common Worship (1)

For those who work on land or sea

Almighty God,
whose will it is that the earth and the sea
   should bear fruit in due season:
bless the labours of those who work on land and sea,
grant us a good harvest
and the grace always to rejoice in your fatherly care;
through Jesus Christ our Lord.

Common Worship (1)

For immigrants

Father, conscious that your Son, while still an infant, made his home in a foreign land, we pray for all those from other countries who now live among us. May their customs and culture be appreciated and may they be offered true Christian friendship and understanding as a token of gratitude for that welcome which was once offered to your only Son.

Michael Buckley (24)

For universities and schools

O God, who dost begin and sustain all progress up to thee in thy kingdom: bless our universities and schools, that they may convey to thy children thy best gifts of truth and godliness, and prepare them for the perfect citizenship alike of earth and heaven; through Jesus Christ our Lord.

Eric Milner-White (16)

For students

Grant, Lord, to all students,
to love and know that which is worth loving and knowing,
to praise that which pleases you most,
to esteem that which is most precious to you,
and to dislike whatsoever is evil in your eyes.

Thomas à Kempis

For animals and for the integrity of creation

Heavenly Father, your Holy Spirit gives breath to all living things; renew us by this same Spirit, that we may learn to respect what you have given and care for what you have made, through Jesus Christ our Lord.

Andrew Linzey (30)

For scientists

Almighty and everlasting God, you made the universe with all its marvellous order, its atoms, worlds and galaxies, and the infinite complexity of living creatures: grant that, as we probe the mysteries of your creation, we may come to know you more truly, and more surely fulfil our role in your eternal purpose; in the name of Jesus Christ our Lord.

Book of Common Prayer 1979, ECUSA (28)

For those who work with their hands

O blessed Saviour, who wast pleased thyself to be reckoned among craftsmen, bless all those who labour with their hands, that their work may be done for thy honour and rewarded with thy approval; for thine own name's sake.

Richard Meux Benson

For prisons and prisoners

Lord Jesus, for our sake you were condemned as a criminal: visit our gaols and prisons with your pity and judgement. Remember all prisoners, and bring the guilty to repentance and amendment of life according to your will, and give them hope for their future. When any are held unjustly, bring them release; forgive us, and teach us to improve our justice. Remember those who work in these institutions; keep them humane and compassionate; and save them from becoming brutal or callous. And since what we do for those in prison, O Lord, we do for you, constrain us to improve their lot. All this we ask for your mercy's sake.

Book of Common Prayer 1979, ECUSA (28)

For the caring professions

We thank you, O God, for all who work in the caring professions:
for police and probation officers;
for youth leaders and school teachers;
for welfare officers and psychiatric social workers;
for doctors and nurses and many others.
We pray that you will give to all such people
   sympathy and understanding,
   love and firmness,
and the deeper knowledge that Jesus Christ
   is the only one who can make people truly whole.
We ask this for his sake,
our Saviour and our Lord.

Peter Markby* (29)

For art and music

We magnify your name, O Lord,
for the vision of your holiness
revealed in works of art and musical performance.
We bless you for the ingenuity of artists and musicians,
the awesome majesty of their imaginations
and the intricacy of their skill.
As our lives are ennobled by wonder,
help us always to look beyond
to the beauty of holiness and the glory of heaven
where you live and reign in eternal splendour.

AB (8)

3 Human Love and Human Need

For families

God, from whom all fatherhood in heaven and earth descends,
Father, who are Love and Life,
ensure that every human family on earth shall become,
    through your Son, Jesus Christ, 'born of woman',
    and through the Holy Spirit, the source of divine charity,
a true shrine of life and love for the generations which are always renewing themselves.
Ensure that your grace shall guide the thoughts and the works of spouses
    towards the good of their families and of all families in the world.
Ensure that the young generations shall find firm support in the family
    for their humanity and their growth in truth and love.
Ensure that love, reinforced by the grace of the sacrament of Matrimony
    shall show itself to be stronger than any weakness and every crisis
    through which our families pass at times.
Ensure, finally, we ask you,
through intercession of the Holy Family of Nazareth,
that the Church, in the midst of all the nations of the earth,
    may fruitfully accomplish her mission in the family and through the family,
through Christ our Lord,
who is the way, the truth and the life,
for ever and ever.

Pope John Paul II (25)

For husband or wife

Bless your servant my *husband* with health of body and of spirit. Let the hand of your blessing be upon *his* head, night and day, and support *him* in all necessities, strengthen *him* in all temptations, comfort *him* in all *his* sorrows, and let *him* be your servant in all changes; and make us both to dwell with you for ever in your favour, in the light of your countenance, and in your glory.

Jeremy Taylor, The Rule and Exercise of Holy Living*

For a father

Heavenly Father,
you entrusted your Son Jesus,
the child of Mary,

to the care of Joseph, an earthly father.
Bless *N* *[this man]*
as he cares for his family.
Give him strength and wisdom,
tenderness and patience;
support him in the work he has to do,
protecting those who look to him
as we look to you,
for love and salvation
through Jesus Christ
our rock and defender.

A.B .
Common Worship (1)

For child and parents

God our Father, we pray to you for all
who have the care of *this child*.
Guide them with your Holy Spirit,
that they may bring *him* up
in the ways of truth and love.
Through their care enable *him* to grow in grace
and become daily more like your Son,
our Saviour Jesus Christ.

Common Worship (1)

For a mother after a miscarriage

O God, the giver of all comfort,
look down on *N* who has known the joy of a new life within,
and the desolation of losing that life;
do not hide your face from her distress,
but hear her when she calls to you;
restore her to health in body and spirit
and renew in her hope, faith and love,
for the sake of your Son
who brought peace to the grieving hearts of mothers,
Jesus Christ our Lord.

Janet Henderson (26)

For a child with special needs

A parent would change 'them' and 'their' to 'us' and 'our'.

Living God, creator of us all,
we thank you for entrusting *N*
into the special care of *N* and *N*.
Give *them* and all who surround *them*
wisdom and understanding, courage and patience;
give *them* grace to put aside fear and anxiety
and to fulfil your purposes;
fill *their* hearts with your unfailing love,
that *N* may grow up secure in giving and receiving love
and in the enjoyment of your presence,
to enrich our lives and the lives of others
in ways beyond our imagining,
in Jesus Christ our Lord.

Common Worship (1)

For an engaged couple

Lord of love,
we pray for *N* and *N*.
Be with them in all their preparations
and on their wedding day.
Give them your love in their hearts
throughout their married life together,
through Jesus Christ our Lord.

Common Worship (1)

For friends

Be pleased, O Lord, to remember my friends, all that have prayed for me and all that have done me good. Do good to them, and return all their kindness double in their own lives, rewarding them with blessings, making them holy with your graces, and bringing them to glory.

Jeremy Taylor, The Rule and Exercise of Holy Living*

For enemies

Almighty and tender Lord Jesus Christ, just as I have asked you to love my friends, so I ask the same for my enemies. You alone, Lord, are mighty. You alone are merciful. Whatever you make me desire for my enemies, give it to them. And give the same back to me. If I ever ask for them anything which is outside your perfect rule of love, whether through weakness, ignorance or malice, good Lord, do not give it to them and do not give it back to me. You who are the true light, lighten their darkness. You who are the whole truth, correct their errors. You who are the incarnate Word, give life to their souls. Tender Lord, Jesus, let me not be a stumbling block to them nor a rock of offence. My sin is sufficient to me, without harming others. I, a slave to sin, beg your mercy on my fellow slaves. Let them be reconciled with you, and through you reconciled to me.

Anselm (27)
Benedicta Ward SLG

For those who are absent

O God who art everywhere present, look down with thy mercy upon those who are absent from among us. Give thy holy angels charge over them, and grant that they may be kept safe in body, soul and spirit, and presented faultless before the presence of thy glory with exceeding joy, through Jesus Christ our Lord.

Richard Meux Benson

At a time of disaster

God of goodness and love,
in whom we can trust in every hour of need;
have mercy on all who are faced with fear and distress
[*through earthquake, tempest, pestilence, flood . . .*].
We ask that help may be given to them speedily,
and that this emergency may be turned into an opportunity
   to strengthen the bonds of love and service
which bind people and nations together;
through Jesus Christ our Lord.

Christian Aid (33)

In pastoral crisis

God of all care and compassion
you take us through deep waters
but never abandon us in the storm;
we walk in the dark
but you never leave us without light.
Be with us in the night of our anxiety
and in the day of our over-confidence
that we may keep faith with each other
as you have kept faith with us
in Jesus Christ our Lord.

Stephen Oliver (26)

For protection

Father, Son and Holy Spirit,
one God, blessed for ever:
expel and put away from this house
all power and presence of darkness.
Watch over and defend this home,
and let no evil come near your servants,
that they may be guarded by your angels
and folded in your eternal love.

Book of Common Order (32)

For the sick

Lord,
it was not the pool that healed the paralytic,
but your word.
The power of your voice was stronger
   than the chronic bond of the disease.
Therefore he cast away the burden of sickness
   and took up his bed as a witness to your abundant mercies.
Lord, glory to you.

Hymn of Praises, Sunday of the Paralytic (10)

In sickness

Lord, you are good and gentle in all your ways; and your mercy is so great that not only the blessings but also the misfortunes of your people are channels of your compassion. Grant that I may turn to you as a Father in my present condition since the change in my own state from health to sickness brings no change to you. You are always the same, and you are my loving Father in times of trouble and in times of joy alike.

Blaise Pascal, tr. Robert Van de Weyer (31)

In sickness

O my Saviour, since I share in some small way your sufferings, fill me to the brim with the glory which your sufferings won for mankind. Let me share in some small way the joy of your risen life.

Blaise Pascal, tr. Robert Van de Weyer (31)

For other prayers for the sick, see pages 95–98.

For prayers for the dying, see pages 99–101.

4. The Dead

For the departed

Receive, Lord, in tranquillity and peace, the souls of your servants who have departed out of this present life to be with you. Give them the life that knows no age, the good things that do not pass away; through Jesus Christ our Lord.

Saint Ignatius Loyola

or

God of faithfulness,
in your wisdom you have called your servant *N* out of this world;
release *him* from the bonds of sin,
and welcome *him* into your presence,
so that *he* may enjoy eternal light and peace
and be raised up in glory with all your saints.
We ask this through Christ our Lord.

Order of Christian Funerals (23)

For one who died accidentally or violently

Lord our God,
you are always faithful and quick to show mercy
Our *brother N*
was suddenly [*and violently*] taken from us.
Come swiftly to *his* aid,
have mercy on *him*,
and comfort *his* family and friends
by the power and protection of the cross.
We ask this through Christ our Lord.

Order of Christian Funerals (23)

5 Conclusion

Trisagion

Holy God
Holy and Strong
Holy and Immortal,
have mercy on us.

Prayer of Saint John Chrysostom

Almighty God, who hast given us grace as this time with one accord to make our common supplications unto thee; and dost promise that, when two or three are gathered together in thy name, thou wilt grant their requests: fulfil now, O Lord, the desires and petitions of thy servants, as may be most expedient for them; granting us in this world knowledge of thy truth, and in the world to come life everlasting.

Book of Common Prayer (2)

The Grace

The grace of our Lord Jesus Christ, and the love of God, and the fellowship of the Holy Spirit, be with us all evermore.

cf 2 Corinthians 13

Evening Prayer

The Office of Vespers on Saturdays and on the Eve of Solemnities

Items marked (+) are also available in traditional language, see Evening Prayer in Traditional Language, pages 649–654.

In The Propers *(see pages 201–431) festal and seasonal alternatives are available for items marked (*).*

Advent — page 203

Christmas
and the Annunciation of the Lord — page 213

Epiphany (until Candlemas)
and Feasts of the Lord — page 221

Ordinary Time
(3 February until Shrove Tuesday) — page 229

Lent — page 239

Passiontide — page 253

Eastertide — page 285

Ascension Day — page 293

Pentecost
(Friday after Ascension until Pentecost) — page 299

Trinity — page 305

Corpus Christi — page 311

Sacred Heart   *page 323*

Ordinary Time
(Monday after Pentecost until the end of October)   *page 331*

Our Lady   *page 363*

Saints   *page 397*

Faithful Departed   *page 419*

The King and the Kingdom
(Christ the King and Ordinary Time in November)   *page 425*

V/	O God, make speed to save us	or	*V/* O God, come to our aid.
R/	O Lord, make haste to help us.		*R/* O Lord, make haste to help us

Glory . . . Amen.

(Except in Lent) Alleluia.

Office Hymn (*)

Phos hilaron

O gracious light, Lord Jesus Christ,
In you the Father's glory shone.
Immortal, holy, blest is he,
And blest are you his only Son.

Now sunset comes, but light shines forth,
The lamps are lit to pierce the night.
Praise Father, Son, and Spirit, God
Who dwells in the eternal light.

Worthy are you of endless praise,
O Son of God, life-giving Lord;
Wherefore you are, through all the earth
And in the highest heaven, adored.

LM
Athenogenes? (3rd cent.) (37)
Francis Bland Tucker
Hymns for Prayer and Praise 242

or

O lux beata Trinitas

O Trinity of blessed light,
O unity of primal might,
As now the fiery sun departs,
So shed your radiance in our hearts.

To you our morning song of praise
To you our evening prayer we raise:
May we behold your glorious face,
And joy in your eternal grace.

To God the Father, God the Son,
And God the Spirit, praise be done;
To you most holy Trinity,
Praise now and for eternity.

LM
Ambrose?(35)
tr. John Mason Neale*
Hymns for Prayer and Praise 252

Psalmody

Either *the psalms for the day*

Week 1	Week 2	Week 3	Week 4
141:1–9 *(see below)*	119:105–112 *(14)*	113	122
142 *(see below)*	16	116	130

or *Psalms 141 and 142*

Psalm 141

1 O Lord, I call to you; come to me quickly; *
　　hear my voice when I cry to you.
2 Let my prayer rise before you as incense, *
　　the lifting up of my hands as the evening sacrifice.

3 Set a watch before my mouth, O Lord, *
    and guard the door of my lips;
4 Let not my heart incline to any evil thing; *
    let me not be occupied in wickedness with evil-doers,
    nor taste the pleasures of their table.
5 Let the righteous smite me in friendly rebuke;
    but let not the oil of the unrighteous anoint my head; *
    for my prayer is continually against their wicked deeds.
6 Let their rulers be overthrown in stony places; *
    that they may know my words are sweet.
7 As when a plough turns over the earth in furrows, *
    let their bones be scattered at the mouth of the Pit.
8 But my eyes are turned to you, Lord God; *
    in you I take refuge; do not leave me defenceless.
9 Protect me from the snare which they have laid for me *
    and from the traps of the evil-doers.
10 Let the wicked fall into their own nets, *
    while I pass by in safety.

   Glory . . .

Psalm 142

1 I cry aloud to the Lord; *
    to the Lord I make my supplication.
2 I pour out my complaint before him *
    and tell him of my trouble.
3 When my spirit faints within me, you know my path; *
    in the way wherein I walk have they laid a snare for me.
4 I look to my right hand, and find no one who knows me; *
    I have no place to flee unto, and no one cares for my soul.
5 I cry out to you, O Lord, and say: *
    'You are my refuge, my portion in the land of the living.
6 'Listen to my cry, for I am brought very low; *
    save me from my persecutors, for they are too strong for me.
7 'Bring my soul out of prison,
    that I may give thanks to your name; *
    when you have dealt bountifully with me,
    then shall the righteous gather around me.'

   Glory . . .

Evening Prayer

Canticle

The Song of Christ's Glory

Refrain: At the name of Jesus every knee shall bow.

1 Christ Jesus was in the form of God, *
    but he did not cling to equality with God.
2 He emptied himself, taking the form of a servant, *
    and was born in our human likeness.
3 Being found in human form, he humbled himself, *
    and became obedient unto death, even death on a cross.
4 Therefore, God has highly exalted him, *
    and bestowed on him the name above every name,
5 That at the name of Jesus, every knee should bow, *
    in heaven and on earth and under the earth.
6 And every tongue confess that Jesus Christ is Lord, *
    to the glory of God the Father.

   Glory . . .

Refrain: At the name of Jesus every knee shall bow.

Philippians 2:5b-11
Common Worship (1)

Scripture Reading

The second reading appointed for the day (see the Propers, pages 203–431).

or

Short Readings (*)

My thoughts are not your thoughts, nor are your ways my ways, says the Lord. For as the heavens are higher than the earth, so are my ways higher than your ways and my thoughts than your thoughts. For as the rain and the snow come down from heaven, and do not return there until they have watered the earth, making it bring forth and sprout, giving seed to the sower and bread to the eater, so shall my word be that goes out from my mouth; it shall not return to me empty, but it shall accomplish that which I purpose, and succeed in the thing for which I sent it.

Isaiah 55:8–11

or

Be doers of the word, and not merely hearers who deceive themselves. For if any are hearers of the word and not doers, they are like those who look at themselves in a mirror; for they look at themselves and, on going away, immediately forget what they were like. But those who look into the perfect law, the law of liberty, and persevere, being not hearers who forget but doers who act – they will be blessed in their doing.

James 1:22–25

Short Responsory (*)

R/ How great are your works, O Lord.
R/ How great are your works, O Lord.
V/ In wisdom you have made them all.
R/ How great are your works, O Lord.
V/ Glory . . . Holy Spirit.
R/ How great are your works, O Lord.

Refrains (*)

Come to me, all who labour and are heavy-laden, and I will give you rest.

Matthew 11:28 (RSV)

God was in Christ reconciling the world to himself.

2 Corinthians 5:19 (RSV)

Gospel Canticle: Magnificat

The Song of Mary (+)

Refrain *(as above or as in the Propers)*

1 My soul proclaims the greatness of the Lord,
   my spirit rejoices in God my Saviour; *
   he has looked with favour on his lowly servant.
2 From this day all generations will call me blessed; *
   the Almighty has done great things for me
   and holy is his name.
3 He has mercy on those who fear him, *
   from generation to generation.

4 He has shown strength with his arm *
   and has scattered the proud in their conceit,
5 casting down the mighty from their thrones *
   and lifting up the lowly.
6 He has filled the hungry with good things *
   and sent the rich away empty.
7 He has come to the aid of his servant Israel, *
   to remember his promise of mercy,
8 the promise made to our ancestors, *
   to Abraham and his children for ever.

   Glory . . .

Luke 1:46–55
ELLC*(15)

Refrain *(repeated)*

Prayers

Intercessions are said.

If set prayers are desired, some or all of the following petitions may be adapted and used (and see pages 597–602):

Govern and direct your holy Church;
fill it with love and truth;
and grant it that unity which is your will . . .

Guide the leaders of the nations into the ways of peace and justice . . .

Guard and strengthen your servant Elizabeth our Queen,
that she may put her trust in you,
and seek your honour and glory . . .

Endue the High Court of Parliament and all the Ministers
   of the Crown with wisdom and understanding . . .

Bless those who administer the law,
that they may uphold justice, honesty, and truth . . .

Give us the will to use the resources of the earth to your glory,
and for the good of all creation . . .

Bless and keep all your people . . .

Bring your joy into all families;
strengthen and deliver those in childbirth,
watch over children and guide the young,
bring reconciliation to those in discord
and peace to those in distress . . .

Hear us as we remember those who have died in the peace of Christ,
both those who have confessed the faith
and those whose faith is known to you alone,
and grant us with them a share in your eternal kingdom.

from the Litany
Common Worship (1)

or

O God, the creator and preserver of all,
we pray for people of every race and in every kind of need:
make your ways known on earth, your saving health among all nations.

We pray for the good estate of the catholic Church;
guide and govern us by your good Spirit,
that all who profess and call themselves Christians
may be led into the way of truth,
and hold the faith in unity of spirit,
in the bond of peace and in righteousness of life.

We commend to your fatherly goodness
all those who are any ways afflicted or distressed,
in mind, body or estate;
comfort and relieve them in their need,
give them patience in their sufferings,
and bring good out of all their afflictions.

We remember those who have gone before us in the peace of Christ
and we give you praise for all your faithful ones,
with whom we rejoice in the Communion of Saints . . .

All this we ask for Jesus Christ's sake.

Common Worship (1)

For the traditional version of this prayer, see page 647.

Evening Prayer

Our Father

The Lord's Prayer is said here or after the Collect.

Collect (*)

The collect of the day (or season) is said

or (+)

O God,
the source of all good desires,
all right judgements and all just works:
give to your servants that peace
   which the world cannot give;
that our hearts may be set to obey
   your commandments
and that, freed from the fear of our enemies,
we may pass our time in rest and quietness;
through Jesus Christ our Lord.

Common Worship (1)

or (+)

Lighten our darkness, Lord, we pray;
and in your mercy defend us
from all perils and dangers of this night;
for the love of your only Son,
our Saviour Jesus Christ.

Common Worship (1)

Ending

The Lord bless us, and keep us from all evil, and bring us to everlasting life. Amen.

The Office of Vespers on Sundays and Solemnities and daily as required

Items marked (+) *are also available in traditional language, see Evening Prayer in Traditional Language, pages 649–654.*

In The Propers, *alternatives are available for items marked (*).*

Advent	*page 203*
Christmas and the Annunciation of the Lord	*page 213*
Epiphany *(until Candlemas)* and Feasts of the Lord	*page 221*
Ordinary Time *(3 February until Shrove Tuesday)*	*page 229*
Lent	*page 239*
Passiontide	*page 253*
Eastertide	*page 285*
Ascension Day	*page 293*
Pentecost *(Friday after Ascension until Pentecost)*	*page 299*
Trinity	*page 305*
Corpus Christi	*page 311*
Sacred Heart	*page 323*
Ordinary Time *(Monday after Pentecost until the end of October)*	*page 331*
Our Lady	*page 363*
Saints	*page 397*
Faithful Departed	*page 419*
The King and the Kingdom *(Christ the King and Ordinary Time in November)*	*page 425*

Evening Prayer

V/ O God, make speed to save us.   or   **V/** O God, come to our aid.
R/ O Lord, make haste to help us.   **R/O** Lord, make haste to help us

Glory . . . Amen.

(Except in Lent) Alleluia.

Office Hymn (*)

Lucis creator optime

O blest Creator of the light,
Who made the day with radiance bright,
And o'er the forming world did call
The light from chaos first of all.

Whose wisdom joined in meet array
The morn and eve, and named them Day:
Night comes with all the darkness fears;
Regard your people's prayers and tears.

Lest, sunk in sin, o'erwhelmed with strife,
They lose the gift of endless life;
While thinking but the thoughts of time,
They weave new chains of woe and crime.

But grant them grace that they may strain
The heavenly gate and prize to gain:
Each harmful lure aside to cast,
And purge away each error past.

O Father, that we ask be done
Through Jesus Christ your only Son,
And Holy Spirit; who as three-
in-one we praise eternally.

LM
6th cent.
tr. John Mason Neale*
Hymns for Prayer and Praise 246

Psalmody: Sunday

Week 1	Week 2	Week 3	Week 4
110 *(see below)*	110 *(see below)*	110 *(see below)*	110 *(see below)*
114 *(see below)*	115 *(see below)*	111 *(see page 515)*	112 *(see page 516)*

Psalm 110

1 The Lord said to my lord, 'Sit at my right hand, *
   until I make your enemies your footstool.'
2 May the Lord stretch forth the sceptre of your power; *
   rule from Zion in the midst of your enemies.
3 'Noble are you on this day of your birth; *
   on the holy mountain, from the womb of the dawn
   the dew of your new birth is upon you.'
4 The Lord has sworn and will not retract: *
   'You are a priest for ever after the order of Melchizedek.'
5 The king at your right hand, O Lord, *
   shall smite down kings in the day of his wrath.
6 In all his majesty, he shall judge among the nations, *
   smiting heads over all the wide earth.
7 He shall drink from the brook beside the way; *
   therefore shall he lift high his head.

   Glory . . .

and *(in Week 1)*

Psalm 114

1 When Israel came out of Egypt, *
   the house of Jacob from a people of a strange tongue,
2 Judah became his sanctuary, *
   Israel his dominion.
3 The sea saw that, and fled; *
   Jordan was driven back.
4 The mountains skipped like rams, *
   the little hills like young sheep.

5 What ailed you, O sea, that you fled? *
    O Jordan, that you were driven back?
6 You mountains, that you skipped like rams, *
    you little hills like young sheep?
7 Tremble, O earth, at the presence of the Lord, *
    at the presence of the God of Jacob,
8 Who turns the hard rock into a pool of water, *
    the flint-stone into a springing well.

Glory . . .

or (Week 2)

Psalm 115

1 Not to us, Lord, not to us,
    but to your name give the glory, *
    for the sake of your loving mercy and truth.
2 Why should the heathen say, *
    'Where is now their God?'
3 As for our God, he is in heaven; *
    he does whatever he pleases.
4 Their idols are silver and gold, *
    the work of human hands.
5 They have mouths, but cannot speak; *
    eyes have they, but cannot see;
6 They have ears, but cannot hear; *
    noses have they, but cannot smell;
7 They have hands, but cannot feel;
    feet have they, but cannot walk; *
    not a whisper do they make from their throats.
8 Those who make them shall become like them *
    and so will all who put their trust in them.

9 But you, Israel, put your trust in the Lord; *
    he is their help and their shield.
10 House of Aaron, trust in the Lord; *
    he is their help and their shield.
11 You that fear the Lord, trust in the Lord; *
    he is their help and their shield.

12 The Lord has been mindful of us and he will bless us; *
    may he bless the house of Israel;
    may he bless the house of Aaron;
13 May he bless those who fear the Lord, *
    both small and great together.
14 May the Lord increase you more and more, *
    you and your children after you.
15 May you be blest by the Lord, *
    the maker of heaven and earth.
16 The heavens are the heavens of the Lord, *
    but the earth he has entrusted to his children.
17 The dead do not praise the Lord, *
    nor those gone down into silence;
18 But we will bless the Lord, *
    from this time forth for evermore.
    Alleluia.

    Glory . . .

Psalms: Weekdays

The Sunday psalms may be used or as follows (see pages 636f.):

	Week 1	Week 2	Week 3	Week 4
Monday	11 15	45	123 124	136
Tuesday	20 21	49	125 131	137 138
Wednesday	27	62 67	126 127	139
Thursday	30 32	72	132	144
Friday	41 46	116 121	135	145

Saturday   (see Evening Prayer, page 627)

Evening Prayer

Canticle: Sunday

Canticle (on Sunday, outside Lent):

A Song of the Lamb

Refrain: Let us rejoice and exult *
        and give glory and homage to our God.

1 Salvation and glory and power belong to our God, *
   whose judgements are true and just.
2 Praise our God, all you his servants, *
   all who fear him, both small and great.
3 The Lord our God, the Almighty, reigns: *
   let us rejoice and exult and give him the glory.
4 For the marriage of the Lamb has come *
   and his bride has made herself ready.
5 Blessed are those who are invited *
   to the wedding banquet of the Lamb.
   To the One who sits on the throne and to the Lamb *
   be blessing and honour and glory and might,
   for ever and ever. Amen.

Refrain: Let us rejoice and exult *
        and give glory and homage to our God.

Revelation 19: 1b, 5b, 6b-7, 9b
Common Worship (1)

or (on Sunday in Lent)

A Song of Christ the Servant

Refrain: Christ committed no sin, *
        no guile was found on his lips.

1 Christ suffered for you, leaving you an example, *
   that you should follow in his steps.
2 He committed no sin, no guile was found on his lips, *
   when he was reviled, he did not revile in turn.
3 When he suffered, he did not threaten, *
   but he trusted in God who judges justly.

4 Christ himself bore our sins in his body on the tree, *
    that he might die to sin and live to righteousness.
5 By his wounds, you have been healed,
    for you were straying like sheep, *
    but have now returned
    to the Shepherd and Guardian of your souls.

  Glory . . .

Refrain: Christ committed no sin, *
    no guile was found on his lips.

1 Peter 2:21–25
trans. A Daily Office SSF (3)

Canticle: Weekdays

Monday

A Song of God's Grace

Refrain: The glorious grace of God *
    is freely bestowed on us in the Beloved.

1 Blessed are you,
    the God and Father of our Lord Jesus Christ, *
    for you have blest us in Christ Jesus
    with every spiritual blessing in the heavenly places.
2 You chose us to be yours in Christ
    before the foundation of the world, *
    that we should be holy and blameless before you.
3 In love you destined us to be your children,
    through Jesus Christ, *
    according to the purpose of your will,
4 To the praise of your glorious grace, *
    which you freely bestowed on us in the Beloved.
5 In you, we have redemption
    through the blood of Christ, *
    the forgiveness of our sins,
6 According to the riches of your grace, *
    which you have lavished upon us.
7 You have made known to us, in all wisdom and insight, *
    the mystery of your will,

8 According to your purpose
   which you set forth in Christ, *
   as a plan for the fullness of time,
9 To unite all things in Christ, *
   things in heaven and things on earth.

Glory . . .

Refrain: The glorious grace of God *
   is freely bestowed on us in the Beloved.

Ephesians 1:3–10
trans. A Daily Office SSF (3)

Tuesday

A Song of Praise

Refrain: You created all things, O God, *
   and are worthy of our praise for ever.

1 You are worthy, our Lord and God, *
   to receive glory and honour and power.
2 For you have created all things, *
   and by your will they have their being.
3 You are worthy, O Lamb, for you were slain, *
   and by your blood you ransomed for God
   saints from every tribe and language and nation.
4 You have made them to be a kingdom and priests
      serving our God, *
   and they will reign with you on earth.

To the One who sits on the throne and to the Lamb *
be blessing and honour and glory and might,
for ever and ever. Amen.

Refrain: You created all things, O God, *
   and are worthy of our praise for ever.

Revelation 4:11; 5:9b-10
trans. A Daily Office SSF (3)

Wednesday

A Song of Redemption

Refrain: Christ is the image of the invisible God, *
 the first-born of all creation.

1 The Father has delivered us
 from the dominion of darkness, *
 and transferred us to the kingdom of his beloved Son;
2 In whom we have redemption, *
 the forgiveness of our sins.
3 He is the image of the invisible God, *
 the first-born of all creation.
4 For in him all things were created, *
 in heaven and on earth, visible and invisible.
5 All things were created through him and for him, *
 he is before all things
 and in him all things hold together.
6 He is the head of the body, the Church, *
 he is the beginning, the first-born from the dead.
7 For it pleased God that in him
 all fullness should dwell, *
 and through him all things be reconciled to himself.
Glory . . .

Refrain: Christ is the image of the invisible God, *
 the first-born of all creation.

Colossians 1:13–20
trans. A Daily Office SSF (3)

Thursday

A Song of the Kingdom of our God

Refrain: Rejoice you heavens *
 and those who dwell in them!

1 We give you thanks, Lord God almighty,
 who are and who were, *
 for you have taken your great power and begun to reign.
2 The nations raged but your wrath has come, *
 and the time for judging the dead,

3 For rewarding your servants, the prophets and saints *
   and all who fear your name, both small and great.
4 Now have come the salvation and the power
   and the kingdom of God *
   and the authority of his Messiah,
5 For the accuser of our comrades has been thrown down, *
   who accuses them day and night before our God.
6 But they have conquered him by the blood of the Lamb *
   and by the word of their testimony,
7 For they did not cling to life even in the face of death. *
   Rejoice then, you heavens and those who dwell in them!

To the One who sits on the throne and to the Lamb *
be blessing and honour and glory and might,
for ever and ever. Amen.

Refrain: Rejoice you heavens *
        and those who dwell in them!

Revelation 11:17–18;12:10b-12a

Friday

A Song of Moses and of the Lamb

Refrain: All nations shall come and worship you, *
        and share in the feast of your Kingdom, O Christ.

1 Great and wonderful are your deeds, *
   Lord God the almighty.
2 Just and true are your ways, *
   O Ruler of the nations.
3 Who shall not revere you and praise your name, O Lord? *
   for you alone are holy.
4 All nations shall come and worship in your presence, *
   for your just dealings have been revealed.

To the One who sits on the throne and to the Lamb
be blessing and honour and glory and might,
for ever and ever. Amen.

Refrain: All nations shall come and worship you, *
        and share in the feast of your Kingdom, O Christ.

Revelation 15:3–4
A Daily Office SSF (3)

Scripture Reading

The second reading appointed for the day (see the Propers, pages 203–431).

or

Short Readings (*)

Blessed be the God and Father of our Lord Jesus Christ, the Father of mercies and the God of all consolation, who consoles us in all our affliction, so that we may be able to console those who are in any affliction with the consolation with which we are ourselves are consoled by God.

2 Corinthians 1:3–4

or

You have come to Mount Zion and to the city of the living God, the heavenly Jerusalem, and to innumerable angels in festal gathering, and to the assembly of the firstborn who are enrolled in heaven, and to God the judge of all and to the spirits of the righteous made perfect, and to Jesus, the mediator of a new covenant, and to the sprinkled blood that speaks a better word than the blood of Abel.

Hebrews 12:22–24

or

If now for a little while you have had to suffer various trials, so that the genuineness of your faith – being more precious than gold that, though perishable, is tested by fire – may be found to result in praise and glory and honour when Jesus Christ is revealed. Although you have not seen him, you love him; and even though you do not see him now, you believe in him and rejoice with an indescribable and glorious joy, for you are receiving the outcome of your faith, the salvation of your souls.

1 Peter 1:6–9

Short Responsory (*)

R/ Blessed are you, O Lord, in the vault of heaven.
R/ Blessed are you, O Lord, in the vault of heaven.
V/ You are exalted and glorified above all else for ever.
R/ Blessed are you, O Lord, in the vault of heaven.

V/   Glory . . . Holy Spirit.
R/   Blessed are you, O Lord, in the vault of heaven.

Refrains (*)

Come to me, all who labour and are heavy-laden, and I will give you rest.
Matthew 11:28 (RSV)

God was in Christ reconciling the world to himself.
2 Corinthians 5:19 (RSV)

Gospel Canticle: Magnificat

The Song of Mary (+)

Refrain *(as above or as in the Propers)*

1 My soul proclaims the greatness of the Lord,
   my spirit rejoices in God my Saviour; *
   he has looked with favour on his lowly servant.
2 From this day all generations will call me blessed; *
   the Almighty has done great things for me
   and holy is his name.
3 He has mercy on those who fear him, *
   from generation to generation.
4 He has shown strength with his arm *
   and has scattered the proud in their conceit,
5 casting down the mighty from their thrones *
   and lifting up the lowly.
6 He has filled the hungry with good things *
   and sent the rich away empty.
7 He has come to the aid of his servant Israel, *
   to remember his promise of mercy,
8 the promise made to our ancestors, *
   to Abraham and his children for ever.

   Glory . . .

Luke 1:46–55
ELLC(15)*

Refrain *(repeated)*

Apostles' Creed

For the Book of Common Prayer text of the Apostles' Creed, see page 594.

I believe in God,
the Father almighty,
creator of heaven and earth.

I believe in Jesus Christ, his only Son, our Lord.
He was conceived by the power of the Holy Spirit
and born of the Virgin Mary.
He suffered under Pontius Pilate,
was crucified, died and was buried.
He descended to the dead.
On the third day he rose again.
He ascended into heaven,
and is seated at the right hand of the Father.
He will come again to judge the living and the dead.

I believe in the Holy Spirit,
the holy catholic church,
the communion of saints,
the forgiveness of sins,
the resurrection of the body;
and the life everlasting.

ELLC

Prayers

Intercessions are said.

If set prayers are desired, some or all of the following petitions may be adapted and used (and see pages 603–23):

Govern and direct your holy Church;
fill it with love and truth;
and grant it that unity which is your will . . .

Guide the leaders of the nations into the ways of peace and justice . . .

Help and comfort the lonely, the bereaved and the oppressed . . .

Keep in safety those who travel, and all who are in danger . . .

Heal the sick in body and mind,
and provide for the homeless, the hungry, and the destitute . . .

Show your pity on prisoners and refugees, and all who are in trouble . . .

Forgive our enemies, persecutors, and slanderers,
and turn their hearts . . .

Hear us as we remember those who have died in the peace of Christ,
both those who have confessed the faith
and those whose faith is known to you alone . . .
and grant us with them a share in your eternal kingdom.

from the Litany
Common Worship (1)

or

O God, the creator and preserver of all,
we pray for people of every race and in every kind of need:
make your ways known on earth, your saving health among all nations..

We pray for the good estate of the catholic Church;
guide and govern us by your good Spirit,
that all who profess and call themselves Christians
may be led into the way of truth,
and hold the faith in unity of spirit,
in the bond of peace and in righteousness of life.

We commend to your fatherly goodness
all those who are any ways afflicted or distressed,
in mind, body or estate;
comfort and relieve them in their need,
give them patience in their sufferings,
and bring good out of all their afflictions.

We remember those who have gone before us in the peace of Christ
and we give you praise for all your faithful ones,
with whom we rejoice in the Communion of Saints...

All this we ask for Jesus Christ's sake.

Common Worship (1)

For the traditional version of this prayer, see page 603.

Our Father

The Lord's Prayer is said here or after the Collect.

Collect (*)

The collect of the day (or season) is said.

or (+)

O God,
the source of all good desires,
all right judgements and all just works:
give to your servants that peace
    which the world cannot give;
that our hearts may be set to obey
    your commandments
and that, freed from the fear of our enemies,
we may pass our time in rest and quietness;
through Jesus Christ our Lord.

                                        Common Worship (1)

or (+)

Lighten our darkness, Lord, we pray;
and in your mercy defend us
from all perils and dangers of this night;
for the love of your only Son,
our Saviour Jesus Christ.

                                        Common Worship (1)

Ending

The Lord bless us, and keep us from all evil, and bring us to everlasting life.
Amen.

Evening Prayer in Traditional Language

O Lord, open thou our lips.
And our mouth shall shew forth thy praise.

O God, make speed to save us.
O Lord, make haste to help us.

Glory be to the Father, and to the Son:
and to the Holy Ghost;
**As it was in the beginning, is now, and ever shall be:
world without end. Amen.**

Praise ye the Lord.
The Lord's Name be praised.

Psalms

Day of the Month	*Psalm*
Day 1	6–8
Day 2	13–14
Day 3	17
Day 4	22–23
Day 5	27–29
Day 6	32–34
Day 7	36
Day 8	41–43
Day 9	47–49
Day 10	53–55
Day 11	60–61
Day 12	65
Day 13	70
Day 14	74

Day 15	77
Day 16	82, 84
Day 17	88
Day 18	93–94
Day 19	98–99
Day 20	104
Day 21	105:23–45
Day 22	110–111
Day 23	114–115
Day 24	119:1–32 *(1–4)*
Day 25	119:73–104 *(10–13)*
Day 26	119:145–176 *(19–22)*
Day 27	126–131
Day 28	136–138
Day 29	141–143
Day 30	147–150

First Lesson

The first reading appointed for the day (see the Propers, pages 203–431).

or

Short Reading

Hear, O Israel: The Lord our God is one Lord alone; and you shall love the Lord your God with all your heart, and with all your soul, and with all your might. And these words which I command you this day shall be upon your heart; and you shall teach them diligently to your children, and shall talk of them when you sit in your house, and when you walk by the way, and when you lie down, and when you rise.

Deuteronomy 6:4–7 (RSV)

Gospel Canticle: Magnificat

The Song of Mary

1 My soul doth magnify the Lord: *
  and my spirit hath rejoiced in God my Saviour.
2 For he hath regarded: *
  the lowliness of his handmaiden.
3 For behold, from henceforth: *
  all generations shall call me blessed.
4 For he that is mighty hath magnified me: *
  and holy is his name.
5 And his mercy is on them that fear him: *
  throughout all generations.
6 He hath showed strength with his arm: *
  he hath scattered the proud in the imagination of their hearts.
7 He hath put down the mighty from their seat: *
  and hath exalted the humble and meek.
8 He hath filled the hungry with good things: *
  and the rich he hath sent empty away.
9 He remembering his mercy: *
  hath helped his servant Israel;
10 As he promised to our forefathers: *
  Abraham and his seed, for ever.

    Glory be to the Father, and to the Son: *
    and to the Holy Spirit;
    As it was in the beginning, is now, and ever shall be: *
    world without end. Amen.

Luke 1:46–55
Book of Common Prayer

Second Lesson

The second reading appointed for the day (see the Propers, pages 203–431).

or

Short Reading

This is the message we have heard from him and proclaim to you, that God is light and in him there is no darkness at all. If we say that we have fellowship with him while we are walking in darkness, we lie and do not do what is true; but if we walk in the light as he himself is in the light, we have fellowship with one another, and the blood of Jesus his Son cleanses us from all sin.

1 John 1:5–7

Gospel Canticle: Nunc Dimittis

The Song of Simeon

1 Lord, now lettest thou thy servant depart in peace: *
   according to thy word,
2 For mine eyes have seen thy salvation: *
   which thou hast prepared before the face of all people;
3 To be a light to lighten the Gentiles: *
   and to be the glory of thy people Israel.

   Glory be to the Father, and to the Son: *
   and to the Holy Spirit;
   As it was in the beginning, is now, and ever shall be: *
   world without end, Amen.

Luke 2:29–32
Book of Common Prayer

Creed

I believe in God,
the Father almighty,
maker of heaven and earth.
And in Jesus Christ, his only Son, our Lord,
who was conceived by the Holy Ghost,
born of the Virgin Mary
suffered under Pontius Pilate,
was crucified, dead and buried.
He descended into hell.
The third day he rose again from the dead;
he ascended into heaven
and sitteth on the right hand of God the Father almighty.
From thence he shall come to judge the quick and the dead.

I believe in the Holy Ghost;
the holy catholic church,
the communion of saints,
the forgiveness of sins,
the resurrection of the body;
and the life everlasting.

Book of Common Prayer (2)

Lord, have mercy upon us.
Christ, have mercy upon us.
Lord, have mercy upon us.

Our Father

Our Father, which art in heaven,
hallowed be thy name;
Thy kingdom come,
Thy will be done, in earth as it is in heaven.
Give us this day our daily bread,
and forgive us our trespasses,
as we forgive them that trespass against us;
and lead us not into temptation,
but deliver us from evil. Amen.

O Lord, shew thy mercy upon us.
And grant us thy salvation.

O Lord, save the Queen.
And mercifully hear us when we call upon thee.

Endue thy ministers with righteousness.
And make thy chosen people joyful.

O Lord, save thy people.
And bless thine inheritance.

Give peace in our time, O Lord.
Because there is none other that fighteth for us, but only thou O God.

O God, make clean our hearts within us.
And take not thy Holy Spirit from us.

Collect of the Day

Collect for Peace

O God, from whom all holy desires, all good counsels, and all just works do proceed: Give unto thy servants that peace which the world cannot give; that both our hearts may be set to obey thy commandments, and that we, being defended from the fear of our enemies, may pass our time in rest and quietness; through the merits of Jesus Christ our Saviour.

Book of Common Prayer (2)

Collect for Aid against all Perils

Lighten our darkness, we beseech thee, O Lord; and by thy great mercy defend us from all perils and dangers of this night; for the love of thy only Son, our Saviour, Jesus Christ.

Book of Common Prayer (2)

The grace of our Lord Jesus Christ,
and the love of God,
and the fellowship of the Holy Ghost,
be with us all evermore. Amen.

2 Corinthians 13
Book of Common Prayer (2)

Night Prayer

The Office of Compline on Saturdays and on the Eve of Solemnities and daily as required

Items marked (+) are also available in traditional language, see pages 649–654.

V/	O God, make speed to save us.	or	**V/**	O God, come to our aid.
R/	O Lord, make haste to help us.		**R/**	O Lord, make haste to help us

Glory. . . Amen.

(Except in Lent) Alleluia.

An examination of conscience follows.

This confession may be used:

Almighty God,
long-suffering and of great goodness:
I confess to you,
I confess with my whole heart
my neglect and forgetfulness of your commandments,
my wrong doing, thinking, and speaking;
the hurts I have done to others,
and the good I have left undone.
O God, forgive me, for I have sinned against you;
and raise me to newness of life;
through Jesus Christ our Lord.

Common Worship (1)

May almighty God have mercy on us,
forgive us our sins,
and bring us to everlasting life,
through Jesus Christ our Lord.

Office Hymn

Week 1

Te lucis ante terminum

To you, before the end of day,
Creator of the world, we pray
In love unfailing, hear our prayer,
Enfold us in your watchful care.

Lord, when we sleep, be in our hearts,
Your Spirit peace and rest imparts;
Then with the light of dawn, may we
Your glory praise unendingly.

Your living power breathe from above,
Renew in us the fire of love;
And may your brightness drive away
All darkness in eternal day.

O Father, hear us, through your Son,
Who, with the Spirit, ever One
Now reigns as living Trinity
In time and for eternity.

LM
7th cent.? (35)
Hymns for Prayer and Praise 260

Week 2

Christe, qui lux es et dies

O Christ, you are the light of day,
Revealing what is veiled by night,
The morning star that gives the pledge
And promise of eternal light.

Watch over us who love you well,
And when our eyes are closed in sleep,
Protected by your strong right hand,
With you, our hearts will vigil keep.

O Father, Son and Spirit blest,
Immortal Trinity we praise,
Give us true sorrow for our sins
And life in everlasting days.

LM
Stanbrook Abbey c1974 (4)
Hymns for Prayer and Praise 261

Psalmody

The psalmody for Saturday (Psalms 4 and 134, below) or Sunday (Psalm 91, see page 499) may be used midweek. Otherwise the daily scheme is used (see below).

Psalm 4

1 Answer me when I call, O God of my righteousness; *
    you set me at liberty when I was in trouble;
    have mercy on me and hear my prayer.
2 How long will you nobles dishonour my glory; *
    how long will you love vain things and seek after falsehood?
3 But know that the Lord has shown me his marvellous kindness; *
    when I call upon the Lord, he will hear me.
4 Stand in awe, and sin not; *
    commune with your own heart upon your bed, and be still.
5 Offer the sacrifices of righteousness *
    and put your trust in the Lord.
6 There are many that say, 'Who will show us any good?' *
    Lord, lift up the light of your countenance upon us.
7 You have put gladness in my heart, *
    more than when their corn and wine and oil increase.
8 In peace I will lie down and sleep, *
    for it is you Lord, only, who make me dwell in safety.

   Glory . . .

Psalm 134

1 Come, bless the Lord,
    all you servants of the Lord, *
    you that by night stand in the house of the Lord.
2 Lift up your hands towards the sanctuary *
    and bless the Lord.
3 The Lord who made heaven and earth *
    give you blessing out of Zion.

Psalms (see pages 437–556)

Monday	86
Tuesday	143
Wednesday	31:1–6, 130
Thursday	16
Friday	88

Short Readings

On Saturday and on the Eve of Solemnities

Hear, O Israel: The Lord our God is one Lord alone; and you shall love the Lord your God with all your heart, and with all your soul, and with all your might. And these words which I command you this day shall be upon your heart; and you shall teach them diligently to your children, and shall talk of them when you sit in your house, and when you walk by the way, and when you lie down, and when you rise.

Deuteronomy 6:4–7 (RSV)

Other days

You, O Lord, are in the midst of us, and we are called by your name; do not forsake us!

Jeremiah 14:9

or

Be sober, be watchful. Your adversary the devil prowls around like a roaring lion, seeking some one to devour. Resist him, firm in your faith.

1 Peter 5:8–9

Short responsory

R/ Into your hands, O Lord, I commend my spirit.
R/ Into your hands, O Lord, I commend my spirit.
V/ For you have redeemed me, Lord God of truth.
R/ Into your hands, O Lord, I commend my spirit.
V/ Glory . . . Holy Spirit.
R/ Into your hands, O Lord, I commend my spirit.

or (in Eastertide):

R/ Into your hands, O Lord, I commend my spirit, alleluia, alleluia.
R/ Into your hands, O Lord, I commend my spirit, alleluia, alleluia.
V/ For you have redeemed me, Lord God of truth.
R/ Into your hands, O Lord, I commend my spirit, alleluia, alleluia.
V/ Glory . . . Holy Spirit.
R/ Into your hands, O Lord, I commend my spirit, alleluia, alleluia.

Gospel Canticle: Nunc Dimittis

The Song of Simeon (+)

Refrain: Save us, O Lord, while waking,
and guard us while sleeping,
that awake we may watch with Christ,
and asleep may rest in peace.

Now, Lord, you let your servant go in peace: *
your word has been fulfilled.
My own eyes have seen the salvation *
which you have prepared in the sight of every people;
a light to reveal you to the nations *
and the glory of your people Israel.

Glory . . .

Luke 2:29–32
ELLC (15)

Refrain: Save us, O Lord, while waking,
and guard us while sleeping,
that awake we may watch with Christ,
and asleep may rest in peace.

Collect

Visit this house, O Lord, we pray,
drive far from it all the snares of the enemy;
may your holy angels dwell with us
   and guard us in peace,
and may your blessing be always upon us.
Through Christ our Lord.

A Daily Office SSF (3)

or

Be with us, O merciful God,
and protect us through the silent hours of this night,
so that we who are wearied by the changes
   and chances of this fleeting world,
may rest upon your eternal changelessness;
through Jesus Christ our Lord.

A Daily Office SSF (3)

or

Lord Jesus Christ, Son of the living God,
who at this evening hour lay in the tomb
and so hallowed the grave
to be a bed of hope
for all who put their trust in you;
give us such sorrow for our sins,
which were the cause of your passion,
that, when our bodies lie in the dust,
our souls may live with you for ever.

A Daily Office SSF (3)

Ending

In preparation for Communion the next day

As watchmen wait for the morning, so do our souls long for you, O Christ. Come with the dawning of the day, and make yourselves known to us in the breaking of bread; for you are our God for ever and ever.

Mozarabic

The Lord grant us a quiet night and a perfect end.

A Final Anthem to the Blessed Virgin Mary follows (see page 668 below).

The Office of Compline on Sundays and Solemnities and daily as required

Items marked (+) are also available in traditional language, see pages 649–654.

V/	O God, make speed to save us.	or	**V/**	O God, come to our aid.
R/	O Lord, make haste to help us.		**R/**	O Lord, make haste to help us.

Glory . . . Amen.

(Except in Lent) Alleluia.

An examination of conscience follows.

This Confession may be used:

My God, for love of you
I desire to hate and forsake all sins
by which I have ever displeased you;
and I resolve by the help of your grace
to commit them no more;
and to avoid all opportunities of sin.
Help me to do this,
through Jesus Christ our Lord.

Common Worship (1)

May almighty God have mercy on us,
forgive us our sins,
and bring us to everlasting life,
through Jesus Christ our Lord.

Office Hymn

Week 1

Te lucis ante terminum

To you, before the end of day,
Creator of the world, we pray
In love unfailing, hear our prayer,

Enfold us in your watchful care.
Lord, when we sleep, be in our hearts,
Your Spirit peace and rest imparts;
Then with the light of dawn, may we
Your glory praise unendingly.

Your living power breathe from above,
Renew in us the fire of love;
And may your brightness drive away
All darkness in eternal day.

O Father, hear us, through your Son,
Who, with the Spirit, ever One
Now reigns as living Trinity
In time and for eternity.

LM
7th cent.? (35)
Hymns for Prayer and Praise 260

Week 2

Christe, qui lux es et dies

O Christ, you are the light of day,
Revealing what is veiled by night,
The morning star that gives the pledge
And promise of eternal light.

Watch over us who love you well,
And when our eyes are closed in sleep,
Protected by your strong right hand,
With you, our hearts will vigil keep.

O Father, Son and Spirit blest,
Immortal Trinity we praise,
Give us true sorrow for our sins
And life in everlasting days.

LM
Stanbrook Abbey c1974 (4)
Hymns for Prayer and Praise 261

Psalmody

The psalmody for Saturday (Psalms 4 and 134, see page 657f.) or Sunday (Psalm 91, below) may be used midweek. Otherwise the daily scheme is used (see below).

Psalm 91

1 Whoever dwells in the shelter of the Most High *
   and abides under the shadow of the Almighty,
2 Shall say to the Lord, 'My refuge and my stronghold, *
   my God, in whom I put my trust.'
3 For he shall deliver you from the snare of the fowler *
   and from the deadly pestilence.
4 He shall cover you with his wings
   and you shall be safe under his feathers; *
   his faithfulness shall be your shield and buckler.
5 You shall not be afraid of any terror by night, *
   nor of the arrow that flies by day;
6 Of the pestilence that stalks in darkness, *
   nor of the sickness that destroys at noonday.
7 Though a thousand fall at your side
   and ten thousand at your right hand, *
   yet it shall not come near you.
8 Your eyes have only to behold *
   to see the reward of the wicked.
9 Because you have made the Lord your refuge *
   and the Most High your stronghold,
10 There shall no evil happen to you, *
   neither shall any plague come near your tent.
11 For he shall give his angels charge over you, *
   to keep you in all your ways.
12 They shall bear you in their hands, *
   lest you dash your foot against a stone.
13 You shall tread upon the lion and adder; *
   the young lion and the serpent you shall trample underfoot.
14 Because they have set their love upon me,
   therefore will I deliver them; *
   I will lift them up, because they know my name.

15 They will call upon me and I will answer them; *
     I am with them in trouble,
     I will deliver them and bring them to honour.
16 With long life will I satisfy them *
     and show them my salvation.

   Glory. . .

Psalms (see pages 437–556)

Monday	86
Tuesday	143
Wednesday	31:1–5, 130
Thursday	16
Friday	88

Short Readings

Sunday and Solemnities

The servants of God will worship him in heaven; they will see his face, and his name will be on their foreheads. And there will be no more night; they need no light of lamp or sun, for the Lord God will be their light, and they will reign for ever and ever.

cf. Revelation 22:4–5

Other days

Be angry but do not sin; do not let the sun go down on your anger, and do not make room for the devil.

Ephesians 4:26–27

or

May the God of peace himself sanctify you entirely; and may your spirit and soul and body be kept sound and blameless at the coming of our Lord Jesus Christ.

1 Thessalonians 5:23

Short Responsory

R/ Into your hands, O Lord, I commend my spirit.
R/ Into your hands, O Lord, I commend my spirit.
V/ For you have redeemed me, Lord God of truth.
R/ Into your hands, O Lord, I commend my spirit.
V/ Glory . . . Holy Spirit.
R/ Into your hands, O Lord, I commend my spirit.

or (in Eastertide)

R/ Into your hands, O Lord, I commend my spirit, alleluia, alleluia.
R/ Into your hands, O Lord, I commend my spirit, alleluia, alleluia.
V/ For you have redeemed me, Lord God of truth.
R/ Into your hands, O Lord, I commend my spirit, alleluia, alleluia.
V/ Glory . . . Holy Spirit.
R/ Into your hands, O Lord, I commend my spirit, alleluia, alleluia.

Gospel Canticle: Nunc Dimittis

The Song of Simeon (+)

Refrain: Save us, O Lord, while waking,
and guard us while sleeping,
that awake we may watch with Christ,
and asleep may rest in peace.

Now, Lord, you let your servant go in peace: *
your word has been fulfilled.
My own eyes have seen the salvation *
which you have prepared in the sight of every people;
a light to reveal you to the nations *
and the glory of your people Israel.

Glory . . .

Luke 2:29–32
ELLC (15)

Refrain: Save us, O Lord, while waking,
and guard us while sleeping,
that awake we may watch with Christ,
and asleep may rest in peace.

Collect

Visit this house, O Lord, we pray,
drive far from it all the snares of the enemy;
may your holy angels dwell with us
   and guard us in peace,
and may your blessing be always upon us.
Through Christ our Lord.

A Daily Office SSF (3)

or

Be with us, O merciful God,
and protect us through the silent hours of this night,
so that we who are wearied by the changes
   and chances of this fleeting world,
may rest upon your eternal changelessness;
through Jesus Christ our Lord.

A Daily Office SSF (3)

or

Look down, O God,
from your heavenly throne;
and illuminate the darkness of this night
with your celestial brightness,
and from the children of light
banish the deeds of darkness;
through Jesus Christ our Saviour.

A Daily Office SSF (3)

Ending

The Lord grant us a quiet night and a perfect end.

A Final Anthem to the Blessed Virgin Mary follows (see below).

Final Anthems to the Blessed Virgin Mary

The versicles, responses and prayers may be omitted.

Alma Redemptoris Mater, Ave regina caelorum *and* Salve, Regina *may be used at any time outside Eastertide.*

From Advent Sunday until Candlemas

Alma Redemptoris Mater

Mother of Christ! hear thou thy people's cry,
Star of the deep, and portal of the sky!
Mother of him who thee from nothing made,
Sinking we strive, and call to thee for aid;
Oh, by that joy which Gabriel brought to thee,
Thou Virgin first and last, let us thy mercy see.

Divine Office (14)

From Advent Sunday until Christmas Eve

V/ The angel of the Lord declared unto Mary,
R/ and she conceived by the Holy Spirit.

Let us pray.

Pour forth, we beseech you, O Lord, your grace into our hearts, that we to whom the incarnation of Christ, your Son, was made known by the message of an angel, may by his passion and cross, be brought to the glory of his resurrection, through Christ our Lord.

From Christmas until Candlemas

V/ After childbirth you remained a pure virgin.
R/ Mother of God intercede for us.

Let us pray.

O God, by the fruitful virginity of blessed Mary you have given mankind the rewards of eternal salvation: grant, we pray, that we may know the intercession for us of the one through whom we were deemed worthy to receive the author of life, your Son, our Lord Jesus Christ.

tr. AB (8)

During Lent

Ave regina caelorum

Hail, Queen of Heaven, beyond compare,
To whom the angels homage pay;
Hail, Root of Jesse, Gate of Light,
That opened for the world's new Day.

Rejoice, O Virgin unsurpassed,
In whom our ransom was begun,
For all your loving children pray
To Christ, our Saviour, and your Son.

Stanbrook Abbey (4)

V/ Grant that I may praise you, sacred virgin.
R/ Give me strength against your enemies.

Let us pray.

Grant us protection in our weakness, O merciful God, that we who commemorate the holy Mother of God may triumph over our iniquities with the help of her intercession. Through Christ our Lord.

tr. AB (8)

During Eastertide

Regina caeli, laetare

Joy to thee, O Queen of heaven, alleluia.
He whom thou wast meet to bear, alleluia.
As he promised hath arisen, alleluia.
Pour for us to him thy prayer, alleluia.

V/ Rejoice and be glad, O Virgin Mary, alleluia,
R/ for the Lord has risen indeed, alleluia.

Let us pray.

O God, by the resurrection of your Son, our Lord Jesus Christ, you have brought joy to the whole world: grant that, with the help of his mother the Virgin Mary, we may obtain the joys of everlasting life; through Christ our Lord.

After Pentecost

Salve, Regina

Hail, holy Queen, mother of mercy,
our life, our sweetness, and our hope.
To you do we cry,
poor banished children of Eve.
To you do we send up our sighs,
mourning and weeping in this vale of tears.
Turn then, most gracious advocate,
your eyes of mercy towards us,
and after this exile
show to us the blessed fruit of your womb, Jesus.
O clement, O loving,
O sweet Virgin Mary.

V/ Rejoice and be glad, O Virgin Mary, alleluia,
R/ for the Lord has risen indeed, alleluia.

Let us pray.

Almighty and everlasting God, who by the co-operation of the Holy Spirit prepared the body and soul of the glorious Virgin Mother Mary to become a worthy dwelling-place for your Son: grant that, as we rejoice in commemorating her, we may be delivered by her loving intercession from present evils and eternal death. Through Christ our Lord.

tr. AB (8)